A Lousy Start

A Realistic Book about the Great Depression in Holland

written by Jacobaris

iUniverse, Inc.
New York Bloomington

A Lousy Start
A Realistic Book about the Great Depression in Holland

iUniverse books may be ordered through booksellers or by contacting:

iUniverse
1663 Liberty Drive
Bloomington, IN 47403
www.iuniverse.com
1-800-Authors (1-800-288-4677)

ISBN: 978-1-4502-6184-5 (sc)
ISBN: 978-1-4502-6186-9 (hb)
ISBN: 978-1-4502-6185-2 (ebook)

Printed in the United States of America

iUniverse rev. date: 10/18/2010

Foreword by the author

This story started around the turn of the 19th Century in the time that the earth was still considered to be flat by some people. The feudal system was still firmly entrenched in The Netherlands and it was an uphill struggle for flying machines and movies. Both were condemned by the clergy.

Only one decade of prosperity had been experienced after World War I when the Great Depression started. Millions of people were dumped into poverty creating a generation of Depression children.

For younger people who are used to living in a prosperous time this book is an eye opener and for the survivors of those terrible times it's a memory!

Language warning

This book deals with quite a different time in a hostile world where it was a constant struggle to survive. The struggling people were by no means Sunday School teachers and their language wasn't the best English. Reader discretion is advised.

All the stories in this book really happened but the names of the people have been changed. If any known name appears in this book it's just a coincidence. Only the names of politicians and leaders have been kept to make the book authentic.

Contents

THE GOOD OLD TIME

A team of two Clydesdale horses was pulling a wagon heavily loaded with potatoes on the soggy gravel road to the town of Stryen. The horses looked awfully tired and the driver Adrianus Demerwe (who was known as Janus Demerwe by the people.) looked worn out as well.

Janus was holding the reins in his iron hands while he was fighting sleep. He couldn't afford to fall asleep with his heavy load of potatoes. The road was in a terrible shape after the incessant rains and whenever the wagon seemed to come to a halt, he jumped from the wagon to go to the front to lead the horses by hand. If he got stuck it might take some doing to get going again.

Actually, it had been an excellent summer with lots of sunshine and rain when it was needed. Now there was lots of rain which was not needed at all for the harvest. There had been a bountiful crop but harvesting had been a disillusion. Right after the grain had been mowed and stoked on the land, it rained for a solid five weeks. Oh, there had been afternoons of sunshine which were followed by more rain showers the next day.

Consequently, everything had deteriorated; the grain was molding and had started to germinate. There was also a lot of water on the land which had prevented the harvest of potatoes and sugar beets. Finally with a week of constant sunshine and wind, harvesting became possible again though it was very difficult.

Normally, to harvest the potatoes, farmers would plow up the hills of potatoes and all that was needed were some people to put the potatoes in bags. The land was still plenty wet and to put a plow with two horses on the land was impossible. This time, the harvesting of potatoes had to be done the hard way with men to dig up the potato hills with a spade. That was a lot of extra hard work and there were not enough hours in the day to do it.

The potatoes had to be delivered to the steam tram station in Stryen from where they would be transported to the big city of Rotterdam which was eagerly awaiting the shipment of potatoes from the island. There was an excuse for the delay of shipping the potatoes but rain or shine, the people were still eating and there was a severe shortage of potatoes in the city.

Janus lived in Heinenoord, a hamlet situated about an hour from Stryen. The steam tram company couldn't afford to lay rails to all the little hamlets, so if the steam tram didn't come to where the farmers were farming, they had to take their produce to the steam tram and that was where Janus came in.

Janus started to yawn; he had gotten up at 3.30 a.m. to milk the farmer's cows and right after that he had been digging up the potatoes and also had to load them. With all the extra heavy work he had to do without getting paid for it, he wasn't amused at all. He worked for Farmer Zwart for one guilder per week, no matter how many hours he worked. As a farm hand he had to do all the work there was and if he couldn't handle it, he could be replaced by a younger farm hand.

However, there were lots of fringe benefits with his job. He lived in a little farm house that was specially built for the farm hand. All farmers provided housing for their farm hands, that way the farm hand was easily called if he was needed, especially if a cow was calving in the middle of the night. Again, whenever that happened, there was no extra pay.

Most of the food was obtained from the farm free: i.e. potatoes, bread, vegetables, eggs, meat, milk, butter and cheese. Sugar, salt, tea, coffee, soap and clothes had to be bought from the one guilder per week he made.

Actually, he didn't have a full guilder per week to spend. On Sundays, he had to go with his family to church twice. That meant that there were two collections each service which cost him with his five children (seven offerings twice each service) 28 cents per Sunday.

Luckily, he didn't have fourteen children as did his next door neighbors. Most of his money would be gone by church collections alone. The neighbor's wife said that the Reverend had told her that it is a blessing from the Lord to have that many children. Janus couldn't see it that way; according to his calculations it was a blessing for the Lord if he had that many children. With fourteen children, the Lord would collect 64 cents every Sunday. A guy could go broke while he was counting his blessings. Of course, when all those 14 children grew up and have fourteen children each, having a church was a booming business. It would make the church rich and also more powerful.

Only the poor people are that stupid to have that many children was the conclusion of Janus. The Reverend, doctor and lawyer had only each two children and the Reverend was telling the poor people that it was a blessing to have an orphanage on your own. Those big shots were certainly not looking forward to be blessed by the Lord with ten to fourteen children.

Twice a year there was some extra money coming in. In early summer when the strawberries were ripe, his wife with the oldest kids would pick strawberries for the remuneration of two cents per basket. That amounted to about 30 cents per day per person which meant that there was a lot more money coming in, if they picked strawberries for a week. They made more money in a day than he made the entire week.

During the fall; they picked up potatoes and put them in bags and were rewarded with the payment of one penny per mud. (A mud is a volume measurement, not a weight. One mud of potatoes weighed 80 kilos and a mud of wheat weighed one hundred kilos.) It translated to about 40 cents per day income.

That was a welcome addition to the low income they had and his wife was already contemplating how she would spend that money long before it was made. Most of the money was spent on clothes. Most of their clothes came second hand from the farmer. When the oldest kid grew out of them, the clothes went to the next oldest kid and so on. By the time the youngest kid was too big for the clothes they were finished. They were living in poverty but they had a roof over their head and were never hungry. Janus was very happy about that.

While he had been thinking about his hard life, he had reached the tram station. It started to rain again and there were two other wagons with potatoes ahead of him for unloading. By the time he was finished unloading it was already 8.30 p.m. It was another long day; it would be 10.00 p.m. before he would be home.

Janus settled himself on the bench of the wagon and soon fell asleep. He wasn't worried about getting stuck anymore, the horses could easily pull the empty wagon and they knew the way home. No matter where they were, they automatically returned home unless they were told otherwise. Even the horses knew: "There is no place like home."

* * * *

Jaap Dalm also lived in Heinenoord. He was twenty years old and worked for Farmer Beet. His task was the same as the task that Janus de Merwe had to fulfill. He had to get up at 3.30 a.m. in the morning because he had to milk the cows at 4.00 a.m. The cows had to be milked again at 4.00 p.m. in the afternoon and furthermore, he had to do all farm jobs that came about.

Officially, Sunday was called: "Lord's Day." It was the day of rest because the Lord had created Heaven and Earth in six days and rested the seventh day. Unfortunately, the farmer's cows didn't know about Lord's Day and had to be milked at 4.00 a.m. and 4.00 p.m. like on all other days.

Milking the cows was not the only job that Jaap had to do on Sunday. He also had to attend two church services if he wanted to keep his job. By the time Jaap was finished milking the cows in the morning, it was about 6.00 a.m. That gave him about three hours to go back to bed because the church service started at 10.00 a.m. and he had to walk half an hour to the church in the village.

Farmer Beet was so good to Jaap by allowing him to milk the cows Sunday afternoon an hour earlier than on other days. Instead of at four o' clock, he could milk the cows at three o' clock. This was not to the benefit of Jaap because he was now finished early enough to attend church services at five o'clock. That was the whole idea: to have Jaap in church twice on Sunday. Actually Farmer Beet didn't allow Jaap to milk the cows an hour earlier, he was told to do it and had no choice. When he was told to do it there weren't any questions, he just had to do it if he wanted to keep his job.

Jaap was sitting in the back of the church and Farmer Beet was sitting in the front of the church; he was one of the elders and formed with the deacons the executive of the church. Only farmers would be in the executive. Farmhands were not considered at all. What would a dumb farm hand know about running a church? All farmers were involved in running the church and the farm hands were only church goers.

To make sure that the farmhands stayed stupid, they weren't supposed to read the newspaper or books. All rich people were reading the newspaper but poor farm hand families were glad to have food on their table. They wouldn't waste money to buy a newspaper. That was exactly what the farmer's clique wanted.

Jaap was a single guy and spent some of the little money he had in cash on books and newspapers. While he was eating, he would read his newspaper. When Farmer Beet saw him reading the newspaper, he pulled the paper out of Jaap's hands and said: "I don't want you to read newspapers because you'll become way too smart."

Jaap went reluctantly to church; he didn't care for the Reverend Young, who was the pastor. His name was Young but the truth was that he was an old Conservative Doomsday preacher that saw nothing but gloom and doom for the world and he danced to the pipes of the farmers. The farmers were the ones that got the people to church, they made sure that their farm hands and family went to church lest they be fired.

The church was built very conveniently for the farmers who were sitting in the benches for the elders and deacons. The pulpit was in the front in the middle and the benches were on either side. They were placed so that the farmers were facing the congregation. That was done on purpose so that the farmers could check if their farmhands with their family were attending church services. There was no roll call but there might as well have been, the farmers didn't miss a thing. Only if you were sick you were excused from attending church services, no other excuses were acceptable. Going to church was an obligation to keep your job.

Jaap Dalm was single; his father and mother had died and he lived by himself in the farm hand house of Farmer Beet. He only had to account for his own actions. Farm hands who were married were also responsible that their wives and children were coming to church twice on a Sunday.

Reverend Young could put society back into the Middle Ages with his Conservative preaching. He was against any progress that was being made, especially in transportation. In the early 1800's traveling was an expensive and slow proposition of 35 miles per day at the most. When the train came to The Netherlands one could travel 35 miles per hour, it was like breaking the sound barrier. It was a great improvement but not to the doom sayers who condemned it from the onset.

It had taken some doing to get the first train on the go as there was a lot of stiff opposition to the project. The farmers didn't want to sell their land; they were not impressed with having a train going across their land. When the pie was sweetened with giving them a lot of money for their land, they finally caved in except some die hards who objected because they thought that the steam from the locomotive would sour the milk of their cows. Whenever they hit a stubborn sour milk farmer who didn't want to sell his land, the railway made a wide curve around his land.

Heinenoord was on an island, not in the middle of the ocean but it was surrounded by rivers. That made a ferry necessary and one of the improvements was to build a bridge. By the year 1900 it was decided to build a new bridge that would also serve a steam tram that would go to the city of Rotterdam which was about 20 miles from Heinenoord.

Reverend Young saw the steam tram as a connection with Sin City where people could go to the movies and was against it. Without a steam tram, only the rich people that had a horse and buggy could travel to Rotterdam and now everybody who had ten cents could buy a tram ticket.

When the horseless car came to Heinenoord he had nothing good to say about it. All he saw was a guy in the open front with a cap backwards on his head so the wind wouldn't blow it off and on the back bench was usually sitting two ladies with long skirts and veils flapping in the wind.

According to him, the horse and buggy beat the horseless carriage by far. If you wanted to go somewhere by car, you had to start it first which was a job and a half. The start motor hadn't been invented yet so you couldn't burn it out which was a good thing. As for the bad thing about it, you had to start the motor by hand with a crank. Luckily they didn't have high pressure engines and there were only four cylinders so they were easier to turn. In spite of that it usually was a job and a half to crank the motor until it started. The gasoline engine had a mind of its own and could kick back like a wild horse.

Many a good guy broke his arm or wrist when he tried to start the engine when it kicked back.

From those exciting days of yesteryear comes a classic poem:

Uncle John cranked his Chevrolet,
The engine kicked back and to his regret,
He got the crank against his head.

That was all hay on Reverend Young's fork to condemn the horseless carriage some more. He saw broken arms and wrists as a punishment of God. His observation was that whoever made those contraptions would go broke. The horseless carriage wasn't going to replace the horse and buggy. "Why do you think that God made horses?" was his final observation.

There were people who weren't satisfied with a horseless carriage, they wanted to fly like the birds and copied the birds. They made wings and strapped them to their body. It was a disillusion; they never got off the ground. Studying the birds it looked so simple, big birds and small birds had no problem and were flying to where they wanted to go.

As long as people tried to make wings for flying purposes they didn't get anywhere but people never gave up. In 1903 there were two bike repair men in the U.S., the Wright Brothers, who had a different approach to the problem, they made the very first flying machine propelled by a gasoline engine and had managed to fly their flying machine a distance of 852 feet. From bike repairmen they became experts in aviation.

Reverend Young had a special sermon to condemn it. His sermon was based on the first chapter of the Bible, Genesis 1 verse 20. "And on the fifth day God said: 'Let the waters bring forth abundantly, the moving creatures that hath life and fowl above the earth in the open firmament of heaven.'"

In the sermon that followed Reverend Young said: "As you can see from your Bible, God created the birds and gave them wings. If God had wanted that man would fly he would have given him wings as well. Men have made wings like the birds have; they strapped them on their body and tried to fly like the birds by jumping off a high mountain. The only thing that it accomplished was that they jumped to their death. That was a punishment of God for interfering with his creation. The last venture of those two bike makers is not a flying machine; it is only a glider that glides a few feet. God will never allow that man will fly and change his creation by flying like the birds. It will never happen."

(The Wright Brothers had an appropriate name, they had done it right. The question was "What was the name of the two brothers who made an unsuccessful flight with a flying machine?" The answer was "Their name was 'The Wrong Brothers'")

In spite of all his Dooms Day sermons, there was a man by the name of Jan Olieslager from Antwerp in Belgium who came to demonstrate his flying machine in The Netherlands. When that happened, Reverend Young had a living fit and preached some more doom: "God has created Heaven and Earth and he made the water for the fish, the sky for the birds and the ground for the people. Not even Jan Olieslager can change that."

Though Jaap was unhappy to sit in church listening to this kind of nonsense, he went to church faithfully twice every Sunday. He had no choice if he wanted to keep his job. Farmer Beet would fire him if he refused to go to church.

One year it had been a miserable Fall with a lot of rain. The crop was wet and couldn't be harvested. Finally, there had been a few nice days to dry the crop and harvesting could commence. Every night Jaap Dalm had to work till eleven o'clock including Saturday night, to get the crop in the barn.

When he went to bed that Saturday night after 11.00 he was very tired. It didn't matter how tired he was, the next morning he had to get up at 3.30 a.m. so he could milk the cows at 4.00. Very sleepy he milked the cows and like always he went to bed for three hours before he went to church. With all the hard work and late hours, he was so tired that he didn't hear the alarm clock telling him that it was time to get up and go to church. When he finally woke up, the church service was almost over so he had missed it.

After he had milked the cows again in the afternoon, the farmer knocked against the window that he wanted to talk to Jaap. "How come you weren't in church this morning?" Farmer Beet asked.

Jaap answered: "I was so tired this morning from working that late on Saturday night that I never heard the alarm clock."

"Tired from what?" Farmer Beet snapped him off. "You don't work that hard! I don't believe in stupid excuses like that. If it happens again, you don't even have to try to explain because you will be fired."

Jaap knew that he meant business and wasn't planning to miss church again. A few weeks later when the wheat, oats and hay were already in the barn, there were still the sugar beets to be harvested. Unfortunately, there had been a week of incessant rain just before the harvest, which had changed farmer's field into a quagmire. Lifting the beets out of the ground with a little fork was very hard work but that was only part of the trouble. It was hard to transport the beets as well; quite often they had to take half loads or the horses couldn't pull the wagons out of the field.

The sugar factory only works for about ten to twelve weeks per year and demands a steady supply of beets once it opens up. After they extract the sugar they are open for a few more months to refine the sugar and that is it. Again, it were long days of hard work; he had worked till 8.00 p.m. one Saturday night and when he almost fell asleep during his meal, he decided to go to bed at 9.00 p.m.

At 10.00 p.m. he was awakened by a loud noise. Some idiot was banging on his door. When Jaap checked what was going on, it was an excited Farmer Beet who told him to get up immediately and come to the stable because a cow was calving. The cow was rather small and had a difficult time to deliver the calf. When part of the calf came out, they tied a rope to the calf to help the cow by pulling.

(Most of the city dwellers are not familiar with pulling calves out of cows. A farmer was in his pasture when one of his cows was getting her calf. The cow needed help so the farmer tied a rope around the calf and started pulling. When he saw a passerby he asked him to aid him with pulling. When the calf was finally out of the cow, the farmer thanked the passerby and the passerby remarked: "That calf must have had quite a speed that it ran that far into the cow.")

It took a long time before the calf was out of the cow and by the time that Jaap was back in bed, it was one o'clock after midnight. There was only two hours of sleep left before he had to get up again to milk the cows. Those damned cows always had to have their calf at the most inconvenient times and buggered up his sleep many a time. They must get their instructions from Farmer Beet to get their calf in the middle of the night so it wouldn't interfere with the regular farm work. If the cow had delivered the calf during the church service everything would have been alright. The farmer and Jaap would have to assist the cow during the church service because the farmer could have lost his cow and calf. Those farmers and the Reverend were just a bunch of hypocrites.

Luckily, he got up to milk the cows but after he returned to bed, he slept like a log and didn't hear the alarm clock to go to church. Jaap knew that there was hell to pay and indeed after he had milked the cows, there was the famous knock against the window; Farmer Beet wanted to see him. Jaap knew that Farmer Beet wasn't calling for him to give him a Christmas present or that he wanted to give him a cup of coffee with a cookie. He knew that he was in trouble and when he entered the farmer's living room the farmer shouted at him: "I warned you that you had to go to church on Sunday but apparently you didn't give a damn. You are fired! I want you to be out of the farmhand house by tomorrow afternoon because my new farmhand has to move in."

Jaap didn't get a chance at all to tell Farmer Beet why it had happened. It didn't matter how tired he was, he had to go to church. This all meant that he was in deep trouble, he didn't have a job and neither did he have a place to live.

His sister Dini was living in Heinenoord as well and her husband Gijs was also working as a farmhand. It didn't take long to convince Dini that he could stay at her place so that problem was solved. All he had to do was to find another job and he was back on track again.

Finding another job proved very difficult if not impossible. Whenever he went to a farmer for a job, the farmer would say: "You were fired by Farmer Beet because you didn't go to church. I don't want heathens to work for me."

Reverend Young had found out that Jaap was staying at his sister's place so he paid her a visit. When the Reverend came in, Jaap was just reading a book he had recently bought that had been written by Multituly with the title "Coffee in Brazil."

There was an outcry about how the plantation owners were misusing their Negro slaves and Jaap could see almost similar conditions in Heinenoord. The farmers weren't using a whip on their slaves but they starved the people if they didn't do what they were told.

When all of a sudden Reverend Young entered the house, Jaap put his book to the side. He didn't think that Reverend Young would appreciate literature like that and he was right. After the introductory topic "The weather," the first thing he did was pick up the book and when he saw the title he said to Jaap's sister: "You shouldn't allow a God blaspheming book like this in your house. Get rid of it!"

Jaap was defending his position stating that he merely was reading different books to learn what other people had to say about different things. The Reverend's fist hit the table while he was shouting angrily: "The Bible is the word of God; only that should be taken as the truth. All other opinions are sinful; they are only the work of Satan to distract the people from worshipping God. Satan wants you to read that trash but God wants you to read the Bible!"

A couple of days later when Gijs walked past the window of the farmer where he was working, there was a knock on the window indicating that the farmer wanted to talk to him. When he entered the living room the farmer said: "I hear that you have Jaap Dalm in your house. I won't allow him to stay at your place. Get rid of him or I'll get rid of you as my farmhand!"

When Jaap was told that he wasn't welcome by anybody anymore in Heinenoord and was practically run out of town, he decided to pick up his suitcase to try elsewhere. There was a shipyard called "Boele" in Bolnes and they were advertising that they needed laborers. Bolnes was a two hour bike ride from Heinenoord, and full of hope, he went to the shipyard to see if they would hire him. Hopefully they had some use for him and if not, he would be starving.

To his great relief, he was hired as a laborer which meant bread on the table. After he worked at the shipyard for a couple of months, the shipyard boss asked for him to come to his office. Jaap thought that he was going to be fired, maybe Reverend Young had contacted him and he was told to get rid of that heathen Jaap Dalm.

Luckily that wasn't the case. The boss had probably never heard about Reverend Young and Jaap wasn't about to introduce him. The boss said: "I've watched you and you seem to be very handy with maneuvering equipment and material. We are training three crane operators and if you are interested you can be one of them."

Jaap couldn't believe it; for the first time in his life he was told that he was doing a good job and offered training as a crane operator. He accepted eagerly and after his training he had a job for life. Actually this stupid cow that had a calf in the middle of the night had been a blessing; it got him fired but it also had given him a much better job. Being a crane operator was a lot better job than pulling calves out of a cow in the middle of the night without pay and being fired for not attending church.

It seemed that all his problems were solved except one. The only unresolved problem was that he had roots in Heinenoord. Before he was run out of Heinenoord, he was going steady with Dirkje Demerwe who was a daughter of Janus Demerwe, and Janus had ordered Dirkje not to see that heathen Jaap Dalm anymore. If he wanted to see his sweetheart he had to bike two hours to Heinenoord. The only time he could see her was between the church services. In the afternoon Dirkje went for a walk and Jaap left early in the morning which gave them a chance to be together for a couple of hours. It was a secret meeting but of course, somebody had seen them together and Janus was told what had taken place.

When Janus found out that Dirkje was still seeing Jaap he almost had a fit and said to her: "Are you out of your mind to date that good for nothing heathen? He is nothing but trouble; he might be a nice talker but he will bring you nothing but unhappiness."

He also forbad her to see him again. Janus had severely underestimated the power of love; she sneaked out of the house anyway to meet her lover. In the afternoon Janus had a nap and at 3.00 p.m. he had to milk the cows for the farmer he worked for. He couldn't keep an eye on his daughter all the time. That gave Dirkje a chance to sneak out of the house.

In spite of her father's objections they had a rendezvous every Sunday afternoon. When Dirkje was 21 years old, Dirkje and Jaap wanted to get married but her father didn't want to give permission. Eloping and marrying by a Justice of the Peace wasn't possible in those days. Nobody would marry a couple without the consent of the parents.

At twenty one years of age Dirkje was of age but she still needed permission from her parents to get married. It meant that Jaap Dalm had to bide his time and wait till she was 25 years old. At that age parental permission wasn't needed anymore and no matter what Janus said, she could marry the man she wanted. Actually Jaap Dalm was a very nice guy in spite what Janus said about him. This heathen Jaap could have made Dirkje pregnant and then what?

As soon as Dirkje was 25 years old they got married without the blessing of her father. He didn't even attend the wedding. Actually, it was in The Netherlands not that much better than in India and Japan where the parents arrange a partner for their children. In The Netherlands you could find your own partner but your parents had to approve of that person. If they didn't you had to wait till you were 25 years old.

After a year they got their first baby and Dirkje, who was still going to church, wanted her children to be baptized. Jaap wasn't going to church anymore after all the things that had taken place; yet, he was a very nice guy and allowed their children to be baptized.

He even went one step further; on the day that his child was baptized, he went to church for the happy occasion to support his wife. There was only one comment that he made after he came home: "That Reverend must be blind; he never said anything to me and didn't even look at me."

The reason for that was that only Dirkje his wife was a member of the church and Jaap wasn't. When a child is going to be baptized, the Reverend will read a Form of Baptism. This includes the history of baptism which goes back as far as Abraham. After the form has been read, the parents bring the baby in front of the baptismal font and then the Reverend will ask: "Do you promise that when this child grows up that you will teach and have it educated in the knowledge of our Lord? As the father and mother of this child, what is your answer to the Lord?"

In this case, only Dirkje was a full fledged member and Jaap wasn't, so the Reverend asked: "As the mother of this child, what is your answer to the Lord?"

No matter how he was insulted, he really loved his wife and for her sake, he went with her when their next three babies were baptized. (This is a real heart warming love story.)

* * * *

It was on a cool day of September 1879 that a long line of people were waiting very patiently their turn to move a switch that was lighting the very first light bulb ever. It was a carbon hydrate bulb invented by Thomas A

Edison. After he had spent more than $40,000 on his experiments, he finally had succeeded to make a lamp and after his invention, he spent a lot of time and money on generation and distribution of electricity.

Thomas Alpha Edison was a great inventor, in 1894 he came up with a kinescope. It was the very beginning of the movies. At that time it was only a peep show which worked on a coin in a slot machine lasting fifteen seconds. There wasn't much to the show itself either, it showed a woman cooking food and a man chopping wood. It became more appealing when the pictures were projected on a screen. People liked to see moving figures and wanted to see more than working and walking people.

They got it in a movie "The Kiss," which was played in 1910. It was a very short film and only once in the entire film the man kissed the woman. The church called it a scandalous movie and demanded screen censorship so that immoral movies like "The Kiss" wouldn't be played on the screen anymore.

Reverend Young saw it as the end of the world because it was immoral. He had an entire sermon about the film and said: "Going to the movies is sinful and the Lord will punish you. When you are sitting in the dark looking at the moving light on the screen, the light will be drawn out of your eyes and you will go blind. Besides movies are sinful and create lust." He finished his doom sermon with a big bang on the pulpit stating: "God destroyed Sodom and Gomorrah because of immorality namely, 'Sodomy' and God will also destroy us if we condone immoral movies to be played."

A lot of church leaders got into the censorship of movies and demanded decency. They called Hollywood "Sin City" and banned the movie "The Kiss" because it was scandalous. Other restrictions were imposed as well especially about the dialogue. Not only were the words "Sex" and "Damn" disallowed in movies, words like "Bed" and "Toilet" were not allowed in movies anymore either. A couple in bed couldn't be filmed as it suggested sex and you never talked about sex. If you were talking about sex, you substituted the word "It" for sex and would say: "I had it." People still say: "I had it." However they don't mean sex, they merely mean that they are fed up with it. The language changes. Sexy women were referred to as "It women."

At the beginning of the Twentieth Century sex was taboo at any time. Only if you were married could you have sex. Men could enjoy sex but women couldn't, they were only there for the enjoyment of men and to provide offspring. If a woman enjoyed sex, she was considered to be a dirty woman. Queen Victoria said: "The only thing that sex is good for is to get children. Having sex means that you spread your legs and close your eyes, you wait till the man is satisfied and carry on." Queen Victoria died in 1901 after having six children.

Even the church with threats of hell fire couldn't stop progress and movies were there to stay. The movie industry supplied some more ammunition to Reverend Young when the movies weren't silent anymore; they were now "Talkies." In the movie "Gone with the Wind," Clark Gable playing the role of Buttler, answered Olivia when she asked: "What am I going to do?" His answer was: "I frankly don't give a damn my dear." Swearing in movies would undoubtedly be punished by God.

* * * *

Janus had worked very hard all his life for his family and had managed to feed them and have a roof over their head. What else could he possibly want? "Security" was the answer to that question. He worried a lot that when he got older he couldn't do all the heavy work on the farm anymore and could easily be replaced with a younger stronger man who could. If that happened he would have to vacate the farm house and then where would they go? Janus didn't have the foggiest idea where he would live. The church would have to look after him which would be no fat pot. As long as his family was grown up when that happened, that's all that counted.

In spite of all his worries, his family grew up fast and all his children got married. There was an empty nest when during a cold winter he got a flu which caused pneumonia and four days later he was dead leaving the worrying to his wife.

His wife managed to make a living by working for the farmers. She was doing the house keeping for an old farmer and lived at the farm. After a couple of years, a man by the name of Adrianus Penning was interested in her and she replaced one Adrianus with another one. The whole town of Heinenoord went to the wedding and she had a rather comfortable living for the rest of her life.

Dirkje was the oldest one in the family followed by Gysje, another daughter. Next came Arie as the oldest boy followed by two boys Teun and Jaap. Arie was working in the flax industry for Farmer van Nes.

People have been growing flax even in ancient times at the time of Moses. It was used for food at first until the Egyptians started to make linen from the fibers. Growing flax to make clothes spread to Europe and The Netherlands became an important producer of flax. In The Netherlands flax wasn't used for food, they made mainly paint and clothes from the flax.

Farmer van Nes had always barns full of flax and knew all there was to know about flax. He told Arie that there were over a hundred thousand seeds in a pound of flax seeds. Arie couldn't care less, to him the only appreciation he had for flax was that it provided him with a livelihood. He wasn't about to check it out if there were indeed that many seeds in a pound of flax, he took his word for it.

Actually, Arie had a steady job. Producing flax started in Fall when the land was plowed and manure had to be spread for the growing of flax in Spring. In Spring the seeding took place, followed by the weeding because God's earth brings forth thorns, thistles and weeds before the crop has matured. The very first thing that came up were the weeds. They weren't seeded but they were the first to appear on the land. All those weeds had to be pulled out by hand a couple of times before the flax had matured.

That was all a lot of work but most of the work came after the flax had matured. The flax had to be pulled out by hand and sheaves had to be tied and set up on the land in stokes so that the flax could dry. That was done so the flax could be threshed to obtain flax seed which was needed to seed flax the next year. Not all the flax seeds were used for seeding; most of the flax seeds were crushed to obtain linseed oil which was used to make paint.

Threshing the flax seeds was a lot of work; when the flax was dry in stokes, the flax bulbs had to be pulled off by hand. There was no time to get the seeds out of the bulbs; that was a winter job when there was more time. The bulbs were stored in a barn and were ready come winter.

That was all very profitable but the straw of the flax was even more valuable. From the fibers they made linen which was an awful lot of hard work. After drying the flax for threshing purposes, the flax had to be wet to obtain linen. The flax had to rot so that the needed linen fibers could be removed from the woody stem.

Nature decays plants and quite often the flax was spread in the field to be rained on. After the flax was wet the rotting process would start. Most of the time, the farmers took a short cut; they didn't depend on rain to get it wet but threw it in the ditches. After a few days, the flax was wet through and through and was stoked on the land again to complete the rotting process.

Growing flax on the land looked beautiful with all the blue flowers but the flax production was a real stink. When the rotting flax was standing in stokes on the land, one could smell it an hour in the wind. Long before the field with flax was reached, the smell would tell you that you were nearing a field of flax. The stench was indescribable and people working the flax weren't smelling all that good either, but it was a way of life.

As soon as the rotting process had been completed, the flax was ready to get the needed fibers out. There was little time to do all that work in Fall, so the sheaves were also put in the barn till winter when there was more time.

When winter came, the seed bulbs were taken from the storage barn to complete the threshing. The bulbs were put on the barn floor and three horses, head to tail, walked over it for a couple of hours to get the seeds out of the bulbs.

Horses were doing a lot of work in those days. The only problem with horses was that they shit anywhere, any time. Since paint and horse shit doesn't mix too well, they had a remedy to avoid such an undesired mixture. There was a guy walking right behind the horses with a big shovel to catch the horse shit that the horses might drop while walking. As soon as one of the horses lifted its tail indicating that a drop was coming, the man would catch it with his big shovel. They even had a big tub to catch the horse piss. All very ingenious!

After the seeds had come out of the bulbs, there was one more job to be done; the seeds had to be separated from the chaff. A wind mill was turned by hand with a big wheel, the chaff was blown away and the seeds remained. Turning the wheel to make wind was usually done by boys that just had finished school. It was a job that showed them the reality of making a living.

Getting seeds to make linseed oil was a big job but that was only the beginning of the work. In order to make linen out of flax, the next step was to flail the flax to get the fibers out. That created a lot of dust which was very hard on the lungs of the workers. When half a dozen of workers were flailing the flax it was so dusty that you couldn't see one another in a distance of a couple of meters. It wasn't only hard and dusty work; the hours of labor were long as well. The daily schedule was as follows:

Start work at 5.00 A.M.	
Work from 5.00 A.M. till 7.00 A.M	2 hours of work.
Coffee break 7.00 A.M. till 7.30 A.M.	
Work from 7.30 A.M. till 9.00 A.M	1 ½ hours of work
Lunch break 9.00 A.M. till 10.00 A.M.	
Work from 10.00 A.M. till 12.00 noon	2 hours of work
Coffee break from 12.00 noon till 12.30 P.M.	
Work from 12.30 P.M. till 2.00 P.M	1 ½ hours of work
Dinner 2.00 P.M. till 3.00 P.M.	
Work from 3.00 P.M. till 5.00 P.M	2 hours of work.
Coffee break 5.00 P.M. till 5.30 P.M.	
Work from 5.30 P.M. till 7.00 P.M	1 ½ hours of work.
Total working hours	10 ½ hours of work per day.

This working schedule was worked six days a week, including Saturday. For a total of 63 working hours they got paid 4 to 5 guilders per week. They had quite a few coffee, lunch and dinner breaks daily. This was necessary to combat the dust and give their lungs a chance to clean out.

By the time the winter work was done it was April which meant that flax had to be seeded again to get another crop. Arie's work in the flax industry was rudely interrupted when on his 20th birthday he got a present from the Government. It was a letter that called him up for military duty.

Military conscription had come to The Netherlands as early as 1898 when Queen Wilhelmina ascended the throne. At the beginning of the 20th Century all was peace and quiet after a century that had seen two major wars, namely the Napoleonic wars and the Prussia – France war. Since there was no war in the often a small army would do.

All Dutch young men had to serve their fatherland for a full year when they reached the age of twenty. Only if you already had a brother that had served his fatherland you were excused from military duty. That was called that you had "Brother Service." It was put in place in order not to put unnecessary hardship on families, especially farm families that needed the labor of the boys.

If there were more than two brothers, the third brother had to serve again and the fourth would have Brother Service. The military took the first, third, fifth and so on. Of course, the soldiers had to be in a good shape so there was a medical examination with a chance that the doctor would say that the young man was a wreck and they had no use for him.

There was one other way that a young man could escape military services but he had to be lucky. The Government had a lottery in place with a certain number of free numbers. All eligible men for military duty had to draw a number, usually at City Hall. They called it that you were "reporting for your number." If you drew a low number it was called "a blank" and you could be sure that you were going to be a soldier. A high number was called "a price;" it gave you a good chance to be free of conscription. They didn't know how many men were going to pass their medical examination, so they would take the lowest numbers first until they had reached the required number of soldiers.

If you had a free number, you could sell your number to somebody with enough money who hated the Army. Of course, rich boys would take advantage of that and money kept them out of the Army.

Even boys that were in prison weren't free of the draft, they simply had to serve their sentence first and had to report for drawing their number right after. The number of soldiers who had to serve was determined by the Government, it depended on how many soldiers they needed and how many they wanted.

Baldness was a reason to be rejected in those days; they figured that a bald guy would have trouble keeping his helmet on his head. Before the boys drew their number, they measured the prospective soldiers. If they were less than 155 centimeters tall, they were rejected. There was no place for shorties in the army.

Some stories came about that boys from the farm were carrying a yoke with two full pails of milk, every day, to make themselves shorter. If you just had made the required 155 c.m., it was possible to ask for a re-measurement in which case the complainant could go to the farm to carry a yoke with two pails of milk to get shorter.

When Arie got his letter, the Government was expanding its military forces. It was 1914 and war was imminent. War could break out any time now. The Big Powers were only waiting for an excuse to grab one another and then all hell would break loose.

A big day in Arie's life came up when he had to go to Stryen to the Town Hall to draw a number. After the number drawing, most of the young men went to the pub and after drinking a lot, numerous fights broke out. It looked as if the war had already started and it didn't take the police long to participate in this war. After the police had made numerous arrests, peace and quiet returned to the town of Stryen.

Arie was far from happy to be drafted into the Dutch army with the prospect of war looming. Happy or not, he drew a low number and unless they rejected him with his medical examination he would be a soldier.

Once he became a soldier he was trained to kill any intruder of The Netherlands in case of war. It didn't take long before the war started and all the land between Germany and The Netherlands was inundated by opening the flood gates. The Netherlands was below sea level and was easily inundated.

Many times when Arie was supposed to go on leave for a weekend, all leaves were cancelled due to increased tension on the front. So far only France and Belgium had been attacked and England had sent some troops to support them to fight the Germans. Any German troop movement could be translated that the Germans were ready to attack The Netherlands as well which meant no leaves.

IT HURTS TO BE POOR

"The clock strikes five, five strikes the clock. The clock strikes five, five strikes the clock."

Arie Cornelis Tamerius woke up to the loud voice of the town crier whose duty it was to tell the time, every hour, to the people who were living on the Nol Dyke in Rysoord. Rysoord was just another small town, about 25 kilometers from Heinenoord. It was close to a one and a half hours bike ride. Rysoord was an insignificant but prosperous farm community under the smoke of the all important city of Rotterdam. Unfortunately, prosperity was only experienced by the rich farmers and a few tradesmen, it wasn't shared with the farmhands and laborers who made prosperity happen.

Arie Cornelis Tamerius was one of the unfortunate citizens of the town of Rysoord, who worked hard like a slave and got paid very little. Sustenance in his family was very poor and the outlook of improvement on those conditions was non existent. His father and mother were poor and poverty was inherited as well as riches. If you were born to have a nickel, you would never have a dime.

Aries Cornelis worked in the flax industry during the winter and worked hard and long hours in a dusty environment. Somewhere in March or April, the work he was doing in the flax industry like flailing and threshing was done and he became unemployed. *(There was no unemployment insurance in those days. If you didn't work, you didn't eat.)* Arie Cornelis went from farm to farm looking for work and most of the time he found nothing.

When everything failed to find work, he put an old basket on his back with a set of clean underwear and a couple of loaves of bread and walked with his friend Jan Pete to the Haarlemmermeer Lake polder. A polder is a low lying area reclaimed from a sea or a lake. First of all they dyked the area in and pumped the water out. Next, ditches were dug for proper drainage. It was a hundred kilometers walk which they managed to do in four days.

The Haarlemmer Lake polder had been recently created. It was one of the largest lakes in The Netherlands until a Dutch hydro engineer with the nick name of Leegwater (meaning "Empty Water") came along. He managed to pump the lake dry and kept it dry with an intricate system of canals and dykes. On the bottom of the former lake were now quite a few farms with fertile fields of grain and other produce.

There was still a lot of work to be done. Ditches had to be dug by hand to drain the land. From the ditches, the water was pumped into the canals and from the canals it was pumped into the rivers. The rivers flowed into the ocean and through this complex system, the land was properly drained. Just before winter started, Arie Cornelis, with his friend Jan Pete, walked back home to reclaim their steady winter job in the flax industry.

With no better prospects in sight to improve his living conditions, Arie Cornelis struggled on. It was a way of life and there was nothing he could do to improve his future. When he was twenty years old, he met a good looking woman by the name of Willempje van der Giessen. She was the youngest one of a twin and had beautiful blond hair and freckles. Her twin sister Truida didn't look like Willempje at all. Truida had raven black hair and black eyes, she was a spitting image of her mother Jaapje who looked more Spanish than Dutch with her dark complexion.

Even poor people fall in love and get married. Somehow he had been able to make a meager living and Willempje was also a hard working woman. Together they must be able to make a go of it. He found a little house on a farm that they rented and they got married.

The farm belonged to Kees Pleiter who had two little farm houses adjacent to the farm for his farm hands. Kees needed only one farm hand and rented the other little house to Arie Cornelis.

Kees Pleiter the farmer and landlord of Arie Cornelis, had one daughter Geertrui who he loved very much. On the other hand he didn't get along with his wife very well. His wife had been a great disappointment; she had given him only one daughter and no son. Of course, she couldn't help that but he blamed her anyway.

Besides this little problem he had with his wife, Kees was a reasonable guy. He was so reasonable that one night he sneaked into the room of his maid. Sjaan was the domestic servant on the farm and served for night and day. She slept on the farm and had her own room. Sjaan had the shock of her life when the farmer entered her room. She was already in bed which was alright with Kees; he said to her: "Come on girl, move up a little to make some room for me in your bed."

Sjaan was a young strong girl who didn't take that kind of attitude and punched Kees right in the face with her fist. Kees left in a heck of a hurry and Sjaan was still trembling in her bed fearing that Kees might come back and try again. There was no lock or bolt on her door so Kees could walk in any time.

The next morning she was planning to pack up her belongings and leave but first she went to talk to her friend Wilempje and tell her about her adventures. Willempje said: "Maybe it's better to stay on to next Spring when your contract will be terminated. You have only two months to go and you were planning to call it quits anyway because you are getting married. I think that Kees has learned his lesson, he might be the farmer, and you sleep in a room on his farm but that doesn't give him the right to sleep with you. After you punched him out, I don't think he has the nerve to try this again."

Sjaan wasn't too sure but when Kees came over to apologize, he promised that it would never happen again and he would leave her alone. She then decided to take the advice of Willempje and stay till her contract was finished.

On December 3rd 1898 Arie Cornelis and Willempje had their first baby. It was a daughter and they called her Jacoba Treintje (Calling name Ko), after the mother of Willempje. With a family to support, it meant a hardship when he was laid off in early Spring, but as always he put his old basket on his neck with a clean set of underwear and a couple of loaves of bread and walked with his friend Jan Pete to the Haarlemmer Lake Polder.

Willempje had known that this was coming and had turned every penny over twice before she spent it. She had enough money till her husband would send her some money by mail and besides she did some work for the farmers for which she got paid.

Then on August 18th 1901 the couple was blessed with a baby boy who was going to be the name carrier of the family. They called him Henk after the father of Arie Cornelis. Girls were usually called after their mother's mother. When they married they would lose the family name anyway but boys would keep their family name and the family name would be carried from generation to generation. Henk was born on the farm but he wasn't a farmer's son, he was the son of poor Arie Cornelis.

Kees Pleiter was jealous of Arie Cornelis who had a son. Other farmers teased him that he should hire Arie Cornelis to get the job done. Two years later in 1903, another daughter was born and they called that one Treintje Jacoba.

Another two years went by before the good old stork returned with a baby girl called Apolonia.

About a year later Kees Pleiter's daughter got married and Kees sold the farm. The new farmer wanted to keep two farm hands so he needed both his little houses. Consequently he told Arie Cornelis to move out. Henk was already five years old and he couldn't understand that the farmer just could come over to kick them out. That was not fair at all, it was their house. How come that they were sitting on a kicking chair?

Arie Cornelis looked around for a place to live and found a little house on the Noldyke that he could rent for 50 cents per week. The house was one of three row houses that had only one toilet sharing. It was an outside toilet like all other houses had. That was a problem in the morning when everybody wanted to use the biffy at the same time. The girls were standing outside with their hands between their legs waiting for their turn. They were shouting: "Hurry up I can't hold it any longer." Boys had it easier; they just peed against a tree.

It was a very small house for a family with four children and one more was on its way. When you opened the outside door there was a little back porch of three square meters for the wooden shoes. The wooden shoes were scrubbed once a week and were standing neatly in a row. The smallest kid put his wooden shoes on the far left and so on to size. With the wooden shoes neatly in a row, Willempje only had to count the pairs of wooden shoes to see if all her children were in the house.

In the little back porch were also two pails of water. Above one of the pails was a little dipping pan hanging on a rusty nail. That pail was for drinking. The other pail was for the dishes and other cleaning. Both pails were filled with water from the ditch which was clean water and unpolluted in those days.

When you opened the living room door there was a ladder, right behind the door; leading up to the attic. In the day time the ladder was in the way, and could be removed to get more room. It could be put against the wall.

In the living room were two cupboard beds. One of the cupboard beds was for Arie Cornelis and Willempje. Arie Cornelis had made a little wooden box at the foot end to put the baby in. On the bottom of the wooden box was some straw on which the baby slept. For a blanket, Willempje used one of her old skirts and during the winter she put an old coat on top of her old skirt to keep the baby warm. There was no money for luxuries like blankets, even the other children and Arie Cornelis slept on straw and covered themselves with old clothes and coats.

It was handy to have the baby sleeping at the foot end of their bed, whenever the baby cried Willempje could just grab it to breast feed the baby. That usually quieted the baby and everything was peace and quiet again.

Between the two cupboard beds in the living room, was a kitchen cupboard and in the second cupboard bed the youngest children slept. When the children were small, four children could sleep in that cupboard bed. The older children all slept in the loft, they could look after themselves. When the children got older, more of them would have to sleep in the loft. The four girls would sleep in the loft and the two boys would sleep in the second cupboard bed. You couldn't have girls and boys sleeping in the same room.

Underneath one of the cupboard beds were the potatoes and underneath the other cupboard bed was the coal which would be needed during the winter. Above the cupboard beds were shelves which were used to put the pee pot and the alarm clock on. Everything was made handy for the occupants of the little house. The toilet was outside and nobody in his right mind would dress himself to go to the outhouse during the night.

Even when Willempje got more babies and the family had grown to six children, they made do with the very small house. They barely got by and there was no money to rent a bigger house. In the living room was the stove and there was also a table that could be extended for the meals. The children were still small and three could sit on two chairs. They also put a board across two chairs which made it possible for four children to sit. One could call it a close family, everybody was very close. A brother might put his elbow in his sister's plate, so close they were.

The Noldyke was a gravel road that was dusty in summer and during fall and winter it was full of water filled potholes. When the farmers were harvesting there was a lot of mud falling off the wagon wheels and soon the Noldyke looked like a farmer's field. The police stepped in and told the farmers that they had to clean the wheels of mud before they entered the Noldyke. If they didn't do as they were told, they would get a ticket.

The gravel road was fixed with loads of gravel. Each year, the road became higher and the houses that were built at the same level as the dyke now needed a step to get onto the dyke.

Henk was 6 years old and had to go to school, but first he had to visit the doctor to get his vaccination against small pox. Smallpox epidemics had wiped out entire villages in the 17th and 18th Centuries and there wasn't a treatment against the disease. In order to avoid a smallpox epidemic in the future, the only hope they had was prevention. Mass vaccinations took place and the disease was more or less under control. Before the children went to school, they had to have a medical certificate that vaccination had taken place. That was the law.

There were nine classes of eight months at school and the second class was in the same room as the first class. After Henk was seated the teacher gave him a slate with slate pencil so he could learn how to write.

The Netherlands was a prosperous country that had colonies in the East and in the West but unfortunately few benefited from the riches. There was the elite clique that kept the laborers poor. It was a conspiracy against the poor. A rich farmer was overheard by his maid, when he was talking to the Reverend. The farmer said to the Reverend: "If you keep the laborers stupid, I'll keep them poor. That way we'll have them under control and won't have too much trouble with them."

Church policy was: "Don't make the labourers wise because you'll never get them dumb again." The church was exploiting human stupidity. The same policy was maintained with the colonies, they never educated the people lest they would start demanding more money.

Laborers were permanently poverty stricken with no hope for a better future. If they had work, they were happy because without work, they would be starving. At the best of times when they were working they were poor but they made a go of it. The poor people were marked by the clothes they were wearing. They were dressed in overalls or a strong Manchester pair of pants because they had to last a long time. Workers were usually wearing a checked shirt that wouldn't show dirt and had a red hanky that wouldn't show dirt either. Office workers had a white hanky and a white shirt. They were also wearing a pair of pants with a sharp crease in them.

Hygiene wasn't a word in the vocabulary of the workers. Saturday night, they went with their dirty faces to the barbershop for a five cent shave. When they came home they put their heads underneath the tap and with a little green soap, they washed their face, hands and feet. The rest of their bodies never saw water or soap. Only when they got soaked in a rain storm did their body get wet. On Saturday, they also put a clean undershirt and underpants on and that was good for the entire week.

(A man was pretty deaf and when he had to visit his doctor he took his wife along so she could tell him what the doctor said. After a thorough check up, the doctor said: "I need a urine, a stool and a sperm sample."

The man asked his wife, "What did the doctor say?"

His wife answered: "The doctor said to leave your under panties.")

Heintje de Weerd had six children and his wife had died. He worked for Besjaan Nuchteren as a loose laborer and got paid for the hours he worked. One week, because of a lot of rain, he made two guilders and fifty four cent which wasn't adequate at all to feed his family. In order to feed his children, he went to the Poor People's Committee for assistance. The Poor People's Committee existed of rich farmers and other well to do business men. He was told that on Saturday he could get two loaves of bread and 25 cents. He had to walk half an hour to the town hall to get it.

When there was nothing to do during the winter Heintje with his six children were starving. Once a week, he could pick up two loaves of bread and twenty five cents at the town hall. With his growing kids, that wasn't enough for two days. What would he eat the remainder of the week? Looking at the hungry faces of his offspring, he had to do something. Finally he was at his wit's end, swallowed his pride and went to the stable of Besjaan Nuchteren to beg for food. He found Besjaan with two other fat farmers with golden watch chains on their big fat bellies, smoking big cigars. Heintje asked: "Besjaan, can I get some of those very small potatoes that you are feeding to your pigs. We are hungry!"

Besjaan's answer to that request was: "Don't my pigs have to eat?"

Heintje left and Besjaan said to the other two farmers: "Those laborers are a problem; you should be able to plow them under in winter and dig them up in spring when there is work."

The farmers took better care of their cattle and the horses than of their workers. As soon as the harvest was completed, the workers were sent home. A situation like this could bring a good honest man to steal. When that happened, they would throw him in jail. That man was a thief and it said in the Ten Commandments: "Thou shall not steal!" Naturally, that man had to be punished. Just throw him in jail and throw the key away, he had it coming.

Those hypocrites knew the Bible so well, but they forgot the most important thing that on God's earth, everything grows for all his creatures. Of course, the judge would never see it that way and had to put up an example to discourage others from stealing. The Reverend read the Ten Commandments every Sunday. That was the law but the Ten Commandments also dictate that we have to love everybody like ourselves. Unfortunately, that part was never considered. Besides, taking advantage of poor people is stealing too.

In the play and movie, "Les Miserables," a man was sentenced for stealing a loaf of bread to feed his hungry family. The man was sentenced to four years of hard labor in a labor camp. This was just a movie but lots of people had unpleasant experiences like that. When you are hungry, the Ten Commandments or laws of the country mean nothing.

When Besjaan's wife got sick, he suddenly remembered Heintje who needed help. His oldest daughter had finished school and could work for Besjaan's wife every day from 8.00 a.m. till twelve noon. A whole day's help wasn't needed that would cost too much money. Besjaan had it all figured out, the girl was finished at noon just before lunch. That way, he didn't have to feed her. That would be too expensive; he already paid her a lot of money. Four hours of work at two cents per hour, every day, amounted to 56 cents per week and moreover, she got every day a cup of weak coffee at 10.00 a.m.

Besjaan was well known to be stingy and he was always figuring ways to cheat people. One day the baker came at the door to deliver bread. Besjaan said: "I need half a loaf of bread."

When the baker gave him the bread, Besjaan said: "Let me check with my wife if we really need bread," and walked inside his house with the half a loaf of bread. When he returned he said: "No my wife said that she still has enough bread, here is your half a loaf back."

The baker knew Besjaan, and felt the cold loaf. That was not the half a loaf he gave to Besjaan because that was still warm and fresh. Besjaan had gone inside his house to change an old half a loaf for a fresh one. The baker said: "I want the half a loaf back that I gave you. I gave you fresh bread and this is stale."

Oh I'm sorry," said the shameless rich man, "I made a mistake."

There was only one smart guy who ever fooled Besjaan Nuchteren. It was Petrie the fruit man who came around with plums and cherries. To praise the wares he had for sale he would shout:

Ripe and round.
Nine cents per pound.

Petrie made a deal with Besjaan and bought all his pears on the trees that were in his orchard. That meant that Petrie had to pick the pears himself. An agreement was made that Petrie would pay half of the agreed upon price when he started to pick and the other half he would pay when he was finished picking.

Petrie picked all the pears from the trees except from one little tree. Besjaan asked him several times to finish picking the pears so he would get paid. Every time Petrie promised to pay Besjaan as soon as he had finished picking the pears. Christmas came and the pears were still on the little tree. By now Besjaan knew that he had been had by Petrie. No matter how much Besjaan threatened to go to court, Petrie wouldn't finish picking the pears. If Besjaan wanted to go to court, it would cost him a lawyer and that was too much money that the stingy farmer couldn't afford. And so, Petrie got away with cheating Besjaan out of some of his money.

Even with working hard long hours, Arie Cornelis made barely enough money to feed the mouths of his growing family. There was enough bread but there was only a token of margarine on it. Willempje would put a little margarine on the bread and then she scraped it all off to put it back in the butter dish. She scraped more butter off the bread than she put on it and consequently the butter dish was always full of bread crumbs.

A token of syrup was also on the bread. A slice of bread with sugar was a luxury and happened only on Sunday if affordable. Sugar was too expensive. Milk in the coffee was also a luxury which was reserved for the Sundays. The whole family looked forward to Sunday which was a feast when you had milk in the coffee and perhaps a slice of bread with sugar.

At noon, the potatoes were dished out on a dish with a cup of salt water in the middle of the potatoes. Everybody sitting around the table took a piece of potato on a fork and dipped it in the salt water for the taste. That salt water came from the water in which the potatoes had been cooked. A delicacy was potatoes with buttermilk. That only happened when the farmer was making butter and sold the buttermilk for two cents for half a pail.

Sometimes, they caught a pike in one of the ditches. That was a feast; Willempje would fry the pike in bear butter. That was a name for margarine, attached by the rich farmers who ate of course, farmer's butter. A cheap way to cook their food, which was mainly cooking potatoes and making coffee, was on the open pit outside. In summer they burned flax straw in the open pit and suspended a kettle on a chain to cook their food. Flax straw was cheap but it didn't come free. A large bag cost ten cents.

In late autumn they started to burn the stove inside for heat and cooking. Willempje worked a lot during summer. She bound the flax sheaves for the farmers and made some money to buy coal and potatoes for the long winter. Because of lack of coal, people used a hay box. They got their food cooking and then put it in the hay box to finish it.

Toys were non existent for the poor children. Willempje made some dolls of old rags and filled them up with sawdust. Old cigar boxes that she got from the farmers served as beds for the dolls.

There was not enough oil to burn the oil lamp all night so when it got dark Willempje would take the youngest one on her lap and the other children were sitting in front of her on the floor. It was singing time. They were singing hymns and other Christian songs together. After a while even the youngest children participated in the singing. An hour after it had become dark, the oil lamp was finally lit.

After the singing, it was bed time. They were allowed to play together for a while until Willempje decided that it was enough. Before the children stepped into their beds, they had to sit on their knees to pray. And after the prayers they stepped into their beds to sleep on the hay and were covered with old sweaters and coats.

Home made toys were made from old rags. Old skirts, pants and shoes they had were gifts from rich farmers and an old squeaky bed came from grandma. They were all gifts and everything was old. That's all the family had. The children were walking in clothes from the children of rich farmers. Those children would wear the clothes for a while and then they were given to Willempje. The oldest children would wear the second hand clothes until they grew out of them and then they went to the next oldest in line.

They were poor but they were happy, they had a very good mother and each other to play with. Used to a meager existence, they didn't know they were poor until some kids from rich farmers started to shout at them: "You are poor!" They were blamed for being poor as if it was a crime.

On the other hand, there were the rich farmers who didn't know what poverty was. They took advantage of their laborers and paid them very little for a lot of hard work. There were two farmers with the name of Bas Visser. In spite of the fact that they had the same name, they weren't related to one another. To keep them apart, the people called them "The Rich Bas" and "The Poor Bas." The Poor Bas didn't have much land but the Rich Bas had large parcels of land and a lot of cattle.

The family of the Rich Bas consisted of two daughters and a son. Both his daughters were married to important people. One of his daughters was married to the Mayor of Barendrecht. His son was an alcoholic who had only one friend, "The Bottle."

The Rich Bas was a Pharisee among the Pharisees. He had made enough money to call it quits and had a beautiful villa built. For transportation, he had a luxury coach with two beautiful white horses. Every Sunday, his servant had to put the coach outside with the horses. Then the Rich Bas would drive the coach, with his wife and daughter, to the church. In spite of the fact that there were four seats inside the coach and two on the front, the servant had to walk half an hour to church. The servant had left after he had put the coach outside and on purpose he arrived earlier than his boss. At the church, the servant waited for his boss to arrive and after the two passengers got out of the coach, he would take the horses with the coach to a nearby farm.

In the church, the servant had a reserved seat on the very last bench. Rich Bas with all the other rich people were sitting in the front of the church with golden watch chains on their big fat bellies. The poorer you were the more you would sit to the back. The church wasn't exactly free, the seats were rented and there were collections. Seats in front of the church were the most expensive ones. That way, all the poor suckers ended up sitting in the back of the church.

Arie Cornelis, with his family, was sitting in the second bench from the rear. The rich ladies were sitting in the middle, at the front of the church. During the winter months, the Verger would bring them a foot stool with a pot in which a piece of coal was burning. That way, they wouldn't get cold feet. For rich people only! Poor people weren't supposed to have cold feet.

When the Reverend announced the last hymn that the congregation had to sing, the servant left the church to get the coach with horses for his master. All what was left was the singing of the last hymn and the blessing. Apparently, the Lord only blessed the ones who were already blessed, "the farmers."

After the ladies got into the coach, the Rich Bas rode in the coach back home and the servant walked again. Back home, the Rich Bas would tie the horses to a tree and when the servant arrived after his walk, he would take the horses to the stable to take care of them.

It was hard to understand why his servant had to walk. There was plenty of room in the coach and even a seat at the front beside the Rich Bas. Of course, the Rich Bas had to keep up his important position in the community and therefore it was beneath his dignity to sit in the same coach as his servant.

One day when Henk passed the pasture of the Rich Bas, he saw one of the nice white horses lying flat on the ground and making difficult painful movements with his hoof. When he looked at the horse, it seemed that it had a broken leg. The vet was called but the leg wasn't curable, so the horse had to be shot and butchered. Killing the horse brought out the tears of Rich Bas, they were streaming down his cheeks and he noisily blew his nose. People thought that it was awful, he never cared for his workers when they were sick but when he lost a horse he cried.

The horse was butchered and the meat was sold to the poor people. Nothing was given away except some peas that the government gave to the poor. Actually, the government didn't give anything. Some rich warehouse master probably found some bags with old peas that were no good anymore. It looked as if the peas had been taken by Napoleon to Russia and he had brought them back. Willempje soaked them for three days in water but when she cooked them they still were hard as a stone. They were so old that they had turned into little stones.

The team of white horses pulling his coach had been the pride of the Rich Bas. He tried desperately to find a matching white horse. When he failed to do so, he sold the one left over horse and his coach. From there on, he walked to the church.

Arie Cornelis' youngest brother, Jan, also walked to the church. He hated farmers and farm work. During the winter he had taken night classes to get a good job in a manufacturing plant. One Sunday, the Rich Bas tried to walk with him for company and said: "Hi Jan, we are walking the same way so we can have company with each other."

Jan turned him flatly down and said: "No Bas, I don't want your company. You had my father working from 5.00 a.m. till 7.00 p.m. for 75 cents per day. When it was raining cats and dogs, you had my father cleaning out ditches. My father told you that he would be wet all over and he might get sick but you told him to go. You called your dog back because it was no weather for a dog to be outside but a farmhand didn't matter, if he died you would just hire another farmhand. I make more money per hour than you paid my father for a long day."

Bas argued: "Working in a manufacturing plant is no good with all those machines that take away work and nowadays with all those red people, those Socialists, a plant is not good for you."

Jan interrupted: "For your information, I'm as red as a red beet but that's not my fault. You and your buddies in crime have made Socialists. When you were 50 years old, you had a beautiful villa built to retire in. That money came from the sweat of our backs, from the money that you short changed us. You are rich but I don't want to change places with you. The Lord will judge you for the wrongful things you've done. The way you farmers cheat us and threaten us, I don't think there is a farmer going to heaven. Good bye Bas, go to the church and sit in the first bench with your solemn face."

The Rich Bas smoked only cigars that cost five for a dime. Those were expensive cigars because most of the cigars cost only one cent each. But he was rich and he wanted to show it. Whenever there was an old shirt, blouse, sweater or any other old piece of clothing, he gave it to his maid who in turn gave it to Willempje. Willempje wasn't a seamstress but she managed to alter or repair clothes for her family. If it was too big, she would take the pants or blouse apart and make it smaller.

Willempje's skill contributed largely to keep her family clad. Once a month, Mr. Sloof came with his boy who pushed a wheelbarrow. Underneath a tarp, there were rolls of material to make blouses, skirts etc. He also sold wool for knitting. Mr. Sloof was a nice guy, if the woman paid half the cost, he would extend credit for the other half.

Black Bet was a neighbor of Willempje, she was called that way because of her raven black hair and was a blessing in disguise. She helped with the delivery of babies and after the delivery she made a glass of brandy, mixed with an egg and sugar for the new mother. That was good to get a lot of milk for the baby, she said. If somebody was sick, she would do the house keeping for the sick person and never accepted money for her services. Everybody was poor and helped one another when needed.

Aunt Trui had a baby every year, as soon as her husband took off his pants, she was already pregnant. She wouldn't mind to pass a year without a baby for a change. Black Bet had the solution and it wasn't the solution of the jokers. A woman who had likewise a baby every year went to the doctor for advice. The doctor said: "That's easy enough to fix. All you have to do is buy a new pair of wooden shoes and put them on before you go to bed. I can guarantee you that you won't have anymore babies."

After a few months, the woman came back and said to the doctor: "I followed your advice to put on a pair of new wooden shoes before I went to bed. How come I am pregnant?"

The doctor asked her: "Did you cut the string that holds the wooden shoes together?"

When her answer was affirmative, the doctor said: "You are not supposed to cut the string of your new pair of wooden shoes. If the wooden shoes stay together so do your legs and if you don't spread your legs when you go to bed, you won't get pregnant." It was that simple.

(For the people who are not familiar with wooden shoes, the wooden shoes are held together with a string when they are sold.)

Black Bet's advice was: "If you don't want a baby every year, keep breast feeding the baby. That way, the baby will suck it off." It's hard to understand "old folk medicine" but it helped. Her last baby Japie was already two years old and she hadn't become pregnant yet. There was only one problem, Japie got little teeth and hurt his mother a lot. Trui decided that it was enough breast feeding and her two year old had to be weaned.

That was easier decided than done, Japie screamed murder when he didn't get his mother's breast anymore and followed her everywhere. He would unbutton her blouse and grab her breast. Luckily, Black Bet knew a way to solve the problem. She put mustard on the nipples and when Japie grabbed her breast again, he spit it out and ran away. Japie was finished with breast feeding and didn't even want to come close to his mother's breast.

Willempje delivered another baby boy in 1907. Unfortunately the boy died after four days. The blinds were closed indicating that there was a death in the house. They made a little wooden box, put some shavings on the bottom and put the baby in it. They carried the box with the dead baby to the church yard. Rich people were buried in the front of the church yard with elaborate head stones. Poor people were buried at the very back of the church yard. At the very rear of the church yard was a little hole dug. Arie Cornelis put the box in the hole and put sand over it. Discrimination was the norm in those days. The rich were always first and in the front of everything.

Willempje was pregnant again and expecting another baby in April 1909. Queen Wilhelmina was also expecting a baby in April. Needless to say, nobody took notice of Willempje's coming baby other than the direct family. With the Queen it was quite a different story. As soon as the happy occasion was announced, the entire world hastened to send presents to the Queen. Within weeks, the Queen received 27 cradles, over a hundred dolls and rattlers from gold. Poor people, like Willempje, wondered what the Queen would do with 27 cradles, the baby could only sleep in one cradle at a time while Willempje's baby would be sleeping in a wooden box with straw, covered with an old skirt.

The entire country got ready to celebrate as soon as the Queen's baby would arrive and Willempje was thinking how she would feed another mouth. Willempje beat the Queen with her baby that was born on April 5th and the Queen came in second when she welcomed a baby girl on April 30th.

People were dancing in the streets and were shouting: "Orange for ever! Long live the Queen." Only the rich people were happy; most of the poor people didn't care too much for the Queen, they only got a tip from all the riches abound and besides, they were only second class citizens, yet they were still part of the celebrations. As a matter of fact they wouldn't dare not to participate.

Socialism had made advances in The Netherlands and Government, church and farmers did anything to suppress it. If you said anything about the Queen or didn't celebrate, you might be called a Socialist. Poor people couldn't afford that because they might be run out of town. Reluctantly, most of the poor people were wearing orange buttons, put orange ribbons in the girl's hair and an orange sash around the middle of the boys. *(Orange was the color of the reigning monarch because of one of her forefathers who was Prince of Orange, a small German state in Germany. Whenever the Queen had a birthday or any other celebration in which the people of The Netherlands participated; all Dutch patriots wore orange.)*

Willempje called her new born baby girl Johanna and the Queen called her baby girl Princess Juliana Louise Emma Maria Wilhelmina. It seemed that the Queen had a way to get rid of a lot of her unnecessary presents. All girls born in April received a present and the children born on April 30th received a cradle. Girls born in the same week as the new Princess received 25 guilders and girls born two weeks before the Princess received 15 guilders. The farther you were from the magic birthday the less you received.

Willempje received 10 guilders; her daughter was born 25 days before the Princess. The police came to deliver 10 guilders, as a gift from the Queen, to

Willempje because her baby girl was born in the month of April. The police man said: "In name of the Queen, congratulations with your new born daughter and as a present from the Queen I have the honor to present you with 10 guilders."

That was all very nice but it seemed that the devil had the habit to shit always on the same pile. The wife of the rich coalman Berkman delivered her baby girl the same hour as the Queen. She received a cradle and 25 guilders. Mrs. Berkman gave her new born daughter the same names as the daughter of the Queen except Princess.

In spite of the insignificance of the town of Rysoord people were feasting. The feast committee had a parade organized with decorated wagons. There were prizes for the best decorated wagon and the first prize was 10 guilders, the second prize 5 guilders and the third prize 2 guilders. Six judges had to determine which wagons were the winners and award the prizes.

For the children, the celebrations started at 9.00 in the morning. First of all, the children were treated with a rusk with orange hail and a cup of chocolate milk. Of course, the children of the rich farmers were treated first, they got lots of orange hail but when the poor children were treated, they had just run out of orange hail. Henk got a rusk with a little margarine on it.

When all the decorated wagons arrived, it was the intention that all the children would be sitting on the decorated wagons. Again, the rich children ran to the wagons of their fathers. The poor children were supposed to ride on the wagons too but when Henk jumped on a nicely decorated wagon, the rich children tried to push him off. When that didn't work, they called their father for help. Their father turned around and shouted: "Go away you tramp," and hit him with the whip in his face.

Henk jumped off the wagon, holding his hand on his aching face. He watched the decorated wagons go by with girls and boys in orange shirts and skirts and waving flags. At the end of the parade was poor farmer Wout with an old wagon. He had decorated his wagon and horse beautifully but he was not counted among the big farmers and was pushed to the back of the parade. There was a place for Henk on this wagon that seemed to be reserved for the poor kids. "Birds of the same kind flock together," they say. Rich and poor don't flock together but poor and poor do.

The judges were seated on a platform at the end of the parade route. They were in charge of judging the decorated wagons and awarding the prizes. Wout was the last one to pass the tribunal with his decorated wagon but the dignitaries didn't even look at his wagon. Such a farmer wasn't considered at all no matter how nice his wagon was decorated. What would the rich farmers say if a poor sucker like Wout would win a prize.

It was too bad that discrimination played a big part in the contest. The richer you were; the more clout you had and the more chance you had to be awarded a prize. Rich people controlled town hall, the church and everything else. Of course, the first prize went to a very rich farmer and the judges of the feast committee didn't even look at the nicely decorated wagon of a poor little farmer. Money was circulated among the rich and a poor sucker never had a chance.

The feast continued with contests and games but Henk was told by the Principal to go out of the way to the back. Henk had his pockets full of the discrimination that was going on. His cheek was hurting and so was his pride. "It really hurts to be poor," Henk thought, "on his face and in his heart."

Willempje couldn't believe that Henk was already home that early and neither could she believe that a rich farmer would lash his whip in Henk's face. Those farmers pretended they were Christians and look what they did. They thought they could get away with anything, just because they were rich. She put a towel with cold water on Henk's marked face while she was still mad. There was not much she could do; there was no use to complain about it to the authorities, because the law would be on the side of the rich farmer. This boy was a real pest; when he was told to get off the wagon he didn't and had to be taught a lesson. Moreover, she couldn't afford to get a farmer mad, if you made one farmer mad, they all would be mad and that could be a disaster. They would get no more work and have no house to live in. All she could do was swallowing her pride and accept the abuse and injustice which was going on in the beautiful town of Rysoord.

The feast ended at night when a bunch of teen agers, who were drunk, were singing on their way home:

Why should I give a damn for Wilhelmien the Queen,
It's only a dame I've never seen.
Orange forever, long live the wild Mien.

ONLY CHANGE IS CONSTANT....

.... So they say. The rich farmers and industrialists didn't want a change, they were sitting pretty. In spite of the desperate struggle of the ruling class to combat Socialism, it seemed that they were fighting a losing battle. More and more people hated the ruling clique and supported Socialism. In spite of the repressive Government, a change was in the offing.

The Government had all kinds of tricks in place to combat Socialism. In towns like Rysoord it wasn't that hard, they just starved the people who wouldn't dance to the pipes of the governing clique. The individual human being counted for little and his personal preferences for less.

Fast developing cities made some changes and undermined the power of the churches. The Netherlands was supposed to be a Democracy with a Constitutional Government. In ancient times, Democracy meant that all the citizens of a community met in the market place and decided on all matters that had to be dealt with. In a modern state Democracy it meant to exclude undesirable elements such as Communists and Socialists. Those people were not welcome and the Communist Party was outlawed in the U.S. and other Capitalist countries as well. The excuse was that Communists were traitors that wanted to sell out their country to the Soviet Union.

Socialism goes as far back as Plato but it had taken to 1848 before Carl Marx came up with his Communist Manifesto. His manifesto stated that there had to be a classless Society with an equal distribution by the State of all goods and services.

This sounded all very good in the ears of the poverty stricken people in Russia who were ruled by the ruthless Tsar who sent people to Siberia for the least disobedience to the State. There had to be a better system in which people wouldn't starve to death and had some rights. When Lenin started to preach Communism in Russia, the people believed in him; besides, it was impossible for them to get it any worse than they had it right now. The people supported Lenin to overthrow the Tsar and expected a better living after the successful Revolution.

Unfortunately, for the Russians, it never happened. Now the ruling clique consisted of the top rulers of the Communist Party which were more ruthless than the Tsar had ever been. Now there was the famous knock on the door in the middle of the night that rounded up people who weren't dancing to the pipes of the Communist regime. Hundreds of thousands of people were banned to Siberia where they suffered a gruesome death.

The Capitalist regime in The Netherlands made hay out of the bizarre situation in Russia. Photos in the newspapers pictured churches that were filled with corpses as a result of the Communist regime that preached that Religion was the opium of the poor people. In order to make Communism work they were hell bent to eradicate Religion completely.

In spite of the propaganda of the Capitalist clique, more and more people made a stand against the Capitalist. The Netherlands was supposed to be a Democratic country after the absolute power of a Monarch had been abolished in a lot of countries throughout the world. People weren't taking the brutality of an absolute ruler anymore; they killed him or banished him out of the country. In order to keep control, the Capitalists had taken away the absolute power of the Queen and had instituted Democratic elections. In this new system, the majority would rule, the Queen would be just a figurehead and the rights of the minorities would be protected.

They made a deal with the Queen on the level that if you scratch our backs we'll scratch yours. She was the Head of State, could keep all her money and palaces and in return the Ministers of her Government would be responsible for the people and the country.

Elections came with all citizens participating. However, there were all kinds of election restrictions with respect to property, residence, sex, education and race. In the U.S. Negroes weren't allowed to vote and women's suffrage was unheard of. That would never happen. Women didn't have any brains to decide on political matters was the argument. It took some doing before the secret ballot was introduced. In the U.S. you could be shot if you didn't vote for the preferred candidate and in The Netherlands you would be run out of town.

In The Netherlands, property ownership was a requirement for voting rights. How could anybody vote who didn't have property? A person without property was a person without brains and wasn't fit to vote at all. After a long struggle everybody could vote but the clause in the Democracy that the rights of the minority had to be protected was adhered to. Rich farmers and industrialists were in the minority, there were more poor people than rich people. Therefore a farmer or an industrialist had ten votes while the poor suckers only had one vote. That was done to offset the sheer number of people without property. If this wasn't done they reasoned, their rights of a minority weren't protected.

Finally, the Capitalists had to yield to a Democratic election where everybody had a vote and even the women were voting. Women suffrage came in 1919 in The Netherlands after the First World War had ended. There was an outcry about the millions of people that had died during the war and women's groups demanded to have a vote as well to prevent it from happening again.

The voting was done by popular vote rather than by ridings. Members of Parliament don't represent a riding like they do in Canada; they represent the entire country so every vote counts. It doesn't matter where you cast your vote, in the city or in the country, your vote counts for the party you voted for.

In The Netherlands there are a lot of splinter parties. Anybody can start a political party; you don't have to be rich although being rich has proven to be helpful. There is no large deposit required that you forfeit if you don't have a certain number of votes like in Canada. The advantage is that everybody has a chance to be elected but the disadvantage is that you seldom have a majority Government.

Voting in The Netherlands was compulsory. With an election, every eligible voter would get a voting card in the mail showing where he or she had to vote. On election days; everybody had to report to the designated voting station to cast a ballot. People who didn't appear were fined. After the struggle that everybody had a right to vote on even terms, the Government went the other way and had decided that voting was a privilege but in order to get a proper Government which represented all people, everybody had to vote.

If you were unable to vote, you had to appoint somebody else to vote for you. In that case you had to fill out the back of your voting card to tell them why you couldn't vote and give them the name and address of the person who was going to vote for you. Some people who didn't want to be told by the Government that they had to vote rebelled and out of protest they voted for the last candidate on the voting list. If you were the last candidate on the last list, you would normally get only your own vote and the vote of your family but now you would get an extra number of votes. Other people who didn't understand the voting system voted for the first candidate on the list so the very first candidate and the very last had the advantage of the dumb people and the rebels.

Socialism increased and the churches had to do something about it. The churches had success by preaching doom if the Socialists took over. According to the Bible there had to be bosses and workers and also rich and poor, that's the way the Lord had meant it to be. And you can't argue with God, can you now? Granted that not everybody can be a boss and that somebody has to do the work. However, the Bible clearly states that the laborer is worthy of his wages and that point was missed by the rich clique. They only read in the Bible what they wanted to read. Most of the working people were poor suckers who believed in their leaders and started to shout, "Red neck" at the Socialists.

Finally, Arie Cornelis found a job at the ship yard of Boele in Bolnes. The hours of work were long from 6.00 a.m. till 7.00 p.m. It was more than an hour's walk to get there so he had to leave his house 4.45 a.m. and he would return home at 8.15 p.m. He had to get up at 4.00 a.m. and that all for 8 cents per hour. It was also hard work because most of the work was done by hand. On Saturday, he was off early; they worked only till 5.00 p.m. If he was lucky and worked all week he made 7 guilders per week but especially in winter when there was a lot of snow and rain they couldn't work. They only got paid for the hours they worked; that it rained the boss couldn't help. After he got paid he would walk past the landlord to bring him 50 cents for the week's rent.

With a little more money coming in, they could afford to rent some land to grow potatoes. There were different kinds of potatoes of which the purple eye potato was grown most of all. That potato was a good tasting potato but grew every year fewer and smaller potatoes. Because of using that kind for hundreds of years, the potato seemed to run out of steam. Moreover, potato blight occurred a lot in purple eyed potatoes and potato blight was a feared sickness among potatoes. The Irish potato blight of 1855 was a disaster remembered by everybody and nobody wanted to take any chances.

Potatoes are native to Peru (South America) and were feeding the people of Peru for over two thousand years before they came to Europe. In 1532 when Pizarro arrived with his Spanish hordes in Peru, he was looking for gold and silver and perhaps diamonds. Pizarro looked for nothing else but treasure, but all the treasure he found was just small potatoes, compared to the treasure he trampled on with his pirate boots. He ran right over potatoes and tomatoes, the very food that would feed the world in the future.

Eventually, the Spanish recognized the food value of potatoes and brought them back to Spain around the early 1600's. It was a great success especially since you could feed more people from one cultivated acre when you were planting potatoes instead of grains. The Irish farmer went all for potatoes, especially since there was political unrest in Ireland and marauders quite often burned the wheat fields which left the population starving. Potatoes were the ultimate solution to that problem, you just don't burn a field with potatoes.

Old Folk medicine had it that potatoes were not only good staple food, they also gave man more vigour with sex and they even cured arthritis. Many people put a small potato in their pocket or purse to combat arthritis pain. The potato was the greatest invention of that time, it wasn't destructible or so it seemed.

In 1845, the potato crop which couldn't be destroyed by marauders was wiped out by potato blight and left the Irish starving. Potato blight is a fungus that destroys the entire foliage and consequently no potatoes are harvested. By that time, the Irish were as dependent on potatoes as the Chinese were on rice. The average Irishman ate about 8 lbs. of potatoes per day and without potatoes the Irish were starving which decimated the population from 8.5 million to 6.5 million, a loss of 2 million people. Many more people emigrated to the U.S. which reduced the population some more. Potato crops were sprayed with copper sulfate to combat blight.

Densely populated, The Netherlands saw the value of potatoes as well and followed the lead of Ireland. What Ireland had England could have, too, and they started to plant potatoes in England as well. Nobody knew anything about potatoes so beginning proved difficult.

The Royal Family had a big celebration in the Palace; it had to be a big splash with an extensive dinner. When the menu organizer put the menu together he thought it plenty smart to put potatoes on the menu. This was something new which would be appreciated by all royal guests, he thought.

The man who was in charge of supplies was ordered to go and get potatoes from a field just outside of London.

He didn't know what potatoes looked like so after arriving at the potato field he was flabbergasted. There were lots of potato plants but where were the potatoes? He didn't know that potatoes were growing underground which made him mighty confused. After a thorough study of the potato plants, he saw small green balls on the plants, which were the seed balls that make a peeping sound when you burn the dead potato plants. They were actually small tomatoes, because tomatoes are a relative from the potato. Only the taste is different, they taste quite bitter.

"Ah," he thought, "Eureka! I have found it!" He started to cut the little green seed balls off the plants and put them in his container. It took quite a long time before he had filled it with the small green balls but finally he had enough potatoes, he thought. Convinced that he had done his duty he returned to the palace.

Even the cook had never seen potatoes, he knew that they had to be cooked which shouldn't be too difficult. When the supplier put the container with the green seed balls on his table, he said: "Hi cookie, here are your potatoes." The cook didn't think much about it and started to prepare them.

After he had cooked the potatoes, he tasted them. They were kind of bitter but this high society was always eating strange things. Those people probably found the potatoes a real delicacy. When the potatoes were served it became a situation of the story like "The Emperor's New Clothes." Nobody dared to say that they didn't see the beautiful costume lest they would be called stupid. When you are at a royal dinner, it is very difficult to say: "Say king, those potatoes are the best crap that I ate for a long time!"

The king would probably not have been amused so everybody pretended that he had never eaten anything like that before. They were right; nobody ate the seed balls before. This sounds very stupid but if you never have seen potatoes, it isn't stupid at all.

Potato breeders had introduced a new potato, "The Eigenheimer." It was a good looking potato with blue eyes and excellent production with plenty of big potatoes. Moreover, it was a good tasting potato and resistant to blight. The only bad thing that could be said was that it took longer to mature and that two potato crops per year were not possible. Actually, that was not a problem because one crop meant less work and the total production, with bigger and more potatoes would give them as much food as with the two crops of purple eye potatoes. They decided to try their luck with the new kind, the Eigenheimer. *(New kinds of potatoes are obtained by seeding them. A potato plant produces potatoes and flowers that become berry like fruits that contain 100 to 300 seeds and the seeds produce different kinds of potatoes. Potato breeders check the seeds carefully and the number and size of the potatoes produced by one plant is very important. What is equally important is that the new potato plant has resistance to potato blight.)*

Willempje took care of the land because Arie Cornelis was home very little. Sunday was the only day he was home to see his kids. When he left for work at 5.00 a.m. the kids were still sleeping and when he came back at night at 8.15. p.m. the kids were already in bed. On Sunday he went twice to church and only Sunday afternoon, he was home for a couple of hours besides his sleeping hours. The youngest kids weren't all that happy with that strange guy in the house, they asked their mother: "Who is that guy in our house?"

Arie Cornelis was a tyrant who demanded respect and service from Willempje his wife. On Sunday morning he went to church and demanded that hot coffee was on the table when he came home and the warm meal had to be consumed right after. He took the two older kids Henk and Tryntje to church and Ko the oldest girl had to stay home to help her mother with the two babies Jaap and Joh and she also lent a hand with the cooking.

The church service started at 10.00 a.m. and lasted approximately one and a half hours. It was about a twenty minute walk from the church back home. The tyrant could be expected home about ten minutes before twelve, give or take five minutes. At a quarter to twelve Willempje got restless and worried if she didn't have the potatoes ready yet and told Ko to go to the top of the dyke to see if her husband with the two children were coming.

Ko went to the top of the dyke and stayed there till she saw her father with the two kids far away. As soon as she spotted them, she ran into the house and shouted to her mother: "They are coming!"

Willempje nervously drained the potatoes and put them on the table as soon as her husband entered the room. The tyrant looked like an inspector around the room and when he saw nothing wrong in his eyes, he said Grace. After that, the meal was consumed in silence, no talking was allowed at the table when they were eating.

The newly introduced Eigenheimer potato didn't let them down. They had more potatoes than they could eat. That was no problem at all; they would sell the surplus potatoes and had some extra cash. The boys were also helpful to make some extra money; they killed moles and skinned them. A mole skin brought ten cents and the skins were used to make fur coats for the rich. It was a tricky business to catch moles; they could dig pretty fast. The art was to stick a spade just in front of them and expose them. (A mole is a furry mammal about six inches long, it lives underground and eats worms and other insects.)

Kors de Gelder had been a farm hand for a rich farmer who had a not that great looking daughter. Eligible bachelors were looking for a girl that was prettier than she was. When years went by and no rich farmer's son asked for her hand, she married the farm hand Kors de Gelder. Kors didn't mind that she was kind of ugly; to him it meant having a farm when the old farmer died.

Unfortunately, his wife was always sick and they didn't have any children. His wife looked healthy enough, yet she always complained that she felt sick and stayed in bed. The local doctor had examined her but found nothing wrong. He gave her some medicine but nothing ever changed. His wife stayed in bed and was always complaining that she didn't feel good. One day, Kors went to see Willempje and said: "You have a daughter that has finished school. I wouldn't mind if she came to work for me. My maid is getting married and my wife is always sick, she needs help with the house keeping."

Working in the household meant for the girls that they had to braid their hair, put it in a bun on their head and do household chores. Ladies that hired household help insisted that their domestic servants didn't have loose hanging hair. Their excuse was that with loose hanging hair there could be hairs in the food. The real reason was that their household help had to be branded as household help; loose hanging hair was reserved for their daughters and themselves. Besides, the lady of the house was working with food too, but that didn't seem to matter; she couldn't have the same kind of hair as her servant.

Serving the rich was by no means easy; most of the rich ladies who hired a maid were far from nice to their servants. When the maid had completed the dusting, she would check it with white gloves on and go over all the areas that had been dusted to check if their maid had done a good job. If her gloves had any indication of dust, the lady would give her domestic servant a scolding and brand her as lazy and incompetent.

And so Ko was the first one to leave the house on the Noldyke. She was a domestic help for day and night and made one guilder per week with board and room. Sunday afternoon was the only time she had off. All mornings, including Sundays, she had to get up at 3.00 a.m. to milk the cows.

Kors had wooden pails for milking the cows. When the pails got dry they would leak milk through the open seams. Before they started to milk, he put them in the ditch for a while. That had two advantages and served two purposes. The wood expanded and the pails were leak proof again but he also left a little bit of water in the pail. That way he always had a little extra milk.

Dr. Bysterveld was a famous doctor in Rotterdam who could determine the illness of a person by looking at the urine. If you had an undetermined illness, people would say: "You better go with your piss to Bysterveld."

When Kors de Gelder heard about this brilliant Dr. Bysterveld, he decided to take some urine of his wife and let the good doctor determine the illness of his wife. Dr. Bysterfeld took the bottle of urine, shook it a bit, held it in the light and studied it for some time. After a few minutes, Dr. Bysterveld said: “Go home, take a whip and let her have it. Your wife isn’t sick at all, she is only lazy. Get her out of bed and put her to work.”

Kors wasn’t all that impressed with the doctor’s proposed remedy but he was going to try it. When he came home, he took his whip, went into the bedroom and said to his wife: “Out of bed or I’ll let you have it. You aren’t sick, go to work and if I see you in bed again I’ll give you some lashes with my whip.”

She saw that Kors meant business; got out of bed and started to work. It was an instant cure.

When Henk had finished school there was a job for him in the flax industry; he had to turn the wheel to make wind to blow the chaff away. While Henk was turning the wheel he often thought about the Dutch sea hero Admiral de Ruiter who had started his career with turning a spinning wheel to make linen. There was a patriotic song about him that after turning the wheel for some time, he had gone to sea and had become a famous Admiral.

Henk wouldn’t mind going to sea as well; at least it wouldn’t be a dusty job as he had now. Actually, it wasn’t a steady job that he had but he was lucky. After the seeds were obtained from the flax bulbs his job was finished. Luckily Kors de Gelder knew about Henk through Ko who was working for him and had a job for him as well.

Some progress was made when the neighboring town of Barendrecht got a water tower. The town had extended the water supply to Rysoord and everybody now had one cold water tap in the house. Of course, people had to pay for the water they used and the poor people couldn’t afford to pay for water. They all continued to drink water from the ditches which was good potable water too and it was free.

Another progress was the steam tram that was going from Rotterdam to Zwyndrecht. Most of the people could do without a polluter like that. Black billowing smoke came from the locomotive and the tram was also making a lot of noise to warn the people that it was approaching.

Kors de Gelder was paid a handsome sum of money to have the steam tram going right through the centre of his pasture. After collecting the money Kors had a problem, because he had quite a few cows grazing in the pasture. To prevent the cows from going on the tram dyke, he had the tram dyke fenced off with barbed wire, yet there was good grass to be had.

That was the job that Henk was offered, to look after the cows while they were grazing on the tram dyke. Whenever the tram came, he had to make sure that the cows were off the rails. The tram came only three times a day and in between, when there was no steam tram coming, Henk had to keep the pasture clear of thistles and nettles. He also had to spread the cow pies or there would be dead places in the grass.

Most of the time, Henk took a nap around noon when the cows weren't grazing. They were lying down cudding (re-chewing) their grass. A cow has four stomachs and when they rechew their grass it goes to the next stomach. (Wouldn't it be nice to go to an open buffet with four stomachs.) Henk worked from 5.00 a.m. in the morning till 7.00 p.m. at night and got paid one and a half guilders per week.

Now the children were making some money, Arie Cornelis could afford to keep a pig. Butchering a pig was quite a chore. To kill the pig, they had a pointed hammer and hit the pig with the point right above the eyes. As soon as the pig collapsed, they stabbed the pig in the throat with a long knife. The blood was caught in a big dish and from the blood, they made blood sausage. Lots of hot water was poured onto the pig to make the hairs supple so they could scrape them off.

Next, the pig was cut open and the guts were taken out. Even the guts were used; they were scraped so they could put their sausage in them. The smaller guts, that couldn't be used to put sausage in, were given to the poor people who would clean, scrape them and chop them up to cook soup out of it. Some of the lard was saved for the winter when the children had a cold. An old remedy was to put some lard on the chest of the children to get some relief. Helping neighbors who had been helping to make hot water would get a piece of bacon as reward.

Henk got a new job; he had to start Sunday at midnight to cut out the lettuce heads for the market, by full moon. His boss wanted to take the lettuce early to the market in Rotterdam which was an hour away by horse and wagon. Later in the year he had to bunch the radishes, carrots and red beets. The produce had to be clean and Henk had to wash it in the ditch. That usually got him quite wet but the wages were good compared to the money he used to make with the herding job with Kors de Gelder. He made now two and a half guilders per week.

Henk had good eyesight. When they were working on the land, he could tell the time by looking at the cathedral church in Dordrecht which was about three kilometers away. One of the other guys that was working with him said that his eyesight was better than Henk's. "I bet you," he said, "that you can't see the fly on the clock scratching his ear."

They got new neighbors who came from the city and had to adapt to small town living. The woman was very clean. Every week she put her mats on the hedge to remove the dust with a rug beater. Willempje said that she was so clean that when she broke a dish, she would dust the pieces first before she threw them in the garbage can.

It was 1913 and more and more alarming news came from the Balkans where Greeks and Turkish people were fighting about border settlements. People from Bulgaria and Bosnia were fighting as well and in the midst of all the problems was the German Emperor who did some saber rattling. Only a little spark was needed to ignite a political explosion.

That spark came in the beginning of July 1914, when the Austrian crown prince was murdered in Sarajevo, the capital of Serbia. On July 18th Austria declared war on Serbia and Germany declared war on Russia and France. Germany invaded Belgium in order to get at France, which brought England into the war. At the beginning of August, The Netherlands mobilized its army.

With the brand new war came brand new war songs. The people were singing:

The English soldiers are marching off to war.
Even when it's raining shells, they sing even more;
It's a long way to Tipperary,
It's a long way to go.
It's a long way to Tipperary,
To the sweetest girl I know.
Farewell Piccadilly,
Farewell Leicester Square.
It's a long way to Tipperary.
But my heart is over there.

The war had its impact on the people. Everything was rationed and the farmers had to deliver all their produce to the Government so they could distribute it honestly. Moreover, the farmers had to supply horses to the Government and the nut trees were cut down, that was good wood to make rifles from.

The Germans had a canon called the "Fat Bertha" that could shoot shells 40 kilometers. When the Germans were within 40 kilometers of Paris, they were shelling it. It made the green grocer sing:

I have nice red radish,
And the Germans are shooting at Paris.

The greengrocer was always joking, when he saw a barking dog he would say: "Shut up, I can't get a wink of sleep with all that noise."

He was an alcoholic and always said: "They didn't brew it for the geese and it helps against the cold and the worms." That was a good enough excuse to drink.

The Minister of Agriculture invented "The common sausage." It was made of all the junk he possibly could find. All the junk of the butcher's places like blood and chopped guts were in it but also black potatoes, ground bones and even a mole's paw was found in it.

Another invention was Eternal Porridge. It looked a lot like oatmeal and when you made porridge you only ate half of it. You added water to the other half that you didn't use and you had a full pan of porridge again. Again, you would eat half and added water to the other half to get a full pan of porridge again. This was supposed to go on for ever and you would never run out of food.

When Arie Cornelis ate a plate of this Eternal Porridge, he got a terrible tummy ache which was unbearable; he thought he was going to die or maybe he had an appendix infection. When he went to the doctor, the doctor told him that the porridge he had been eating was the culprit. The porridge was made out of fibers that would expand tremendously and therefore you could add water to get another pan of porridge. That was all very nice but when this expansion took place in your stomach, terrible cramps were the result.

Arie Cornelis said: "I have made one mistake. Before I ate the porridge I should have given some to the cat. If the cat eats it, it's good and if there is something wrong with it she wouldn't eat it. From now on I will give some to the cat when I eat something new."

In 1914, the stork visited again and delivered a boy Cornelis. Unfortunately, he didn't live long. It seemed that 1914 was a disastrous year. It was just another disaster when the house in which they lived was sold. The new owner wanted to move in the house and they were notified that they had to move out.

Next, also in 1914, Arie Cornelis had an accident at the shipyard where he worked. Some steel plates fell on his leg when a crane was moving them. His left leg was broken and he was transported to the hospital. He didn't do well at all, he got infection in his leg and it had to be amputated underneath the knee. Half a year later he came home with an artificial leg.

Arie Cornelis had accident insurance through the newspaper he was reading. If he lost a finger they would pay him 25 guilders, loss of a thumb would give him 50 guilders, an arm or leg 250 guilders and loss of two legs or arms 500 guilders. In case he became an invalid, he would get 750 guilders and if he died his family would get 1000 guilders.

That sounded great but unfortunately, the insurance company had a loophole to make sure that a lot of claimants wouldn't qualify. The accident had to be reported within four days of the accident and his accident was reported after five days. Just one day too late. That Willempje had just a baby and that they had to move were good excuses to be one day late but not to the insurance company. Too late was too late, which translated in no payment. The shipyard where he worked did a lot better, they paid his wages of 15 guilders per week right through without any deductions. They paid his wages until he died.

That accident had been foretold by a fortune teller when he was young. When they were working in the flax, one of the other workers was telling a story about a fortune teller in Rotterdam. Jan Piet, his friend, dared Arie Cornelis to have their fortune told. One Saturday night, they plucked up enough courage and walked to Rotterdam for a visit to the fortune teller.

The fortune teller had the usual deck of cards that she shuffled and exposed some of the cards. Then she said: "Arie Cornelis will get a blond wife and Jan Piet will get a darker type. Both of you will get eight children and both of you will get into an accident and lose a limb. In spite of the accident, you will both be very happy."

At the time, they didn't think much about it, this was just a joke. Time would tell. After Arie Cornelis came home with his artificial leg, he started to think. His friend Jan Piet had lost an eye when a sliver of steel hit his eye in an industrial accident and now he himself had lost a leg. Both had an income from the place where they had worked because of the accident and both were relatively happy. Moreover, Arie Cornelis had married a blond woman and Jan Piet a darker type and both had eight children. Two of Arie Cornelis children had died but he had still six left, four girls and two boys. Two boys had died. Was there something to this gypsy that she could foretell the future?

It seemed that the laborers made some headway to get a better existence. In 1916, for the first time, the free Saturday afternoon was introduced. In the beginning, people didn't know what to do with all that free time; they were used to working from early in the morning till late at night. However, they soon got used to having some time for themselves.

Babies born out of wedlock were a deadly sin; an unwed mother was unheard of. When a single woman who lived by herself was expecting a baby, the Reverend wanted to know who the happy father was. When she refused to say, the Reverend said that he wouldn't rest till he had the culprit. Unfortunately, he rested earlier than he thought and died suddenly. It was never revealed who the father was.

There didn't seem to be an end to this war and more incidents of unwed mothers happened. More and more Belgian refugees came to The Netherlands and the Dutch authorities distributed the refugees throughout the country. Most of them were young guys and the girls were attracted to them.

Nees Broekman became pregnant but didn't want anybody to know. She tied herself up so her big belly couldn't be seen. One day, she collapsed and brought a dead baby into the world and died herself, too.

Marie, a daughter of Madam the Stallion, was pregnant as well. Madam the Stallion was her nickname because her husband used to go from farm to farm with a stallion to breed horses. Marie was smarter, she said: "What was put in at the bottom of my body will get out at the bottom. What will be, will be!" She brought a healthy baby girl into the world and returned to work after a couple of weeks.

THE SILENT KILLER

Through the ages there had been all kinds of epidemics with the Plague Epidemic during the Fourteenth Century being the worst one of all. Plague was also called "Pest" or "Black Death" and was actually a rat disease. Plague outbreaks usually started in India where rats are considered to be holy. Buddhist Priests kept thousands of rats in their temples and treated them with cakes in their religious ceremonies. Fleas on rats spread the Plague fast by sucking blood and moving from one rat to the next one. It is like a mosquito spreading Malaria and other infectious deseases like Yellow Fever etc. by moving from one person to the next.

When many rats died it was an indication that Plague was coming. The fleas that were on the dead rats had no blood to suck anymore and moved onto humans. Keeping rats out of the houses was the best answer to avoid Plague Epidemics. There were more Plague Epidemics through the ages but luckily they were never as severe as the 14th Century one.

The Plague had killed almost one third of the world population with England taking the brunt of this outbreak losing more than 50% of its population. Over one thousand of England's villages had been completely wiped out. It had taken over 300 years before England's population had returned to the old pre-plague level. Not even a war had killed that many people.

Seeing that so many villages were wiped out by the Plague, the people in Oberammergau, Germany, prayed to God to spare Oberammergau and they promised to perform a Passion Play about the crucifixion of Christ. The village was spared and the people still perform the Passion Play.

There were also severe epidemics of smallpox through the ages but nobody expected a Flu Pandemic that started in March 1918 while the world was still at war. The war had a lot to do with the spreading of Flu so fast to different countries. People were quite familiar with the Flu, it occurred steadily as clockwork during most of the winters and a few people died of complications like Pneumonia. Influenza wasn't taken seriously at all, if you had it you went to bed with an aspirin and within a week you were back to normal again, that's all there was to it.

It started in an army camp in the U.S.A. which was a bad place to spread disease. With the war going on those troops were shipped overseas carrying the deadly Flu virus which killed more people than the war. U.S.A. soldiers who were infected spread the deadly virus to the soldiers that were fighting in the trenches, even the Germans were infected. It seemed that the Flu got nastier all the time; there was no stopping of the epidemic. When it spread to Spain, for the first time the press reported it. That's why it was called the Spanish Flu, in spite that it had started in the U.S. Old people, children and weak people were usually the victims of an epidemic but not this time. This deadly killer Flu virus had no selection and killed young and old with no preference. There was no cure, once infected, all you could hope for that you would survive. After attracting the deadly Flu virus, it spread to the lungs causing pneumonia and within days the victim died.

It seemed that the Flu became deadlier all the time, in less than a month all of Europe was infected and it spread at an alarming rate through the rest of the world. More than a billion people were now sick and within a month over 20 million people had died, twice as many as from the war. Once more the world population was decimated.

Then at the end of 1919, the Flu virus disappeared as mysteriously as it had come after killing more people than the Plague. Graveyards throughout the world expanded rapidly to bury all the victims of Flu and were a grim reminder how many people had died of the Spanish Flu.

In The Netherlands the Flu outbreak was severe and many people died. Willempje and her son Henk were both sick but survived. They recuperated very slowly. With the severe fever they had experienced, they were completely dehydrated. It took a couple of weeks to get their strength back.

It was busy in the Town Hall of Rysoord where the Spanish Flu had also killed a lot of people. Besides the regular day to day business, the town register had to be updated every day to account for the people who had died. The Town Hall staff had also been decimated; a couple of people had died and some were sick. There was only one man left to do all the work, so everybody said: "Hopefully you don't get the Flu because if you do there will be nobody to do the work."

He replied: "Don't worry; I'm way too busy to get sick."

In spite of his optimism, he was dead three days after he had said that. Now there was nobody left to do the work and the town hall closed for the next three weeks until one of the Town Hall workers had sufficiently recovered to do some work.

It was November 11th 1918. General Von Hindenburg suggested to the German Emperor to head his troops in the last battle. That way, he could die with his soldiers and have an honorable death. It wasn't in the plans of the German Emperor to die and he wasn't going to stay in Germany to find out what they were going to do with him either. Just in time he escaped to hospitable The Netherlands. When the Allies asked the Dutch Government to hand him over so he could be tried for war crimes, the Queen said: "We are neutral, he is our guest."

Apparently he had transferred a lot of money to Switzerland and was doing alright for himself. He bought a castle in Amerongen, married for the second time, lived like a real millionaire and expected to be addressed as "Sire." *(He became 84 and died during World War II when The Netherlands were occupied by Germany. He got a full military burial from Adolph Hitler.)*

Grandfather Hein got a visit from his oldest sister Marie. She was already 84 years old and had two sons in South Dakota. Her sons wanted her to come to the States to live with them and were going to pay for the trip. She didn't speak English and was kind of scared of engaging in such a trip by herself. Grandfather Hein said: "You should go; it's the chance of a life time."

"If I just had somebody to travel with and help me with the language," she said.

Jan, who had recently married his cousin Stein had been listening. He had always wanted to leave narrow-minded The Netherlands to go to the land of opportunity. He had learned English and wouldn't mind going with her to help her. Unfortunately he didn't have the money to pay for the passage to the States. Jan told her: "I could go with my wife and help you out but we don't have the money."

Marie said: "I'll write my sons to see what they think."

It took a couple of months before she got an answer to her letter. Her sons were willing to pay the trip for Jan and his wife. It was a deal and Jan prepared to leave The Netherlands. A few days before he left, the Rich Bas came to say good bye but Jan wasn't home. He said to Grandfather Hein: "Your son was cheesed off with me and told me what he thought about me. It took a while for me to realize that he was right. Let bygones be bygones. Tell him I said good bye and here is a box of cigars as farewell present."

Grandfather Hein was so surprised that he almost fell off his chair and

Jan was no less surprised. It looked like Jan's lecture had paid off and put the Rich Bas on the Road to Damascus.

The landlord came to tell Arie Cornelis that his daughter was getting married and she was going to move into the house that he was renting. For the third time they were kicked out of the house they were living in. Henk couldn't believe that they were chased out of their house for the third time. He vowed there and then that he would work hard and save enough money to buy a house for himself beside the river Waal in Rysoord.

Ko got a new job in Zwyndrecht. Once per month, she had a free weekend and came home on the steam tram Saturday morning and had to return Sunday night.

Tryntje found a job as a household aid with a teacher in Limburg where she later got married. She already had a boy when she was expecting her second child. There was a problem with the delivery of the baby and in the middle of the night, her husband had to go out to get the doctor. It was a miserable cold rainy night that turned into wet snow; he got soaked, got pneumonia and died a week after her second son was born.

There she was with two babies and no husband. That could have meant a life of extreme poverty if it hadn't been for the boarder that they had been keeping. The boarder was all alone as well and asked her to marry him. That was an offer she couldn't refuse and they lived happily after.

When Henk became unemployed again, he had a good look at his life. If he ever was going to succeed in life, he was on the wrong track. Poverty was a way of life; it was as if he was caught in a vortex from which he couldn't escape. It was a constant cycle of poverty. His parents were poor and though they were still living he had already inherited their poverty. The clique of rich farmers looked after their own offspring and those youngsters had a bright future while he didn't have much of a future at all.

When he found out that the Dutch Navy was recruiting young people like himself, he signed up for five years. The most important thing was that he had a job for five years and maybe he could start saving some money to make his dream of his own house at the River Waal come true. It had to be a house that nobody could kick him out of. With low paying jobs or no job at all, he would never get a house but with a steady job there was a chance. For starters, they paid him six guilders per week with a raise in sight as soon as he ranked a class higher.

As soon as he entered the Navy camp, they cut his hair bald and he had to take a shower. They gave him three sets of clothes and a coat free. Whenever he needed clothes later, he had to pay for them. Monday and Thursday were laundry days, washing clothes and darning socks.

The training took place on an old sailing ship. They learned how to climb the main mast which was 40 meters above water. Target shooting was also an important part of their training and, of course, painting and cleaning. Lots of sailors were sailing on a never come back line but the Dutch navy maintained the ships well.

After six weeks of training, they left for Batavia, the capital of the East Dutch Indies. It was going to be a five week voyage. Henk, who had seen nothing but the tram dyke with cows and vegetables he had to clean, was enthusiastic about it. Now he was going to see the world.

First they passed the Rock of Gibraltar which is the key to the Mediterranean. It was one of the important strategic possessions of England and they protected it with 1800 cannons in order to control the Mediterranean.

In the Straight of Messina were two giant eddies. They were called by their names Scylla and Charibdys. On a quiet night, one could hear some murmuring that the sailors thought was the singing of sirens that lured unsuspecting sailors to their death.

The Greek saga tells us that there were two beautiful sirens which were nymphs that were part bird and part woman that lured sailors to their death on rocky coasts, by seductive singing. The truth was that when sailors were entranced by what they thought was singing, they forgot about their ship and ended up in the two giant eddies. Consequently, the ship was lost with men and mice. The Greeks had a God for everything. Eolus was the God of the Wind and Eos was the Goddess of the dawn etc. If they didn't understand things they figured that some God had something to do with it.

Port Said was the entrance to the Suez Canal and all ships were equipped with a search light on the fore ship. While the ship was made ready for going through the canal the men were allowed to go ashore. As soon as they went ashore there was a magician who drew a big crowd with his big stories. He asked the audience for a ten guilder bank note. "You'll get it back," he said.

He threw the ten guilder bill into the air and pulled it from underneath his shoe. That was very impressive! For the gentleman that had given the ten guilder bill it wasn't impressive at all; he later found out that the bill he got back was a counterfeit.

They went to a lecture to hear all about the Suez Canal. The idea of the Suez Canal wasn't new. An old Egyptian Pharaoh managed to dig a canal between the Mediterranean and the Red Sea. Later on too much sand made it unusable. The Persians fixed it up so that it could be used again. Even Julius Caesar had been working on it.

Ferdinand de Lesseps statue stands at the beginning of the Canal. He started digging in 1859 with shovels and wheelbarrows. Hygiene was not existent and more people died than the number of cubic meters of sand that had been moved.

After ten years, in 1869, the Canal was officially opened for shipping. It was 168 kilometers long and 55 meters wide with a depth of 11 to 12 meters. There were 9 wide places for the passing of ships going in the opposite direction. Thirteen signal posts gave directions as to who could sail and who had to moor in the passing places. Big ships that went more than ten meters deep were not allowed to go faster than 6 miles per hour. It was a lot of convoy sailing.

With a speed of 8 miles per hour it took 21 hours to pass the Suez Canal. It was cheaper than going around Cape of Good Hope. Kaapstad used to be the place to land to get fuel, food and fresh water and some passengers. With the making of the Suez Canal, they lost a lot of business and had tried desperately to prevent the building of the canal.

One of the older members of the crew had landed once in Kaapstad. He said: "Before we went ashore a policeman came aboard to tell us the law of the land. It was forbidden to have sex with a colored person and imprisonment of 2 years would follow for trespassers."

The crew wasn't all that happy with the cook; he wasn't able to make more than a mediocre meal and when they were eating endive there was a lot of sand in it. After a lot of complaints the captain investigated. One of the sailors said: "I'm in the Navy to serve my country and not to eat it."

When they came to Batavia, they had reached their destination. This time Henk saw the tropical splendor of the Dutch Indies. He was supposed to be there for two years before returning home for leave. It was a lot of money for the Dutch Government to get all the Navy staff back to The Netherlands for a leave after two years of service in the Tropics and therefore they made it attractive for the men to stay for another two years without leave. If they stayed without leave those two years would count double for their pension. Henk was still single and had nothing important to do in The Netherlands so he signed on.

After four years of service in the Dutch Indies, he finally got home. He was already 30 years old and figured that it was time to get married and start a family. There was a good looking neighbour girl by the name of Pietje Bredius who was interested in him and in October 1932 they got married.

Henk bought a house for 3000 guilders in De Helder where the Dutch Navy base was. He wasn't going to rent a house because his parents were kicked out of a rented house three times. With his double time in the Indies he had saved over 5000 guilders so he had lots of money to buy furniture. It was very nice to have money. He felt very happy with his wife and considered himself lucky as there were a lot of people unemployed.

* * * * *

Jaap, Henk's younger brother, was a horse of a different color. He was born on a Sunday afternoon, one year before the Titanic, an unsinkable palace, went to the ocean bottom. It was the largest ship ever built that had to show the competitors how fast it could go. The Captain was ordered to go on maximum speed while he was crossing a large area frequented with icebergs. From the 2000 passengers there were only 705 survivors after the Titanic hit an iceberg. There were only lifeboats for one third of the passengers and two thirds of the passengers drowned. The Titanic was an unsinkable ship so what do you need lifeboats for? Titanic showed that there is no unsinkable ship.

After Jaap's delivery, the midwife said to his mother: "There is a veil over his head, we will burn it in the fire; otherwise the child will have second sight in his lifetime which could bring much unhappiness." People were very superstitious those days.

When he went to school he was frequently punished with the cane that maintained strict discipline in the school. The children had to sit with arms folded and chatterboxes were silenced by having sticking plaster put across their mouths. They were also frequently banished to the corner.

There were sixty children in his class and the first three grades were in one class room. He was in the first grade so there were quite a few older boys in his classroom. Jaap was a fighter and constant fights gave him countless bleeding noses.

Yet, he liked school days a lot better than Sundays. On Sunday, everyone that appeared outdoors wore a suit and highly polished boots. His boots were old ones that his brother and his sisters had worn but since there was no money for new boots, they had to do. His suit had been made by his mother from an old suit that had belonged to a rich farmer. In spite of that, he looked great because Willempje was an expert in making good looking things out of discarded items from the farmers.

His problem was that there was nothing to do for a young boy except going to church two times a day which was mandatory. Playing outside was not allowed and the richer kids who had a bike were told that biking on Sunday was a deadly sin. God made Heaven and Earth in six days and he rested the seventh day. You didn't see God go biking after he was finished working.

Jaap always went through Sunday with sullen resignation and Monday school was a dawn which he faced with the utmost fortitude. He envied the few Roman Catholics in his neighborhood who went to early mass in the morning and were allowed to do what they liked to do the rest of the Sunday. It was a much better approach to get the children interested in religion, but the grown ups damned them if they were even thinking of it.

Besides going to church twice on Sunday, he had to go to Catechism one evening per week and also to Boys Club. He didn't mind the Boys Club as much because he could borrow books and he became an avid reader.

Once he had finished school, he wondered what he could do in the world to make a living. He certainly didn't want to work for the farmers; that had been poverty for his parents. Working in the transportation business wasn't possible because he had to be eighteen years old before he could drive a horse. Ship building was becoming a major industry and there were many repair yards that were looking for workers. As a boy of under sixteen years of age he was allowed to work 48 hours per week. Older people could work 52 hours per week in the industrial sector.

He couldn't make up his mind and it was still a sixty four guilder question what he was going to do until one day when he was looking curiously at a 600 ton barge that had been just re-outfitted. The skipper saw that he was interested and offered him a job as a deckhand for $2.50 per week with full board. That was it, his brother Henk was sailing with the Navy and he could take a short cut if he accepted. There was no need for a medical examination, as long as he could do the jobs they gave him, he was in business. And so the second son of Arie Cornelis was leaving to see the world. It was remarkable because at that time most people never got away from home more than 25 miles lest they became homesick.

Jaap was not yet fifteen but he was strong and sturdily built and could easily pass for sixteen. Brought up in strong Reformed Church surroundings with brimstone and hell fire, he eagerly accepted his first job in spite of the fact that the skipper was a Roman Catholic.

The skipper had a wife with two children who were sailing with the skipper. In the bow were the quarters for the hands and in the stern was a good modern house for the skipper with his family. A blow pipe telephone connected the quarters. All the skipper had to do, if he wanted his deckhand, was to blow in the pipe to attract the attention of his deckhand and command him as to what he wanted him to do.

When he had to go to the toilet Jaap was told that the toilet was on the campagne deck where he could launch his excrement into the waves of the ocean. The ocean was rather rough and was so good to wash his behind when he was finished. Cleanlessness was the all important thing Jaap thought, this sure was different than the old out house he was used to, although he was far from being amused.

They took on a load of coal for Basel in Switzerland and were the first one in a long line of six barges behind a tugboat. On that trip Jaap woke up to the smuggling and stealing that was going on. The coal cargo couldn't be sealed as it was too high. Every evening in the dark, the tugboat came alongside, took a load of coal and went back to the place in front. From there it was sold to interested parties, which was a lucrative racket for both sides.

When a ship was loaded with coal, there was a Plimsoll line on the outside of the ship indicating the water level to which the ship may legally be loaded. That was done to prevent dangerous over loading. Whenever the ship was loaded they loaded it until the water level was at the Plimsoll line. Of course when the tugboat took out a load of coal the ship wasn't loaded to the Plimsoll line anymore, which gave away that theft had taken place. The next day, the skipper had Jaap hand pump some water in the bilges to stay on the Plimsoll line.

Jaap discovered other thefts that took place in the harbors. When wagons with barrels of wine came in the harbor, some guys came and drilled a little hole in the barrel. After they had filled their can with wine, they just put a little wooden plug in the barrel.

When they were anchored at night, Jaap quite often had to row the skipper ashore and wait aboard for his whistle to haul him back. One time after he had rowed the skipper ashore, Jaap had come back to the ship. The blower telephone summoned him to come to the skipper living quarters at once.

After he had entered he called: "What do you want madam?"

She answered: "Come in and rub my back."

When he entered, there she was stark naked in the bathroom. There he was, not quite sixteen, could pass for seventeen, good strong built with curly blond hair. Brought up with hell and doom for sinners on sex. Subject to daily Bible reading at home, he found himself in the Joseph versus Potifar's wife situation. (Bible story of similar contents.) He never had seen a naked woman and retreated hastily slamming the door on his way out. Jaap was shocked and terrified, his mind in turmoil.

He never told anyone but after the incident he could do no good anymore. The skipper's wife was ridiculing him all the time that he as a Protestant was a bad influence for the kids because he didn't make the cross sign when saying Grace.

When he was back in Rotterdam, he had to deliver some parcels from the Holland America Line to the S.S. Rotterdam. When he delivered the parcels, the steward told him that they were a fellow short and if he went to the office they would take him on. He went to the office on an impulse and was hired. All he had to do was to go back to his skipper to tell him he was through with his job and report back to the S.S. Rotterdam.

The ocean liner was sailing to Southampton first to pick up some more passengers. After that was accomplished they were on their way to New York and from there they were going to make a cruise to the West Indies called

Caribbean Cruises. There was prohibition in the U.S. and cruises to the Caribbean were very popular. As soon as the ship was in International waters, the bars opened and they could drink as much as they liked.

There were 600 passengers on the ship and Jaap's job was to wash the dishes. The dirty dishes came down from the salon tables by service lift and after they were cleaned they were sent up again. There were a few portholes in the roomy work place that couldn't be opened and soon it was very hot with all the steaming water around.

There was on a lower deck a small place that was well screened off to get a little bit of fresh air if there was time; the rest of the ship was off limits for the staff. One of the other dishwashers had been around on the ship for a while and told Jaap that he had to be very careful not to break clean dishes because that was stupid. If he broke dirty dishes that was alright. Jaap always had thought that he was in a very good shape but at the end of the day he was very tired. As soon as he felt his mattress he fell asleep, they sure made him work for the money they paid him.

A great disappointment was waiting in New York when he was told that he had to stay on the ship. He had figured that he was going to see the world like his brother Henk but the staff wasn't allowed to get off the ship. The only thing he saw of New York was the Statue of Liberty from the porthole.

As soon as the ship returned he called sailing quits, he had been too impulsive and it had gotten him nowhere. He followed an electric welding course and when he passed his exam he found a job in a ship yard. His first job was welding the steel letters of the ship's name on the ship. This had to be done from a rowing boat which made it very difficult. He had a helper who was supposed to hold the rowing boat steady. Unfortunately, the waves from passing ships made it very difficult. One moment he was hugging the ship and the next moment he was far away from it. His helper learned quite a few new words when he said some friendly words to the rowing boat. Those words he had learned when he was at sea from the other sailors. It was a very trying job but he managed to complete it satisfactorily.

One day, he was caught in a rainstorm that had erupted suddenly. A nice young girl by the name of Johanna offered to share her umbrella with him. He was smitten with her charms and managed to get a date with her. After dating her for a year, they got married.

In spite that Jaap had a steady job as a welder, there was lack of money to set up a household. They bought some real cheap furniture that looked as if it was made out of old orange boxes. Grim humor made them say that they had Spanish furniture because that's where most of the oranges came from.

Jaap didn't go to church anymore and when his first baby was born he wanted to have it baptized. That was only possible if he became a full member of the church. Remembering the power they had used when he was growing up he refused that, stating that he wasn't going to promise things that he couldn't keep. Consequently his children couldn't be baptized.

THE OLD BUCK

There seemed to be no end to this terrible war. Arie Demerwe was supposed to serve his fatherland for twelve months and a popular song had it, that twelve months in the army were thirteen months too many. His military service hadn't ended with twelve or thirteen months, he was already 4 years in the army because of the war that was still raging.

At the end of 1918 the war was finally over and the Government started to let the soldiers get back to civilian life. When Arie was released he went back to his home town Heinenoord and picked up where he left off. He worked in the flax again.

He was already 25 years old when the Queen had another birthday on August 31st which meant a holiday. Arie had also a holiday because of the occasion and wondered what he would do. In Heinenoord there was little to do but Rysoord was a progressive town where they had elaborate celebrations. It was more than an hour biking which was O.K. with Arie. In spite of the 12 miles he had to pedal, he wouldn't miss it for the world. In those days there wasn't much entertainment. This was fun and it would be a long time before another opportunity came along. He wasn't married yet and was in no hurry to get home, he had all the time in the world until the next day when he had to get back to work.

Rysoord was a farmer's community which meant that there had to be entertainment for the farmers. They put some kind of a farmer's fair together on a pasture. All they had to do was to go with a pooper scooper to scoop up the fresh cakes the cows had deposited in the pasture so that the visitors to the fair wouldn't be dancing in the poop. After that little hurdle had been over come the terrain was ready for the celebrations.

Especially for the farmers there was a "Tilt at the ring contest." The farmers came from far and near to participate to show their skills in this contest. There were twelve giant bows and from each bow was a ring suspended in the center. The fat farmers would ride with their horse and buggy underneath the bows and their wives would sit on the box beside their beloved husbands, with a little stick in their hand, to catch as many rings as possible while they were driving underneath the bows. As there were twelve bows, the one that had the most rings at the end of the track was of course the winner. It required a keen eye and a steady hand but it was fun.

There was also a bandstand where a farmer's band, with all kinds of copper musical instruments, would blow the favorite tunes of that time. It wasn't only the farmers who joined the party; it was a feast not to be missed by anyone. For the youth there were all kinds of games with prizes to be won. There was an obstacle course, a sack race, a greasy pig that had to be caught and even a greasy pole with a wheel on the top with prizes. And for the older youth, this was an opportunity to find yourself a girl and if you were a girl to find yourself a boy. There was something for everybody.

After arriving in Rysoord, Arie went straight to the feast pasture because that's where the action was. He looked at the greasy pole but he wasn't a climber at all and just watched other people do their thing until he came face to face with a beautiful girl named Ko Tamerius. This was the girl he liked and at the end of the day, he tried to get another date.

If this had been a Hollywood movie, they would have fallen in love with each other, gotten married and lived very happily ever after. Unfortunately, this wasn't Hollywood, this was Rysoord. Though he was smitten by Ko, she had some objections because Arie was four years older than she was. When Ko was growing up, she always had dreamed of being swept off her feet by some handsome Prince. She just couldn't fall in love with an old buck that wanted a green leaf and she had no intention of marrying an old guy like that.

In her mind, a couple shouldn't be more than one or two years apart in age and Arie didn't qualify at all as a suitor. Arie wondered what the problem was with that Amor fellow they were always singing about. He was the God of Love. What was he doing? He probably had taken a day off because he sure wasn't on the ball. And how about this Cupid and his henchmen, where were the arrows he was supposed to shoot in Ko's heart. He didn't have help at all and had to do everything by himself. Good help was hard to get in those days.

Arie sure hadn't swept Ko off her feet and quite disappointed he biked back to Heinenoord to resume his work the next day. While he was weeding the flax, his heart was in Rysoord, he had to go back to Rysoord to get that nice girl Ko. She worked in Zwyndrecht but was usually home on the weekends.

In spite that he wasn't too sure about himself, he biked on Sunday to Rysoord to see her. He managed to see her but he got a cold shoulder again. She told him that she had to think this over a bit because she couldn't fall in love with an old buck. Arie was certainly not the guy she had been looking for.

In spite of all the negative response he got, Arie kept going to Rysoord to his unanswered love. He had to give it a heck of a try. After all "Perseverance wins the game," he thought.

It seemed that Cupid's bow took finally aim at Ko's heart and Amor lent a helping hand as well. They probably felt sorry that they had messed up this love affair and Ko had a change of heart. She probably thought that he wasn't really that old, he was only mature. Everything worked out in the end and they got engaged.

Then one day, she met the old farm hand that worked for Kors de Gelder. When she had left he had stayed and was still working there. Looking at her engagement ring he had the shock of his life and said: "I see you are engaged. That's too bad because I always had a crush on you and fell secretly in love with you. Now it's too late, I could hit myself on the head that I missed this opportunity. I never dared to ask you because I was scared to be jilted by a girl."

Ko never had known that she had a secret admirer and told him: "It's too late now, you should have asked me. It might have worked out but we'll never know now. I promised another man."

After being engaged for a year, they decided to get married and rented a small house in Heinenoord where Arie was still working in the flax industry. Ko didn't want children the first year of their marriage, she thought that they should get to know one another better before they had to care for children.

Arie had two brothers, Teun and Jaap who never came over to visit. They lived close enough for a visit but they were mad at Arie, their brother, because they couldn't borrow money from him without paying it back. Both of them were big spenders and Arie wasn't, he managed to spend his money wisely and though he never had much money, he was never short of money. That attracted his brothers who wanted to borrow money from him. After they had borrowed money from Arie they never paid it back and to top it off they wanted to borrow some more money. Arie wasn't going to give them any more money unless they paid first back what they had borrowed. They both got mad and called him a cheap skate who refused to help his poor brothers. As soon as there was nothing to be gained by visiting Arie, they never showed up anymore.

Arie had also two sisters, Dirkje who was married to Jaap Dalm and Gysje who lived about forty miles away. That was too far to visit regularly, so once in a blue moon they came over. Gysje was married to a guy by the name of Bertus who was a practical joker. He was chewing tobacco and when he had extracted the juice, he disposed of his old tobacco plug on the handle of the coal shovel.

The coal scuttle was right beside the stove in a dark corner. When Gysje was going to shovel some more coal on the stove, she grabbed right in the wet disposed tobacco from Bertus. After she had done that a couple of times, she checked before she grabbed the coal shovel and removed the tobacco first.

The trick of Bertus didn't work anymore so it was no fun and he quit putting his tobacco on the shovel. Gysje didn't check the coal shovel anymore because Bertus didn't put his wet tobacco plug on the shovel anymore. Then, all of a sudden he got back to his old tricks and she grabbed in the wet tobacco again.

Bertus had a copper tobacco juice spit bowl in the middle of the living room; he could spit from any angle of the living room right into the bowl. With the guys from his neighborhood he had a tobacco juice spitting contest to see who could spit the farthest. He won the contest several times.

Arie got along with his sisters and his brother in law Jaap Dalm quite well. Jaap Dalm was known by the family as "The Fat Dalm." He didn't receive that nick name because he was the runt of the litter; he was a big guy who liked to eat bacon right out of his hand. Moreover, he had a job as crane operator and was sitting all day in his crane. All those things added up to a Fat Dalm.

When Ko and Arie were married for a year and a half, they were blessed with a son who was called Adrianus after Arie's father. Unfortunately, when the boy was two months old he died suddenly because of crib death. Shortly after Ko got pregnant again she was hopeful that the stork would deliver another healthy baby.

In the meantime Arie started to cough and had a hard time breathing. His chest was all plugged up and he coughed up a lot of slime. At first they thought that it was just a bad cold but when it didn't improve a visit to the doctor was on the agenda.

Arie was sitting forlornly opposite his doctor when he heard the verdict that his promising future in the flax industry was over. The doctor's verdict was: "You have asthma which has been triggered by the dust that you are inhaling when you are flailing the flax. Your lungs can take this abuse only for so long and then difficulties will develop. It is the same with men that are working in the coal mines. The coal dust enters their lungs and after a few years they get Black Lung. They have to quit working in the mine or they'll die. It's the same with you; you'll have to find some healthier work."

It was easy for those doctors to give advice like that. There was another older man in Heinenoord who had bronchitis and the doctor's advice was to go to the mountains. Where the heck did you find mountains in The Netherlands? The country is as flat as the chest of a sparrow. Moving to

Switzerland was impossible because what was he going to do for a living? Travel costs were also high; he couldn't even pay the costs of moving there.

However, the verdict was in and Arie's future was completely in jeopardy. When he told Ko she was plenty worried. She was expecting a baby and her husband had to quit his job or he would die. What were they going to live from?

Luckily he found a job in the irrigation works to drain the land. A lot of ditches had to be dug by hand and there were also dykes needed to protect the low lying land from flooding since it was below sea level. Now he had an outside job with lots of fresh air, just what the doctor had ordered. There was also a lot of fresh rain coming down on him which wasn't appreciated at all. His lungs cleared out but he still had trouble with his chest.

Kees van Nes was a rich farmer in Rysoord who had become rich in the flax industry and Arie would have problems with his chest his entire life thanks to the flax industry. Kees van Nes was never around in the barn with the flailing of the flax when you couldn't see each other from the dust. The only thing he ever did was stash away his money.

Arie's new job in irrigation work wasn't as steady a job as he was used to. During the winter they shut it down for three months and then he was unemployed. Besides, they started to use more and more machines in the irrigation works and when the trenchers, tractors and trucks made their debut there were many layoffs. There was no future in doing ground work by hand; he needed a job with a future.

When he was unemployed, he had no income as there were no social insurances in place at the time. He delivered the newspaper, dug up the gardens for older people and even had a temporary job on a building project as night watchman. When the building was finished, so was his job. He had managed to make a few bucks here and there to stay alive during his unemployment. Unfortunately, it was a time of great uncertainties.

Arie tried to improve his chances for work by taking night classes. They taught him some more arithmetic and he had to write hymns in a scribbler. That didn't cut the cake in a fast changing society from agricultural to industrial.

On September 9th 1926, Willempje, Ko's mother, died suddenly of scarlet fever at the age of 48. And four months later, Ko's baby girl was born who they named Willempje after Ko's mother. They called her Willie.

With a baby Arie sure could use a better job and when he was reading the newspaper one night, he saw that they were asking for laborers in the harbor of Rotterdam. He decided to apply for a job and biked to the harbor the next day. Luckily, he was hired and was very happy to have a steady job. Ko was also thrilled that her husband had a job without layoffs in winter. At least there would be bread on the table.

Working in the harbor was an eye opener for Arie; he couldn't get over the dirty practices of the people who were unloading grain ships. They were urinating in the grain. When Arie said that they shouldn't do that bccause the grain was going to be consumed, the answer was: "Man we can't sweat it out."

"Why don't you go to the urinal?" Arie asked.

"Are you kidding, the foreman will fire me if I leave the ship."

"How about overboard, that's better than in the grain that we have to eat," Arie argued.

"If I urinate overboard, the women from the house boats will be watching all day with binoculars," was the reply he got.

It seemed that Arie got help from the other workers who said: "What's wrong with that, it's good advertising when you display your merchandise."

There was another incident in the harbor. One of the workers suddenly collapsed, he had been unloading bananas from the hold of a ship into white painted banana wagons from the railway. Wagons for transportation of bananas were always painted white to reflect the sun so the bananas stayed cooler.

When the doctor checked the worker over, he found a red spot in his neck caused by a poisonous spider. The spider had been between the bananas and when it was disturbed it bit the worker.

It was an hour and a half biking to his work and an hour and a half back home. That was three hours of biking every day and the weather wasn't always nice. Quite often it was raining and there was a strong wind. With his asthma that was hard to take and he figured that he would be worn out before his time. Besides, he had to work nine hours every day. He talked it over with Ko and they decided to move closer to Arie's work.

Arie and Ko were both raised in the country which made city living not very attractive. City living was nothing for them; they didn't like a suite in an apartment block. What they really wanted was a house with a garden in the back to grow their vegetables and potatoes and a flower garden in the front.

Such a demand couldn't be fulfilled in the city of Rotterdam but there was a solution to this problem. Just under the smoke of Rotterdam was a fast growing town Yselmonde. It was a town situated on the mouth of the River Ysel. *(Mond is mouth in English, so it was a town on the mouth of the Ysel. Yselmouth in English.)* That's how the town got the name of Yselmonde.

Yselmonde was still rural in spite of its big neighbor Rotterdam and Mayor Hazenberg was the administrator of this fast growing town. There were all kinds of farmers and vegetable growers around. The houses had a front and back garden, it looked exactly like Heinenoord but it was much bigger. Since Yselmonde was still rural, people could keep chickens, a goat, a pig and even a horse. In Rotterdam you weren't welcome to do those things but in Yselmonde it was a way of life.

There was a house on the Smeetlandse Dyke for rent and they decided to rent it for the time being. The rent was kind of high and Arie figured that he would pay for the house five times during his life time if he kept renting from those house milkers. *(People who were renting out houses to other people were called house milkers because they collected the rent every week.)* Even if he paid five times for the house there wasn't going to be one two by four he would be able to call his own.

He talked it over with Ko and they decided to try to buy a house. There was a house on Hordyk 121 that was for sale. It was only a few years old and it had a flower garden in the front and a large garden in the back. There were three pear trees in the front and one plum tree, two pear trees and four apple trees in the back. It was perfect, just what they always wanted.

The owner wanted 6000 guilders for the house and Arie had only eight hundred guilders saved. It meant that he needed a mortgage which was hard to get. He had a steady job but his income was low as a laborer and the banks weren't even listening, they didn't want to take the risk.

There was a money lender who was willing to give him a mortgage provided he had a guarantor. When Ko mentioned it to her sister Ploon who was working for Jan Lems, a farmer, she said she would ask her boss. He knew Arie Demerwe well enough and knew he wasn't trying to pull a fast one, so he agreed to be the guarantor that in case Arie failed to make his payments, Jan Lems would be responsible. That was very nice of him because he didn't get paid for being a guarantor and could lose money if something went wrong.

It was 1928 when they moved into their own house and they were both very happy. They had accomplished a lot in a relatively short time. For that time, it was a modern house; it had a kitchen and a livingroom with two cupboard beds. The living room was also the bedroom which was very common in those days. There were two doors to close off the cupboard beds; when the doors were closed you didn't see the beds anymore. If you didn't have time in the morning to make the beds you just closed the doors and nobody could think that you were a lazy housewife.

The cupboard bed was actually a handy invention. When you wanted to go to bed all you had to do was open the doors and your bed was ready instantly. Sleeping in the living room had an added advantage; there was a potbelly stove in the living room for heat and cooking purposes. At night Ko would fill up the stove with coal and turn it down so it would burn slowly during the night. That way it would give heat all night and by morning there were still a few glowing embers that could easily be revived to make a fire again.

The cupboard bed was more than just a bed. Houses were very small in those days which made it necessary to use all possible space. Even the space underneath the cupboard beds was used to store potatoes, beets and carrots. In the shed they would freeze during the winter but underneath the beds they stayed good. Besides, it was pretty handy to have carrots underneath your bed in case you got hungry during the night.

When you got up in the morning, you just closed the doors of your cupboard bed and you couldn't see the potatoes, carrots, beets or pee pot. You would swear those people didn't have any beds but at night they were instantly available. If you went early to bed and other people didn't, you could close the doors if the light was bothering you.

Over the foot end of the bed was a plank which had a multi purpose function, it was used to put the pee pot on and Ko put also the alarm clock on it. She couldn't see what time it was in the dark but that didn't matter. When the alarm clock went off, it was time to get up.

Even Arie had good use for the shelf; he put his baton in the corner on the shelf, just in case burglars entered the house during the night. A man had to protect his home, and with the baton, he could beat the hell out of potential burglars. His baton was a good weapon; it looked as if it was made of rubber, but inside it was filled with lead. He had bought it when he was night watchman to defend himself. Fortunately, it never happened that burglars entered their home; they had nothing worth stealing anyway. It would have been interesting though, to see Arie running after burglars, with his baton in his hand, like a bobby runs through the streets of London with his billy club after criminals. Arie put also a glass of sugar water on the shelf. With his asthma he coughed a lot during the night and a couple of swallows of sugar water usually quieted him down so he could get some sleep.

The most modern feature in the house was the toilet which was indoors. Most of the houses still had an outhouse which was a curse in winter time. Unfortunately, in winter it was freezing in the indoor toilet too. The only two rooms in the house that could be heated were the living room and the kitchen. When you had to go to the bathroom you still had to put on your winter coat.

A pee pot was still a handy thing to have around during the night. It was the greatest invention of that time and ranked only second to the invention of barrels of beer. The only thing they didn't do on the peepot was a big job; that was too much of a stink, but people with an outdoor biffy didn't hesitate to do that in the pot as well. A pee pot could be a life-saver. Of course the draw back was that somebody had to empty and clean the pots. Some people might be so poor that they don't have a pot to pee in but not in the time of outdoor biffies. A pee pot was a must.

When they were living in Heinenoord and on the Smeetlandse Dyke, they had an outdoor biffy like everybody else. If it was forty below with a snowstorm in progress, it was bad enough to go to the bathroom in the day time but during the night it was a disaster. You would cool off completely and never warm up anymore during the night. In spite that a pee pot is dirty, unsanitary and stinks, you can change your mind in a hurry when you wake up in the middle of the night and you got to go. Instead of putting two sweaters and two winter coats on, you could have a pee pot on the shelf or underneath your bed and you wouldn't freeze up. People worshipped the pee pot in those days and considered it to be a blessing from above.

In winter layers of hoar frost covered the seat of the out house and sitting on an icy seat was enough to make a Spartan sob. People wore so many clothes that it looked as if they were going on an Arctic expedition instead of to the out house. The job was made more difficult when you had to horse around with numb fingers to get your fly open. There were no zippers on the man's flies in those days and to loosen buttons was plain murder.

Some people were inventive and had the toilet seat hanging beside the stove to keep the hoar frost off it and to keep it warm. When you had to go to the biffy you simply took the toilet seat off the wall, used it and put it back on the wall when you were finished, where it was ready for the next user.

The toilet has had a dramatic evolution which is not going to be completed for a long time. Adam didn't need a toilet; he went behind the bush. When more people dwelled together they did their business in the river. Waste was carried off with the current of the river and everything was well. Of course, it's not too refreshing if you live down river and you see excrement floating by.

Drinking water was also supplied by the river which made it necessary to keep the river clean. In order to do that, the outhouse was born. You don't need a blueprint to build one, they all look the same. All you have to do is dig a hole, build a plank with a hole over it and enclose it with a little house to be out of the wind and out of sight when you are using the outhouse. Don't forget to cut out a moon in the door; else you can't see that it's an outhouse. The moon indicates that this is the place where you moon. When you take down your pants you moon.

In The Netherlands they had to be different; they cut out a heart in the door which meant that you could do your business to your heart's content. Actually the moon or the heart in the door served two purposes; it gave you light and fresh air. You didn't need a window or a bathroom fan.

Even the name of the toilet had an evolution, they started to call it an outhouse, and next it became an in-house toilet which was called in old times, "The poop box."

When the kids went to school they told the teacher that they had to go to the poop box. The teacher wasn't amused; she called it boorish language which she wasn't going to tolerate in her classroom. W.C. was the proper word which means Water Closet.

Besides that an out house is very cold in winter, there are also advantages. When the hole is full, you dig another hole right beside the outhouse, cover the old hole and move the out house over the new hole. On the farm and even in small towns, you never ran out of room to dig another hole.

Naughty kids were sometimes locked up in the outhouse for punishment but sometimes the outhouse had some involuntary adult prisoners. The outhouse had a wooden spindle for an outside latch. Most of the times; it was no more than a piece of wood with a nail driven through the middle which caused trouble sometimes. It could also happen that somebody played a prank on you and locked you in. More often it was just an unfortunate accident that you were locked in. If the nail wasn't driven exactly through the middle, one half was heavier than the other half and sometimes fell half down.

Of course there was no panic hardware and to make it worse, things were sturdy in those days. You could push, boot the door or fling your body against it but the door didn't budge. You could be easily trapped like a wild animal in a cage or as a tame human in an outhouse. People who had seen somebody who was locked in the outhouse used care that it wouldn't happen to them. Once inside there was a bolt to lock the door from the inside for privacy. Privacy or not, quite a few people kept the door ajar and held the bolt so the door wouldn't blow open by the wind.

An outhouse in winter was a problem but in summer it created a different problem. The outhouse attracted a lot of flies which created worms in the pit. The flies had also the unpleasant habit of landing on your behind to sting you while you were trying to do a job.

There was quite a bit of row housing in The Netherlands with out houses. The developer was cheap and only provided one outhouse for two houses. Sometimes you went to the toilet and the neighbor was sitting on the throne. In that case you had to wait till he was finished. Waiting in summer might be annoying when you had to cross your legs while you were waiting. In winter it was a disaster but when it was cold enough, the neighbor made a rush job out of it.

To prevent congestion of the outhouse, people had a urine corner; with a little gutter the urine was transported to the ditch. Men could use the corner, that way they didn't occupy the out house and somebody else could sit on the throne. The family bathroom had usually two holes in the plank and that way it had a double capacity.

Toilet paper hadn't been invented yet, so people used the old newspapers instead. They were cut up in pieces that were big enough to do the job and were put on a string to hang them in the biffy. The only good toilet tissue came with Christmas from the orange wrappers that were so soft, compared to the cut up pieces of the newspapers and were much cleaner too. Newspapers left black marks on your behind from the ink that came off the papers.

It always was a long way to Tipperary but it was also a long way to the modern toilet. To invent the indoor toilet took a long time. Even a pig doesn't shit where he eats. Naturally, the indoor toilet was invented in wintery countries where the need was great. Tropical countries had no problem when they had to go to the bathroom.

Eventually somebody figured it all out; he built a toilet inside the house against the outside wall and right behind the outside wall, he dug the hole. A little piece of drain pipe connected the toilet with the cess pit which was lined with concrete so it wouldn't cave in. The early toilet bowls were made out of brown pottery which was considered the best. White toilets were for the birds, they showed when they were dirty. Even when excrement was stuck on the brown toilet bowl you wouldn't notice it. For the first time the outdoor biffy was replaced by an indoor biffy.

The first indoor bathroom was received with mixed feelings. Some people said it was indecent while others thought it was unsanitary and a stink in the house. On the other hand there were a lot of people who welcomed the indoor toilet because it was handy on a rainy night and more than handy when it was 40 below in the middle of the night.

An outhouse had some advantages; it didn't need a fan to get rid of the smell, the wind would do the job. Once the toilet was inside the house there had to be a window to vent the toilet room. Another disadvantage of the indoor biffy was that you couldn't fill in the cess pit; you couldn't dig another hole and move the house over it. Besides emptying the pee pots, there was now another smelly job, emptying the cess pit.

In those early days, nothing was wasted, not even waste was wasted. The night soil of the cess pit was usable as manure when you spread it on your land. Farmers were saying that manure of meat eating animals wasn't good manure. Compost is only good without meat or fat, the little creatures that break down the compost hate fat which means no fat in compost. Horse and cow manure were the best because they were grass eating animals.

That was no problem for the Demerwes, they only ate a little piece of meat on Sunday and for the rest they were vegetarian. Their manure was as good as from a cow. They had the rich people beaten because they had better manure. At least there was one thing that they had better than the rich people who were eating steak.

A no flush toilet bowl attracted a lot of flies. When you went to the bathroom you took an old newspaper along and made a fly swatter out of it to kill some flies. That was a cheap fly swatter; you didn't need a three guilder fly swatter to do the job. The flies were just as dead when you hit them with an old newspaper as when you hit them with a three guilder fly swatter. Most of the flies were sitting on the wall and it didn't take long to have a bunch of dead flies laying on the floor indicating that Kilroy had been in action.

In The Netherlands they hung a birthday calendar in the bathroom indicating what date everybody in the family had a birthday. It only gave you the date because the calendar wasn't renewed every year so you had to consult the normal calendar for the day the birthdays were. When the neighbor went to the bathroom, he ran out of old newspaper and used the birthday calendar. His wife wasn't happy with that because she had to buy another calendar and fill in all the dates of the family again.

The cess pit had a cover over it so nobody would fall into the pit. Inspection of the pit was necessary to see if it was almost full. If the pit wasn't emptied in time, the sewage would back up in the toilet bowl. Most of the time nobody checked the cess pit; when the sewage stayed in the toilet bowl, it was time to empty the pit.

Most people knew about when the pit would be full and emptied it before the sewage backed up. There was a guy in the neighbourhood of Arie and Ko who was known as Patrick. One day he wondered how full the cess pit was. He took the cover off the pit but couldn't see it because it was dark. When he lit a match, he saw the sewage and even tasted it; the whole cess pit had blown up in his face. A cess pit can create explosive sewage gas when the cover is closed, so fire should be avoided at all times.

The poet described this event in a beautiful poem, just the way he saw it.

Patrick almost said good bye,
When he flew with his shit-house through the sky.
He was wounded only a little bit.
His only problem was; he was full of shit.

Finally the toilet was inside which was a great improvement. Yet, it was still primitive. There was no heating, and in winter it was still a cold job to take your pants down. It wasn't a flushing toilet so there was no water in the toilet room, not even to wash your hands. The toilet couldn't freeze for lack of water but it required rinsing to keep it clean. Rinsing the toilet bowl was on the housewife's work roster but it was only done once a week. If you had to rinse or flush the toilet bowl every time you used it, the cess pit would have been full every month.

Rinsing the toilet bowl was a smelly job and it wasn't easy either. With the use of old newspapers as toilet paper there was a problem. The drain pipe wasn't all that big so a lot of times the pieces of newspaper clogged up the drain pipe. To get the drain pipe unplugged there was such a handy tool which was called "The Shit House Stick." Of course, this was a smelly stick; you couldn't throw away the stick after use either. If you threw the stick away you would need a new stick every week. You rinsed the stick in the ditch, put it in the corner of the bike shed and it was ready for use again.

Of course, no matter how much you rinse a shitty stick, it will still smell. The stick had a double function. If you had mis-behaved, they would give you a licking; you guessed it, "With the shit house stick." The one who handled the stick wouldn't grab the smelly end; he would hold the clean end and hit the subject with the shitty end. If you received a spanking with the smelly stick, you would get it with the shitty end of the stick.

All those expressions in our language were born in a different time in a different world. The stinking stick disappeared but the expression is still used. Whenever somebody is chastised they say: "He got the shitty end of the stick." Few young people know where the expression came from, but older people remember.

Besides a smelly stick, there was also a smelly pail. It was attached to a stick to make it possible to dip it in the cess pit to empty the pit. That way you didn't have to lie on your tummy to fill the pail. Most people tried to time the emptying of the pit when there was need for night soil. They just spread it on the land and delicious vegetables would grow.

Some vegetable growers over-did it; they spread too much night soil on the land and when they were growing cauliflower, they dumped some more night soil beside the growing cauliflower. When you cooked the cauliflower you could smell the night soil. "Cauliflower has to grow fast," the grower said. That's understandable as long as you don't have the plants standing in the nightsoil while they are growing, because they pick up the undesirable flavor from the manure.

Arie and Ko only spread night soil on the land in fall. That way there was a whole winter with rain and snow to absorb the unpleasant odour. All you had to do in spring was dig up the garden and it was ready for seeding and planting. If you didn't over do the use of nightsoil the cauliflower smelled and tasted like cauliflower and not like the contents of the cess pit.

Even with a small household, the cess pit had to be emptied twice a year; once in Fall when the contents could be spread on the land and once in

Spring when they would dump the contents of the pit on the dung hill. The dung hill was good for everything; the chicken manure with straw from the chicken coup was also dumped on it and the weeds that were pulled out of the garden. Of course, you had to pull the weeds before there were seeds in, otherwise the dunghill would be full of seeds, which you would seed when you were spreading the manure. You had to think of everything.

Over-population had a lot to do with the development of the toilet and the sewer system we know today. Back in Paradise, with only two people, there was no need for a sewer system or toilet. Adam would squat behind the apple tree; he didn't even have to pull his pants down, because he had no pants. Paradise was a nudist colony; he just crouched behind the tree and looked the beautiful apples over in the same time. After Adam and Eve were booted out of Paradise people lived in caves; they would go outside the cave to relieve themselves. Soon people got organized and started to use the same place all the time to prevent running through their own dirt. They learned that from the devil; it is said that the devil always shits on the same pile. (uneven distribution of goods)

In the old days plumbing was easy to understand. There was a hole in the ground, a plank with a hole, and a shack with a half moon or heart in the door. Even today plumbing is simple; all you have to know to be a plumber is; that shit doesn't run up-hill and payday comes on Friday. The early plumber knew all about it that fluid runs down hill. Plumbing for urinals was very simple; he dug a little trench from the urinal to the ditch and another plumbing job was finished.

Farmers cared less about those things; they weren't going to waste any money on a plumber, they could pee in the ditch and even if they did it on their land it would sink into the ground anyway. With the growing cities, the problem to supply the citizens with potable water became worse.

The outhouse was superb; when the hole was full, they just dug another hole and covered up the old hole. They learned that from the cat; the cat always covers up his dirt. People were observing and learned a lot from other creatures. The cess pit, which had to be emptied, was followed by the flushing toilet which dumped the sewage in the river. Some improvement that was when you consider that people were drinking from the river.

Because of the cold houses with unheated bedrooms, people had all kinds of contraptions to keep warm during the night. Of course, you could take a warm water bottle but that didn't prevent your ears from freezing. You could wake up with white frozen edges on your ears like the cat. To prevent that from happening, people put a night cap on their head, i.e. the fabric night cap and not the alcoholic night cap in a glass. The alcoholic night cap might have worked too, because alcohol doesn't freeze.

They even had night socks to go to bed; the hot water bottle stayed only warm a certain time and socks would keep your feet warm longer. When a child misbehaved in those days, a parent might say: "If you don't behave, I'll send you to bed bare feet." Nowadays children wouldn't know what you were talking about because all children go bare foot to bed.

The house of Ko and Arie didn't have a medicine cabinet, all the medical supplies were in a little table drawer. There was ample room for the bottle of aspirins, the little box of ointment and the few rags that served as bandages. Bandages were made from old pillow cases and bed sheets.

The house also had a loft which could be developed into one or two bedrooms in the future. They had only one daughter but were planning to have at least one more child, preferably a boy this time. When the kids were growing up, they needed a bedroom and with the open loft they should be able to fix that somehow.

There was a little sink with one cold water tap in the entire house. That's where all the cleaning took place. Everybody washed himself right there, they stuck their head underneath the cold water tap and used soap if necessary. Other parts of the body were cleaned with a wash hand instead of a wash cloth. That was handier; you could stick your hand in it. In case of real dirty hands people would boil a kettle of water to make cleaning with hot water easier. They knew about a dishwasher but the one they knew had two hands. The dishes were cleaned with a kettle of hot water.

There was no electricity yet. However, they had a modern oil lamp with four wicks. Most of the time, they only lit one wick but with reading they could light four wicks if they so desired. And the wicks could be turned up or down to get more or less light. It was like a dimmer on an electric light. It was better than an electric dimmer because each flame could be individually dimmed or turned up. When you had four wicks burning and you wanted less light you simply blew out one or more wicks. No switch was necessary, everything was simple and effective. With an electric light that has four bulbs, you dim all four bulbs at the same time so an oil lamp was easier in controlling the output of light.

A portable oil lamp was used in the other areas of the house. Many houses burned down because of oil lamps and if you turned the wick up too high, the lamp smoked which would release soot into the room. If you knew what you were doing, oil lamps were rather safe. In those days a house never burned down because of faulty wiring.

Most of the people used gas for cooking and also for light. They had a gas mantle as light which was a problem. If you weren't careful it would break and then you were without light until you had it replaced. It was so fragile that when the kids were playing above it on the loft the mantle would break.

Whenever the kids were playing on the loft the parents would shout: "Don't bang on the floor, if you break the mantle we will have no light."

That was a nuisance and also cooking with gas had a problem. Some accidents had happened with gas leaks when people died because of inhaling the deadly gas. Arie and Ko didn't have natural gas hooked up. They had decided against it because of the accidents that had happened with gas leaks that had killed people, sometimes in their sleep.

The gas company had taken steps to warn the people of gas leaks by making the gas smell like rotten eggs. Before it was odorless and now it was noticeable as soon as there was a gas leak. If you smelled rotten eggs, you had to phone the gas company unless it was Halloween. In that case the kids had probably thrown rotten windows against your egg; or was it that they had thrown rotten eggs against your window? Anyway, in that case you had to get the water hose to clean it all up. In spite of the smell that would warn them, Arie and Ko didn't trust it, gas was dangerous and scary, they were rather safe than sorry.

Gas can be very dangerous at the best of times. One guy even managed to blow up his house when he smelled gas in the basement and tried to find the gas leak. Since he couldn't see very well in the corner, he lit a match which was followed by a loud bang. Incidentally, he found the gas leak!

A familiar saying is that the kettle is telling the pot that it's black. It's a saying that isn't too well understood today because we don't have black kettles and pots. In the old days the pots and kettles were sure black because they were used on the kitchen stove which had three openings on the top that were covered with three rings. When you needed hot water you took some of the rings out so that the kettle would be partly inside the stove. The kettle was made that way with a flange resting on the outside of the stove. That would give you a black kettle.

There was more than one function for the kitchen stove; it also had an oven with a dual use. First of all the rather damp wood was put in the oven to dry it out and on a cold day you could open the oven doors to stick your feet into it to warm them up. Even the margarine was put in front of the oven in winter to get it soft enough so that you could put it on your bread.*(There was only one kind of margarine called "Blue Band," in those days which was used for frying and to put it on your bread. In winter it was too hard to smear it on your bread so it had to be warmed up.)*

(This Blue Band margarine became a joke. A guy woke up in the middle of the night because of a terrible noise. He checked the entire house but couldn't detect what made the noise. Finally he opened the fridge and saw where all the noise came from. It was the Blue Band.)

The kitchen stove was a marvel of ingenuity made for different functions but in summer when there was no need for heat; Ko was looking for a way to cook her food without lighting the stove. She didn't want gas in the house so she bought a petroleum cooker. A petroleum man came once a week from door to door to sell petroleum. All she had to do was keep her can filled and she was in business.

Ko and Arie had a nice house with little furniture and decorations. On one wall were hanging two portraits, Ko's father and mother. There was also a photo frame in which the whole farmer's family was represented. That way you could look at your relatives even if they weren't visiting.

The other wall had two "Still Life" paintings. They were not real paintings, they were just cheap paper copies but they were nice. Ko and Arie weren't rich enough to buy a real Rembrandt or a Van Gogh painting, thus those cheap copies had to do to decorate their house.

On the chimney mantle were three Delft's Blue vases and there was a striking clock hanging on the wall. Those were all the decorations they had. Of course, there is a great advantage when you have few possessions, you don't have to do much dusting.

As for furniture, they had wooden chairs and one upholstered armchair. This had an advantage as well; if you had luxurious furniture you had to pay luxury tax. Once a year, an inspector came to check your furniture and if you had nice furniture, they figured you could afford to pay more taxes. Ko and Arie never had a problem; the inspector looked around the corner and disappeared to greener pastures, to people who were luckier and richer than they were.

There is another benefit if you have few possessions; you don't have to spend sleepless nights worrying that people will steal them. Ko and Arie were blacklisted by the burglars as being unworthy of their visit. Arie was the only one to sit in an upholstered armchair because he was the boss of the house. Mind you that was a long time before Woman's Lib. If you try that today, you are guaranteed to have a riot on your hands. Today you'll need two armchairs to avoid a conflict.

All the furniture was very old; wear and tear was showing and the wood was full of termite holes. Those termites needed air so they drilled little holes to the outside, to make sure that enough oxygen could enter their domain. Otherwise those creatures would have died of suffocation. There were lots of termites in The Netherlands; old furniture showed lots of tiny holes. It's a shocking fact to chew on that the average termite lives to a ripe old age of twenty years. The average dog lives only eleven years.

It looked as if those termites were taking fertility drugs; they spread like wild fire to other furniture. Once you see little holes in your furniture there is already extreme damage. One day when you are sitting down, your chair will collapse and you can throw it into your fireplace.

When the little holes appear, people think there is sawdust underneath their furniture but they got that wrong. The termites wouldn't waste any good food; what you see are turds which are discarded by the termites. Even a termite has got to go and he pushes the dirt out of the little holes he bored in order to eat. Termites make an instant sewer line when they eat. In The Netherlands they have brick houses. Nothing to eat says the termite and eats your furniture.

After they lived four years in their house, the town of Yselmonde decided to put in electric lamp posts for the streets. The old gas lanterns had done yeoman service and they had to be replaced. Gas lanterns had to be lit every night by a man who had the honorable occupation of gas light lighter. Actually he didn't have to light the lanterns at night because they had a pilot flame. In the morning he just turned the lanterns to pilot operation and at night he only had to turn the lights to light. That man lost his job because the electric lights would be put on and off at the Town House.

At the same time they were making electricity available to the houses, they hooked up the houses for free but of course everybody had an electric meter and the bills had to be paid or they would disconnect your power. In the beginning when electricity was hooked up to the houses you had to put a dime in the meter to get electricity for a certain time. Those coin meters were a nuisance, when you were reading the newspaper and the light went out. When the coin was used up, the light would suddenly turn off no matter what important things you were doing. In the dark, people had to look for a dime and put it in the meter.

With the supply of gas, it was the same; except instead of a money coin, you had to insert a gas coin which the gas company had especially made from copper. The coin was engraved with the word "Gas" which made it a gas coin. Those special made up coins were even a worse nuisance than the money coins because you had to buy the gas coins in the General Store which meant that you had to keep a few gas coins on hand or you would be caught with your pants down or worse, you would be caught without a gas coin when your gas went out. As soon as the allotted cubic meters of gas had been consumed, the gas would go out without a warning.

The gas company could have used dimes as well for the supply of gas but they probably didn't want to copy cat the electric company. They had to be different. (Maybe the electric company had patented their invention of dime meters.) After a lot of complaints, the gas company had another great invention; it was a meter that worked on quarters. That was smart because quarters were also classified as being money. It was so smart that one wonders why they didn't invent a meter that worked on quarters in the first place; it would have saved them the trouble to make special gas coins.

A coin would give you light or a gas flame to cook your food but only for a certain time. When the coin had given gas or electricity for a certain time, you were suddenly in the dark. It was even worse when you were cooking your food on gas. All of a sudden the gas flame would be out and your food would stop cooking. When the woman was checking if her potatoes were done, she found that they weren't done because the coin was finished and there was no gas anymore. In order to restore the gas supply again, you had to insert a coin first before you would see a gas flame again

The attitude of the suppliers of electricity and gas was that they wanted money in advance. "Butter with the fish," they said which translated as "butter before the fish." Actually, for the electricity and gas providers this was the best way to get paid for the supplies. Everybody paid in advance and if you didn't put a coin in your meter you were out of luck. What was good for the utility suppliers wasn't good at all for the consumers but that's the way it was, until somebody invented the white yarn before the black yarn was invented.

Finally, the electric and gas companies saw the light at the end of a long dark tunnel and the light they saw wasn't the light after they had inserted a coin in the electric meter. No, they invented the coinless gas and electric meter. Real smart! It would give you an unlimited supply without putting you in the dark or without the potatoes not being done in time.

They also saw the light of how to put people in the dark who didn't pay their gas or electric bill. First of all, you had to pay a deposit which stayed in, just in case you didn't pay your bill and if you didn't pay your bill they cut off your supply until such a time that you had paid up. There was a trick to get electricity again; you had to pay a re-connection fee in order to avoid a repeat in the future. That in itself was probably the greatest invention of all times, after the invention of electric light.

New jobs were created because somebody had to read the meters and the bills had to be sent to the consumers. Of course, if you didn't pay your bill in time, the light would be disconnected and you would be scrambling for your candles. In case it affected your gas, you had to eat raw potatoes until you had paid your gas bill.

When the city provided electricity to the houses, the electric meter was already inside of the house and that's as far as the supply of electricity went. Wiring of the house had to be paid by the owner. Arie and Ko decided to have electric light with three lights in the entire house; one in the living room, one in the kitchen and one where the sink was. Outside lights weren't necessary, there were only few street lights but they had to do and a light in the bathroom was absolutely unnecessary. You could perform that business in the dark as well as with light.

There was only one plug in the entire house and they didn't even have use for it because they didn't have any electric appliances. They had no radio, fridge, vacuum cleaner or T.V. *(The T.V. was still twenty years in the future.)* They hoped to have a radio in the future so with a plug in the house they were ready. All three lights and the plug were all wired to one fifteen amp fuse.

The winter of 1929 was a very cold winter with extreme low temperatures; it looked as if they were returning to the Ice Ages. During the month of January, the River Maas froze solidly and horse pulled wagons went across the river. Ko was thinking back that she had lost her first baby and was scared that her second baby Willie would freeze to death. She put old coats on top of the blankets to give her extra warmth but wasn't sure that it was enough. During the night she got out of bed a couple of times to check if Willie was still warm.

One day Arie's brother Teun came to visit him; he had left Heinenoord as well and was hired as a postman in the town of Oud Beyerland. He said to Arie: "It's good that you went out of the flax industry when you did, most of the people are now without a job."

"How did that happen?" Arie wanted to know.

"It's because the cotton gin was invented in the U.S." Teun said. "When people heard about the cotton gin they were licking their lips, they all like gin. When they found out what it really was they were biting their lips instead of licking. The cotton grows and produces hairy cotton seed balls. Of course the seed is needed for the next crop but the hairy fibers surrounding the seeds are even more important because they can be spun into cotton.

The process to separate the seeds from the fibers is called ginning. Basically a cotton ginner is an apparatus with two rolls that let the lint pass through but not the seeds. The hand ginning has been replaced by a saw type gin which does a much better job in a lot less time. Cotton is conquering the world and it is a disaster for the flax industry."

"Maybe Kees van Nes should grow cotton instead of flax," Arie replied.

"Impossible," Teun said. "You can't grow cotton in The Netherlands; the climate isn't suitable for cotton at all. Cotton is a tropical plant and is thriving best with high temperatures and lots of sunshine. The temperatures are too low in The Netherlands; there isn't enough sunshine and too much rain. We are up the creek without a paddle with our flax production. We still are making some linen but most of the people buy the cheaper cotton products."

(Cotton has been a long time around. When Columbus landed in the West Indies in 1492, the people were already wearing cotton garments. They even were

fishing with cotton fishing lines. Cotton was already used around 3000 B.C. It probably replaced the fig leaves that Adam and Eve were wearing. Use of cotton probably was a disaster for the people who were in production of fig leaves as it was a disaster for the Dutchmen who were involved in the flax production. After the war, artificial fibers such as nylon, rayon and other 'ons' got even the cotton pickers in the States in trouble,)

INSTABILITY

Prior to the collapse of the stock market in 1929 there was an election in The Netherlands which showed how unstable the political situation was. The result was as follows:

Roman Catholics: 30 seats.
S.D.A.P. Socialist Democrats: 24 seats
Anti Revolutionary: 12 seats.
Christian Historic Union: 11 seats.
Liberals right wing: 8 seats.
Liberals left wing: 7 seats.
Communists: 2 seats.
Other splinter parties: 6 (each one seat)

The Anti Revolutionary Party was actually the Christian Reformed party. They called on the voters for support to fight Socialism. They insisted that the Socialists were going to cause a Revolution and they were against it. From there on they called themselves the Anti Revolutionary Party.

There were no National Socialists in Holland yet. Hitler was just coming out of the mothballs and had started National Socialism in Germany.

There were 100 seats in the Government at the time and no party had 51 seats. That meant that there had to be a coalition Government. The strongest Party was the Roman Catholic Party with 30 seats and therefore the Queen summoned the leader of the Roman Catholic Party to her Palace for an audience. She ordered the Leader to form a Government.

That was easier ordered than done. There had been several coalition

Governments in the House of Representatives before but this time it was a very difficult task to form a Government that had 51 % of the votes which was necessary to pass a bill that was presented in the House.

The best Government would be a Government which was backed up by two thirds of the votes, that was the only way that the Constitution could be changed. That was wishful thinking, the Roman Catholic Leader could be happy to get 51% of the votes.

His Party had 30% of the votes so he needed another 21% from the other Parties in order to form a new Government. Usually it was some kind of horse trading to get other parties interested in participating in the Government. All he had to do was offer a lot of carrot and hide the stick.

The needed 21% of the votes could be obtained from the other Christian Parties which had a total voting power of 23% which was more than he needed. If they participated he would have a Government backed up by 53% of the votes.

Unfortunately, the Roman Catholic Leader had a problem. In the last Government he had those two parties participating in his Government but something had been going awfully wrong. There had been a mutiny on one of the merchant ships of the East Indian Company. The mutineers had taken over the ship, had put the Captain and his faithful ones ashore and had continued the voyage. Not for long did they continue the voyage because the Government ordered the ship bombed. There were many casualties and the survivors were imprisoned.

This drastic action had raised a furor in the Dutch population and the Roman Catholics were the scapegoat for this unpopular way the trouble had been handled. No Party in its right mind wanted to be associated with the Roman Catholic party. It would be political suicide. When the other Christian Parties were asked to participate in his Government they had flatly refused.

The Roman Catholic Leader weighed his only remaining option by asking the Socialist Party Leader to participate. That way he would secure 54% of the votes in the House. However, that would be trying to mix water with fire, it would never do. Even the Pope might condemn him for such a gesture and take his chair in Heaven away. Without the support of the two Christian Parties or the Socialists he was sunk and could forget to form a Government.

The Queen had ordered him to form a Government but since he had been unsuccessful he asked an audience with the Queen to tell her in a polite way about the other parties that were a bunch of creeps that weren't willing to cooperate. Next he asked the Queen to be relieved of his duties.

Normally, the Queen would have asked the next strongest Party to form a Government. The problem was that it was the Socialist Party which was condemned by all other Parties except the Communist Party. It would have been a futile attempt and such an effort would have been a failure from the onset.

The Queen ordered the Socialist Leader to her chambers but didn't ask him to form a Government. They must have seen the writing on the wall and didn't want to waste any more time.

Next, the Queen ordered all the Party Leaders to her chambers one by one. This time the topic was "The political stalemate" and the question was how this could be resolved. It seemed hopeless, so her Majesty summoned her Political Advisors to her Palace. She asked them for a briefing on the possibilities to resolve this political impasse. If no Government could be formed, the Queen could order new elections. It was very well possible that new elections would give the same result and would have resolved nothing.

After lengthy discussions, she ordered all the Party Leaders to her chambers again for a debate. She probably told the Party Leaders to smarten up and be more flexible. When the Roman Catholic party and the Socialist Party couldn't form a Government, the time was ripe to let the smaller Parties give it a whirl.

This time the Queen ordered the Leader of the Christian Historic Union, Mr. de Geer to her chambers and ordered him to form a Government. The Christian Historic Union had only 11% of the votes, yet he was asked to form a Government. Mr. de Geer was a born diplomat but without the cooperation of the other parties it would have been in vain to even try to form a Government.

Mr. de Geer had a lot of political clout and after visiting many times back and forward to the different Party Leaders, he finally presented his new cabinet to the Queen. It was almost identical as the Government that the Roman Catholic Leader had proposed with the exception that he was the Minister President instead of the Roman Catholic Party Leader.

The Roman Catholics were strongly represented in de Geer's Cabinet but they kept a low profile in order to repair the damage to their image that had been caused by bombing the ship. All three Parties had enough portfolios and enough power to satisfy their ego. This was the way it was possible that a small Party which only represented 11% of the population could govern the country.

HAPPY DAYS AND INSANITY

After four dreadful years of World War I the soldiers went home except the ten million who had died by shelling, gas or other causes. Governments tried to cope with the postwar years which were far from prosperous. A war is never won with the sword alone; the country that has the most money to spend on warfare is the victor. Unfortunately when victory is obtained it comes at a high price. Most of the countries were near bankruptcy, the warring nations had spent over $185 billion to fight a war that was supposed to end all wars. Most of the financing of the war had been done by the U.S. and everybody was indebted to the U.S. Long after the war ended bills hadn't ended yet.

In the immediate post war years everything was in short supply which caused years of inflation. There was a lot of money around but no goods to buy and whatever was for sale was very expensive. Quite a few farmers who had two or three sons had a problem. The farm was too small to divide between his sons; if he did they all would be starving.

Most of the time there was a way out of this predicament, one of the sons would get the farm and for the other sons he bought land. Like everything else land was very expensive so he had to borrow quite a bit of money to do that. It wasn't really a worry because the price of produce was high too and the return from farming was lucrative. Enough money was being made to make the required payments to pay off their loans and make a comfortable living at the same time. Everything that people undertook worked rather well.

In the mean time, the world was gradually speeding up in spite of the predictions of Reverend Young that the horse wouldn't be replaced because God had made horses to do the work. Slowly but surely the steam engine was taking over. Old threshing machines and other farm machinery were all running on steam. It was a time that steam was king.

From this lovely time comes the most beautiful song in the world with the best lyrics:

Jingle bell, everything goes on steam you see.
Except the little babies, who are growing on a tree.

Yes, that was good poetry; you don't see that anymore today. Probably there is a crop failure of poets.

This song is derived from the classical song Jingle bell, Jingle all the way. Oh what fun it is to ride in a one horse open sleigh.

However, today's teenager believes that riding in a 300 H.P. open Porche is a lot more fun than riding in a one horse open sleigh.

(Some people have another opinion about the babies. It was after the war when everything became possible in the Western World. A lot of things were unknown in the Soviet Union and when one of its citizens visited the United States he was perplexed.

When he got to the grocery store with his friend, he saw orange powder. He asked what it was and his friend explained that all you have to do is mix it with water and you'll get orange.

Next he saw milk powder and he was told that all you had to do was add water to get milk. When he looked in a different aisle he saw baby powder and said to his friend: "Really, you Americans have a way with powder.")

Everything had to go faster to make it cost less to produce goods and food. It used to be that potatoes were harvested by hand. Usually this was team work, a man would dig up the potatoes with a fork and his wife would pick up the potatoes and put them in the bag.

The farmers knew a faster method, they planted the potatoes in hills so they could plough them up and all what you had to do was pick up the potatoes. It went faster but not better. People who were hired to pick up the potatoes weren't paid per hour, they were paid per bag. The more bags of potatoes they had picked up the more money they would make. Consequently, it became a rush job and the potatoes that were still covered with dirt stayed in the field. Farmers got more work for less money out of the people but they paid for it in the long run by getting fewer potatoes from their field.

It was the steam engine that started the industrial revolution and had a dramatic development. In the beginning of steam, the regulation of the steam was done by a man who was sitting on the locomotive. The man opened a valve so that the steam would enter the cylinder under high pressure and the steam would push the piston to the other side of the cylinder. As soon as the piston was on the other side, the open valve had to be closed and the valve on the other side of the cylinder had to be opened so the steam could push the piston back. The man on the locomotive did this for many years, close one valve and open the other. Then one day, a clever man on the locomotive had it all figured out to make life easier. He put a rod between the valves; if he pushed one valve close the other one would open with the same movement. That was a considerable improvement; it was only half the work.

Yes, that was a smart guy; the only problem was that he was so smart that he out-smarted himself. He dug his own grave; his invention was only the beginning of automation. The next step was to let the steam engine do the closing and opening of the valves which made a valve man unnecessary. Now they could tell the man that his services were no longer required.

Steam engines were rapidly improved and wherever an engine could do the job, it was used. Consequently, more and more jobs disappeared and many people became unemployed. The time of the horse and buggy came to an end.

When the motor bike was introduced it ran on gasoline but in The Netherlands, they called it a steam bike. Everything else worked on steam, if it went without pedalling it must go on steam, the people thought.

Arie couldn't figure out how the motor bike could go on steam if there wasn't a coal box with a shovel on the back of the bike. They were shovelling coal on the fire of the locomotive but he didn't see any fire or steam either. When Arie was studying the motor bike, the owner returned and was so friendly to explain that it was wrongly called a steam bike. Most of the people don't have the foggiest idea what the difference is between a steam engine and a gasoline engine.

In spite of the popularity of steam, the steam engine had to make way for the gasoline and the diesel engine. Steam was probably the greatest invention after the wheel but it's hard to imagine a steam airplane.

One of the greatest disasters happened in the automobile industry. At first when you bought a car, it was a masterpiece made completely by hand by a master in his trade. Henry Ford changed all that when he invented the assembly line. He said you can get an automobile in the color of your choice, as long as you want black. On the assembly line, cars could be made faster and soon there were more cars than buyers. That brought on the Depression, just before Adrie was born.

The end of the Industrial Revolution was by no means in sight; it was only the beginning. It had been thought that with the invention of the machine, God's curse to Adam of having to work by the sweat of his brow, would be erased. Nothing was less true; the cure was worse than the sickness.

Finally, the worker saw that the machine, which he had hailed as the promised Messiah, was a curse. It had looked as if the machine could have produced food and products easier and faster to make life easier for the labourers. Something went terribly wrong, machines could produce an abundance of food and other goods but people didn't have money to buy them. Goods and food had to be destroyed to keep up the prices while people were starving and were living in poverty. Even at the farm, farmers couldn't afford a hired hand anymore; they were so poor that they couldn't even afford a hired finger. One out of every four farmers went bankrupt.

Prior to the stock market crash, farming was quite lucrative but people who had their money invested in industrial investments did a lot better. After the war had ended in 1918 people had a hard time to make a go of it. Slowly but surely things had improved and by 1924 everything went well, it signaled that "The roaring twenties" had started.

People made money hand over fist; they all had work and had few worries. Especially investors in the stock market had been doing alright. If you had shares in the automobile industry or oil it was like having a gold mine. To invest your money in the stock market seemed to be the thing to do and when more and more people invested, the stock market kept going up.

Indeed those were the roaring twenties. People were happy and were singing "Happy days are here again," and they were. The four terrible war years had long been forgotten and life got better all the time.

Since 1924 the stock market had been rising consistently but in 1929 the stock market was rising at an alarming rate. This attracted a lot more investors all the time which of course made the stock go up some more to the tune that some automobile stock and oil went up with 50% per month. The demand was greater than the supply and people thought that the sky was the limit. Even people who didn't have money borrowed it and hopped on the bandwagon of the lucrative stock market. With the huge profits they paid off the borrowed money in no time. They couldn't go wrong.

It was always said that if you wanted to become a millionaire, you had to start as a dishwasher or a newspaper boy. With the big money making stock market it was now possible to take a short cut to become a millionaire and live a care free life.

A self made millionaire man could be made very easily during the 1920's. Any person with one thousand dollars to invest could do it because of the way the stock market worked. If a person wanted to buy stock he bought it on option and paid 10% down. The rest would be due after thirty days.

With the $1000 he could buy $10,000 worth of shares and with the increase of 50% per month, they would be worth $15,000 at the end of the month. All he had to do was phone his stockbroker to sell his stock, pay the balance on his investment which was $9,000 and he had $6,000.

With this $6,000 it was possible to buy $60,000 worth of stock on option. Only 10% down needed. At the end of the second month his $60,000 stock rose by 50% and was now worth $90,000. He sold his stock again, paid off the $54,000 that he still owed on the stock he had bought on option and he had $36,000 of his own, at the end of the third month.

When he repeated this again by buying $360,000 of stock on option, the value of his stock went up to $540,000. He paid of $324,000.00 and had $216,000 of his own with which he could buy $2,160,000 worth of stock with 10% down.

His stock went up by 50% and was worth now $3,240,000. He now paid off the remaining 90% on his stock which was $1,844,000. After he had paid that amount there was still $1,396,000 that was his own after five months of playing the stock market. In five months time he was a millionaire. That was, of course, provided that every month his stock rose by 50%. If it went up less, it would take longer but in a year's time of investing, there were many millonaires made that way.

Where did that million dollars come from is a million dollar question? The answer is very discouraging, "There was no million dollars; the stock that was bought was only a piece of paper with a certain value attached to it. If people believed in it and were willing to pay a million dollars for it, that's what it was worth. On the other hand if people lost confidence in the stock, one could lose his million of dollars in a matter of a week or less."

Everybody enjoyed the prosperous world that had come after a few meager post war years and figured that this would last forever. During the industrial revolution people started to believe that it was normal to have abundance; it was there right. When they had reached a comfortable level of existence, they still wanted more. The industry kept manufacturing and people kept buying more stock in order to make more money. It was a million dollar question if this prosperity would continue forever?

Nothing lasts forever and the stock market, which is always fluctuating, is certainly unreliable at the best of times. The highest point of the stock market was reached in September 1929 and everybody who had invested in the stock market had become rich, almost overnight. They could have cashed in their stock and would have been rich indeed. Some smart people, who figured that good times would come to an end, sold their stock while they were ahead.

For the first time since its fabulous rise that started in 1924 the stock market went down because people were selling. This was quite a normal reaction of the stock market and nobody was worried. Most people were hanging onto their stock figuring that the stock would undoubtedly go up again.

They were right with their figuring; a lot of speculating investors were just waiting till the market had bottomed out and bought up the stock that was offered at bargain prices. Consequently the stock market rallied and went up again. However, some people saw the writing on the wall and were holding back to invest in the stock market again which slowed down the rise of the stock. No more fabulous profits were made in a month, like had happened in the past. That era had ended.

The slowing down of the stock market should have warned the people that the end of the bull market was in sight and a bear market would be next. Investors still could have sold their stock but they didn't want to believe that the worry free world of making money hand over fist had come to an end. Especially the old people who had saved some money for their old age had used that money to invest in stock to become rich. By investing every penny they had, they had made a fortune and wanted to keep it that way. Nobody was selling because the future looked bright and they were sitting pretty, they thought.

Those people were real millionaires if they had sold their stock and there was an extra bonus when a hefty deflation set in. Money became more valuable and a lot more goods could be bought for a dollar than ever before.

Unfortunately those new millionaires weren't going to sell their valuable stock, every month more dollars were added to their fortune. Why would they consider selling, that would be stupid. This was a wonderful world to live in when you were making money while you were sleeping.

All this was possible as long as millions were made in the oil and automobile industry. The only problem was that there had to be a market for the cars and other things that were made. Unfortunately, the big industrialists had never heard about sharing the wealth; all they knew was to rake in the wealth. They didn't pay the laborers, who made the cars and created the wealth, very much, so the laborers would never be in the position to buy a car. As soon as everybody who could afford to buy a car had one and cars produced in those days would last a long time, the manufactured cars couldn't be sold anymore.

Car manufacturers usually have a surplus of unsold cars but when the surplus keeps increasing they hold off for a while and cut production. If you cut production you don't need that many people to make cars so you lay off some people. Less cars produced was interpreted by the investors that the automobile industry was in trouble and consequently no dividends would be paid. They got nervous about their investment and sold their shares but because of the vast selling of stock, the stock market went down.

At the dawn of October 23rd nobody had ever heard about Black Thursday but that was just about to change. The day started like all other days, the sun got up and people went to work. Other people had more serious business to attend to, it was the investors who weren't quite happy with the shares they had in the automobile industry. The shares had gone down and they were losing money, they had to do something about it. They were going to sell their stock and find a different way to make money with their money.

When quite a few shares were offered in the automobile industry, the shares dropped quite a bit more. Other nervous investors saw what was happening and tried to sell their stock as well. This triggered another downward move on the stock market.

When the senior citizens heard the bad news, they hurried to the stock market in order to sell their stock and salvage whatever could be salvaged. Whenever you want to sell something you'll have to find a buyer who is interested in what you are selling. Unfortunately, it was too late to sell, everybody saw doom and nobody in his right mind wanted to buy worthless stock in the automobile industry anymore. All they could do was watch the stock ticker to find out that they were ruined. The senior citizens all had figured to have a worriless old age and had made the bad mistake of putting all their eggs in one basket. Too late they discovered that they had harbored a cobra that had consumed all their eggs.

Panic broke out among the investors; they blamed the stock brokers for the disaster that was happening. The stockbrokers were far from happy and demanded that their customers pay up the stock that they had bought on option with 10% down.

Paying up was impossible because the stock had dropped by 20%. People who had bought $100,000 worth of stock on option with 10% ($10,000) down found out that their $100,000 stock was now only worth $80,000 which meant that their $10,000 was lost and they still owed $90,000. They all had figured to pay for the stock with the profits that they were going to make but in no way could they pay with the losses they had sustained. All investors were broke.

It didn't take long before the angry shouting people grabbed one another and when fights broke out the police were called in to restore order. The police closed the stock market and everything was quiet within the building but it didn't stop the shares from dropping some more. A record of thirteen million dollars on shares was sold on the New York Stock Exchange on that day.

Stability seemed to return to the stock market on Friday and hope was restored that this all would pass. On Monday the opposite happened when the stock market kept dropping at the rate of one million dollars per minute. The major companies were losing $100 million each and the trend of the stock market was still downward.

The worst had yet to come on Black Tuesday. People hearing the news of the fast decline of the stock market wanted to sell their shares in a hurry, but nobody wanted to buy the worthless stock. There was a steady downward trend of the stock market for over two years and when it finally bottomed out two thirds of all the shares had been wiped out.

Where did it go? The answer is: It was never there, it was only imaginary riches that could be wiped out with the stroke of a pen. Most millionaires had become millionaires by the spectacular rise in the stock market. The stock market gave it and the stock market took it away.

It had taken most of the stock market made millionaires four to five years at the average to go from rags to riches. It took only one day to go from riches to rags without hope for the future when the stock market collapsed. Many ruined people turned on the gas and stockbrokers jumped out of their windows. It was a calamity the world had never seen before. The roaring twenties had lasted less than a decade and finished with a big roar, the stock market crash and the following Depression.

In one of the movies that dealt with the stock market crash, a family made rich by the stock market found out that they were ruined. While they had their family meeting, their butler came in and said: "Sir, your stockbroker is on the phone, he wonders if there is anything he can do before he jumps out of the window?"

That was kind of funny but the fallout of the market crash was far from funny. Nobody had been prepared for the stock market crash and the world was even less prepared for a major Depression. It happened almost overnight to change a prosperous world to a desperate one.

"Daddy, how come we have a Depression," a little boy asked his father. The father shrugged his shoulder and answered: "I haven't got the foggiest idea; they say it started in the automobile industry and it spread like wild fire."

Even the world leaders were puzzled what had happened and how they could end the Depression which no one had asked for. They had some explaining to do and they did. Most of the leaders in the Western world blamed the Communists whose intention had been to create chaos so they could take over Government.

Other explanations made more sense like the assembly line, the Gold Standard and tariffs but one explanation was far off base when they blamed the weather. With leaders like that how could the world expect not to go wrong?

According to the Marx Manifesto, "Capitalism is self destructive because the workers will starve within the system (He had that right) and the Proletariat will inherit the power." (Bull, that will never happen.)

When President Hoover of the U.S. was elected in 1928, he promised prosperity forever. All world leaders have a speech at the end of the year and President Hoover was no exception. He had some explaining to do and he pictured the catastrophe as an unfortunate incident that wasn't real and unemployment was only temporarily. All the problems would have been resolved before spring. He ended his powerful speech: "Prosperity is just around the corner." He was wrong, thousands more people lost their jobs and went on relief.

Unfortunately, the hundreds of thousands of people who were standing in long soup lines were real; they demanded action and blamed the Government for the disaster. The opposition also blamed the Government. They charged that in the midst of plenty people should be well fed and properly dressed, yet the opposite had occurred.

The stock market crash was only the beginning of a lot of trouble. Cars are made out of steel and when fewer cars were made, there was less steel needed. Steel manufacturers did the very thing that the car manufacturers had done; they cut production and laid off workers. This caused the stock in steel to tumble as well. Tires, glass and upholstery plants went the same route with cutting production and laying off workers. The snowball effect became an avalanche that gained momentum with no way to stop it.

The 1929 Depression wasn't the first Depression in the U.S. There had been several depressions before but they weren't world wide. And since they were mild Depressions they were called Recessions. A Recession means that people have to do without a lot of things their parents had never heard of.

A recession is nothing new; it's part of our system, it starts when there is an over supply of goods and services and ends usually when a population increase demands more goods and services. Population increase or other increases of activities can change the picture fast. However, the 1929 Depression beat them all and was therefore called "The Great Depression."

The 1929 market crash wasn't the first market crash in history either. The stock market was developed for business people in need of a large business capital for their enterprises. If they couldn't raise the money on their own they went Public with their business and sold shares. If the company did well; so did the shareholders who owned part of the company and shared in the profits. Of course, if the company lost money so did the shareholders.

Throughout the years there have been many fraudulent companies with owners who collected the money and mysteriously disappeared before the police could arrest them. One of those swindlers of the past was John Law who was in charge of commerce and trade for the French Government in Louisiana.

John Law made all untrue claims about Louisiana. According to him it was a Paradise on earth with an abundance of gold, all you had to do was mine it. The climate in Louisiana was so perfect that people never got sick. Everything was just great; you couldn't lose even if you tried.

The shares of the company were rising at a fabulous rate which attracted business men from all over the world. Everybody was hurrying to Paris to get into a good deal and people lined up to buy shares. Because of the tremendous demand for the stock, people indeed got rich very fast. There was even a fabulous story about a hunchback who had made millions by renting out his back to people so they could use it as a desk to sign their papers.

Once the truth came out that there was nothing to be had in Louisiana, people dumped their worthless shares. Instead of riches there was only ruin and people who had been rich for a while were now poor again.

In England they had the fraudulent South Sea Company which claimed to have invented an air pump for the brain which would increase the ability of the brain by one hundred percent.

Furthermore they claimed to have invented a perpetual motion wheel. Unfortunately the brain air pump and perpetual wheel of motion were never supplied. Once people demanded delivery they found out that it was just a scam and in less than three months the company was bankrupt leaving the shareholders to hold the bag.

There have been some ingenious contraptions that came close to perpetual movement. One was shown on the trade show; it was a wheel with weights attached. Every time a weight reached the top, it would tumble down and give the wheel a push. In spite of the clever design, the wheel lost speed eventually and came to a standstill. If you want to create a device of perpetual motion you'll have to wipe out resistance. The best bearing will have resistance even if it's very little and this resistance has to be overcome which takes energy. The only perpetual the world had achieved is perpetual commotion, not motion.

One of the swindles of our time was with the Bre-X Mineral Company in 1997. They claimed that they had bought a lot of land in Indonesia which contained a lot of gold. Many investors bought shares in the company and expected to make a lot of money. When it became known that all there was on the land they had bought were a bunch of mosquitoes and snakes, the stock was worth only pennies.

Those crashes had occurred because of fraudulent entrepreneurs but a crash can also occur if supply outstrips demand. One of the earliest crashes like that happened in The Netherlands with tulip bulbs. The tulip isn't even native to The Netherlands, it originated in Turkey. Some smart guy brought them to The Netherlands and started to cross different kinds of tulips until he had developed the Viceroy bulb. It was a beautiful tulip and of course in the beginning they were in short supply which made the price soar. People who were dealing in the bulbs made a lot of money which made the price go up some more. The price for one tulip bulb amounted to hundreds of dollars and the price went up by the day.

Old people who had money invested took their money out to buy a few tulip bulbs in order to make a lot of money. Indeed they made a lot of money if they had sold them when they were ahead but why sell when you are making a lot of money? When supply caught up with the demand; the tulip bulbs dropped by 97% leaving financial ruin behind.

There can be a craze in anything; whatever tickles people's fancy. If ever for some reason fried spider legs become a delicacy on the dinner plate and go out of whack with pricing, there is money to be made. If you must get in on the opportunity of a life time, buy them early at $100.00 a spider leg and sell them as soon as you can get $200.00 a spider leg. Don't wait till they are

$400.00 because once the frenzy for spider legs is over, they might drop to $10.00 and you'll be left with holding the bag or holding the spider leg. In that case, you'll be selling pencils at the street corner before you know it.

When the stock market crash took place, the average John Blow cared less. It was the rich people who got it in the neck for a change, why would he care? However, when millions of people became unemployed, the situation changed drastically. With less industrial orders, competition became so severe that it caused quite a drop in the commodity prices. Some people had not invested in the stock market; they had invested in commodities like tea and coffee. With the drop in prices they sustained severe losses as well.

With fewer activities, companies sharpened their pencil and cut prices which translated in fewer profits. To combat this problem business men started to economize on the wages they paid their workers. Wage cuts were made several times and to top it off, the employers demanded more production out of their workers. Business was down everywhere and 25% of the people became unemployed. All those unemployed people had no money to spend which caused a lack of sales all around. This in turn caused more lay offs and more cuts in wages. It worked like an avalanche which couldn't be stopped and looked like a nightmare without wake up.

All political opposition leaders made hay out of this bizarre situation and everybody promised the electorate to be a reformer and turn the fortunes of the people around. If the people got rid of the present Government there would be a rosy future again.

Roosevelt, the leader of the opposition in the U.S. told the people that there was something really wrong with the system that had caused this tragedy to take place. He blamed President Hoover and his henchmen for the disaster and the only way to correct it was to do things differently. A bunch of ruthless international bankers were the culprits of this disaster, they had made millions of profits without sharing a nickel of it with the working people who had created their profits. He promised the people "A New Deal" and a prosperous country again.

It didn't take much to convince the millions of unemployed people who were starving that there was something awfully wrong with the current system. Roosevelt was in a wheel chair because of Polio and the people wondered if this crippled man could change things for the better.

The millions of starving people were willing to give Roosevelt a chance; he couldn't do any worse than President Hoover had done. Consequently Roosevelt won the election by a landslide.

Once in power it wasn't all that easy to deliver on his promises, Roosevelt found out. He had to take some drastic steps and the first problem to attend to was the banks. Several banks had gone bankrupt with the market crash which scared the people. They had a run on the banks, took all their money out and put it in an old sock.

Nobody had ever heard that banks could have a holiday but President Roosevelt changed all that. He closed the banks until further notice when he would have the Emergency Relief Act passed. Depository Insurance also came into being, with the Government guaranteeing that deposits would be repaid if a bank went bankrupt. That measure restored confidence in the banks and people re-deposited their hoarded money, to the tune of one billion dollars, in the banks as soon as they re-opened.

The next problem was to convince the people that everything was under control and they had nothing to worry about. He traveled through the country to have some pep talks with the people telling them over and over again: "We have nothing to fear but fear itself! It was fear that collapsed the stock market when people dumped all their stock because they feared to lose their money!"

President Roosevelt came up with all kinds of Federal work programs to get the economy going again. It took him till 1936 before some improvement was seen. However, the investors were careful investing in stock which had proved a risky business. Consequently there was little activity and 8 million people were still unemployed.

It looked that the steps that had been taken were successful when the stock market went slightly up in 1937. World leaders had a sigh of relief, they were confident that the end of the crises was in sight and that everything would be normal again.

Unfortunately it wasn't going to be, nothing had changed in the attitude of the Capitalist. Major companies were still not willing to share the record profits they had made with their workers who had made the profits for them. On the contrary they were trying desperately to make higher profits the next year at the expense of the labourers. They cut the wages of the workers several times in order to economize.

General Motors was making a profit of $200 million, the largest profit ever but that wasn't good enough. The management decided to freeze the wages of the workers and speed up the assembly line so that the profits would increase over the next year.

For a while it looked that the problem was licked and Government and business leaders popped the champagne corks to celebrate their success with the measures they had taken. They put the champagne away in a heck of a hurry when there was another market crash at the end of 1937 and wondered what had happened.

Exactly the same had happened as in 1929, labourers were kept poor and the auto makers raked in all the huge profits. Business and Government leaders had learned nothing from their mistakes. They never had heard that money that goes around comes around, if they had given the labourers the money they could have sold cars to them. Consequently, with not enough money coming around, car sales were down and production had to be cut again. For the second time in eight years the investors dumped the shares in the automobile industry causing another collapse.

It was worse than in 1929, even the people who had managed to buy a car couldn't afford to drive it; they didn't have money to buy gas. Very conveniently they put a horse in front of their car so they could use it. They had hailed the car as a horseless carriage; ironically they now had a horseless carriage pulled by a horse. It was the greatest invention of all times.

The main culprit of the Depression was that the workers were underpaid and didn't have money to spend. The capitalist made more and more money all the time and used that money to build more manufacturing plants so they would make more millions. Who is going to buy all the manufactured goods if nobody has money? Only an idiot would think that you can build more manufacturing plants to make more money which you use to build more manufacturing plants so you can make more money.

When the workers found out that they didn't get anywhere, Unions came into being. It became more than an ugly struggle when the Government tried to break the Union. Early members had many accidents; all of a sudden a load of steel fell accidently out of a crane right on top of a Union member.

Strikes were very difficult in the beginning; they couldn't last very long because of lack of funds. When the strike fund was exhausted people had to go back to work because of starvation. However, the Unions were determined and with a fourteen day strike they did get a wage increase for their members. They also had obtained a seniority system. It was the first victory against Capitalism.

The next victory the Union obtained was Unemployment Insurance. It wouldn't benefit the people who were unemployed already but if the people who were working became unemployed they had at least some kind of income.

Working in the automobile industry was bad but working in the garment industry was worse. In order to economize, they operated sweat shops with 13 year old girls who were working 55 hours per week for $10.

After several strikes, the sweat shops were forced to pay minimum wage. A lot of good that did! It didn't help the girls at all because the shop owners had an answer to that; they increased the daily quota that had to be delivered. If a girl didn't deliver her quota, she had two choices, she could stay longer to reach her quota or she was fired for poor performance. If they were fired, they were also blacklisted and nobody would hire them anymore. Nobody complained because the ones who had been complaining before had been fired.

The Great Depression changed the world forever. Governments toppled and Socialism and Communism were on the rise. The Financiers and Bankers Associations stated that the unemployed were idle loafers and a blight to society. It was time to have another war to get rid of them. *(That other war was in the making in Germany where Adolph Hitler had risen to power, thanks to the Depression.)*

Other suggestions of the Ruling Class were that all male applicants who applied for relief should be sterilized before they would get relief payments in order to get only good people who wouldn't be unemployed. The stand of the Government was that the poor were the authors of their own fate. They were a bunch of idle loafers who only wanted to collect relief payments for doing nothing. Those people were a menace to society. That insult to the hungry people who wanted to work did it. They supported Socialism and opposed Capitalism.

The Government spent a lot of money to fight Socialism and Communism but all the steps they were taking were useless. If they had given the people clothes to wear and food to eat they would have been a lot more successful than spending a lot of money fighting a losing battle. With more and more people becoming unemployed and the insults they had to take, the world was overwhelmed by Socialism and Communism. People went by droves to meetings of Socialists and Communists to hear their propaganda speeches that made a lot of sense. According to the orators of those meetings, Capitalism was a curse to the world and they used this story about the dying donkey caught between two hay stacks over and over again.

"A donkey that was stuck between two hay stacks was heading for one of the hay stacks when he got hungry. Once he was on his way he realized that there was another hay stack. When he looked back he realized that there was a lot of good hay in the other hay stack. The donkey turned around and was now heading for the other hay stack. Still he was thinking about the hay stack he had been heading for in the first place. Again he looked back and decided to go back to his original plan. He turned around again but wasn't sure that he had made the right decision. After turning continuously back and forward, the donkey didn't reach either of the hay stacks and starved between them.

The moral of this story is never to look back because it gets you into trouble. When the wife of Lot looked back at Sodom and Gomorrah when it was destroyed, she became a salt pillar. (Biblical story.) And when the donkey looked back he couldn't make up his mind which one was the better hay stack and died in the midst of plenty."

The orator cleared his throat to finalize his speech with a big bang: "A donkey is known never to get his leg hurt by the same stone twice so it's hard to believe that a donkey would be stupid enough to die between two hay stacks in the midst of plenty. That brings me to the point that I'm trying to make that people are more stupid than a donkey. They are in the midst of plenty walking between not two elevators but between dozens of elevators filled to the brim with the best grain in the world. Yet they are starving. Now if that's not stupid, what is? How in the world can a cow go hungry in a pasture with tall green grass and how can a worm starve in a big apple? They don't, but people starve and are making skirts and pants from old flour bags while the stores are filled with clothes that nobody can buy because of lack of money. People are walking in flour bags without underwear and with worn out shoes. This is most scandalous and unheard of."

They made a poem out of the bizarre situation:

To understand what's going on takes more than a brain.
Our people are starving while we have elevators full of grain.
We also have a Government that doesn't seem to care,
That we are walking in old flour bags without underwear.

Socialism is supposed to be a system in which all goods are evenly distributed by the State instead of by private enterprises. Production and distribution of goods are done by the State and private ownership of businesses and even ownership of houses is completely eliminated.

Communism goes a few steps further than Socialism. Everything is owned by the community in a classless society and everybody shares equally. The State is responsible of planning and control of the economy. Individual liberties are non existent in a one Party system and opposition is a no, no. Any attempt to start another party is doused by bullets instead of ballots.

No matter how many wrongs Communism had, during the Great Depression people wouldn't believe it. They only saw the wrongs in Capitalism because they were poor and starving. In all Western countries Communists popped up like mushrooms in a damp forest. The conditions were right. Communism looked good to the starving people who didn't have a penny in their pocket. The State would take care of its people from the cradle to the grave. Communism looks so simple; everything is for everybody. To the millions of hungry people, Communism looked like a better system to have the State divide the goods evenly. It looked like a Utopia but it wasn't. From the onset it looked like the idea of Robin Hood; you take from the rich and give it to the poor except the Communist leaders took it from the rich and put it in their own pocket.

Various types of Governments work in different ways:

- Socialism: If you have two cows, you give one to your neighbor.
- Communism: When you have two cows you give both cows to the Government and with a lot of luck they might give you some milk.
- Fascism: If you have two cows, you give all of the milk to the Government, and the Government sells it.
- Nazism: If you have two cows, the Government shoots you and takes both your cows.
- Anarchism: If you have two cows, you keep both cows, shoot the Government agent and steal another cow.
- Capitalism: If you have two cows, you sell one cow and buy a bull.

(A crocodile wanted to start a Socialist Political Party. He walked into the forest and asked a bear to become a member of his Socialist Party. The bear thought a while and answered: "I can't, I walk in a fur coat, my wife and children walk in a fur coat so I can't become a member of a Socialist Party."

The crocodile walked farther into the forest until he saw a snail and asked him to become a member. The snail thought it over for a bit and said: "I can't because I have my own house and my wife and children have their own house. That won't do!"

When the crocodile wanted to leave, the bear and snail asked: "Why in the world do you want to start a Socialist Party?" The crocodile answered: "I have a big mouth and my wife and children have big mouths too.")

(There was a Communist rally which was held for the purpose of attracting some new members. The orator had some opposition from a young man that kept ridiculing the Communist Party. When the orator asked the young man why he wouldn't want to be a Communist; the young man said: "My grandfather was a Democrat, my father was a Democrat, so I'm a Democrat!"

"That's sheer nonsense," the orator said: "If your grandfather was an idiot and your father was an idiot, would you be an idiot as well?"

"No, in that case I would be a Communist," the young man answered.)

SOMEBODY'S DEATH IS SOMEBODY'S BREAD

In spite of the political upheaval in the country and the Stock Market crash, life went on and in 1930 the stork was good enough to deliver a baby boy to Arie and Ko. That was exactly what they had hoped for to have a girl and a boy.

The baby boy was called Adrianus again and his every day name was Adrie. People were very superstitious; most of the people wouldn't name their baby after a baby that had previously died because that child would die as well. Ko and Arie didn't believe that and were more interested in naming their children after the grand parents so their names would continue.

If the first Adrianus baby hadn't died, this baby would never have been born. Arie and Ko were pretty good at birth control and only if the second baby had been a girl would they have tried one more baby to see if they could get a boy. Because the first Adrianus died, the second Adrianus was born, which makes the title of this chapter make sense. "Somebody's death is somebody's bread." Some people might have thought that this was an undertaker who makes bread if somebody dies.

In those days, women didn't go to the hospital to have their baby; the baby was delivered at home by a midwife. So Adrie was born in Yselmonde on the Hordyk by his mother in the cupboard bed with the pee pot standing on the shelf that was over the cupboard bed.

The midwife had one good look and said: "Oh boy, it is a boy." Arie and Ko were very proud and called it quits. It was said that having a girl and a boy was a rich people's wish. Arie and Ko didn't see it that way, when you were poor two children was about all you could handle to bring them up and when you were rich you could afford to have more children.

Adrie's birth was only spectacular for his parents; it didn't attract any headlines in the newspaper like the birth of the daughter of the Queen when she was born. When Princes Juliana was born they shot a cannon 51 times, when Adrie was born they didn't even ignite a fire cracker.

Princess Juliana was born in pink and gold,
And Adrie was born to wet his diaper because he was cold.

On the occasion that Princess Juliana was born, the people were dancing in the streets and shouting: "Orange Forever, long live the Queen." *(The Royals were of the House of Orange, and had adopted an orange flag.)* They were celebrating and happy. The only people that were celebrating when Adrie was born were his parents. His sister Willie had nothing to celebrate; she was neither excited nor impressed with her brand new baby brother. When she saw her mother with another baby on her lap, she wanted nothing to do with him. She was jealous.

Willie was used to having all the attention but now with this little screamer around, when he opened his mouth, they rushed to the cradle to take care of him. She was used to being the center of attention but suddenly she had become a second class citizen. No, she wasn't amused at all with the new arrangements. It took some doing before she accepted her baby brother; you just don't talk a three year old girl into understanding that she wasn't the only one in the world her parents loved.

Adrie wasn't annoyed with the hostile attitude of his sister; he spent the day with sleeping, filling his stomach and filling his diaper. Filling his diaper was a big job; his mother must need that stuff desperately. As soon as he had filled his diaper his mother came to take it away on him.

Of course, all of the family came to see Ko's new baby. Uncle Jaap Dalm already had four daughters and was hoping that he would get a baby boy as well. Arie had him beat but he was still hoping.

Adrie wasn't impressed with his Uncle Jaap Dalm who came to look at the brand new baby boy. He realized that he was little but he had a lot of power, one scream out of him made the waiter appear with a bottle of milk and when he screamed murder, his mother hurried to the cradle to see if perhaps a pin was sticking in his body. When she couldn't figure out what the problem was, she picked him up out of the cradle to tap his back. "Maybe he has gas," she said.

Jaap Dalm who saw all the excitement had listened to the conversation of the women, he had it. "Why would a baby have gas?" was his remark. "If he had gas He would open up a service station."

That was worth a laugh or two and people said: "You have to be Jaap Dalm to come up with something stupid like that."

It looked like Adrie had the right idea with all the unemployed people around; he was providing work for at least one person who had a job to do looking after him. He was a big help.

THE MURDERER

From Rotterdam to the island of Hoeksewaard, a steam tram service was maintained for the benefit of the people living on the island who wanted to do their shopping in the city. The steam tram had the unpopular name "Murderer." That name came about after the tram had won its spurs by killing many people on unprotected level crossings in the city of Rotterdam and on country roads. Many a biker was crushed under the murderous wheels of "the murderer." Because of the many accidents, the tram always made a heck of a noise with its steam whistle to warn people of the oncoming tram. In spite of that many accidents kept happening.

It was a sunny day in May; actually the weather was nice enough to go for a walk with the children Ko thought. She had done her work in the morning and a walk would do her and her children a lot of good. She got the baby carriage ready for her two children Willie and Adrie. Adrie was only two years old, he had to be put into the carriage and Wilie was already five years old, she could sit on the front of the carriage.

Actually, Willie was old enough to do some walking but she refused to do even one step when her baby brother had a ride. Right away, she started to bellyache about her sore feet. There was not a thing wrong with her feet and Ko knew it. Her only problem was that she still was jealous of her brother and she wanted to have the same service as he had. It didn't matter to Ko to have her in front of the carriage. Small children don't walk that fast anyway and if both children were in the carriage she could walk as fast as she wanted. That way, everybody was happy like a pig in the sty.

On that very day that they went for a walk, at least Ko was walking, she enjoyed the beautiful weather and nature around her. There were lots of green pastures with butter cups and daisies, and she was happy like a lark with her two children. Everything had come up roses, what else could she possibly want? Thinking about her good fortune, she was absent minded and pushed the baby carriage across the rails of the murderer that was approaching. She hadn't been paying attention while she was thinking.

Luckily, there was a man on a bike who saw the danger that the mother with her baby carriage was in. He jumped off the bike, jumped up to Ko and pulled her and her baby carriage back, just in time not to be crushed under the murderous wheels of the Murderer.

Ko had the shock of her life when she realized that all three could have been dead if it wasn't for the man on the bike. Her heart was bouncing in her throat and she was as white as a sheet; that was a close call, too close for comfort. She had to sit down for a bit to get over this incident. Great accidents can spring from small causes. In her mind she could see it all if this God sent man hadn't pulled her back just in time, there would have been headlines in the newspaper: "Tragic accident. Mother with two children killed on level crossing by 'The Murderer.'"

Still trembling on her feet, she continued her walk back home. She sure had to take better care of her children and herself. From there on, she was always warning her kids to be careful on the road and pay attention to the steam tram. They had crawled through the eye of a needle in the struggle "To be or not to be."

Now Arie and Ko had a beautiful house and a girl and a boy. They even had survived the Murderer and should be very happy. And they were! Unfortunately, their happiness wasn't going to last very long. Nobody had paid much attention when the stock market crash happened in 1929 except the people who had lost a lot of money. Only when the repercussions washed ashore did the people become alarmed.

THE DOLDRUMS YEARS

Dead calm regions in the Pacific were a problem in the time of sailing ships, they were called Doldrums. Sailing ships were dependant on wind to get them where they wanted to go and when they got into the doldrums they didn't get anywhere. They had to wait it out till some wind came back to fill their sails and push them out of the doldrums. Meanwhile the ship's crew was totally inactive and couldn't do anything.

The First World War years were eventful and the post war years had been exciting as well with the stock market crash that did everybody in. People went from riches to rags and stockbrokers jumped out of the windows to be freed from earthly suffering.

After the repercussions of this calamity had washed ashore, everybody settled in the doldrums years. Nothing happened anymore, every day was the same. The sun would rise in the East and set in the West and nobody got anywhere because the wind was taken out of everybody's sails. Years went by and most of the people got poorer and poorer. People couldn't go anywhere since they barely had dry bread on the table. They were completely inactive and nothing exciting happened in their lives.

It was so bad that the newspapers had a problem finding a daily headline for the front page. That was a real problem, and the newspapers were holding off to the last possible minute to print the newspaper. They made up a headline for the paper about some uneventful event hoping that something important or terrible might happen which would make a better front page headline. There was so little world activity that the newspapers were dull, uninteresting and also thin. If you have a dull newspaper, who is going to buy a newspaper especially during the Depression when very few people had any money?

On many days, the editor had to be satisfied with a little accident which had happened, with two people transported to the hospital with bleeding wounds. They had to use their imagination and lay it on so the newspaper boy had something to yell about when he tried to sell his papers. The newspaper boy would scream: "Terrible accident, come see come sa, daddyo is butchering a herring, the blood is splashing against the wall."

Sometimes it was a speech of a politician that made the presses roll. Of course, if you have to wait for politicians to say something interesting, you can wait a long time. They never say anything important, they are content to dust off the old saw and repeat the same message over and over. Politicians only promise things in order to pay lip service to it later. They talk like chickens without a head, as most people know.

During the dull years of the Depression there was very little excitement. The only cheerful news was the birth of the Dionne quintuplets in 1934. People were impressed with the five cuddly babies and thought that Mr. Dionne was the greatest lover of all times. They figured that he had an extra ordinary long penis to make five babies with one shot. He lived at the farm and whenever he went to the outhouse, some curious people were peeking if they could get a glimpse of the master penis that had made it all possible. Dionne got all kinds of letters from women who couldn't get pregnant and wanted him to provide stud service. Mrs. Dionne wouldn't allow it.

(When a woman was delivering a baby, the doctor asked the husband to hold the light so he could see. After the baby came, the doctor said: "Hold the light closer there is one more baby coming."

After the second baby was delivered, the doctor said: "Come closer yet, there is one more baby coming."

After the third baby had been delivered, the man said: "I better put the light away because they come towards the light.")

The doldrums years lasted for about five years; they then disappeared and never returned. Adolph Hitler was the first one to bring a lot of news to the world. It didn't take long to make the thin newspaper disappear; they had to print extra editions to report all the news.

With the Great Depression on the go there was a love story second to none; it even surpassed Romeo and Juliet. The entire world was talking about a Fairy Tale Romance. King Edward had started to romance Mrs. Simpson, a divorcee and when he wanted to marry her, the English Church wouldn't allow it. When he insisted on marrying her he had to abdicate. At that time England ruled roughly a third of the world and King Edward gave up a third of the world to marry the woman he loved. This was a heart warming love story in a desperate time.

In 1937 there was the World Boy Scout Jamboree in The Netherlands which was world news but Spain stole the stage when Civil War broke out. The Spanish King had fallen in love and embraced Communism, making Spain the only Communist Kingdom in the world. This was rejected by the generals and General Franco pulled his army to the Canary Islands from where he was planning a landing on the mainland. General Franco had the backing of Hitler and Mussolini who sent a constant flow of weapons to Spain. Germany even bombed targets in Spain for General Franco and consequently he won and took over.

The word news is not the plural of new, it came from the first letters from all four corners of the world N orth, E ast, W est and S outh. The letters represent the first letters of the four compass points. Suddenly, when the nations prepared for war, there was lots of news with thick newspapers that lasted till the last year of the war and then, because of lack of paper and electricity, paper printing came to a halt in most of Europe till the end of the war.

The Chinese say: "That you may live in interesting times." The Doldrums years were far from interesting, they were dull and uninteresting.

Adrie's life wasn't dull and uninteresting, the Depression didn't bother him a bit; he was innocent like a lamb and had a lot of exploring to do. While he was sleeping most of the day, the world around him changed drastically and not for the better. His father became unemployed with no hope to find work. Adrie was going to be one of the children growing up in a desperate time of poverty.

A lot of people became unemployed with the severe Recession setting in and when the Recession deepened it became a severe Depression called "The Great Depression." It was a Depression with proportions the world had never known before. Arie hadn't been immediately involved with his work in the harbor, he was still working. Unfortunately, the harbors got more and more mechanized and loading and unloading of ships was done with cranes instead of manual labor.

Crane operators and truck drivers were in demand and some people managed to get training for those jobs. Unfortunately, Arie was almost forty years old and was considered to be too old to be re-trained in a more modern job. "You can't teach an old dog new tricks" was the opinion of the bosses.

When Arie was laid off, he tried to find another job and was always on the road to prospective bosses. Unfortunately, he wasn't the only one to look for work and most of the offices where people applied for a job had a sign posted; "No workers needed."

Whenever there were workers needed he didn't have a hope in hell of being hired. The boss would look him over and asked what his age was. When Arie told him, the boss would say: "Just what I thought, you are almost forty years old. You are too old for this job."

And so, Arie became unemployable and not needed which was a terrible position to be in with two little children. However, Arie was brushed aside but he wasn't giving up that fast and wasn't about to be cast aside like an old boot. If nobody wanted him he would just go into business himself and decided to go from door to door to sell herring. That was a great idea but it was a disillusion. His enterprise was already doomed before it started. Money had become as scarce as teeth in a hen and people were economizing. Few people would buy herring from him. He didn't even make enough money to buy the salt for the porridge.

Money had to come in for a family with two children, what was he going to feed his family from? There was a relief fund for the unemployed people, so he had to go on the pogey whether he liked it or not. Arie didn't like to accept handouts but when you are hungry and desperate you have to swallow your pride.

Of course, there was a lot of bureaucracy involved to get money from the Government. A bunch of forms had to be filled out for a starter; they wanted to know where he had worked his entire life and his qualifications. They were also looking critically that he had an owned house. People with an owned house were rich; they had money invested in a house. That house had to be sold and the money of the sale of the house had to be consumed first before they would consider supporting him. That was a slap in his face, he had worked so hard to get an owned house and now he was going to lose it. He had to eat his house and he wasn't a termite.

A house wasn't the only thing that had to be sold to get relief payments. All other possessions and other assets had to be eaten first. There were also Government inspectors in place that could come to check your house in and outside at any time. If you refused to give the inspector access to your house you were automatically disqualified from relief payments.

A brick layer went for relief and after he had filled out the forms, they sent an inspector to his house to verify his statement. The inspector found a couple of wheelbarrows and a few shovels on his property. He was told to sell first his wheelbarrows and tools before they would give him anything. The inspector estimated the value of his possessions and told him how many weeks he had to live on the money of the sale of his possessions. If you had an equity of 1000 guilders in a house, they allowed you to live on 20 guilders per week so you didn't have to come back for fifty weeks.

However, Arie had a lucky break, he had bought the house for 6000 guilders and there was only an equity in the house of 1400 guilders. With the Recession, a severe Depression had set in and everything was depressed including the price of houses. A severe devaluation of Real Estate was the consequence. If that 6000 guilder house had to be sold it wouldn't even bring up 5000 guilders; that was if they could sell it which was very doubtful.

The economy was caught in strangulation and nothing moved anymore. Nobody in his right mind would buy a house with the devaluation going strong and being stuck with a mortgage that he had to pay off while everybody started to make less and less money. A guy could lose his shirt and of course his house in the same time.

When the authorities were convinced that absolutely nothing could be gained if the house was sold, they decided to give him relief money. He received 8 guilders for himself and his wife and one additional guilder for each kid. A total of 10 guilders was going to be his weekly income.

The Government wasn't about to trust the unemployed people and were determined to check up on those crooked people so they weren't making money on the side with another job. They issued Stamp Cards to all the people who claimed relief money. The stamp card would contain the name and the address of the person. It also had six squares, one for each day and also a designated time that he had to report to Town Hall to get a stamp in the square of the day. The earliest people had to report was at 9.00 a.m. A few people reported at that time and a few people reported 9.05 a.m. and so on.

If your reporting time was 9.00 a.m., you couldn't report at five minutes to nine. That wasn't acceptable and you had to wait till nine. It was worse when you reported late; if you were two minutes late you would get a scolding like a kid that's late for school. You also would get a warning that if it happened again you wouldn't get paid for that day. It meant that at the end of the week you would get less money. If you missed two stamps on your stamp card you were disqualified from receiving any money. People hardly received any money so they couldn't afford to get less.

No excuses were accepted when you were late. A person could get a flat tire on his way to Town Hall which was a good possibility. People had barely enough money to buy food and coughing up enough money to replace a worn out tire without money was hard to do. A flat tire was no excuse; you were on relief and had all the time in the world to be in time for your appointment.

In order not to be late, everybody left his house half an hour early just in case they had a flat tire. If that happened, they still could walk to be in time. Of course, normally when nothing like that happened, they would be half an hour early which meant they had to wait. There was a park near the Town Hall with a large pond with a bridge across it. All early people would go to the park, stand on the bridge to spit circlets in the water, just to waste half an hour of their time. When they arrived early, they would say to each other: "Let's go to the park to spit some circlets."

This daily trip to get a stamp was unpopular called, "Stamping." Before the Depression, the word stamping would mean stamping on the floor when you had cold feet or maybe the post man would stamp the stamp on the envelopes. During the Depression hordes of people had to go stamping in order to receive relief money.

When you were on relief and made a few extra bucks on the side, you had to report it so they could deduct it from your relief payment. The full one hundred percent of what you had made was deducted which was not encouraging to do anything at all. You might as well do nothing and get the same relief payment as if you worked. It didn't prevent people from making some illegal income, they just didn't report it. There was no reward for honesty so people cheated. The Government jerked people around and made liars and dishonest people even out of religious people that were threatened with hell fire if they cheated.

According to the Reverend you were facing hell if you cheated on your income, it was against the law and the Ten Commandments. People were desperate, their philosophy was that if they were going to hell they would at least be warm and if they were honest, they wouldn't be able to buy coal for winter so they would be cold. One guy who was threatened with hell fire said to the Reverend: "Don't you threaten me with hell fire. I lived in the Outback of Australia for 15 years where the temperatures were 41 degrees Celsius. Hell couldn't be any worse."

Missionaries in the Painted Desert didn't do much better with trying to get the Indians interested in Heaven. The Indian Chief asked: "Does Heaven look like this desert?"

"No not at all," the Missionary answered. He had the shock of his life to think that Heaven would look like this God forsaken desert.

He had mis-figured the Indian Chief who said: "If Heaven doesn't look like this desert, I don't want to go there." He sure loved his desert and wouldn't change it for Heaven.

Arie and Ko had long discussions as how to make ends meet on the little income they received. First of all, Arie added all the bills that had to be paid for sure. The very first thing that had to be taken care of was the mortgage on the house, if they didn't pay that they would be without a roof over their head. Emergency steps had to be taken to make sure that the mortgage could be paid at the end of the year.

With being on relief Arie received at least a little bit of money and they didn't make him sell his house. That saved his house he thought but only for the time being. Mr. Veldhoen was the mortgage holder who had to be paid at the end of the year. The arrangement was that he had to pay off the mortgage at the rate of 300 guilders per year plus the interest which was 4% per year. Interest had to be paid at the end of the year, when the year was up the mortgage holder had earned his interest and that's when it had to be paid.

With a mortgage on the house that was still 4600 guilders the interest of 4% on that amount would be 184 guilders. It meant that he had to pay the mortgage holder 300 guilders on principal plus 184 guilders on interest which amounted to a total of 484 guilders. When he worked in the harbor, he had made 22 guilders per week which was more than twice the money he raked in now. That amounted to a loss of income per year of 620 guilders which was more than he had to pay the mortgage holder.

By paying off part of the principal every year, his payments were decreasing every year because there was less interest to pay. This way, it would be easier every year because his payments were lower. Arie had calculated all this and it looked good. There was only one thing wrong, he hadn't figured that his income would dwindle.

In the meantime there were other bills that had to be paid or else! There was medical insurance which was a must and the electric and water bill, if they didn't pay those bills they would disconnect the utilities.

The Netherlands already had Medicare before the war, which gave the people pretty good coverage. It wasn't exactly free; it was a mutual insurance for which everybody had to pay one guilder per month for the entire family. One guilder per month was a lot of money for those days; most workers made about twenty guilders per week. It was expensive alright, but everybody was fully covered for doctors and hospital expenses. It also covered medicine, glasses and dental work.

No cuts could be made on the medical insurance. Even with the little money they received, they couldn't afford not to have it. Every month, a man by the name of A de Boer came to collect the one guilder for the insurance. All subscribers had a card with twelve squares and when A de Boer came, you gave him your card plus a guilder. He would then put his stamp with A de Boer in the appropriate square and hand the card back to you. That way you could prove you had paid.

The medical insurance worked a little differently than most Health Plans worked. When you were in the health plan, you could choose your own doctor. This doctor got paid a certain amount of money for each client whether he or she was sick or not. He just had to take care of his clients for that money which made abuse of the plan by over-charging, impossible. In most health plans, the doctor just bills the insurance for each visit you make to your doctor, which makes abuse easy. A doctor can keep you on the line and let you make some extra unnecessary visits for which he gets paid.

It is the same for patients; some people are going to see the doctor when they think they have a pain, they always have imaginary pains and problems. In The Netherlands, a doctor would get you out of his office quite fast; he didn't get paid more if he saw you, so he wouldn't put up with it. On the other hand, if you weren't happy with your doctor, you could take a different one. Therefore the doctor would take good care of you or he would lose his customer.

The middle class and rich people weren't in this insurance because it was sponsored by the Government and those people could pay their own bills. Of course a doctor could take advantage of those patients.

(An old doctor had a son who became a doctor as well and took over his dad's practice. One day, he said proudly to his father: "Do you remember Mrs. Johnson, whom you have been treating for over twenty years? I cured her; she doesn't have to see a doctor anymore!"

His father said: "Are you some kind of an idiot to cure that old lady? For over twenty years I treated her, she put bread and butter on my table and you heal her; you must be out of your mind!")

Most people in The Netherlands believed that the rich, who had to pay the doctor themselves got better treatment but as you see, that wasn't necessarily true.

In those days, hospitals were places with strict rules. Visiting hours were restricted to two hours per day and only two visitors at a time. Children had no visiting privileges; a sick person had to rest and a bunch of children running through the patient's room, kicking the bed, didn't do the patient any good they reasoned. All those rules were strictly enforced by nurses in traditional nursing uniforms which consisted of a starched white uniform, accompanied with a big white cap with a black band.

Jaap Dalm said the medical insurance was a rip off; he had four daughters and they only had two times that they had to call the doctor in during an entire year. A doctor's call cost 2 guilders so for that year the insurance paid only 4 guilders while they had collected 12 guilders. He closed his argument by stating: "That insurance company was making 8 guilders off my back and is cheating us while we have our eyes wide open. If I had pocketed those

8 guilders I could get rich while I was sleeping. I don't need that darned insurance company. I'm going on my own."

"That's very risky," Arie said, "We had the doctor coming over a few times last year and we needed some medicine. What if the kids have to go to the hospital, it will cost you an arm and a leg."

"Oh, that's not going to happen," Jaap replied. "The kids are healthy and are seldom sick. Look at all the money I'm going to save without that insurance."

"I don't mind," Arie said, "if the insurance doesn't pay anything for my family. It means that we are all healthy, so what's wrong with that?"

For the first year it looked as if Jaap was right, nobody got sick and he pocketed the 12 guilders insurance money. Then all hell broke loose. First, one of his daughters got sick. When he checked with the doctor, his diagnosis was a severe throat infection due to tonsils. "The tonsils will have to come out," the doctor said.

A few months later his other daughter got severe belly cramps and she had to have her appendix removed. After paying a couple of big bills that were higher than ten years medical insurance payments, Jaap decided to go back into medical insurance. Luckily, he made good money with being a crane operator so he had the money to pay it but Arie would have been in real trouble if he had to pay bills like that.

That was a great relief to be in Medical Insurance that took care of everything as long as you lived. Unfortunately it didn't cover the cost when you died. A burial was very expensive and a death in the family could be a calamity to get the burial costs paid.

They had to stay in the medical insurance and burial insurance, rip off or not. The burial insurance had already picked up the tab when their first baby died prematurely and another death in the family could easily happen. If that happened without having Burial Insurance, they would be stuck to pay for the funeral themselves.

Besides Medical Insurance and Burial Insurance, there was also Fire Insurance for the house itself and contents. A fire could wipe out everything they had so fire insurance was also a must. Having an own home was nice but there were also taxes to be paid and paying those was also a must; if they didn't pay their taxes, they wouldn't live long in their own house. Adding all those musts, there was little left over for food and clothing. Besides they had to pay the utility bills or they wouldn't have utilities.

All those expenses occurred in their summer budget but for winter they needed coal to heat the house or they would sit in a cold house with freezing temperatures. It looked hopeless to get all the bills paid with the low income they had, yet, they had to economize one way or another.

Arie looked meaningfully at Ko and said: "We receive too much money to die but by no means enough money to live on. I have sharpened my pencil half a dozen times but we can't do it. I get relief payments of 10 guilders per week which will give me 520 guilders per year. I have to make my house payment of 480 guilders at the end of the year. That means that I have only 40 guilders left for the other expenses. The Medical Insurance amounts to 12 guilders per year, Burial Insurance to 8 guilders, Fire Insurance to 12 guilders and taxes for the house 10 guilders. I'm already 2 guilders short and we didn't pay the utilities yet. We just don't have enough money to pay the all important bills, let alone to have food on the table.

I can't put all the bills that have to be paid on the table and say: "eeny - meeny – miney – mo. All of those essential bills have to be paid or we'll be in trouble."

We have enough vegetables in the garden for the entire year which is an enormous help but the garden isn't big enough to grow enough potatoes. However, I can do some potato gleaning in fall after the farmers have harvested their potatoes. There are always lots of potatoes left that the potato harvesters miss. That will give us most of our staple food so we only have to worry about bread, margarine and perhaps cheese or jam if we can afford it. In summer we have strawberries in the garden which we can put on our bread and we can also slice apples and pears on our bread instead of jam. Jam is made from fruit too and fresh fruit is a lot better than jam. It doesn't look as though we'll have money to buy meat at all unless we make some extra money.

We can't save on insurance, that's impossible. If we do, we could be in severe trouble. There is no ands, buts and ifs about it; we have to save on our utility bills."

In summer when it was light long there wasn't much consumption of electricity but in winter when it was dark at five o' clock, the electricity bill was much higher. At night, they didn't even dare to switch on the light because light had to be paid or it would be disconnected.

Arie and Ko never wasted electricity. They had only three lights and one plug in the entire house. The lights were in the living room, kitchen and hall. All bulbs were 10 Watt except the living room that had a 20 Watt bulb. You needed good light in the living room because you had to read the paper and do all kinds of chores.

Of course, the parents hammered into the children to switch the lights off and they watched the children like hawks all the time to see if they did. They had to because the bill had to be paid in the prescribed time or else! In spite of all the light saving measures they had taken, the electricity bill was still too high and had to be reduced some more.

Everybody tried to cut costs and to cut the cost of light some more; they managed to do that by buying a transformer. This transformer transformed the 220 volt they had in their house to 6 Volt. They mounted the transformer and a bulb holder on a little piece of board from an old cigar box and used a little bulb that used less than 1 Watt. There was a cord with a plug on the transformer so you could plug the contraption in. That was the first time that the one plug they had in the house was used. Before, they didn't have anything to plug in and now they did.

At night when it got dark, they wouldn't switch any light on for an hour. It was twilight hour which was the handiest invention of the time. It was cozy they said and actually it was because it was the time that the family would talk to one another. They would tell a story or would sing a few hymns. They did things together which is lacking in today's society. Singing songs in the dark is unheard of. If you suggested it, they would think you were crazy; they simply switch on the tube and watch their favorite T.V. program. People are living at the same address but they hardly know each other.

When it was time to eat, the light wasn't switched on, that wasn't necessary at all. Everybody could find his or her mouth in the dark was the argument and everybody managed. After supper the big light went on for half an hour so they could read the newspaper. The 20 Watt bulb in the living room was replaced with a 10 Watt bulb to save electricity. They just couldn't afford it anymore. After half an hour the big light went out and the 1 watt bulb took over. Arie and Ko would play checkers with the little bulb right beside the checker board. There was just enough light to play a game. Sometimes they played a card game to while away the night.

While Arie and Ko played their games, the children were playing on the floor. Willie was playing with two raggedy dolls she had and Adrie was playing with the foot stool. He had only two toys, a rabbit and a duck that had been hand made from old rags and straw but his favorite toy, which was not really a toy, was the foot stool. He could make a toy of everything and let his fantasy go.

During winter when it was very cold in the house, the foot stool was used to put a small stone pot with some glowing coal in it. There were five holes in the foot stool and the hot air would rise through the holes giving the person that had his feet on the stool warm feet.

Arie and Ko had always slippers on and only used the foot stool when it was extremely cold. To Adrie the contraption that his parents called a foot stool was a toy. He put the foot stool on its side and pushed it across the floor pretending that this was a ship. There were even passengers on his ship, he pushed some clay marbles through the holes and the passengers were aboard now. After his ship was pushed to the other side of the room, the passengers were at the place of destination and could come out of the ship. Adrie didn't have a lot of toys but he had a vivid imagination. He could play with anything for hours and did a lot of pretending which gave him a lot of fun.

Everybody was relatively happy at night under the bad circumstances. There was only one person that wasn't happy. It was the electric meter reader. With the 1 Watt bulb on all night, it took 1000 hours to use one Kilowatt hour which was costing ten cents. Even the big light wasn't that big; it only burned a 10 Watt bulb and took 100 hours to burn up 1 Kilowatt hour. The only other light in the house was the light in the hall where the bathroom was. That light was never burned, you can do your business in the dark on the toilet; you don't need light for that.

When the meter reader came, he couldn't believe it that people used less than 2 Kilowatt Hours per month. There was something wrong there. At the office of City Electric, they couldn't believe it either. They sent a bill for the consumption of electricity at the amount of eighteen cent for that month. They also sent Inspector Bright Nose to catch those people red handed that were bypassing the meter. It wasn't possible that people used that little electricity.

When he came, Ko was home by herself. Inspector Bright Nose told her that he came to check the electricity meter and the fuses because there was something wrong. He checked everything and went even outside to check the overhead wiring to see if there wasn't a cord hooked up before the electricity went to the meter. Bright Nose couldn't find anything wrong but he was convinced that those people were stealing electricity so he asked Ko, "How do you do it to get electricity that isn't registered by the meter?"

"What do you mean?" Ko asked.

"I mean that you are using electricity you aren't paying for. It isn't possible that you only use eighteen cents of electricity in an entire month," Bright Nose said.

Ko got the transformer with the little bulb to show him that they were using that at night because her husband was unemployed and they were on relief. They had a very hard time to make ends meet and had to economize where ever possible.

It seemed that Bright Nose saw the light at the end of the tunnel when he saw the transformer they were using in order to cut electricity consumption. He was very much impressed with their efficiency and said: "If there was a Nobel price for efficiency, you people would certainly qualify for it.

You people are so efficient that you could impress the Tsar of Russia like the famous chess playing farmer did. One day, the Tsar invited the famous chess playing farmer to play a game of chess with him in his palace. When lunch was served, the farmer used only one dairy product on his bread, he either put butter on his bread without cheese or if he used cheese he wouldn't put butter on his bread. The Tsar was so impressed that he wanted to reward the farmer for his efficiency and said: "I'll reward you for your efficiency. Ask anything you want and I'll give it to you."

The farmer took his time to think this over and finally he said: "If I can get from you anything I want, I would like a chess board with one kernel of wheat on the first square, two kernels of wheat on the second square, two times two kernels on the third square, four times four kernels on the fifth square and so on.

The Tsar was again very much impressed with the efficiency of the farmer, he found that a very small reward and ordered his servants to give the farmer what he had asked for. His servants got busy to do what they were told. There would be 16 kernels on the fifth square, sixteen times sixteen kernels on the sixth square which would be 256 kernels, 256 times 256 kernels or 65536 kernels on the seventh square and 4294967296 kernels on the eighth square. They were only on the eighth square and soon they ran out of wheat. When the staff of the Tsar reported that there wasn't enough wheat in the entire country to fulfill the request, the Tsar found out that the chess playing farmer wasn't only efficient, he was also a master in arithmetic and very smart."

Ko had been listening intensely to the story and for a while she had forgotten about her misery. This Inspector Bright Nose was actually a nice guy in spite of his looks. Bright Nose looked at his watch, apologized to Ko for not trusting her and said: "I've got to go, I'm very sorry that you people have such a hard time, I hope your husband finds work soon."

"It doesn't look like it," Ko replied. "My husband is forty years old, nobody wants him and there doesn't seem to be an end to this Depression. People are saying that the Depression will only end if we get a war."

"That's a shame when you are unwanted when you are still in the prime of life", Bright Nose replied. "I think you are right that a war will end the Depression and we might be heading for one. Adolph Hitler is now in power in Germany, he is very defiant and he might trigger a war."

Consumption of water could also be cut if they had a rain barrel. A rain barrel cost a few bucks but once you had the barrel, it would save you money all the time because it rained a lot in The Netherlands. It used to be that the water in the ditches was potable but the new houses had flushing toilets that were connected to the ditch.

It was a stink when the excrement was flushed to the ditch, it would go to the bottom for a while and after a few days it would float to the top. To Adrie it looked like little islands and he was going to bomb those islands with big stones into the Stone Ages. The only use for ditch water was for watering the garden.

Ko knew another way to save water. She put a pan underneath the only tap she had in the house. By letting the tap drip into the pan, she thought she saved money because a dripping tap wouldn't register on the meter. She probably had that wrong because it will still register but you don't see it when only drops go through the meter. Anyway, she believed in it. Amazingly, the water department didn't think that those people had fixed the water meter and by passed it. Their department probably had heard about rain water.

Arie and Ko had another discussion about the chronic money problem. They didn't do good at all to get the mortgage payment together in time. Arie said: "We'll have to make illegal money no matter what the Reverend or the Government says."

"I agree," Ko replied. "The Reverend has talking easy with a good steady income and a nice parsonage that's paid for by the church. In spite of the Ten Commandments that requires honesty; we have no choice but make extra money without reporting it. If we report it, they'll deduct all of it from our relief payments. We need some extra cash desperately to relieve the chronic shortfall of money. Survival is at stake, we'll have to do anything to survive in this desperate time, including committing sin. The Reverend said: "You have to be honest and don't worry how to pay your bills, the Lord will provide. I haven't seen the Reverend come over with money the Lord is providing so we have to provide for ourselves or we'll starve!"

And so desperation triumphed over honesty and religion. Without extra money it was impossible to survive. Making unreported extra money didn't have a good start for Arie. People in the Government were a bunch of crooks themselves, so they thought that the unemployed people would be cheating. There were Government inspectors who followed unemployed people on relief. They would just select a guy who was on relief and follow him all day to see that he didn't work somewhere to make extra money. They also went by tips of jealous neighbours who gave away the unfortunate people on relief. There were lots of Judases around who would give you away even without the thirty silver shillings that Judas had received for his betrayal of Jesus. They were plain jealous.

With the very first job that he tackled Arie was caught. He had cut the hedge for an old lady for which she had given him twenty five cent for his effort and still somebody that had seen it had told Inspector Wiersma about it. Inspector Wiersma came to take the twenty five cent off his hands because he wasn't allowed to make any money.

Wiersma had caught a few more people who made some extra money. It almost was his death. One day they had found him in a back alley with a gaping head wound. Somebody had an account to settle with him and had hit him over the head. That was the end of Wiersma, nobody ever saw him again but that didn't mean that there weren't any other inspectors around.

Arie found another way to supplement his meagre income. In spring; he would go from door to door to take orders for seeds for flowers and vegetables. His reward was 15% commission of what he sold. That was only in spring and it was a long year with the little relief payments.

He also was seeding red and white cabbage, cauliflower, Brussels sprouts, onions and endive plants and sold the plants to people who wanted to do some planting. That way he yielded some extra cash which he needed desperately. A big sign on the house stated: "Cauliflower and cabbage plants for sale." In the proper time he changed it to onion, Brussels sprouts or endive plants and he was in business.

The sign on the house that there were plants for sale could have done him in, it was a plain give away. Government Inspectors could have seen it and demanded the money or he would get less relief payment. Arie didn't have a choice and took his chances.

A package of seeds cost only three cents in those days and you could get well over a hundred plants from the package. The plants were dirt cheap; he charged only 10 cents for 20 plants. Going back to elementary school arithmetic, it proves that he made about 50 cents on a package of seeds. He probably made ten guilders per season which was a lot of money for that time. It was exactly as much as he received for a whole week of relief money. Of course, he didn't report that income. It was a lot of work and he needed that money. He wasn't going to work so the Government could deduct it from his relief payment, he didn't have a hole in his head.

Selling plants became a family enterprise like everything else. When Adrie was only 6 years old, he already helped the customers who came for plants. Nobody ever told him that he had to do it and nobody told him how to do it. At that age he was always where the action was and was standing, with his long nose, right on top of it. There was a long knife, standing in the ground, right beside the beds with plants. Adrie's father and mother would stick the knife in the ground, underneath the plants, and lift them out with some dirt. Most people brought a basket or a little box to put the plants in and if not; his parents rolled them in a piece of newspaper. It was so simple that even a kid could do it, Adrie thought.

His chance to prove that he could do it came when his parents weren't home and a customer called for plants. It was no problem; Adrie did exactly what he had seen dozens of times. The man wanted 40 plants; so Adrie charged him 20 cents and then he put the money on the table.

"Where does that money come from?" his mother asked his father but he didn't have an answer. The mystery was solved when Adrie came in the house and told them that he had done 20 cents worth of business. They were very pleasantly surprised and said meaningfully to each other: "Small children are getting big."

That was the nicest compliment they could have given him because he was just a little kid and wanted to be big more than anything else. His parents were glad that they could rely on him to help the customers when they weren't home. In those days you had to grow up fast so you could lend a helping hand.

THE SMALLEST BARBER SHOP IN THE WORLD

Adrie's mother was the proud owner of that shop. A hair cut would cost five pennies in those days. That was a lot of money if you need a hair cut every five weeks. If you waited longer to get a hair cut people would ask "Is the barber dead?" *(Looking at today's young people with their long hair, one could come to the terrible conclusion that there must have been a horrible contagious epidemic, which wiped out half the barbers. Almost all young men have long hair, it is in fashion.)*

Ko figured that she could save that money if she cut the hair of Arie and Adrie. All she really needed was a pair of scissors and a comb. In the beginning her hair cut wasn't as good as a barber's haircut which made the other boys think that it was a home job. They asked Adrie: "Where do you have your hair cut?" He had a good answer: "On my head."

Later on, Ko bought a pair of clippers, they weren't electric but it improved the haircut a lot. She improved fast and eventually you couldn't tell that it was a home hair cut. It looked really professional.

They weren't the only ones to cut their own hair. Some people made a heck of a mess of a haircut. It looked as if they had put the peepot on their head and had cut everything outside the peepot. It was a step up hair cut. At the lower part there was no hair and all of a sudden there was a lot of hair.

Ko had the smallest barber shop in the world with only two customers, Arie and Adrie. She and Willie had braided hair and didn't need a barber. It seems that there is always somebody who can do better and one day

Adrie's mother found out that somebody had her beat and had even a smaller barbershop than she had.

This guy that really had the smallest barbershop in the world was a guy who had only one customer, himself. He would sit between two mirrors to cut his own hair. All this was done to save money and consequently the barber had fewer customers.

Barbers used to have a lot of work when they were still shaving most of the men. The only shave you could have was with a large shaving knife which was a dangerous weapon in unskilled hands. One could get hurt pretty easy. Saturday night was the time that all men got shaved because the next day on Sunday they had to go to church well shaved, lest the Reverend might think that the razor hadn't been invented yet.

When the safety razor blade was invented, most of the men started to shave themselves to save money and consequently the barber's business dropped by seventy percent. Arie was shaving himself three times a week namely on Wednesday, Saturday and Sunday in order to look good when he went to church. Shaving more than three times a week was too much trouble and too costly, he couldn't afford to buy that many razor blades.

When Adrie was small, he wasn't tickled to get a haircut. To make it more interesting his mother would tell him a story about the legendary Tom Thumb, who made a track of bread crumbs in the bush so he could find his way back home. That was very stupid because he hadn't figured on the birds, which were for the birds, and ate all the bread crumbs so he got lost. All this was very educational, you sure could learn a lot from that.

However, the most favorite story was about Red Riding Hood and the bad wolf. This bad wolf ate grandma and Red Riding Hood both, according to his mother. It must have been quite a big wolf to swallow them whole like the whale swallowed Jonah. As a matter of fact the story of Red Riding Hood and Jonah run parallel. In the case of Red Riding Hood a hunter in red shining armour came by. He heard Red Riding Hood and Grandmother cry from within the stomach of the wolf. Can you imagine? This wolf was probably from the time that dinosaurs roamed the earth.

After the whale had swallowed Jonah he was also crying from within the stomach of the whale but there was no hunter around to hear and help him, so Jonah started to pray and God heard the prayer of Jonah. The hunter butchered the bad wolf and got Red Riding Hood and Grandmother out of their predicament and God made the whale sea sick so he puked Jonah right on the shore and that way Jonah got out of his predicament.

The Red Riding Hood story was probably the most favored story by the kids. One of the kids wanted to know if Red Riding Hood and Robin Hood were related.

(The authorities have decided that this story of Red Riding Hood with a man eating wolf is a lot of violence. {Tell that to the wolf that has to make a living some how.} It was not very good for young kids so they had to change it. Today the story of Red Riding Hood is non violent and much better for the development of young kids. The reformed story goes as follows:

"On a nice summer day Red Riding Hood went with a basket of eggs to visit her sick grand mother who was living in the forest. On her way she met a real nice wolf that asked her where she was heading for. When Red Riding Hood told the wolf about her sick grandmother, he got tears in his eyes and got into action right away. He picked some herbs and spices and put them in Red Riding Hood's basket. Hand in hand they went to grandma and while Red Riding Hood was boiling the eggs for grandma, the wolf made some tea from the herbs and spices for grandma's arthritis. When the wolf left with Red Riding Hood, Grandma felt a lot better.)

Wolves make good stories. There are many wolf stories and the kids were also told the story about the three pigs that built a house from straw which the wolf blew down. With the collapse of the house, one of the pigs died and the wolf ate the dead pig. This was murder the game warden said, and arrested the bad wolf. However, the wolf hired a very smart lawyer and in his trial the wolf was found not guilty, due to the fact that after the wolf blew the house down the pig was dead anyway and when you eat a dead pig you can't call it murder.

Arie was in business too; he was the proud owner of the smallest shoemaker shop in the world and had twice as many customers as Ko; four customers in total because he repaired the shoes of Ko and Willie as well.

Whenever new shoes were bought, they had to last an awful long time. It took some doing to save enough money for a pair of shoes and there were four people who needed shoes. All Arie needed was a hammer and a last to start his business. Ko didn't need any materials in her barber shop but Arie wasn't that lucky, he had to buy a piece of leather and some nails. He also bought a sharp knife to cut leather with and a file to file the sole round after he had nailed it on the shoe.

Arie and Ko kept a close eye on all the shoes to prevent the soles from wearing too thin. Arie put a lot of soles on all the shoes and only when the top leather needed repair did the shoemaker get involved. A stitching machine was needed to do that kind of work.

Even underneath the wooden shoes, he nailed a piece of leather. If you think that this was overdoing it, you should have seen the people across the street. They nailed the wood of cigar boxes underneath their wooden shoes.

At least Arie used leather. With those two enterprises they saved money too, and in their book, "A penny saved was a penny earned."

Ko did some work in the household. It wasn't a fat pot but Ko made off and on some extra money when a rich woman delivered a baby. Then she had to do the house keeping for a couple of weeks till the woman had regained her strength. That woman needed help. Whenever Ko had a baby, her sister came to help her a few hours a day for a couple of days and after that she did her own again with the added work of taking care of a baby.

Besides the savings on utilities, further savings were obtained by saving on food. There was a large garden at the back of the house with fruit trees to supply an over abundance of fruit. Fruit comes in fall and if not eaten in a certain time, it will rot. One of the apple trees was a Goudrenet Apple with apples that could be kept throughout the winter. As long as you kept them in a cool place in the loft they would keep. It was a big help to have at least apples during the long winter.

There was also a way to conserve the other apples and pears for the winter. Ko peeled a lot of apples and pears, put them in a bag and gave them to the baker to put them on top of his oven. When he was baking bread, there was plenty of heat to dry the apples and pears. When you wanted to use them you just soaked them in water overnight and you could cook them. Dried apples and pears were a treat during the long winter when there was little fruit available. Even the fruit that was available was too expensive to buy. One of the pear trees supplied cooking pears that were as hard as a rock and couldn't be eaten unless you cooked them. Once they were cooked they were as red as a lobster and were very delicious. (Cooked apples and pears are used as a vegetable in The Netherlands.)

Jan Lems had an orchard with all kinds of apples that he sold. When there was a storm, a lot of apples and pears fell on the ground and bruised a bit. Those couldn't be sold and Ko was welcome to come over and pick up the bruised pears and apples. She would just cut out the bruised or rotten spot and the rest of the fruit was still edible. With the added supply, she had enough to last them through winter.

The garden was a great help in the battle to put more than dry bread on the table. Arie grew potatoes and vegetables. He also had made a small hot house, from some old windows, which was powered by the sun. In the hothouse he grew radishes, lettuce, spinach, beans and carrots which effort gave them fresh vegetables early in spring. In the rest of the garden he grew peas, French beans, red beets, onions, cauliflower, red and white cabbage, Brussels sprouts, and a host of other things.

There was also rhubarb in the garden but you don't really have to grow that. Once you have it in your garden, it's like weeds; you can't get rid of this hardy plant. All that you really have to do if you want rhubarb is, you run the disc over it once a year and you'll have more rhubarb than you ever want. Rhubarb is a hardy perennial; it comes up by itself every year and grows like cabbage. "That is strange" Adrie thought because he thought it was rhubarb.

One year, Adrie dug up the rhubarb plant by mistake. The year after, there were all kinds of rhubarb plants in a large area of the garden. Arie couldn't figure where all that rhubarb came from. The answer was simple. When Adrie dug up the rhubarb plant, the roots were cut in many pieces and those pieces were spread over a large area of the garden. And each piece of root was growing a rhubarb plant.

Arie also grew his own seeds such as beans, peas and onions but he bought the more difficult to obtain seeds such as lettuce, carrots, cabbage and cauliflower. There was also a strawberry patch, some gooseberry bushes and red and black berries. From the red berries, Ko made berry juice which was used to pour over the pudding on Sunday. Some of the red berries were eaten with sugar which was a delicacy at the best of times but during the Depression it was the cat's meow. Blackberries were used to make blackberry gin. Those darned Dutch people will always make gin, even during the Depression; that comes naturally to them.

Being poor brings problems to put food on the table every day in summer. Come winter, there is even more trouble, when nothing grows on the land. People couldn't go into hibernation for a winter sleep or go dormant; they needed food in winter as well. The squirrel has no problem with winter; he has pouches in his mouth where he can store food for a short time. Just long enough to reach his cache where he stores seeds and nuts for later use. What the squirrel could do, Arie and Ko could do too. There was no need for pouches to carry their food; they had baskets and bags to carry their potatoes to their cache, the potato pit.

In The Netherlands, they call it a potato pit but it is actually a potato hill. The potatoes are dumped on the land in hills which are covered with old gunny bags and a layer of straw. They put a bit of ground over the hill and just before freeze up they put some more ground over it, to make sure that their winter supply wouldn't freeze.

You could let beans grow until they had real beans in them and shell them. If you wanted to eat green beans or endive during the long winter, you could preserve those vegetables in clay pots or jars. Ko had three large clay pots which were filled with the veggies she wanted to preserve.

She always preserved one pot of endive, one pot of green beans and one pot of French beans. The vegetables were cooked a little, cooled and a layer of the veggies was put into the pot. Then Ko put a layer of salt over the beans or endive and when she had some more of the veggies, she would repeat the procedure. When the pot was full of endive or beans, she would put a piece of cloth over it and on the cloth she put a board and a heavy stone to weigh it all down so that the veggies stayed underneath a layer of brine.

The results were terrible; it was something to eat, but for taste it was the pits. When you wanted to eat your beans or endive, you had to take it out of the brine, soak them overnight in water to get rid of most of the salt and cook them. In the beginning of the winter the beans weren't too bad tasting but at the end of the winter, when the veggies had been underneath the salt for half a year they were terrible. The white beans in the green beans were all discolored and were now purple in color. Also the smell and taste were horrible; you could hardly stand the smell when they were cooking.

Sauerkraut was the best preserved vegetable as for taste. Bacon and sausages were smoked in those days but Ko never had the problem that she had to keep bacon and sausages for some time. She only saw bacon and sausages sporadically and they were eaten the same day they entered the house.

Keeping eggs good for some time was also a problem; they were put into a chalk solution. The result was that the preserved eggs tasted like chalk.

(For centuries, people have preserved beans and endive in brine. They didn't understand how food spoiled. As soon as they had figured out that it were enzymes and microorganisms that spoiled the food, a solution was on the way. That solution came after the war in the late 1940's, when the glass sealer with pressure cooker was introduced.

Preserving of fruit, vegetables and meat can be done if you destroy the enzymes and the microorganisms that spoil the food. The food has to be heated and the bottles have to be hermetically sealed. When there is no air inside the bottles, the outside pressure is greater than the inside pressure and the lid will stay on, you hope.

Most older people have been involved with sealers and found them a pain. They quite often opened and the food spoiled. The metal can you can buy in the store solved all problems and today you can also throw your meat and vegetables in the deep freeze.)

WITH LEAD IN HIS SHOES

In spite of all the savings they managed to obtain, the scraping they were doing continuously and the extra work they had done, at the end of the year there wasn't enough money to pay Veldhoen. It didn't matter that they would receive the Nobel Prize in Efficiency if there was such a thing; Veldhoen wasn't going to be impressed if they didn't have the money. They had a little more than the interest but were still 260 guilders short on the equity payment.

With lead in his shoes, Arie went to see Veldhoen at the end of the year. This could be it, Veldhoen would very likely foreclose on the mortgage and they would be kicked out of the house. There were already a lot of people that had their mortgage foreclosed by the banks and they had lost their house.

There were also quite a few young farmers who had lost their farms. They had bought expensive farms after the First World War when the price of produce was high. There had been plenty of money to pay off the mortgage but that all changed with deflation when they got a lot less for their commodities while the mortgage payment remained the same. Consequently, there wasn't enough money to pay off the mortgage, the mortgage was foreclosed and the farmers were without a farm. People who are playing a game sometimes say: "I think I just sold the family farm." Real life wasn't a game, it was serious business. Those farms weren't sold, they were repossessed. Only the farmers who had paid cash for the farms and the ones that had paid off the mortgage before the Depression set in made it, the other ones went under.

When Arie called on Veldhoen, the reception was cordial as always which was a foregone conclusion. He came to bring money so why shouldn't he be nice. Arie wondered how long Veldhoen would be nice after he had told him that he couldn't pay off the mortgage.

While Vedlhoen was talking to Arie, his wife made some tea and gave him a cup of tea with a chocolate. Arie started to sip his tea and wondered how he would tell Veldhoen that he couldn't pay. Veldhoen had first asked how his wife and children were and Arie had told him that everybody was still in good health. Next Veldhoen asked: "How are things?"

"Not good at all," was his reply. "I am unemployed and can't pay off the mortgage. I have a little bit more than the interest but on ten guilders per week, I couldn't get more together."

He looked at Veldhoen to see what his response would be and to his surprise Veldhoen wasn't mad at all, he said: "It's a terrible time with this Depression; there are a lot of people in financial difficulties when they are without work. But you say that you have the interest which is O.K. with me.

As long as you pay me the interest, that's alright. Paying off the principal can wait till times improve."

It was as if a heavy load fell off Arie's shoulders, all of a sudden he had no lead in his shoes anymore and could have jumped with the cow over the moon. Arie hadn't figured that he would still have a house after his visit to Veldhoen. He was lucky that he had borrowed the money from a private lender. If he had borrowed the money from the bank they would have foreclosed for sure. Those banks were thriving on somebody else's troubles and were just waiting to repossess and take over.

Ko had been waiting anxiously for the return of her husband and as soon as she saw him she asked: "What did Veldhoen say? When do we have to move out?"

When Arie told her that they only had to pay the interest and that they could keep the house, she was relieved. At least they would have a roof over their head and with the ten guilders per week they received from relief they could manage to get three and a half guilders per week on interest together. If they had rented a house it would have cost them four guilders per week so they were still better off.

To pay only the interest was a brilliant idea, that way the equity in the house didn't go up. If that happened, the Relief Committee would insist on selling the house if they thought there would be anything left. This way, it satisfied the Relief Committee, Veldhoen and Arie as well. It was a good deal for everybody.

It looked as if Veldhoen did Arie a favor but actually it was in his own interest to make this deal. As a matter of fact it was a heck of a good deal for Veldhoen. Arie paid 4% on interest while the interest rate had gone down with the deflation to 2.75%. However, a deal is a deal, once the interest rate is set up in a contract, you are stuck with it. If Veldhoen had repossessed the house he would have lost a lot of money. There was a hefty deflation and the 6000 guilder house was now worth only 4200 guilders; yet, Arie owed still 4400 guilders on it. Veldhoen would have lost 200 guilders by re-possessing the house and it would be questionable if he could have sold the house again during the Depression. He also would get less interest on his money. As long as Arie paid his 4% interest he was sitting pretty.

MENU DURING THE GREAT DEPRESSION

(It was the year 2000 when Adrian was sitting in the Granada Restaurant where they were always dining on Saturday night. He looked at the menu with dozens of attractive dishes. There were all kinds of steaks, fish and even steak and lobster. Whenever he was faced with exravaganzas in the years of plenty, he always thought back about the years of poverty when there was barely enough food to keep them alive. Looking at his menu he didn't see "Shoving cheese." It was a long time ago that he ate that and he certainly wasn't looking forward to seeing it return.)

In the year 1935, the daily menu looked quite different from today. All dishes were non fattening and the only good that they did was avoid heart attacks. The rich had heart attacks because they didn't have enough exercise and over indulged themselves with fattening food. Candidates for heart attacks were the managers who were driven to work by their chauffeur. When the manager arrived at the building where his office was, there was a door man who opened the door for him and there was an elevator boy who even pushed the button of the elevator. A porter would open the office door for him and once in his office his private secretary took over to take care of everything.

The manager was sitting in his office all day with a big Havana cigar in his head and his secretary brought him coffee with whipping cream and rum. He gave orders to everybody and if he wanted something he just pushed the bell button which made his secretary appear to get him whatever he wanted.

The manager made a good salary, he believed that as a good business leader he must look substantial and must have a girth like a pig so success would show. Therefore he devoured substantial breakfasts, lunches and 12 course dinners with a bottle of good old Port. He over ate, was under exercised and smoked and drank too much. Yes, he had a good job and everybody envied him until one day he collapsed with a big Havana cigar in his head. When he arrived in the hospital, he was pronounced dead because of a massive heart attack. He had had it too good for his well being and died in the prime of his life. It was all over!

The teacher at school said that everything that has "too" in front of it is no good. Too long or too short is no good but even too good is no good, it can do you in like the manager in his office. Heart attacks were called "Managers Illness" or "Prosperity Illness." Poor and unemployed people didn't have to worry about getting it, they were neither managers nor did they experience prosperity. People who were unemployed were candidates for tuberculosis, they ate poor quality food and all meals were non fattening.

It was the rich people who got the heart attacks; poor people were smarter than that; they skimmed the milk and gave the cream to the rich so they could drink coffee with whipping cream and drop dead, while the poor people were living happily ever after. Bacon and eggs and lots of fat meat contributed to the troubles of the rich.

The same thing happens in India today, the rich have the heart attacks but the poor bugger who sleeps under a gunny bag, in the streets of Calcutta, gets tuberculosis. A guy, who pulls a rickshaw with a fat rich guy in it all day, while he is starving, has little trouble with coronary disease. On the other hand, the guy sitting in the rickshaw thinks he is so well off but come again; he'll be dead long before the guy that's pulling the rickshaw.

When Adrie was growing up, he never heard about most of the items on the menu of to day. He didn't even know what lobster was and he didn't know a heck of a lot about steak either. All he knew was that beef came from a cow and he knew that steak existed but T bone steak and New York steak, what the heck was that? He seldom ate beef, if he was eating meat it was usually from a pig or a horse. That was cheaper! Horse meat was the most likely meat to show up on his dinner plate.

People couldn't afford to be critical about meat. There were many countries where people ate mice and rats so you were better off to chew on an old horse. If they had meat at all, it was the cheapest parts of the animal they consumed. Ham and steak wasn't within reach of their empty purses.

You are all familiar with the lavish restaurant menus of today. As an eye opener I would like to show you the menu we had to face when we were growing up. It wasn't in a restaurant, it was at home.

Breakfast menu:

Tea.
Three slices of bread.
Margarine.
Jam.
One fried egg.

Remarks about this: "save your heart breakfast!"

There was only one fried egg; never two. They never ate bacon and eggs or ham and eggs. People never had heard about such an abundance of eating bacon and eggs together. In the beginning of the Depression, they didn't even have an egg for breakfast. Later on, when they started to keep chickens there was an egg for breakfast. Instead of jam, they also put sugar or grated cheese on their bread. Both items were very cheap and very cheap was all they could afford.

The warm meal was consumed at noon. During the Depression Arie was home unemployed, and the kids went to school. Everybody was home at noon.

Lunch menu:
Coffee.
Potatoes with "Little eyes gravy."
Vegetables.
Desert. Potatoes with buttermilk.

Remarks about this save your heart lunch!

There was seldom meat, bacon or fish on weekdays, except on Monday. Ko saved a little piece of the little piece of meat they had on Sunday so they would have a little taste of meat on Monday.

Few people have heard about "Little Eyes Gravy." It's very easy to make. The gravy that was made on Sunday when Ko fried the meat had to last all week. On Monday she would stir some water through the left over gravy from Sunday. On Tuesday, she would stir some more water through the left over gravy from Monday. And on Wednesday, she would stir some more water through the left over gravy from Tuesday. By then the gravy was pure water with a few droplets of fat floating on the surface. Those droplets looked like little eyes, from where the name originated "Little Eyes Gravy."

For desert, they ate potatoes with buttermilk six days of the week because it was cheap and easy to make. All what they had to do was to boil a few extra potatoes. They mashed a few potatoes on their dinner plate and poured buttermilk on the potatoes. Instant desert and cheap as borsch, except it was potatoes with butter milk. It was the desert of the day; only on Sunday would they eat vanilla pudding.

Another lunch menu for variety.
Coffee.
Hotch potch.
Bread porridge.

Remarks. Hotch potch is supposed to be a thick stew made out of carrots and onions with various meats, according to the dictionary. They didn't have a dictionary so they couldn't know about that. Their hotch potch was simply mashed potatoes with onions and carrots, the various meats were lacking. Of course, that's why this lunch qualified to be heart saving. Try it and you'll never have another heart attack!

Bread porridge was also easy to prepare. Whenever there was bread that was dried out, it wasn't thrown in the garbage; instead they made porridge from it. The recipe is very simple. Crumb the dry bread and pour milk over it. One shake of cinnamon over the porridge will enhance the taste.

They had quite a variety of vegetables so they could eat a variety of dishes. The meat was left out for the convenience because there was none. To get more variety for lunch, Ko sometimes made rice pudding with raisins.

Menu:

Coffee.

Rice pudding with raisins.

The rice was cooked, solid as a pudding, with raisins in it. It was a great lunch, everybody loved it. They would fill their plates with hot rice pudding and make a little dip in the centre of the rice with the spoon. In the dip, they put a little lump of margarine and over the melting margarine they threw a spoonful of brown sugar. Now they were ready to eat. A spoonful of rice was dipped in the mixture of margarine and brown sugar and they ate it that way. Delicious!

When they ate rice pudding with raisins, everybody had his own plate. In the farm district, the farmers probably hated to wash all those dirty dishes so they took a short cut. The rice pudding was eaten out of a common dish. A big bowl of rice pudding was placed in the middle of the table and the whole family was seated around it. In the middle of the rice pudding was the dip with the lump of butter and sugar in it. Everybody would dip his or her rice in the same butter, sugar mixture and eat it.

(On one occasion, the Parish Priest made a call to one of the farms and was invited for dinner. The dinner was rice pudding and everybody was dipping their rice in the same dip. All of a sudden, one of the kids said: "Father, you have the whole lump of butter on your spoon!"

The farmer said: "It doesn't matter, Father, I had that lump of butter already three times in my mouth." Bon appetite!)

At the farm, they might have had real butter, but of course the Demerwes had margarine. It was much better for their hearts. The supper menus were of the same ingredients as the breakfast and lunch menus.

Supper Menu:

Coffee with skim milk and half a lump of saccharine.

5 Slices of bread with margarine.

Fried cow udder.

Shoving cheese.

Actually, this was a pretty good menu. Most of the time supper didn't come with meat at all and was confined to cheese and jam. Cow udder might not be the kind of meat that people want to eat today, but during the Depression they were glad to have it.

If Ko had worked a lot to make extra money, she would buy horse meat. There were a lot of horses around. Most of the merchants had a horse and wagon to deliver the merchandise to their customers from door to door. The farmers had work horses as well.

The old gray mare isn't what it used to be.

This was a famous song but the truth was that such a condition was bad for the mare. When a horse was too old to pull his own weight, he ended up on the butcher's block. Horse meat was cheap on the market because it was from discarded horses which meant that it was plenty tough. That was hardly a problem for the people, they were glad to see meat at all so they gnawed on it a bit longer. Luckily everybody had a good set of teeth because they never had money to buy candies and cookies to ruin their teeth. Tough horse meat was better than nothing, so why should the people complain?

(Once at school the children were singing the song "The old gray mare isn't what it used to be," The teacher asked the children: "Is there anybody who can tell me what we mean by the old gray mare?"

A little girl said: "Yes Sir. We mean the old gray gentleman at City Hall.")

Remarks. Before they struck a deal to buy milk from the farm, they had always skim milk. They couldn't afford homo milk and neither could they afford sugar. That's why they used saccharine in their tea and coffee. Saccharine is used in diabetic diets as a non calorie sweetener. They were not diabetics but they used saccharine anyway, just to save money. It was easier on their purse and it saved their hearts as well. It sounds like an old saw to repeat that same cliché all the time but saving money was for ever in their minds during the Depression. People never thought about saving their hearts but that came along as a reward and was a bonus!

Anyway, saccharine is 500 times sweeter than cane sugar. Even the saccharine lumps were quite sweet so they cut the sugar lumps (Actually the saccharine lumps) in half. That way they got twice as many lumps which translated in a saving of fifty percent.

In The Netherlands they used beet sugar since it was too cold to grow sugar cane. A lot of farmers were growing sugar beets which were harvested in fall and shipped to the sugar plants. You can't keep sugar beets very long, so the sugar factories only operate for about six weeks per year. They make sugar and molasses from the beets and the by-product is pulp which is used for cattle feed.

Cow udder, "yuk," you say. "Delicious," people said during the Depression. Cow udder is of course the tit of a cow and is very tough so that the calf can't pull the udder apart when sucking. If you want to eat it, there is some work to be done to make it edible. This calls for a recipe.

Trim all fat from the udder (Don't throw it away because it's Depression time and the wasteful society hadn't been invented as yet.)

Cook the udder for half an hour in water.

Take a frying pan, melt the trimmed fat and fry the udder in it until it has a medium brown color.

Now you are ready to eat fried cow udder, you dip your slice of bread in the hot grease and slice the udder on your bread. Yummy, delicious!

Cow udder was a lot better than "Shoving Cheese." Oh, you don't know what shoving cheese is, which demands some more explaining. During the Depression you would only get a very small and thin slice of cheese on your bread, about one inch wide and three inches long. It didn't cover much of your bread, so you had to be a smart operator to get the benefit of the cheese. You put the cheese on your bread, just far enough away that you don't touch it when you take a bite. After taking a bite the cheese is still there, so you shove it up a little and with your next bite you miss the cheese again. Keep shoving up the cheese till the cheese covers the bread, remember it's shoving cheese. Now you are ready for a taste of cheese and eat bread with cheese.

Shoving cheese wasn't all that great, but it was better than "Bread at point." Many people ate "Bread at point" which was plain, dry bread. While you are eating your bread, you point your finger towards the spot where the jam or cheese was supposed to be.

Sunday's Lunch Menu:

Coffee.
Vegetable soup.
Potatoes.
Vegetables. (Only one kind, usually cooked apples or cooked pears)
Fried beef. (which came in cans from Argentina.)
Pudding with red berry juice.

Remarks! That's more like it for lunch but only on Sunday would they eat like that. Red berry juice was home made from the red berries they grew in their back yard.

If they had an old chicken that didn't lay any more eggs, they would butcher it and in that case they would have chicken for meat and chicken soup instead of vegetable soup. The gizzards of the chicken went into the soup, including stomach, heart, liver, kidneys and the pope's nose.

Their soup was better than in the restaurant; when they ate chicken soup, there was at least chicken in it. Usually when you eat chicken soup in a restaurant, it is broth.

(A gentleman, who was dining in a restaurant, complained to the waiter that he couldn't find a trace of chicken in the so-called chicken soup. The waiter said: "That's not strange at all sir; if you order Queen Soup, you don't expect to see pieces of the Queen floating in your soup.")

Occasionally, they ate fish if it was a hot bargain. This happened usually on a Saturday. The Roman Catholics ate fish on Friday because they weren't allowed to eat meat on Fridays but the Demerwes ate fish on Saturday because they were poor. Even though they weren't Roman Catholic, they never ate meat on a Friday or on a Thursday, Wednesday, Tuesday or Saturday. This situation was dictated by an empty purse.

During the lean years, there were seldom luxury items on the dining table. The unemployed people didn't even know that steak and lobster existed; to them herring was a luxury item in the land of the herring.

Every spring the Dutch herring fleet sailed out to the North Sea to catch the Dutch people's favorite food. Unfortunately Ko had no money to buy herring no matter how much everybody liked it. On Saturday the fish man came through the street; he tried to sell fish to the people for the weekend. Ko couldn't afford to buy fish unless it was almost a give-away. That give-away happened on Saturdays when the fish man hadn't sold all his fish. There was no refrigeration so come Monday, the fish would have been spoiled and he had to throw it away. In order to get a little money for the fish, he offered it to Ko for half price.

It was attractive; it would be a welcome change in their dreary menu. Ko tried to figure out within herself if it was possible to put fish on the table and hesitated. The fish man said: "I know you are poor; give me one third of the price and treat yourself."

It was a deal, so once or twice a month, Ko bought 4 herrings which meant that each one of the family would have one herring, on Saturday night, as a Saturday night special. Even at one third of the price, Ko had to scrape over the bottom of her purse to pay for it.

The same happened with dried cod fish; if they wanted to get rid of some old supply, Ko bought it for a couple of pennies. She was a real artist to make a delicious meal out of dried fish. She cooked potatoes and rice and mashed those together, put some peas and fish with it and they ate like a king.

Ko could have been a magician. When it was very hot in summer, she managed to come up with a bottle of fizzy lemonade, in spite of the hard times. It was very hard for her to put proper food on the table that was nourishing and would keep the members of the family in good health. In spite of the poor meals there were some benefits to lean meals. In the meagre menu they ate very little bacon which was beneficial to the health of the family.

Eating bacon could give you a tape worm when the bacon was undercooked and once you had a tape worm it was hard to get rid of it. Tape worms grew to well over six feet in length and quite often they were lost by vomiting. Some people choked because of lack of air when a six foot long tapeworm had to go through their throat by vomiting.

There was a remedy to catch a tapeworm. It was said that if you were fasting for three days, all you had to do was hold some good food in front of your mouth and the tapeworm would come out to eat it. When the worm comes to eat the food you just grab it and yank out the worm.

Unfortunately, this is just a myth and no matter what food you put in front of your mouth, the tapeworm isn't coming out to eat it. Nowadays there are medicines you can swallow to kill the tapeworm.

To prevent tape worms, the bacon had to be well fried or cooked but even then eating bacon could give you boils. People who ate bacon regularly had quite often trouble with boils. The boils were sometimes as big as a ping pong ball and were usually in a very inconvenient place like on your behind. If a visiting person was standing uneasily at the table as if he couldn't get rid of his egg and he was asked to sit down, he would point at his rear with a painful grin on his face, announcing: "I have boils."

EXTRA, EXTRA!

Not an extra edition of the newspaper but something extra to supplement the meagre meals. Most of the extras were seasonal and came mainly from the garden, like strawberries to put on their bread and red berries and gooseberries as an extra before they went to bed. Those were healthy extras and were a lot healthier than the junk food that people take in as extras nowadays.

Once a year, Jan Lems butchered a pig at his farm. Ko was the recipient of the head of the pig from which she made head cheese. Adrie never understood how she could make cheese from a pig's head, as far as he knew a pig's head is made of meat so how can you change it into cheese? However, Adrie's mother knew how to do it.

She also got a piece of bacon and the pig's feet from which she made delicious pea soup. Ko was like a bottomless pit, she could use everything for her family.

(A young woman wanted to make pea soup and went to the butcher shop. She said to the butcher: "Have you got pig's feet?" The butcher looked stupefied at his feet and said: "No madam, I'm happy to say that I haven't.")

The farm of Jan Lems supplied Colostrum a few times a year, which was obtained from the first two milkings after the cow had calved. Milk of the first two milkings was much thicker than normal milk. It was heated, crumbled rusks and a little bit of cinnamon was added and another great meal appeared on the table.

Milk cost 4 cents a litre which was a lot of money in those days but there was a cheaper way by buying skim milk which was only 2 cents a litre. Unfortunately, the skim milk was not much more than water, it looked blue. It could very well have been that in the plant, where the milk was pasteurized against bacteria, that they added water to get more skim milk.

Ko bought every day a quart of skim milk to be used for the coffee and a cup of cocoa before they went to bed. Buttermilk cost also two cents per quart and Ko bought a quart for the desert every day.

Between the quart of skim milk and the quart of buttermilk she bought, she saved four cents per day which amounted to 28 cents per week which was a significant amount of money. Many of those penny pinching ways made a world of difference; it made them get by with the little money they received. There was a lot of skim milk in those days because the rich needed whipping cream to put in their coffee.

With the high price of milk, a lot of people who lived on a dyke with grass kept a goat for milk supply. Adrie hated those goats. If by accident he came within reach of a goat, she would charge and stick her horns on his rear end. When Adrie went screaming to his mother the darned goat was holding her belly while she was shaking with laughter.

Adrie wasn't the only one to complain about the behaviour of the goats. The doctor who made a house call to a little farm, where they were keeping goats, saw to his consternation that one of the goats was walking on top of his brand new car.

When the teacher asked the kids: "Where does the milk come from that we put in the coffee?" One of the kids answered: "From the store!"

The scientist invented cow milk to put in the coffee. That way, they have an excuse to steal milk from the cow.

(Mother milk is better than cow milk for the baby. Why?

It's always fresh, it comes in nice unbreakable containers and the cat can't touch it.

Which bees give milk? The answer is "Boobies.")

When Ploon came over for a cup of coffee after the church service, she saw and tasted the blue skim milk Ko was using in the coffee. She found it a disgrace that her sister and her children were drinking that kind of milk. Especially for growing children that was bad, growing children have to have proper food and not blue looking skim milk, she said and added that she was going to talk to Jan, her husband, about this.

The farmer would receive two cents per litre for the milk he delivered to the milk plant and by the time the milkman sold the milk it would cost 4 cents per litre. Between the milk plant and the milkman there was a one hundred percent mark up. When Ploon came back, she said: "If you want to buy milk from the farm for two cents per litre, you can do so. That's all we get paid from the milk plant."

It was a deal that Ko would pick up every day two litres of milk for two cents per litre. It was the same she paid to the milkman for blue skim milk and now she had full milk. Every day, Ko was going to the farm to get two litres of milk which was a great improvement. Of course, the farmers weren't supposed to knock out the middle man so the transaction to buy the milk from the farmer had to be done secretly.

In the early times there were no mosquito repellents or spray against worms or caterpillars. That kind of world was just about to change when the potato bug appeared. The potato bug had been very common in the Americas but Europe was free of those pests. With increased shipping of food and other goods, from different countries, the potato bug made its debut in The Netherlands. They were called Colorado Bugs since that was the origin of the pests. The Dutch Government was hell bent to wipe them out before they would spread and passed a law that if you were growing potatoes that they had to be sprayed against the bugs. In vain they tried; it was a lost battle from the onset. Even with strong killing sprays the insect always survives and becomes immune to the spray.

There were lots of home remedies against pests that cost virtually nothing. Cabbage worms were combated with spraying the soap suds of the laundry over them. It was very effective, cheap and also safe because soap was still made of natural matter rather than chemicals that wash whites whiter and blacks blacker. That's all very nice but the chemicals kill birds and other useful insects and the soap suds from the early days didn't.

There were lots of flies around which were caught with sticky fly catchers which were covered with a mixture of glue and molasses.

(If you drive a car you can see numerous flies and other bugs smashing against your windshield. The question is: "When a fly hits your windshield, do you know what the last thing is that enters his mind?" The answer is "his rear end.")

Mosquito repellents were unknown at the time and mosquitoes had a hay day in The Netherlands with all the water around. There are lots of mud and water holes which are excellent nurseries for mosquitoes. People blamed Noah that there were mosquitoes, in their opinion Noah could have swatted the two mosquitoes that he had in his ark.

It looked as if people were feeding the mosquitoes with their blood so they wouldn't become an extinct species. Their program was successful with their donation of blood to the female mosquitoes. It is the female mosquito who does all the biting; the male mosquito feeds on juice from plants. The female mosquito needs blood to produce eggs and because of the people's help they were successful in doing just that.

It was bad enough to have those pests outside, but when they came inside they devoured you. Of course, there were some screens in the open windows during the summer but the mosquito got in between the window frame and the glass. The mosquitoes are attracted by the smell of your sweat and know that there is blood to suck. They found any opening to get in the house as a hockey player finds the opening in the net to score. This called for action and the openings were plugged with old newspapers. Swatting mosquitoes was very unsuccesful; it seemed that if you killed one mosquito there were ten other mosquitoes coming to her funeral.

There was also a lot of trouble with moths which were eating the woollen clothes. Nowadays the moths are going hungry with all the nylons and other fabrics there are today. In those days when you were hanging away your suit you would put mothballs in each pocket and everybody put lots of moth balls in the drawers with socks, sweaters and other clothes. One day Ko opened up a drawer with woollen socks and quite a few moths were present in the drawer. Those moths were actually small compared to the mothballs which made Adrie wonder how a little insect could have such a huge balls. No wonder that the mothballs were in the drawers without a moth, those moths picked up their balls when they needed them.

(There was a new salesman in the General Store and a lot of customers took a shot at the unsuspecting clerk. An older man entered the store and asked for an ounce of spider tits. The salesman went to his boss to ask where he might find spider tits.

His boss said: "You have been chaffed my boy, those people can make a fool of anybody. Have you ever seen a spider with little spiders on her lap sucking her tits? Smarten up please!"

A little later, an old lady entered the store and asked for a package of moth balls. The sales clerk said: "Ha, ha, nice try lady, but I don't fall for crap like that because a moth has no balls. Did you ever see a moth scratch his balls?")

Even with the little extra money they made and the money they saved, there was still not enough money to pay all the bills. Economizing was a way of life in the 1930's, the Government was in it and so was everybody else. Everything was under close scrutiny to see if some money could be saved. In the 1930's, everything but everything had a double or triple function. The word recycling hadn't been invented as yet because they used things over and over and when they were finished with it, it was finished. Glass jam jars, lemonade bottles and other containers were all returned to the store. A jam jar yielded 10 cents when it was returned and that was a lot of money in those days.

There was no money to buy gauze or bandage to dress a wound, so they used old bed sheets or pillow cases. They just cut them to proper size and there was the bandage and it was cheap. Today's woman has a wide choice of kotex, maxi pads for heavy days and mini pads for light days.

(I never knew that the women were weighing the days. Why should Monday weigh heavier than Tuesday?)

Also available to today's woman are Super Maxi, Curved Maxi and Curved Super Maxi Pads. There is also Oval Thin, Ultra Thin and Ultra Thin Longs. Furthermore there are different manufacturers; there is Kotex, Freedom and a few other brands. You can also get perfumed and non perfumed Kotex. Perfumed Kotex is especially made to divert the police dogs if they are chasing you; you don't need a red herring if you have perfumed Kotex.

None of them had been invented yet during the 1930's and even if they had been available, it would only have been for the rich women. Everybody used the same brand "Old Bed Sheets," cut to maxi and mini pads for heavy and not so heavy days.

Since bed sheets were of good quality in those days, it took a long time before you would stick your big toe through it and mother would say: "That's good for bandage!" The supply of bandages was tied to the wearing out of bed sheets and was limited. To make bandages last until the next old bed sheet was worn out, the bandages for the monthly periods were laundered so they could be used over and over again, month after month. That might sound dirty and unhygienic but in those days it was a way of life. If there is nothing else, you have little choice.

Paper to write on was never bought; old paper grocery bags were used if you had to do some writing and also the white edges of the newspapers were used for that purpose. They never threw a piece of paper away unless they had written on both sides of it and even then they would throw it in the old paper basket. That old paper was good to light the stove every day. They were great inventors and improvisers; everything was recycled.

In order not to carry mud into the house, the rich people would buy a load of gravel for around the house. Concrete was too expensive so the less expensive gravel had to do. Even gravel was too expensive for Arie so he made his own gravel. The houses in The Netherlands are built of bricks and there are lots of old and broken bricks around. Arie collected the old and broken bricks and chopped them up in sizeable pieces. It was instant home made gravel and was cheap as borsch. Since bricks came in different colors, red, yellow, grey and white, the gravel was a lot more colorful than of their neighbors, who had just plain gravel. It was the most economic and colorful gravel in the world.

There were many needed things for which there was no money, so they had to do without. Toilet paper hadn't been invented in those days and the reason that they were reading the newspaper was that they needed toilet paper. The newspaper was cut up in sizeable pieces which were put on a string and suspended from an old nail in the bathroom. After newspapers and Eaton's catalogues in the bathroom, they invented toilet paper. Not all toilet paper is created equal either, and some toilet paper isn't much better than newspaper.

They could use everything from old paper to light the stove, old bed sheets for your sore finger and monthly periods, old bricks to make gravel and they even had some good use for horseshit. In those days the milkman, baker and other merchants would deliver the required goods to your door by horse and wagon. The horses weren't house broken, they weren't even street broken and since they couldn't sweat it out they dropped their digested food on the street, where it served as food for the sparrows.

The horses ate a lot of oats which didn't digest completely and along comes the sparrow to eat the oats out of the horseshit. It was the horse that brought the sparrow to Russia. When Napoleon invaded Russia with his armies, the horse was there to ride on and to pull the cannons and wagons with ammunition. The sparrows followed Napoleon over the open steppe; actually they followed their food supply.

However, the sparrows had competition from Ko who had also use for horseshit. She came with an old pail and a shovel, to shovel the shit into the pail and throw it on the dung pit. Most of the people who were growing a garden had a dung pit, again for economic reasons. There was no money to buy fertilizer so they had to use manure and making it yourself was the cheapest. That's where the horseshit came to good use. Ko said: "Horseshit broods, it heats the plants." Nobody knew where she got that wisdom from, but if Ko said it, it was true. It was probably knowledge that had passed from father to son or in this case from mother to daughter. What the horse threw away, Ko picked up and grew snow white cauliflower from it and other delicious vegetables. Those old people knew their land and plants, whatever Ko said you could take as Gospel.

This story shows you that they were so poor that what the horse threw away, they picked up.

(That brings me to the next question. What does a beggar throw away and a rich guy put it in his pocket? The answer is, "The mucus of the nose." A beggar blows it out on the street because he has no hanky and a rich guy blows it in his hanky and puts his hanky in his pocket. Incredible!)

Ko and Arie were so economical that they were almost misers and could have taught Scrooge a lesson or two. They weren't stingy and they weren't poor, the only thing that was wrong with them, they didn't have any money. Actually there wasn't any difference between rich and poor people, the rich people were only poor people with money. Everything that the Lord provided was used and the Lord provides; whenever a man plants a tree, the Lord provides a dog to water it.

Ko had to think a long time ahead to make sure that there was money to buy coal for the coming winter. The coming winter ruined their budget which they didn't have. Long before winter, Ko put every week a little money to the side so she could buy coal to heat the house. The rich people burned anthracite a high quality coal which gave little dust. Anthracite was too rich for Ko, she couldn't afford it. She bought ovoids that were made from coal dust in the same way as briquettes. In The Netherlands they were popularly called "egg coals" because they were round and were as big as an egg. Some coal mines had high quality coal but others had just coal dust from which they made briquettes and egg coals. It was coal so it burned well.

There was also "coke," not the stuff that you drink from a bottle but the stuff you burn in the stove. In The Netherlands they had very little natural gas so they made their own gas from coal. A gas plant put coal in giant cylinders and heated it from the outside. Since there was no air in the cylinders the coal changed into gas. This gas was led through pipelines to the houses where it was used for cooking food. Heating of the houses was done at that time only by coal, since gas was too expensive. After the gas was taken out of the coal, there was a poor quality coal left since the best had been taken out of it. This poor quality coal was called coke. It didn't burn as well as egg coals so Ko never used coke coal.

Those were desperate times for the people in The Netherlands and it's hard to believe that there were places in the world where people were worse off than in The Netherlands. Some people lived in the U.S. where it was so bad that people were waiting patiently in line ups of three blocks long to get a plate of soup or a slice of bread.

Even that wasn't the worst. In Saskatchewan, Canada if you applied for relief, an inspector would come to check your cupboards and only if there was no food at all, relief kicked in. No money was given to the unemployed people. The only help they got was food coupons which were far from adequate to feed a family. A family of three, man, wife and child would receive $3.00 in food coupons. That didn't even put dry bread on the table. In many cases people took turns to eat breakfast, if it wasn't your turn you just didn't eat. Consequently kids that went to school collapsed because they hadn't eaten.

People on relief only received inadequate food coupons, but no money was given to buy clothes or pay the rent. The landlord was up the creek without a paddle when his tenants didn't pay the rent and consequently he fainted in the street because he didn't eat. There were no food coupons for him because he was a landlord and was rich.

Without money people couldn't buy clothes either and school children had to share their clothes with brothers or sisters. They took turns to wear the clothes and to go to school. Without money to buy clothes, people were walking around in rags and without underwear. The clothes they were wearing were made from flour bags. Skirts or shirts made from flower bags were the norm instead of an exception.

By 1932 the Depression had become more depressing by the day and the cost of welfare kept increasing. That made the Government act by setting up a Relief Department that investigated people on relief who had made fraudulent claims. The investigators of the Relief Department were receiving a bounty of two dollars for every family they could cancel their relief. They were quite successful and found even five men who had claimed the same woman as their wife. If there were unreported earnings as low as twenty five cents they were cut off relief. Men on relief were not allowed to buy alcohol and if the investigators found out, it was the end of relief payments. Some people were working for shirts or socks instead of money. If they were found out they wouldn't receive relief payments anymore.

Moreover, claimants had to sign an agreement that they would repay the money they had received if they found work and a couple had to be married for a certain time to receive relief money. This was done to prevent people of getting married in order to get relief payments.

They thought of everything. Immigrants who had been in Canada were forced to sign deportation orders before they would receive relief and could be deported any time. Fearing deportation they refused and consequently they were living without income.

Bank hold ups and robberies were on the increase and a lot of desperate people were stealing food to stay alive. If they were caught they were fined $10 and landed in jail if they didn't pay their fine. Consequently most of those people landed in jail, they stole food because they didn't have any money, so how can you expect that those people can pay a $10 fine.

There were also public work programs where the people had to work for the municipalities. Those workers had a hard time; they worked for little money and were working like slaves. People who were working watched them all the time and even if a worker went to the bathroom they phoned City Hall to complain that those lazy bums should work for the money they were paid. It was their tax money that paid their wages and they expected them to work for it instead of lazying around.

At least in The Netherlands people on relief received some money. Before the war The Netherlands was a rich country with their colonies in the East and West Indies. The poor people never benefitted of that but apparently during the Depression it helped some what.

NEW HORIZONS

Ko went to the store and she saw something she had never seen before, "Peanut Butter." Curious as she was, she turned the jar around and when the shopkeeper told her that it was made solely out of peanuts and you could put it on your bread, she decided to try it out. Everybody liked peanuts so that should be right up their alley. Instead of a jar with jam she bought a jar with peanut butter. It was a good decision, everybody liked it and Adrie liked it so much that he ate all his bread with peanut butter.

At night his whole body was covered with itching big, red spots. Ko couldn't figure what had happened to Adrie and called the doctor in. He listened for a while to the banging of his heart, from which he came to the conclusion that he was still alive. The next thing he had to say "Ah." Adrie hoped that he didn't want him to say the entire alphabet. Next, the doctor asked Ko: "Did he eat or drink something new?"

Ko thought for a while and said: "Yes, we tried out peanut butter for the first time."

The doctor came to the conclusion that Adrie was allergic to peanut butter so he had to quit eating it for a while and if he tried it at a later time, he shouldn't eat too much of it at once.

Even the beautiful red tomatoes made their debut just before the war.

Ko wanted to try them so she bought some. The green grocer told her to slice them on bread and eat them with pepper and salt. Everybody tried it but it surely wasn't the taste of peanut butter and nobody liked it. Later on Ko was told to put sugar on them and that was more to everybody's liking. Apparently everybody had a sweet tooth!

The tomato is a relative of the potato and scientists are busy crossing the potato with the tomato which will give us "Pomatoes" or maybe "Totatoes." Scientists aren't quite sure. It sounds terrific but how they will taste we will find out when they come on the market. We have to adopt a wait and see attitude and be patient.

When the tomato made its debut in The Netherlands, just before the war, the potato was known in Europe for only a couple of hundred years. Tomatoes and potatoes weren't the only things Europe got from the New World. Chocolate and tobacco came from the Americas as well. It didn't take long for Europe to drink hot cocoa and puff away after tobacco had been introduced.

Last but not least, Columbus managed to bring syphilis from the New World to Europe. This Columbus was a real smart cooky; he already had proven to the Spanish king that he could put an egg straight on the dinner table without having it topple over. At a royal banquet, Columbus let the royal guests try to put the egg straight on the table. After everybody failed, it was Columbus' turn. He took the egg and put it with a bang on the dinner table. The egg yoke ran all over the fine damask table cloth but the egg didn't topple over. It was so simple that this trick became known as "The Egg of Columbus." There are many eggs of Columbus but unfortunately there was only one Columbus.

This Columbus wasn't only smart; he could talk radishes out of the garden and had more balls in the air than a Ringling Brothers juggler. Columbus said to the Spanish king that he was going to China. He went the wrong direction but that was just a minor problem which you couldn't shove in Columbus' shoes.

In those days, the general belief was that the earth was flat and at a certain point you would fall off the world. Columbus told the Spanish king that the earth was round and he was going to prove it by going to China, the wrong way. Instead of East he was going West.

Ferdinand, the Spanish king, wasn't all that impressed but Queen Isabella saved the day by selling some of her jewels to pay for the expedition. Isabella adored Columbus; he could put an egg straight on the table so he probably could do this too. And so:

In Fourteen Ninety Two
Columbus sailed the ocean blue.

He didn't fall off the world when he passed the Madeira Islands in the Atlantic Ocean. That's as far as anybody had dared to go, everybody was convinced that if you went farther you would drop off the world. Columbus was very confident but he almost had a mutiny on his hands when he sailed passed the Madeira Islands.

Columbus had thought of everything; he had even a letter from the Spanish king in his pocket, which was addressed to the Chinese king. This was a precautionary measure because Columbus didn't mind to be at the dining table with the Chinese king but he had no interest to be on the Chinese table as Columbus Chop Suey, the main dish of the banquet. He would have done a lot better if he had taken along, as precautionary measure, a pocket full of condoms. (more than 400 years away.)

On his way to China there was a little piece of land in the way, which they later would call "North and South America." Actually, he didn't land in America, he landed in the Bahamas but that was only a small miscalculation in all his miscalculations. When he landed in the Bahamas, he thought for sure that he had reached China. He didn't see any Chinese people yet, but that would come later. All what he saw was a bunch of Indians running around with chicken feathers on their head.

Actually, those people were not Indians. However, Columbus thought that he was in India, judging by the people he saw. The people from India and the American Indian are both from the Mongolian Race, so they have some similarities. If he was in India those people were Indians. All of a sudden the poor people from the Americas had a name: "Indians." Because of the mistake Columbus made, we have Indians in America while India is on the opposite side of the world. Nice going!

Columbus reached the Americas too early to go that way to China. The Panama Canal was more than 400 years away and the Straight of Magellan, the only other way to go to China, wasn't discovered yet because Magellan was only twelve years old at that time.

Columbus hadn't accomplished what he set out to do but he wasn't unhappy about that; he was a great discoverer. The only problem was that he had to show the Spanish king what he had discovered. He put a couple of Indians in an oversized bird cage which would prove that there were people in this far away land. In order to show the king that he had discovered syphilis, he bandaged his penis. He didn't have to put it in a bird cage, and unfortunately it wouldn't escape before he reached Spain.

When Columbus and his men came back with Syphilis, it was called the Spanish Sickness. Spain was where Syphilis originated in Europe. Mercury was used to treat Syphilis which was called "Blue Salve." Side effects were playing havoc with the kidneys and people succumbed. If you didn't die from

Syphilis, the treatment with Blue Salve was deadly as well when the kidneys collapsed. The cure was as bad as the Syphilis.

Of course, we all know that it was Leif Erickson who discovered North America in the year 1000. Leif was on his way from Norway to Greenland but lost his way because of a storm. He by-passed Greenland and landed in North America, somewhere on the Labrador coast. When he realized that he wasn't in Greenland he promptly turned back and reported his discovery. In spite of all this, Columbus got the credit for discovering America.

THE CHICKEN ENTERPRISE

After Arie had made the deal with Veldhoen that he only had to pay the interest of 184 guilders per year which amounted to 3.5 guilders per week there was still 6.5 guilders per week left for all the other expenses. Of course there were the insurances, taxes and utilities that had to be paid first of all but with all the cuts they had made there was still a little bit more money left for food. Ko managed to buy every week a very little piece of meat for Sunday but that was all.

Even eggs were a luxury they couldn't afford with a relief income of 10 guilders per week. "There is more than one way to skin a cat," said Columbus and put his egg on the table with a bang so it wouldn't roll over. Arie knew about the egg of Columbus and he figured that there was a way to eat eggs with his little income.

At night Arie said to his family: "We are going to raise chickens. The chickens will lay the eggs and all we have to do is to gather the eggs and eat them. When the chickens are too old to lay eggs we aren't going to be that good hearted to put them in a home for aging chickens, we'll put them on the butcher block and eat them. A chicken can easily lose her head when she is getting old. That way we have off and on some meat on our plate."

That sounded as simple as "The Egg of Columbus," but come again, it wasn't. Raising chickens requires a capital investment and being on relief means, "No capital." "I like that idea," Ko said, "but where are we going to get the money to buy the chickens?"

Arie had thought about that problem too, and said: "Now I only have to pay the interest on the house, I have enough money to buy three chickens to get us started."

Ko said: "Whenever I'm working, I can save that money to buy chickens, too. I'll get enough money to buy three chickens as well and we'll have six chickens. In no time we'll have a chicken farm."

That was one important problem solved but there were two more problems. There had to be a hen house, if they didn't want to keep the chickens in the bedroom. And there was also the problem that chickens have a terrible habit of eating. If you were planning to gather eggs at the rear end of the chickens, you had to throw food at their front first before you could expect eggs.

It was up to Arie to build the hen house which wasn't that easy without wood. Buying wood wasn't even mentioned because that was out of the question. Arie didn't have his eyes in his pocket; when he was biking to Town Hall to go stamping; he had seen an old barn at one of the farms that had been blown over by the wind.

There was a lot of old lumber there from which he could easily build a hen house. He wondered what the farmer was going to do with all that old wood. Maybe he could get some of the wood if he cleaned up the old barn for the farmer. When he asked the farmer, he had a deal. If he cleaned up the old barn, he could keep all the old lumber. That was a cheap way to get rid of the old blown down barn and Arie thought it was a cheap way to get wood for his hen house. Everybody was cheap in those days.

Suddenly he was a very busy man to get all the old lumber home and de-nailed. When he was finished, he had all the ingredients to build a hen house. The only thing he had to buy was some chicken wire for the run. There were even enough nails after he had straightened out all the old nails he had pulled out of the wood from the barn. It was a lot of work which didn't matter at all. He had nothing else to do other than going stamping every day. Every inch of wood was used, even the rotten pieces he cut off the planks served to heat the house and the ashes of the burned wood were used in winter around the house when it was slippery. Nothing was wasted.

It was a hen house that looked as if it had been designed by an architect. There was an over capped area where the chicken feed was dumped and there was a chicken run surrounded only by chicken wire. "That's where the chickens can run for the next election, get some fresh air and a sun tan," Arie said. "We are going to buy White Leg Horns and a little color on their cheeks will improve their appearance."

There was also a night compartment, the chicken's bedroom, with sticks for the chickens to roost on. Furthermore there were some nests with peat moss where the chickens could lay their eggs. Over the nests was a hinged door which could be opened from outside the henhouse for the purpose of egg gathering. Everything was dirt cheap but practical and strong.

When Arie was finished building his hen house, Jaap Dalm came to have a look at what his brother in law had been building. He viewed the henhouse from all sides and asked: "Say Arie, I thought you said you were going to keep chickens in this hen house? The way you have built it, it's so strong that it looks as if you are planning to keep lions and tigers in it."

Arie sure deserved the feather in his cap. It was a well deserved compliment after all the hard work he had been doing. As soon as the henhouse was finished, it was ready for the first chickens to arrive. The favorite kind of chicken was the single combed white leghorn which was bred to a high level of egg production and the eggs were white. White eggs were favored in The Netherlands while the English people preferred brown eggs. Of course, this is all malarkey, white eggs or brown eggs, they all taste like eggs so what does it really matter? However, they liked white eggs so six white leghorns were bought with the money Arie and Ko had saved.

Arie had made nests for the chickens to lay the eggs in and had thrown peat moss on the bottom to prevent the eggs from breaking when they fell out of the chicken's behind. You can't tell the chickens anything, they have their own habits and in the wild they usually lay their eggs in a dip in the ground. There is a trick to everything if you know the habits of the chickens; you can use it to fool the chickens. The chickens are in business to preserve the species the same as people are. They usually make a nest of their own, lay six to eight eggs and start brooding. Arie put some stone eggs in the nests which made the chickens think that it was brooding time and laid some more eggs in the same nest. When the eggs were gathered, the stone eggs were left in the nest as a decoy for the chickens.

The stone eggs looked like real eggs but the person who was gathering the eggs could tell the stone eggs because they were heavier than the real eggs. It fooled the chickens because they never lifted the eggs out of the nest to weigh them and consequently didn't know the difference between a stone egg and her own eggs.

There was a lot about the eggs that the chickens didn't know. Her chicken's instinct tells her that she has to brood a bunch of eggs to get chicks. Fat chance! The chicken could sit till Dooms Day on the stone eggs and even when she was brooding on her own eggs, there never would be baby chicks as there was no rooster to fertilize the eggs. Tough luck, if there is no rooster to do some cockledo there will never be baby chicks.

(Even at the best of times when there was a rooster present, it could happen that there were no baby chicks if the rooster did a sloppy job.

At the farm, a rooster was busy jumping from one chicken on top of the next chicken to do his thing. As soon as a little girl came to throw some bread crumbs on the ground, the rooster got off the chicken and started to pick up the crumbs of bread. An old man who had been watching the chickens said: "Holy smokes, I hope I'm never going to be that hungry.")

It wasn't really the chicken's fault that they didn't know their business. Man buggered up the chickens by taking them out of their natural environment. When chickens live in the wild there are always roosters around to see to it that the eggs are fertilized. No, you can't blame the chickens because they never had sex education so how were they supposed to know?

Neighbor Immerzail was keeping chickens too. He had trouble having the chickens lay their eggs where he wanted them. When he saw that Arie had stone eggs as decoy for the chickens, he was going to trick the chickens to lay in his nests as well. He was some kind of a cheapskate and decided not to buy stone eggs. "Buying stone eggs is a waste of money," he said. "I have a lot better use for my money than to buy stone eggs. I'll put some real eggs in the nest, that's much cheaper."

He marked the eggs that he was going to use as decoy to indicate that those eggs had to be left alone because they weren't fresh eggs. Everything went good for quite some time. After the decoy eggs had been in the nest for months, the marks he had put on had worn off and one day he couldn't see which ones were the old eggs. He had a good look and found that a couple of eggs were kind of dirty which was explainable when the eggs had been in the nest for a couple of months. He left the dirty eggs in the nest and took the others out.

His wife was going to cook some eggs for lunch. "That would be nice," she said. When Immerzeel shelled his egg, it wasn't nice at all. It was one of the decoy eggs that had been in the nest for a couple of months. The smell was unbearable, the egg was stinking an hour in the wind when he opened it up.

For the next three months he had lost his appetite for eggs, even to look at an egg turned his stomach upside down. After they boiled a stink egg, he bought stone eggs after all. It was a typical case of closing the barn door after the horses have escaped.

Chickens are not that smart at all; even when the eggs are fertilized, who in the world wants to sit on a bunch of eggs for six weeks? The cuckoo is much smarter; she actually is a parasite that lets somebody else do the work. When the cuckoo is looking for another bird to brood her eggs, she makes sure that this other bird doesn't get suspicious that she is brooding eggs that are not her own. For a beginner, she makes sure that her eggs are the same size as the ones that are in the nest and also throws an equal number of eggs out of the nest, just in case that the host counts the eggs. That precaution should do the job as there would be still the same number of eggs and they were the same size.

As thanks for the hospitality, the young cuckoo is a real pain and throws all the other birds out of the nest in order to get all the food and attention alone.

Beside stone eggs there also had to be rings for the chickens. Rings are needed to be able to tell the age of the chickens because the chickens only produce a lot of eggs for about two to three years. A chicken keeper isn't a philanthropic institution, as soon as the chicken lays less than 220 eggs per year it costs too much money to keep her.

If you want to know the age of a horse, you look at its teeth. That won't work for chickens. As the saying goes, "They are as hard to find as hen's teeth." So looking at the teeth won't work and with all the feathers on a chicken you can't see the wrinkles either. There is a solution to the problem. If you want to know the age of a tree you count the rings of the tree. With chickens it's exactly the same; you count the rings on the chicken to determine her age. The only difference is that you have to put on the rings yourself because the rooster is not going to put a promise ring on the chicken when he does his cuckledo.

When the chicken is one year old you put a ring on her leg and the next year you put one more ring on the chicken's leg. Even without Grade 12 education everybody can tell the age of a chicken by counting the number of rings on her leg.

Only one more problem had to be resolved. What were the chickens going to eat? Some people kept a couple of chickens on table scraps but six chickens can eat more table scraps than there are available. With the Depression there weren't that many table scraps either, any leftovers were always consumed the next day.

Everything was geared to get food for the chickens. As soon as they were finished eating, the pots and pans were scraped out and the scrapings went to the chickens. They never had thrown away food before but now they had even candidates for the scrapings from the pans. There were also the outer leaves of the lettuce which were not good for consumption. They went to the chickens as well.

The chickens were good for everything. When Arie was digging up the garden, he had a little can beside him to put the worms in that he was digging up. Those were also for the chickens. He had to be careful not to give the chickens too many worms because if he did, the blood from the worms would show up in the egg yoke.

Actually, chicken feed was everywhere, even in the ditch. The ditch at the back of the garden was covered with duck weed which contained a lot of feed for the chickens. Between the water plants and the duck weed it swarmed with leaches, snails and other water bugs that were devoured hungrily by the chickens.

The snails were living in a little house which was devoured as well. It contained a lot of calcium which came to the good of the shell. If the chickens didn't get enough calcium they would lay wind eggs with only a fleece. Without the protection of the shell, the eggs were very fragile. Most of the time the fleece would break and the egg was lost.

There was another trick that wasn't missed. Actually, the chickens provided their own calcium. After the eggs were consumed, the shells were returned to the chickens for a refill. The empty egg shells were also devoured by the chickens and they made a brand new eggshell out of it for the next egg. All the chickens had to do was provide a refill. It was recycling at its best.

With all the tricks they had up their sleeves to feed the chickens, there was still a lot more chicken feed needed if they were going to expect any eggs. Arie knew a way to solve that problem. There were a lot of farms around that were growing wheat and after the harvest there were always quite a few wheat heads lying on the land. That was good chicken feed; all he had to do was pick it up.

After all the problems to keep chickens had been resolved, the egg gathering could start and of course the egg eating. For the first time things started to look up slightly.

TOO YOUNG

Willie was already six years old and wanted to come along with her father to pick up the wheat heads. Adrie was only three years old and was too young to help. He surely felt left out; he was always too young to do anything. When his sister came home after he had been bored to his gills all day, she had always all kinds of exciting stories. Adrie wondered how many more nights he had to sleep before he could do anything worthwhile in this world.

Ko understood that Adrie was bored and took him out in the afternoon to pick flowers. There was a gravel road with grass on the side that was covered with yellow butter cups. Adrie liked picking flowers, as soon as he saw all the flowers he said that he was going to pick them all. That would take him several days, Ko thought, but for the time being he was busy and forgot his loneliness.

All the flowers were put in the baby carriage that filled up pretty fast. Ko wondered where she was going to put all the flowers when she came home and threw a hand full of flowers in the ditch a few times. When she told Adrie that it was time to go home he wouldn't hear about it. He said: "I'm not finished yet."

"You can't pick them all," Ko said.

"I have to," Adrie said. "I love flowers."

Ko knew how she could talk him into going home and said: "We have to go home to put the flowers in water or they will die."

That helped, he got worried about his flowers and wanted to go home. At home, Ko had to fill pails and a tub with water to put all the flowers in.

Willie and Adrie played well together most of the time. They had their little arguments but were depending on each other for playing all day. Their mother wouldn't allow them to play in the street until they went to school. She was over protective and looked after her children as a hen looks after her little chicks. Her opinion was that when children play in the street they don't watch the traffic and can get easily into a deadly accident or be maimed for life.

Their father backed her up, he said: "You can lose an arm or a leg and later when you grow up you'll blame us for it because we didn't look after you better." That made a lot of sense to a worrying mother but the kids didn't see it that way. However, their mother was the boss and besides she was bigger and stronger, so that's the way it was.

They had no choice but to play together and that they did. Adrie learned a lot from his older sister who came up with all kinds of games to play. One time she had visited her cousin who had a little slide in the garden. She was much impressed and when she came home, she announced to Adrie that she was going to make a slide.

In spite that Adrie never had heard about a slide, he liked it already. It sounded like a lot of fun and he was all in favor of it. Willie took an old plank and put it with one end on the gate. "Here is your slide," she said to Adrie.

Adrie was amazed; he had thought that making a slide was a project that would take hours. When Willie admired her master work, she knew that the plank had to be made slippery in order to slide down.

She had an answer to that problem, she could make mud to smear on the plank and the slide would be perfect. An old can with water and some clay from the yard made a substance that would do very well. To Adrie, his sister looked some kind of a magician who had an answer to everything. Unfortunately, Willie ran into some kind of trouble after she had put all the mud she had on the plank. She came to the terrible discovery that she didn't have enough mud to cover the entire plank.

Willie wasn't discouraged; it was easy enough to make some more mud. Unfortunately, she couldn't find any more water. No matter how she looked, the place was bone dry; it looked like a desert without an oasis. Even this wasn't a problem to her; she just peed in the can and had water to make mud. Adrie was perplexed; he had heard that Jesus made wine out of water but making your own water was incredible. His sister never disappointed him; she always had an answer to everything. In Willie's humble opinion that was water, too. With a new supply of mud it didn't take long to finish the project and soon the slide was ready for testing.

All that was needed now was a volunteer for the test run, who wasn't hard to find. Adrie was the lucky candidate to be the first one to slide down the just completed slide. To Adrie, this was a great honor and undoubtedly he would go down in history, if his mother didn't kill him.

Willie got an old pail for Adrie so he could climb to the top of the slide. Everything was perfect; the slide was second to none and Adrie was very happy with the result. Only one problem, most of the mud that had been on the slide was now on Adrie's pants. It looked as if he just had crawled out of the swamp.

That was funny, Willie thought, so she started to laugh very loud. Since his sister was laughing, Adrie started to laugh too. This was fun! The only one who didn't think it was fun was their mother who had heard all the laughing. She wondered what was going on and came to check what was so funny. When she saw Adrie covered with mud she had nothing to laugh about, she probably didn't understand humor. To her it meant a lot of work. She said: "No more playing on that dirty slide and come inmediately inside for a thorough cleaning."

That was a blooming pity, Adrie thought; the slide was a master piece and it hadn't cost any money to make it. He only had one slide down and now they had to abandon the invention of the century.

Ko shook her head, it was almost impossible to keep Adrie presentable. Whenever she visited her father she had to use a lot of saliva on his hair just before he entered the house or she would get comments. Adrie didn't like the comments of his grandpa at all. His grandpa was a man of the clock who had to eat at five o clock sharp. At 4.30. p.m. he would get up from his chair to make preparations for supper which meant set the table, make coffee and slice the bread. (Sliced bread hadn't been invented yet.)

At five minutes before five he was finished with his chores. Then he would just stand beside the grandfather's clock to let the time lapse and wait till it would strike. You couldn't eat a minute earlier than five o clock. While the clock was striking he would pour the coffee, say Grace and then you could eat. You weren't allowed to talk during supper time and if you were moving a little on your chair, he would say: "Have you got pins in your butt that you can't sit still?"

Adrie wasn't impressed at all; he was too lively to sit still. To him his grandpa was just an old sour puss who only said hi and bye. He never sat on his grandpa's knee. What was there to like about his grandpa?

When the kids were growing up, they had an ostentatious way of boasting about everything. There was the usual sheer nonsense: "My father is stronger than your father" or "He is much bigger." They had no lack of ways to express themselves. If there was an enormous quantity involved, they wouldn't talk about millions, billions or zillions. No, they had a much better and bigger indefinite number; they knew the quantity of "cat million." The origin of this nonsense is unknown. There was even a greater quantity, "So many times to the sky." If somebody was exaggerating, he would say: "I have 999 hundred thousand cat million times to the sky." Well, you can believe that this is an awful lot, much more than a zillion.

When Willie had to go to school, it made quite an impact on her life. It made even a greater impact on Adrie who had lost his playmate all of a sudden. His life had changed for the worse and he wished that he could go to school, too. He had learned a lot from his big sister and now she was in school, he was all alone by himself locked up in his own little world which was very small. His domain stretched from the ditch at the back of the garden to the gate in front which separated the flower garden from the street. The gate was bolted and closed because the street was off limits to him. With his big blue eyes, Adrie would stand at the gate looking longingly through the openings of the gate.

Some kids from the neighborhood would come off and on to ask if he was coming to play with them in the street. His answer was always the same: "No, I'm not allowed to play in the street."

The kids would just walk away from lonesome Adrie who was all alone in his little prison because the streets were taboo for him. When convicts are in jail, they say that they are on the inside. Well, Adrie was on the inside alright, he looked through the openings of the gate from the inside out to the wonderful street that was all fun.

On the first day that his sister went to school, he was waiting impatiently all day for his sister to come home. When she finally came home, she brought some girl friends with her to play with. They played hopscotch and were skipping rope. When Adrie tried to get into their game, the girls said: "No, you can't play with us because you are just a stupid little boy and we don't play with boys."

Unhappy that he was banned from participating, he looked for sympathy from his mother which wasn't hard to get. His mother shouted at his sister: "Let your little brother join."

That made it worse, the girls said: "Let's go and play in the street, then we are rid of that little pest."

With treatment like that and discrimination, he got an inferiority complex. Suddenly he wasn't a human being anymore; he had changed into a little pest. They say that boredom can kill you but Adrie wasn't going to kill himself, he was going to do the next best thing and make himself disappear. It would be a lot of fun to hide himself, his father and mother would be plenty worried when they couldn't find him and look all over the place for him. All he had to do was find a good hiding place to make sure they couldn't find him. Yes, he knew a good place behind some boards in the shed, that way he could hear what was going on.

Adrie's mother kept a good eye on him all the time; he was seldom out of her sight, but suddenly: "Where did he go?" She looked in the house and outside, he couldn't have gone in the street because the gate was still closed. He could reach the bolt with which the gate was closed, on the inside, but by no means could he have reached the bolt from the street side to close the gate. His arms were too short to do that, so he must be on the property. His mother looked in the shed again. She was standing right beside him, only the board was between them but to her he was invisible. Boy this was fun, it was exciting! Finally he had some action in this dead place.

His mother got real worried and called his father. Adrie could hear them discussing the problem and according to them the only place he could be was in the ditch. He could have fallen into the ditch behind the garden and drowned. His father grabbed the rake from the shed; he could have touched him had he extended his hand behind the board only a few inches. He ran to the ditch with the rake, to dredge between the weeds, to see if he could find him.

Even the neighbors had been drafted to join in the search of the lost kid. Nobody thought about looking behind the board in the shed because they didn't figure that he was playing hide and seek. After a while, he decided that he had caused enough commotion and it was time to get back to earth. He came out of his hiding place and said: "Peek-a-boo" to his mother. Was she glad to see him, she shouted at his father: "I found him!" Everybody was happy like a pig in the sty, including Adrie. He had caused a lot of consternation and for a while he hadn't thought about his loneliness. Feeling quite a bit better after all the commotion, he could face the music again and there was lots of music to face on the Hordyk.

Some more excitement in his lonely life came about when his father had taken a few trees down on the farm for firewood. The trees had to be sliced with a cross cut saw on the saw horse so they could be chopped up. When his father and mother were doing this, Adrie was running around, and stumbled over a piece of wood. Unfortunately, he fell right against the sharp corner of the saw horse. The result was a gaping wound right above his left eye. If it had been an inch lower he might have lost his eye. It took twelve stitches to put that Humpty Dumpty back together again. Luckily, he wasn't depending on all the king's horses and all his men because they couldn't do it. Fortunately, he had a good doctor that could do it.

POLITICAL UNREST

With the deepening of the Depression, more and more people became unemployed and were treated with disdain. The Government stated that the unemployed people were too lazy to work; all they wanted was handouts and trouble. All unemployed people had to go on relief and were consequently very unhappy.

People who were still working weren't very happy either; they were abused by their employers. A person who was working made about 26 guilders per week which was the average wage. On Saturday they would get paid in cash and the cash would be in an envelope. One week there was a note in the envelope beside the cash. The note read: "The management regrets that due to the severe Depression, the competition has forced prices down. If this business is to survive, we have no alternative but to meet the prices of the competition. Therefore everybody will have to tighten his belt to make this possible. Next week your wages will be cut from 26 guilders per week to 25 guilders per week. We understand that this will mean hardship to you. If you are not in agreement with the lowering of your wages, your employment will be terminated effective immediately."

Nobody was in agreement but wisely kept his disagreement for himself, he knew he could be replaced very easily. The workers were even less in agreement when three months later the management had some more regrets. This time, the wages were slashed from 25 guilders per week to 24 guilders per week. And half a year later the wages went down to 23 guilders per week.

To top it off, the bosses were insisting that their employees would perform their tasks in less time than before. If you couldn't keep up with the tempo, you would soon be out of a job. The boss was constantly pushing the workers, he didn't have a whip in his hand but the whip was behind the door. If you dared to say anything about this slavery, you were dismissed immediately. All the unhappy people were muzzled and clung to their job as a drunk clings to a lamp post in spite of the brutality of the boss. If you lost your job, you were finished working because nobody would hire you anymore.

There were always lots of people hanging around the gates of the manufacturing plants waiting till somebody was fired for obvious reasons and had to be replaced. The replacement was willing to accept that job for a couple of guilders less than the kicked out person had made because he was desperate. Social unrest became intense, angry and violent. People can only put up with such extreme despair for so long and ongoing deprivation will bring out the worst in the people. Democracy was on shaky grounds and with worsening conditions it showed up in the 1933 elections that the people were angry. Consequently the three Socialist Parties in The Netherlands were gaining more supporters by the minute.

Socialists and Communists were singing the same tune that the free enterprise system had failed and Capitalism wasn't working for the people at all. The Capitalist system hadn't provided people with enough money to buy the goods they had produced. Manufacturers had made excess profits instead of legitimate profits. Those profits had to be taken away from them and be given to the unemployed people.

That sounded mighty good to the unemployed people who figured that only the Communists and Socialists cared for the people. They were the only ones that could change their hopeless future. The Communists stated that only Communism could provide full employment for all.

National Socialism under Hitler worked a little differently. Hitler wanted the big industrialists to continue because he needed them to make war material for him. Everybody was working in Germany and people were prosperous. The contrary was true in The Netherlands, where people were unemployed and starving.

It seemed that The Netherlands was following the lead of Germany to go for National Socialism. Before the stock market crash nobody had heard about Hitler. All businesses did rather well and the citizens were prominent. Nobody in his right mind would go for Hitler and his National Socialist Party.

That changed when a world wide Depression dumped everybody into poverty. Hitler was a great orator and his speeches attracted more and more disillusioned people who started more and more to vote for him. In 1933 he had so many votes that he became the Reich Chancellor.

Hitler had great plans for Germany; he started to build Autobahns throughout Germany. That was done because every German would have it so good that everybody would be driving a car and of course for that many cars you needed highways. The real reason was that he was preparing for war for which he needed good highways to move tanks, cannons and all other military equipment speedily throughout Germany to where they were needed. Re-arming Germany was also on his agenda. With all those activities on the go, the Germans went back to work and the industrialists were making lots of money. Everybody in Germany was happy with Hitler and supported him.

Across the border, in The Netherlands, people were still unemployed and suffering. People who lived close to the German border went across to work in Germany and thought the world of Adolph Hitler. Other people in The Netherlands were looking with envy at Germany and wished they had a man like Adolph Hitler to get the country going again.

There was such a man in The Netherlands by the name of Anton Mussert. He was a real bright man; at school he had top marks and his future was promising. The only problem was that his parents were poor; they didn't have money for Anton to continue studying. However, Anton had an aunt with lots of money, her only problem was that she was as ugly as the night and nobody wanted to marry her.

She had an idea that could help Anton and herself in the same time. She had all the money she ever needed and Anton had none. Anton wasn't married yet and she wanted to get married but had no admirers. His aunt told him: "If you marry me, I'll pay for all your studies."

For Anton it was the only way to study and for her it was the only way to get married. It was a deal provided they could get permission from the Queen. There were laws against inbreeding and only the Queen could approve a marriage between relatives.

The Queen probably thought that they couldn't do any harm because Mussert's aunt was already 47 years old and wouldn't get children anymore. She gave her approval and Anton married his aunt and started with his studies. They never had any children but they were married. When Anton Mussert was finished with his studies, Hitler had just scored victories in Germany and Anton Mussert thought that National Socialism would be a good thing for The Netherlands.

He started the National Socialist Party and participated in the 1933 elections. Mussert promised jobs for everybody like the Germans had in Germany. Many unemployed people without hope thought that the National Socialist Party was the Messiah for The Netherlands and voted for Anton Mussert. For a starter the brand new Nazi Party obtained 8 seats with the election which was quite an accomplishment.

The Communist and Socialist Parties gained also considerable strength.

That had happened at the expense of the right wing and splinter parties. After the elections, the all important question was; "Who would form a Government?" The Queen had a good look at the situation and asked Mr. de Geer from the Christian Historic Union to form a Government. He had managed before and hopefully he would succeed again.

Dr. Hein Colein was the son of a rich farmer and had studied law. He had become the leader of the Anti Revolutionary Party and had gained prominence in the de Geer Government. When de Geer failed to form a Government, the Queen asked Dr. Hein Colein to give it his best shot. Again, a minor Party with only 12% of the seats managed to form a Government.

For the second time, Troelstra of the Socialist Party wasn't asked to form a Government. He had gained two seats and had now 26 seats. If it hadn't been for the brand new National Socialist Party that took 8 seats, he probably would have those people vote for him as well and he would have had 34 seats. That would have made him the strongest Party in the House. Now there were three Socialist Parties in The Netherlands; The Socialists, The National Socialists and The Communist Party.

Troelstra was a lawyer who started out by trying to improve the living conditions of people on the bottom of the ladder. In order to do that he started the S.D.A.P (Socialist Democratic Arbeid {*Labor*} Party) of which he was the leader. That was a new twist to Socialism; they wanted to abolish the Monarchy and have Democratic elections.

When Troelstra started his Socialist Party, he was more Marxist than Marx had ever been. The S.D.A.P. party was Revolutionary instead of Reformist. Troelstra's goal was public ownership of resources and he wanted to nationalize the banks and manufacturing plants without compensation to the bankers and industrialists because they had stolen everything from the Proletariat. Capitalism had to be eradicated as it was the evil of Society. The State would take care of its citizens from the cradle to the grave.

It sounded great to the tens of thousands of people who were starving while the Government only cared about the weakness of the guilder and a balanced budget. One problem only! There was Queen Wilhelmina who was called "The Mother of the Fatherland." She was the millstone around his neck if he wanted to do all those things.

The only way that this could be obtained was with a revolution. All the unemployed people would go for it; they were ready to fight. They were only Proletaries which were propertyless citizens of the lowest class who served the State only by having children. Why were they the dispossessed while the Capitalists were bathing in riches? Of course, the ruling class was not prepared to hand everything over on a silver platter.

(Patrick was cutting a tree down on an estate. Soon, the owner appeared to raise hell to Patrick. Patrick asked: "What makes you the owner of this tree?"

"The tree is on my land," was the answer.

"And what makes it your land?" Patrick wanted to know.

"I inherited it and my forefathers fought for it," was the reply.

Patrick took off his coat and said: "Let's fight for it again."

This is just a joke but people can easily see it that way and are ready to change the unfair set up.)

Troelstra had it up to his gills with the other parties that pretended that there was no Socialist party; he was never asked to form a Government or to participate in the Government. When the Social Democrats had gained strength again in the last election, Troelstra thought that the time had come to throw the Queen out and make a Republic out of The Netherlands. The Socialists had their main support in the big cities which he could get under control hands down. Once that was accomplished, the rest of the country would follow automatically.

Troelstra had it wrong; he had misfigured on the power of the Roman Catholic Church which drummed up all farmers from the Southern provinces of The Netherlands. Those provinces had an 80% Roman Catholic population and they were told to go to The Hague, which was the Seat of Parliament, to demonstrate and fight for God and Queen if necessary.

The farmers heeded the call of their leaders and marched to The Hague armed with pitchforks and shovels. They were going to make mincemeat out of those red neck Socialists. Soon, The Hague was occupied by angry farmers that were marching with spades and pitchforks on their shoulder singing "Forward Christian soldiers," and other patriotic songs. With their disorderly behavior they provoked the citizens of The Hague and it didn't take long for fights and riots to break out. When the situation went out of control, the Government called in the army to restore law and order.

With great difficulty, the army got finally the upper hand and regained control of the Government City. Getting control of the city didn't mean that the argument was settled. Tensions were still high and police and soldiers were patrolling the streets continuously in order to prevent a repeat of what had taken place. A full scale Civil War was threatening and it looked as if The Netherlands was going to turn into a bloodbath, never experienced before, in the struggle that would follow.

When Troelstra saw the terrible consequences of his policy, he had a change of heart like Saul had on the Road to Damascus. He changed his policies, called off the takeover of Government and devised a policy to make The Netherlands a welfare state with a governing Queen. The change of the course in history happened at the eleventh hour. The Netherlands could have been a second Russia, but for once wisdom had prevailed.

If all people would be wise,
And also would be doing well.
The world would be a Paradise.
Now, so often it is Hell.

The Government had quite a scare when a Revolution almost broke out. They were going to do something about the plight of the unemployed to save their own neck. Next time they might not be that lucky. All the unemployed people dumped into poverty were the main worry and Colein had a remedy for them. He threw a small bone to the unhappy poor people.

As all Good Governments do when there is trouble, he appointed a committee, a Crisis Committee to take care of the unemployed. The first miracle from the Committee was that the people on relief could get half a package of margarine per person per week and a quarter pound of canned meat. For the very first time canned meat was introduced in The Netherlands. It was something new from Argentina where they were raising a lot of beef and it was the very beginning of the "Everything in cans society." The margarine and meat were not completely free; it could be obtained at half the cost in the stores.

On Saturday morning when the unemployed were collecting their relief money, they could buy their margarine and butter at the same time. Arie got two packages of margarine and one can with a pound of beef every week.

The Crisis Committee was supposed to relieve the misery of the unemployed but didn't help all that much, it helped a little bit and according to a famous Dutch proverb: "All little bits help said the fly that pissed into the ocean."

In spite of the fact that the unemployed still had to pay for their meat and margarine, everybody went for it. It was the only way to get a piece of meat at least once a week on the table, usually on Sunday. Ko baked her meat from the Crisis Committee in the margarine of the Crisis Committee and saved a little bit of the little bit of meat she had for Monday. That way they had a taste of meat for one more day.

From this miserable time originated a famous song with great lyrics:

We are living from relief,
The Crisis Committee and grief.
We are eating meatless pea soup,
Which looks a lot like cow poop.

It looks like Governments throughout the world are very good at taxing their people. The Dutch Government was good at it too. In spite that The Netherlands was a prosperous country with its colonies in the East and the West, the Dutch Government had bike taxes in place. The Netherlands was the land of the bikes so this tax netted the Government a considerable sum of money.

If you were riding a bike you had to have a little tax plate with you. The copper tax plate came at the cost of 1 guilder and had the year engraved in it. That was the proof that you had paid your bike taxes for that year. At first the people pinned the little tax plate to their coat with a safety pin. That was a problem because if people put on a different coat or somebody else would ride the bike they didn't have the tax plate with them. The police were constantly checking the bike riders to ensure everybody had complied and had no mercy for people who had forgotten their tax plate. If you were caught without a tax plate when you were biking you would get a fine.

To avoid that problem, people mounted the tax plate on the bike frame, that way they had it always with them. It didn't solve the problem because the bike plates were stolen when you left your bike on the street. You could lock your bike but the tax plate could still be removed. The tax plates weren't numbered and looked all alike, a tax plate was a tax plate whether it was stolen or bought.

A new almost fool proof tax plate holder made its debut. In order to get the plate off a bike it required tools. Nothing is one hundred percent fool proof. If you couldn't get the tax plate off the bike you could always steal the bike, tax plate and all. The unemployed got the blame for stealing the plates and the bikes. Probably, some unemployed people stole the tax plates because they didn't have the money to buy one.

Anyway, the Crisis Committee had a bright idea to give some of the unemployed people a free bike tax plate. If you were unemployed and lived half an hour or more walking from Town Hall you were entitled to get a free tax plate because you had to go stamping. If you had to walk less than half an hour you could walk. Also, if you could prove that you needed your bike to look for a job, you could also get a free tax plate. That left the door wide open and a lot of people claimed that they needed their bike to find work.

If you qualified, you could go to Town Hall to pick up your free plate. To identify the free plates there was a hole punched in the center of the plate and it also had an inscription "Free." That way, the owner of the tax plate was identified that he was unemployed. This was actually adding insult to injury. It was bad enough to be unemployed but with the tax plate with a hole in it the unemployed people were branded like a cow.

Arie went one more time to the Town Hall to pick up his free bike tax plate with a hole in it. He was a good customer at the Town Hall, he came every day there to do his stamping, picked up a can of meat and two packages of butter every week on Saturday and he came for a free tax plate every year. In spite that he was such a good customer, he didn't have any clout. He had to be every day exactly in time for stamping or he would be disqualified from getting relief money.

In some cases it could be beneficial to have a tax plate with a hole in it. Biking was a big thing in The Netherlands, everybody had a bike. With a mixture of bikes and motorized traffic; the bikes had to be illuminated. A bike that was operated between half an hour after sunset and half an hour before sunrise had to have proper lighting.

One night that Arie had to go out with his bike after dark, he had a problem with his light. He still had a carbide lantern that worked by having water dripping on the carbide. That created carbide gas which you could light and you had light from your lantern.

Light on your bike was a must during the dark hours; if you didn't have it you would get a fine. That night Arie had trouble to keep his light burning, there was quite a bit of wind that blew his lantern out all the time. When a policeman stopped him, he was going to give him a ticket. That it was windy was no excuse, for some time there were little dynamos available that were running on the front wheel ribbed tire. Those lights ran on electricity which couldn't be blown out by the wind.

Arie had wanted an electric light on his bike but he didn't have the money to buy one. Because he was poor he would get a ticket for riding his bike without light. At the same time the policeman checked if he had a bike tax plate. Quite often he could kill two birds with one stone As soon as he saw the tax plate with a hole in it, he said: "I see you are unemployed, you have enough trouble the way it is so I won't give you a ticket."

That was a relief that he didn't get a ticket because he would have a hard time to cough up the money to pay for it. When he came home he said to Ko: "For once it pays off to be unemployed. If I had been working I would have had a ticket."

LITTLE BROTHER

It looked as if the Princess Juliana School had been built with Willie, Adrie and a whole bunch of other kids in mind. Just before Willie had to go to school, it was built out of necessity. From the town centre sprawled long dykes that were heavily built with houses. There was a Christian and a Public School in the town centre which couldn't accommodate the growing population. Since there were many children on the Hordyk and around, the School Board had decided that a school was necessary.

Luckily, it was a Christian school. If it had been a public school, it wouldn't have done any good because the church dictated that children of Christian parents had to attend a Christian school. In that case, Willie and Adrie would have had to go to the town centre to attend school. There was a bus going to the town centre but it was unlikely that there was money to have the kids go by bus and walking forty minutes would have been a daily occurrence.

There was no Public School on the Hordyk so the parents that wanted their kids to attend the Public School had to let them go by bus. A lot of people were lacking money to do that and sent their children to the Princess Juliana School which was closer and the children could walk to school.

Most of the Christian people were real fanatics; they called the kids who went to Public School "Public Frogs." Whoever had dreamed that up was supposed to be a Christian but certainly didn't behave like a Christian. Those people were hate mongers; they could create a riot as well as a Holy War.

Adrie was looking forward to going to school to expand his horizon which was the street. For Adrie going beyond the safety of the yard was expanding his horizon because the yard was all he knew. His sister went to school; she had all kinds of friends and could play in the street. As soon as Adrie went to school, his mother had to let him walk to school and he could play with other boys in the street.

Adrie was lucky with the way the rules were. The school year started the first day of March and you had to be six years old before you could attend school. There was a rule that when a child had his or her birthday before April 1st, he or she could start school March 1$^{st.}$.

Adrie's birthday was March 23rd, so he was lucky to start school March 1st. Others were not so lucky and had to wait almost a year before they could go to school when they were almost seven years old. One girl had her birthday on April 1st (she was probably an April Fools Day joke) and her parents tried to enroll her for school on March 1st without success. They argued with the

Principal that it was only one day but the Principal was firm, he said: "A rule is a rule, if I let your daughter get away with one day, the next parents will say: 'You allow that girl to go to school and my child is only one day younger than she is.'"

"Yes," they argued, "but it's so close. If the stork had flown a little faster, she would have been born on March 31st." In vain they tried to persuade the Principal and their daughter had to wait a year because of the slow stork.

Finally, the big day arrived when Adrie stepped into the wide world though it was still on his mother's hand. Actually, he was ill prepared for a big step like that. His mother had always taken care of him and he had lived a sheltered life. She had kept him under her wings and made sure that no harm would come to him.

Adrie only knew a handful of people beside his parents; he never went out and didn't have any friends. He hadn't been allowed to play in the street and few people visited his house. The only ones that came frequently were Aunt Ploon and Aunt Joh who provided a break in his lonely life. If there was somebody else coming, Adrie withdrew in his private corner of the room and was glad when that stranger left.

At the school yard Adrie was welcomed by a bunch of bigger boys from higher grades who were throwing corn and wheat right on his shoes while they were shouting: "Chick, chick, chick!" The kids who came for the first day to school were chicks and the boys in higher grades were the chickens. Chicks had to be fed and they did a good job, the entire school yard was covered with corn and wheat.

After arriving at school, his mother handed him over to Miss van Dyk. She was real friendly and asked if he knew some of the kids that had come to school this first day. A boy from across the street, Adrie van der Linden was the only boy he knew. He had sometimes talked to Adrie when he saw him.

"Good enough," said the teacher, "We'll put the two Adries in one bench. That will make it easy for me; at least I know where the Adries are." She surely had a way with kids, Adrie liked her already.

Many kids who went for the first day to school were crying, especially the girls but there were also some boys crying. This drama was aggravated when their mothers left. Adrie looked the battle ground over and decided not to cry, he could see the girls cry because they were sissies but a big boy that was already going to school didn't cry. He had to act like a big boy now.

When he saw his mother leave, he changed his mind about being a big boy. Here he was all alone by himself with total strangers and he wasn't sure that the natives were friendly. The real world looked more hostile than when he was observing it from behind the gate at his home. Moreover his mom wasn't present to take care of him anymore so he had to take care of himself.

In spite that crying was closer than laughing, he managed to keep his tears away.

To make the school more attractive, the teacher started the kids off with something they all liked to do, "Eating cookies." She had brought a bag with cookies and soon all children were eating cookies, it was their favorite pastime. That helped to dry some of the tears that had been so readily flowing. Eating cookies wasn't all that bad and the school looked a lot better when you were eating cookies.

In spite of the fact that the teacher was very nice, he couldn't help liking his mother better. Did he ever miss his mother! Miss van Dyk had all kind of tricks to make the first morning of going to school easier to take; all that they did was eat cookies and get to know one another. And to top it off, she ended the class ten minutes early.

Willie was supposed to take Adrie back home. No chance; as soon as he was outside he took a run for it, straight to his mother. He had been looking forward to the freedom of the street, the way it worked out he didn't see the street at all when he was running home to his mother.

Adrie's mother had expected that she was going to have a problem to get him back to school in the afternoon. To her surprise, he swallowed his food and was ready to go back to school. He had a job to do before his classes started, there was an awful lot of corn and wheat lying in the school yard which was good chicken food. At an early age, he was already thinking of how to get the chickens fed and he was going to pick it all up.

While most of the chicks were busy wiping their tears, Adrie was the only one who had responded to the call of "chick, chick, chick;" he was going to pick up all the food in the school yard. Feeding the chickens was his job at home and this way he would have chicken food. Going to school benefited him already because he was thinking.

This food gathering for the chickens was a very bright idea for a five year old boy. Unfortunately, it went sour. Early in the afternoon, he was standing in the Principal's office to watch the Principal bandage both his bleeding hands that were covered with cuts.

Besides the corn that he could use for feeding the chickens, he could also use the old razor blades his father had discarded. When Arie discarded his old razor blades, they were finished, because he sharpened them in a glass to make them last longer. Of course, it didn't matter to Adrie that they were old blades, he could use everything. He put the old razor blades in his pockets where they would be ready to cut his hands. When he put the corn and wheat on top of the razor blades he ran into trouble. After a while he wondered how much chicken food he already had and went with his hands through his pockets.

That was a lot of chicken food he thought, the chickens would for sure appreciate his hard work. He had to show that to his sister how much corn and wheat he had gathered. When he showed his sister, he also showed her two bleeding hands with multiple cuts. He was bleeding like a pig; it looked as if he had tried to make blood sausage from his fingers. His sister took him right away to the Principal's office to get both his hands bandaged.

For the second time that day he was trying to hold back his tears. In the morning he had to hold his tears back when his mother left him alone and in the afternoon he had to hold his tears back when the Principal put iodine on all the little cuts. Slowly but surely he started to understand that being a big boy is plenty tough.

Soon he was back in the school yard where he looked dumbfounded and a little forlornly at his bandages. So much for gathering chicken food, a boy could get easily hurt while he innocently tried to take care of his chickens.

That was a hard day's work with a lot of adventure; he hadn't been bored at all the first day at school. The worst thing had to come yet when his mother took his valuable old shaving blades away and told his father to discard his old blades in a way that Adrie couldn't find them. No matter how Adrie argued with her, his mother said: "Shaving blades are not toys, you can't have them. They are way too dangerous. Just look at your hands."

This lecture made Adrie mad like a hornet. Why can't a boy have anything besides toys? And dangerous, what the heck was she talking about and where did she get that dumb idea? It had been only a minor accident and accidents are bound to happen.

After the incident with the razor blades in Adrie's pocket, he still piled everything in his pockets. One day, he found some snails with colorful houses. "Wow," they were beautiful, he could use those and they went straight into his pockets. When he went to bed, the snails woke up; they crawled out of his pockets and started exploring their new environment.

When Ko found the snails crawling around the next morning, she wondered where they had come from. Maybe sonny had brought them in. When she asked Adrie, he wanted the snails back which triggered another lecture. "Don't put all that junk in your pocket, your pockets are only to put your hanky in."

A hanky was a totally useless thing as far as Adrie was concerned; if he had a dirty nose he could use his sleeve. That didn't go over too well with his mother either, she just shook her head and kept trying to talk some sense into him.

With the favorite birthday Adrie had, only one week before the crucial deadline, he was the youngest pupil in the class and also the smallest. In spite of that he was certainly not the dumbest kid in the class. The contrary was true, he was the brightest. His mother and his sister had taught him to write the numbers from one to ten. Once he had mastered that, he became interested in how you could tell time on the clock. His mother had drawn a clock on a piece of paper with a long and a short hand and in no time he could tell time.

The first thing the children had to learn was to write the numbers from one to ten which was a piece of cake for Adrie, he could do that already. Most of the teachers didn't have a watch and were depending on the hall clock. One day the teacher asked who could tell time.

Only one hand went up, it was Adrie's hand. "Go to the hall," she said, "and look on the clock what time it is."

Adrie was very proud that he was the only one who could tell time and from there on he had a steady job as the "Time Keeper." Adrie was very much impressed with the standing clock in the hallway that was tick tocking constantly. Most of the students didn't admire the clock the way Adrie did. They thought that the clock in the hallway was the slowest clock in the world when it was school time. It took almost for ever before it was noon when they could go home for lunch. In the afternoon it took even a lot longer before the magical hour of 3.30 p.m. was reached indicating that the school time was finished for that day.

Arithmetic was Adrie's favorite subject. Most of the kids had to count on their fingers to find out how much two plus three was which took time. Adrie knew that all by heart which saved him a considerable amount of time and consequently he was always first to have his assignment finished.

That was no problem for Miss van Dyk, she always had something to do for him. Cleaning the blackboard and collecting the papers from the other students were part of his duties.

It was the custom in those days that when the kids of the lower grades had a birthday that they would treat the class with candies. The teachers got treated as well and since they were special, they usually got a couple of chocolates. It seemed that the teachers who made up the rules looked after themselves pretty good. In order not to make it too suspicious, they allowed brothers or sisters in another classroom to eat a candy too. Otherwise, eating candies was prohibited at school.

Miss van Dyk always offered one of her chocolates to the kid that had finished the assignment first. It was a foregone conclusion who would get the candy. Adrie could win that candy hands down. He sure loved his teacher and would do anything for her including behaving. Love went both ways and Miss van Dyk loved her bright student; even after school; she would look after him. At one time, they were sitting in the bus and like usual Adrie had the backseat so he could look out of the window. The bus was quite full and all seats were taken. In those days, there was a sign in the front of the bus stating: "Young people under the age of 21 have to surrender their seat to older people."

(Nowadays quite a few young people refuse to give up their seat to an older person or a pregnant woman. They simply state: "Why do I have to give up my seat? I paid for my ticket too. What the heck those old geysers think they are?")

That included Adrie and when at the next stop more people entered the bus, the bus driver walked through the bus telling the younger persons to stand up for the older ones. All of a sudden, Adrie was without a seat but not for long. His mother had kept an eye on him and called him to sit on her lap. He had a better offer; his teacher was also in the bus and moved up a bit to make room for him.

Adrie was basking in the good relationship he had with his teacher and if anybody would have told him that this relationship would end, he wouldn't have believed it. That it happened had everything to do with the scandalous way the Government took advantage of the student teachers.

If you wanted to become a teacher, you went to Teacher's College. That was already a hardship for the parents of the prospective teacher since they paid for the study costs. After finishing their education, they were fully qualified teachers. The problem was that with the severe Depression, there was a surplus of teachers which made it hard to clinch a job.

The Government lent a helping hand graciously and instituted a program in which there were assistant teachers. There was only one problem when a person was an assistant teacher, he or she had a full time job but didn't get paid at all. That was an added burden to the family of the teacher. A teacher had to wear respectable clothes and a lot of times, the teaching job was too far away from where they lived. That meant that the teacher had to rent a place or have board and room without making a plugged nickel.

In order to cut education costs, the Government had a rule in place that all schools with seven grades could have only six teachers plus a Principal. The Principal usually was teaching Grade Seven because it had the least students. A lot of students went to a different school after Grade Six. Actually, the Principal had a lot of other things to do besides teaching and that's why the Government allowed a school to have an Assistant Teacher without pay. That way, the Principal could attend to his Principal duties instead of also teaching a class. And the price was right; it cost absolutely nothing to have an extra teacher.

A young teacher without a job would take on a non paying job in order to get experience. Whenever there was a job opening for a paying job, the teacher could apply and claim experience. Miss van Dyk was such a teacher who had been teaching without getting paid. No wonder she couldn't afford to buy a watch.

Whenever there was a paying job available, she would apply and hope for the best. It seemed that finally the best had delivered and she had a paying job. That was very good for her that she could leave for greener pastures but it was not good at all for Adrie who saw his favorite teacher leave. She left a vacuum behind that would be filled with a new teacher.

Love and hate are never far apart especially in romance. In Adrie's case, love and hate were apart exactly two days from Friday night when they said good bye to Miss van Dyk till Monday morning when the Principal came to introduce the brand new teacher Miss Kouwenhoven. That's how he called the beast.

Miss van Dyk was actually scrawny but this was a big woman and unfortunately bigger is not necessarily better. She looked more like a wrestler than a teacher, she had a forefront like a Chevrolet and had the kind of ample bosom one could serve a tray of drinks from. That was Adrie's mild observation but his friend had an opinion as well, he said: "Miss Kouwenhoven has a bust on which a cat with nine kittens can lay on quite comfortably and there would be lots of room left."

There were a lot of jokes about Miss Kouwenhoven but as a teacher she was a joke as well, if there ever was a joke. Quite often, big fat people are very soft of nature but this wrestler was a real pain. Adrie hated her; she was some kind of a person who only a mother could love. He had liked Miss van Dyk and she had liked him but this tyrant didn't like little bright boys which was very unlucky for him. Miss Kouwenhoven liked little girls with snow white starched ribbons in their hair. From far it looked as if you saw a bunch of white butterflies on their way to a cabbage patch to lay their eggs on the cabbage leaves.

That was discrimination alright and Adrie was sure that she was the inventor of discrimination. Very likely she had had an unlucky love life and took it out on the entire male population. It was no wonder that she had an unlucky love life; Adrie wouldn't marry her even if she was the last woman on earth. Like Solomon said: "It's better to be alone than to be with a quarreling woman." Solomon should have known because he had one thousand wives.

It sure was a change compared to Miss van Dyk; the morale in the class room had changed overnight and was at its lowest. She was always yelling and was singing stupid songs about frogs in a ditch that was frozen over. According to her song the frogs were almost dead. She probably had been standing near that famous ditch with frogs hoping that if she kissed the right frog a handsome Prince would appear, so she could get married and live happily ever after.

When she was singing those childish stupid songs, she sounded more like a cross between a squeaking wagon wheel and a neighing horse. You couldn't call that singing, it made Adrie laugh. Unfortunately, his laughter turned into sorrow when the teacher got mad, grabbed his ear and pulled him to the corner. "Now you can laugh," she neighed, "while you are standing in the corner, ha, ha."

There wasn't much to laugh about when he was standing in the corner. This teacher was a real sour puss and took it constantly out on Adrie. Her singing got him in constant trouble because she certainly wasn't a Caruso.

One of the other great songs she was singing; was a song about two kids who were walking in the rain underneath their mother's umbrella. After singing this song for about thirty times Adrie got fed up and changed the lyrics slightly. Instead that the rain sounded tick, tack, tick on mother's umbrella, the rain sounded now like stick, stack, stick.

Of course, the old goat had to hear it and before Adrie knew it, he was standing in his favorite corner again with his hands on his back. It looked as if that corner was reserved for him. She was probably thinking to put a sign in the corner "Reserved for Adrie." The other kids from the class knew exactly how Adrie's back looked because he was always standing in the corner. They seldom saw his face.

Another dumb song was:

Mother our crow is dead.
He fell from his stick on his head,
We tucked him into his bed,
Mother our crow is dead.

No matter how homesick Adrie was for Miss van Dyk, she would not return. She probably had found another little boy who had fallen in love with her and Adrie was left with this useless monster. Why did she have to go and why was she replaced with this useless teacher? There were a lot of unanswered questions which were all part of growing up and coping with life itself.

With the changed position in Adrie's life, he was no longer the favorite student of the class but the pest in the corner. If that wasn't bad enough, there was another problem brewing. As the smallest kid in the classroom, he was abused by the bigger boys who called him "Little Brother."

Calling names wasn't a problem for Adrie, his mother always said: "Sticks and stones can break your bones but calling names doesn't hurt any." The problem was that they didn't only call him little brother; the big boys treated him as their little brother. They kicked him around all the time which caused some kind of an inferiority complex.

Whenever Adrie crossed the school yard, the big boys would be sitting against the fence and some other big boys would push him against the fence where the big boys were sitting. The big boys would grab him and would pull his pants off his behind. It made the big boys laugh while Adrie was close to crying.

There was no fun left in Adrie's life, in the classroom he was the outcast and in the schoolyard he was the laughing stock. When Miss van Dyk was still the teacher, he had loved to go to school but pleasure had turned into a daily recurring nightmare, especially now the big boys made fun of him. In order that he didn't have to put up with the indignity of losing his pants, he started to arrive late in the schoolyard so he didn't have to put up with this harassment too long. The school bell didn't bring any relief as he was harassed by his teacher as soon as he entered the classroom.

Scared like a little bird by the pussycat, he would hide in his favorite corner of the schoolyard. Sooner or later he had to cross the schoolyard and it looked as if Big Brother had been watching constantly. The big boys were always ready to make him lose his pants and make fun at his expense which made Adrie nervous. He had liked school very much but now he hated it, there was no fun left in his life.

The pests in the schoolyard kept up their annoying game until they threw him too hard against the fence. With his knees he slid on the schoolyard and he hit his head against the fence. That gave him bleeding knees and a big lump on his forehead the size of a golf ball with his pants down.

Being caught with his pants down had been a regular occurrence but now he was injured he had enough of this foolishness and had it up to his gills with those pests. This time his blood started to boil and he forgot that those boys were big. With the damage to his knees, head and pride and with his pants still down he jumped up to the biggest bully, who was a head taller than he was and floored him before the boy knew what happened to him. Adrie jumped right on top of him and beat the heck out of him with his wooden shoe. Blood squirted out of the bully's nose; he was bleeding like a pig and was screaming murder.

Adrie didn't know when to stop, he was so furious and determined to make mincemeat out of that bully if it was the last thing he would do. A large circle of school children had formed around the fighting boys. This was good entertainment especially when blood was flowing abundantly through the arena. Apparently, the big boy had never experienced such an onslaught and was screaming for help. Help was on the way, there were always kids that would go to tell the Principal when there was a fight in the schoolyard and this time was no exception.

The Principal had a hard time to pull Adrie away from the big boy and after he succeeded he had them both in his office. It was hard for the Principal to believe that the youngest and smallest kid of the school yard had tackled a boy from Grade Four. It looked to him as if the underdog had become the bully.

Of course, the Principal wanted to know what had triggered the fight. Adrie still mad told the Principal what had happened and added to his story that it better not happen anymore. He wasn't going to stand idle when they threw him against the fence to pull the pants off his butt and was going to kill the bastard if he did. Adrie had still enough adrenalin left in his veins that he wasn't even scared of the Principal and used unorthodox words that weren't allowed at school.

Usually fighting in the schoolyard drew some kind of a punishment and using coarse language wasn't appreciated either. This time, the Principal shook his grey wise head; he probably had never seen and heard anything like that before. He was speechless and instead of the usual sermon he would preach, he just got his first aid kit to take care of the bleeding nose and knees and the lump on Adrie's head. When he was finished all he said was: "Go to the schoolyard and play with each other instead of fighting."

Luckily, Adrie never had to make good on his threats, he had gained immediate respect and admiration. This little brother was a little kid alright but that didn't mean anything. You were better off not to cross him or make him mad because he would beat the crap out of you with his wooden shoes. The name Little Brother also disappeared, Adrie had demanded respect and it never happens that big boys respect their little brother.

All of a sudden Adrie had all kinds of friends. Two boys of Grade Four came to call on Adrie to walk with them to school. They always had hated that bully but never had dared to touch him and here was Adrie, the most insignificant kid in the schoolyard who had tackled this bruiser. They didn't mind having a friend like that.

Of course, Adrie was by no means as strong as the big kid but surprise and adrenalin had worked in Adrie's favor. Because of his anger he could call up powers of the primeval age that he possessed but didn't know about. He didn't know a thing about adrenalin but it was there; ready to be used if needed.

If Adrie had had to depend on his hair like Samson for strength, he would have been in trouble. Because of the lice plague that was prevalent, all boys had the latest fashionable hair cut, a forelock. It looked like a sod of grass on a desert plain but it helped to combat the lice when there was no place for them to hide.

The lice plague was aggravated by not having the means to combat the lice. Girls and women had awful trouble to get rid of their lice. Washing your head with green soap was the usual procedure and once it was soaked you put a tight towel around your head that made you look like a fakir. After a couple of hours, the lice were dead you hoped.

Mr. Mulder, the old Principal had retired and a new Principal Mr. Haspels took over. It had been a disaster when Miss van Dyke was replaced with Miss Kouwenhoven. She was a proverbial pain and so was Mr. Haspels, the new Principal. This new Principal ran the Princess Juliana School like a military camp and Miss Kouwenhoven fitted right in as prison guard.

The only good thing about the Princess Juliana School was that it was only a five minute walk to school and the kids had their education but that's where the good things ended. From the outside the school looked like a prison with a high iron fence at the front. There was a high iron gate that was closed and locked after school hours because nobody was supposed to play in the school yard after school hours. The Principal was afraid that with playing football a ball would be kicked through a window.

Both sides of the school yard were protected by concrete fences, which like in jail, nobody was supposed to climb. There were no armed guards to shoot the kids if they climbed the fence but anybody who was caught doing it was taken off the fence, spanked and scolded by the Principal.

In the centre of the play ground was the Tree of Knowledge of Good and Evil from which the kids weren't allowed to pick fruit to eat or climb on. It was a chestnut tree that provided hundreds of chestnuts. They were off limits for the kids unless they fell on the ground by themselves. If you were a good kid you would comply with the rules and if you were an evil kid and climbed the tree you had to face the consequences.

It was a long wait for the kids before the tree dropped its chestnuts voluntarily and the boys would lend the tree a helping hand with throwing rocks into the tree so the chestnuts would drop prematurely. If the Principal saw that, the kids weren't kicked out of Paradise. (the school yard) No, he kept them within the boundaries of Paradise and made them write a hundred times in the sweat of thy face, "I'm not allowed to throw rocks."

If the rock went by accident through the window, the culprit had to pay for the window out of his piggy bank. The Principal found out easily enough who had broken the window, there were always kids who were the teacher's pets and they blabbed. At school the Principal had the kids coming and going, they couldn't do a darned thing or they were punished.

Inside the school, the rules weren't any better than in a concentration camp. The Principal functioned as the General while the teachers did their best to fill the role of drill sergeant. Five minutes before the school started, the General blew his whistle which meant that the kids had to line up for the polonaise. The First Grade kids lined up in twos closest to the school door followed by the Second Grade and so on. There were Seven Grades so the

Seventh Grade formed the rear guard and had to walk the farthest before they were inside.

Three minutes before school time the General blew on his whistle again and this time it meant: "Forward, March." It looked like a regular well disciplined army. After walking through the double doors, there was a little front hall. On the walls there were some wood etchings with educational inscriptions. On one side the etching said; "Never go with a stranger." That sign was put on the wall after a little boy had gone with a stranger and was later found murdered.

On the other side of the hall was an etching with a motto: "Labor ennobles!" To the chagrin of the Principal, some smarty pants had scratched underneath this beautiful maxim: "But nobility doesn't labor!" This hit the nail right on the head but of course the Principal didn't see it that way. He didn't appreciate a smart aleck, even if he was right.

The Principal asked in vain in all class rooms if anybody had seen who ruined this irreplaceable masterpiece. It seemed that the culprit had probably worked alone when he finished his masterpiece. There were no traitors to give him away, even the telltales didn't have a clue who the sinner was.

Exactly on time, the General pushed the button of the school bell announcing that the lessons were starting. To the kids it meant that they had to sit straight up on their bench with their arms folded in front of them. The teacher said: "Everybody has to sit nice!" She probably thought that the kids were her dogs that had to sit nice and shake paws. With a flat ruler, she walked through the classroom and anybody that didn't have his or her arms folded to her satisfaction got the fingers hit with her ruler.

The next item on the agenda was to sing a hymn followed by a prayer furnished by the teacher. This was followed by a general inspection as in a regular army camp. The hands of the children were the main target of close scrutiny; the children had to turn their hands over so they could be inspected on both sides. Hankies were also inspected, they had to be clean.

Of course, the children washed their hands before they went to school in order to pass the inspection. However, on the way to school it could easily happen that there was the necessity to throw a stone against a friend's head as a friendly gesture. That could easily result in failure to pass the general inspection which resulted in spanking of the hands with the flat ruler. It was a miracle that some kids still had hands left after the many spankings they received.

What was even more miraculous was that the teacher had any rulers left. Quite often the kids would pull back their hands when the teacher was trying to hit them with her ruler and she would hit the bench. That would infuriate the teacher and she would give the kid a spanking with the stick on the behind.

The stick was always waiting patiently in the corner of the classroom, as a sentry who was on duty all the time. Use of the stick was considered a very private business between teacher and school kid to settle the argument of who was the boss and was therefore administered in the privacy of the cloakroom or the coal shed.

One time, the stick had mysteriously disappeared and when the teacher asked the class who had taken the stick away, one of the babblers told the teacher who had done it. The stick came back and the culprit got a few whacks with it in front of the classroom. No wonder that he had been trying to get rid of the stick.

As a deterrence for other trouble makers, the kid would get sometimes his whacks with the stick in the presence of his classmates just to show them that they had to behave or else. The number of whacks the kid would receive depended on the seriousness of the offence and how mad the teacher was.

Some students faked injuries after they had had some whacks with the stick; they limped and walked as cripples. Other students put red ink on their hands after the teacher had spanked them with the ruler, to pretend that they were bleeding. The teacher was never impressed; she had seen it all before.

Authority of the teacher wasn't limited to the classroom, the school or the school yard. Big Brother was watching the kids everywhere, even when they walked home. You would think that a teacher's jurisdiction ended after the kids left the school property; whatever they did on their way home was none of the teacher's business. "Not so," said the teacher, "You have to behave whenever you are in public."

After the general inspection, there was the opportunity for the sissies to tell on their class mates and reveal their evil deeds which included fighting, swearing, making unchaste remarks, doing damage to properties, smoking, stealing etc.

Offenders were punished with detention after school, slapping him some smacks on the bum or spanking of the ears. The stick was reserved for the major offences or when a kid had committed the same offence a second time. Then the teacher would give the kid a few whacks on the bum with the stick and said: "Who doesn't want to listen will have to feel it!"

The authority to do all those things came from the Bible that said: "Spare the rod and spoil the child." Christian education meant that the students had to endure a lot of spankings and other kinds of punishments.

After all the spankings and punishments had been administered, the lessons could finally start. In the morning the first lesson was a beautiful Bible story. With burning buttocks and sore hands from the spankings the kids had just received, they were listening to a story that Jesus loved them very much, despite that the teacher had just beaten the heck out of them. But then Jesus loved sinners and sinners they were.

After the prayer, the teacher would say in a sanctimonious manner: "That the blessings of the Lord may descend on all of you."

Adrie couldn't help but think that in this class room with this dumb teacher, the only blessings the Lord had descending on them were the spankings that this mad teacher gave to them. If that's all the blessings the Lord had to offer, he didn't need them.

Telltales were encouraged by the teacher, she didn't have eyes in her back so she had created a network of spies who would report all the evil deeds anybody would do. There was a whole army of spies around which the K.G.B. in Russia could be jealous of. Before the lessons started, everybody was under the crossfire of her spies who put their stupid little fingers up to squeal on everybody. "Miss, I have seen Adrie Demerwe hang on a moving cart." For that he got a slap on his ears, "You can't do that because it's dangerous."

Adrie was kept on thorns, pins and needles, scared that one of the sissies would put her finger up and squeal on him. The authority of the teacher stretched as far as the tattlers could watch him. He hated the teacher and the tattlers even more than the teacher.

His opinion about the teacher was that she had stupid ways of teaching. At one time, they had to practice to write the letter M. Most of the kids had a problem with that difficult letter and when most of the class didn't get it right, she had all the kids who had failed to write a proper M staying after school to practice. Everybody was upset, especially the girls who had never to stay after the classes; they cried their heart out.

Even Adrie had to stay to practice writing M's. He had written all perfect M's except one, that one had one too many legs which was good enough for the teacher to punish him. Of course, he was furious; she had found an excuse to punish him unfairly. Besides, he couldn't see that a kid should be punished if he couldn't write an M.

Miss Kouwenhoven had cruel ways to educate the children. She forced left handed children to write with their right hand by tying the left hand on their back when they were writing.

A year goes fast, especially when you are enjoying yourself. At the end of Grade One, Adrie received his report card that said: "Advanced to the Second Grade." Somebody else was advanced to the Second Grade as well. It was Miss Kouwenhoven who was going to teach Grade Two. He now had the privilege to be taught by his unfavorable teacher in the Second Grade. He hated it already.

It happened that some kids failed their tests on purpose because they wanted to stay with their favorite teacher. Miss Kouwenhoven didn't have to worry that Adrie would do that. If he had known that she was going to teach Grade Two, he might have been tempted to fail his tests in order to get rid of her. She was the most hated woman in his life.

Being advanced to Grade Two meant that they weren't little chicks anymore, they were now chickens. However, being chickens didn't give them the privilege to cackle in the classroom. As a matter of fact there wasn't a heck of a lot they were allowed to do in the classroom but sitting pretty with their arms folded in front of them.

All chickens knew the traditional National School Anthem:

The school is only a monkey cage, hurrah.
The biggest monkey heads the class, hurray.
He hits the small monkeys on their ass
And pretended that he the leader was.
Hurray, hurray, hurray.

It might take a week for the children to learn the words of a hymn that they had to sing but everybody knew the National School Anthem by heart after they had heard it only once. In spite of their contempt for school, everybody had to have his or her picture taken as a remembrance of their school time. It took some doing to coax the children into sitting in front of this mysterious monster with the operator hiding behind it underneath a black cloak. *(In those days they took the photos on glass plates that served as negatives. Those plates were light sensitive and the camera was covered with a black cloth. The photographer was looking from underneath the cloak.)*

Especially the girls didn't trust it at all, the boys were more daring. Adrie had no problem with it because his sister from Grade Four was joining him in the picture. All the kids of a family that went to school were in one picture. They also took a picture of the entire class.

That picture didn't sell too well; Adrie's mother wanted the picture from Willie and Adrie but not from the entire class; they didn't have money to waste, she said. It seemed that the class picture didn't go over at all and the teacher tried to praise the picture in order to sell some. She said; "After you are grown up, you'll treasure this picture. You can look back on your school time and say: 'Here is Marie, she works in the grocery store and here is Piet he is now a lawyer.'"

One of the boys said: "Yes and we can say: This was our teacher who is now dead.'"

That remark didn't go over with the teacher at all; she put the picture away immediately saying: "Very well then; don't have a picture to remember the class."

After the kids had learned to read and write, the teacher had a new punishment in store. She had the children write fifty lines if they had misbehaved. There were many apple and pear trees around in the gardens and Adrie couldn't resist tasting them for the owner. Because of some traitors in the classroom, Adrie had to write fifty times: "I'm not allowed to steal apples."

Many more kids were stealing apples from the gardens and had to write lines. One of the thieves forgot the word not in his lines and had written: "I'm allowed to steal apples." That didn't go over very well with the teacher who made him write it the right way fifty times. So he wrote one hundred lines, fifty lines wrong and fifty lines right. You couldn't get away with anything.

Kids brought burrs to school to throw them on the teacher's back and one time, somebody had hung a clothes hanger on her back. When she found out she was furious and tried to find the culprit. For once her traitors disappointed her; they hadn't seen who did it. When she couldn't find the culprit, she announced that the entire class had to stay half an hour after school time to write fifty times: "I should respect my teacher."

There was a rhyme in Dutch that condemned the telltales. According to the rhyme, "If you were a telltale, you better not walk through the street because the dog will bite you, the cat will scratch you and the birds will shit on you." You sure had it coming when you were a tell tale.

Adrie was not depending on the dog, cat or birds to punish the telltales, he had his own way to deal with them. He punished the squealers by punching them in the nose; why wait till the birds shit on them? He had an instant cure.

Corrie Oorschot and Rika Veer had both failed to pass Grade Two. To say that those girls weren't very bright would be an understatement; they actually were too dumb to dance in front of the Devil. The only thing they were good at was when it was telltale time and Adrie had been the beneficiary of their unfavorable reports of him to the teacher, many times.

Corrie Oorschot was the leader of the pack, she was short, shapeless, her eyes were watching each other and she wore thick glasses in a dark frame. Moreover when she was walking, she bent over like an old granny which had given her the nick name of "Granny bakes a cookie." Another fitting name was "The Ugly Duckling." That name was derived from the Danish writer Hans Christian Andersen. According to this writer "Beauty is only skin deep," and being ugly was skin deep too. People who are ugly in appearance can be very nice people. In Corrie Oorschot's case being ugly didn't stop skin deep, it went as far as her heart. Adrie thought that she was a misprint by nature.

One day, those two girls were airing their frustrations again and Adrie was their innocent victim. When they kicked him in the shin, he responded with some friendly words, such as: "Damn you, bugger off."

Adrie had figured that this unorthodox language was going to be reported to the tyrant of a teacher and of course, he was right. In the next treason session their stupid finger went up and the accusation was: "Miss, I've heard Adrie Demerwe swear."

The teacher asked: "What did he say?"

The way it looked to Adrie, she probably was trying to learn a few new words that she could use in future at an opportune time. He could only hope. After his well chosen words for the occasion were repeated to the teacher, Adrie could see by looking at her gloomy face that she didn't like the powerful words that he had used.

Slowly but surely the teacher was sneaking up on him like a tiger would sneak up on his prey through the banana fields. For a starter she spanked his ears and said: "I will not tolerate abusive language like that when you are addressing girls. Those are nice girls and no troopers."

Adrie's second opinion that it had been an entrapment wasn't asked for, he was found automatically guilty without having a trial. He had also something to tell the teacher that the girls had kicked him in the shin but the teacher never listened to that accusation. She used the same methods as Hitler did in Nazi Germany who shot people first and then gave them a fair trial.

When Adrie looked hatefully at the girls' faces he could see their satisfaction, they must be thinking: "We got you."

They got him alright but the Lord says: "Vengeance is mine" and if the Lord can have vengeance so could Adrie.

He couldn't get even the same day because he had to stay after school to write fifty lines: "I am not allowed to swear." But there was always another day to punish those girls for the misfortunes which they had caused.

With a brand new day, Adrie had some unfinished business to attend to. After school, he made sure that the girls wouldn't escape their punishment. It wasn't difficult to catch the girls; it was like shooting ducks in a pond. Wildly he jumped in front of the girls, shouting angrily: "You thought you had me yesterday by squealing to the teacher. Well, today I got you!"

He kicked both girls in the shins while he was still shouting: "Here, now you can feel how it hurts when you are kicked in the shins."

Both girls started to cry but he had no mercy for them, they had made him suffer and it was now their turn to suffer. He wasn't finished yet and spanked their ears while he was shouting: "This is from the teacher who spanked the wrong person, now you can feel how it feels when you receive a spanking and you can go to the stupid teacher to tell her what I've done to you!"

The girls surely didn't need any encouragement to tell the teacher, they didn't disappoint Adrie at all. He cared less at this stage and was going to get even with those girls even if it would kill him. A boy could only take so much.

After the girls had reported the evil things Adrie had done to the complaint department, he had to stay after school.

The teacher gave him a sermon that could have paled the Sermon on the Mountain. In this sermon Adrie found out a lot about himself; the teacher said: "You are without a doubt a bully that has to be taught a lesson. You never learned a thing when I punished you before. You should be ashamed of yourself for beating up on nice, soft cuddly girls."

That was worth a big laugh that those monsters were called cuddly girls; you were better off cuddling a cobra than those creeps. The teacher was going to punish Adrie in a very degrading way, she said: "I want you to ask the girls forgiveness for what you have done to them in front of the entire class."

"That will be the day," Adrie said. "I was the one that was abused by the girls in the first place and they weren't punished for that."

Needless to say the teacher didn't agree; she said: "Either you apologize or you'll have to write a hundred lines "I can't beat up on girls."

Adrie wasn't going to do either one and said: "I don't see the girls write lines so why should I?"

"Go immediately to the Principal's office, he can deal with characters like you," the teacher said.

So Adrie told the Principal his story and after he had heard everything, he said: "I'll look into this, go back to your class room."

The Principal was probably too busy to figure it all out and Adrie never heard about it anymore. When he saw the girls the next day, the results were remarkable; they made sure that they didn't come close to Adrie, they had had enough of him. That was just what the doctor had ordered. If those creeps stayed far enough away from him, they couldn't hear him swear and they wouldn't have anything to squeal to the teacher about.

THE THREE TONE REPORT CARD

Adrie had taken a demotion with the change of teachers from Miss van Dyk to Miss Kouwenhoven. From the teacher's favorite pet student, he had been demoted to the outcast of the class. Miss van Dyk had always chores to do for him when he was finished with his task but this dumb teacher wanted him to sit with his arms folded when he was finished.

When you say that to a six year old boy who is full of pep, you can expect problems. Most of the time, Adrie was finished fifteen to twenty minutes early. The tempo of the class was set by the slow students and Adrie had nothing to do. While he was sitting with his arms folded waiting impatiently for the slow students to finish their task, he had lots of time to think which got him into trouble.

One day after he had finished his task, he was looking with great interest at his inkwell. If this inkwell was the ocean, he pretended, he could create a storm in this ocean. More or less a tempest in a tea pot. He could create a storm by blowing in the inkwell and study the results. That way he could see if his own made storm had the same effect as a storm at sea in which the low lying areas were inundated by the rising flood water. There was only one way to find out for sure by just trying it.

Yep, he had that figured right; it was a good comparison and worked very well. As soon as he blew into the inkwell the ink acted like the water of the sea; it came up inundating the land adjacent to the sea. It worked better than he had expected; even the howling of the storm was present, except the howling came from an irate teacher who wasn't impressed with his experiment at all. Adrie had great help from his teacher; she even imitated the lashes of the waves on the beach, except the lashes missed the beach completely and were hitting his behind instead. This all happened due to his successful experiment which wasn't appreciated at all.

A couple of weeks later he was again inspired by the mysterious inkwell. The teacher had told a story about the Haarlemmer Lake which was the largest lake in The Netherlands. A Dutch hydraulic engineer by the nick name of "Empty Water," had drained the huge lake and where once high waves were dashing were now pastures with cows and fields of grain. It was a Dutch success story and instead of "Haarlemmer Lake" it was now called "Haarlemmer Lake Polder."

That was quite a story that had impressed him very much. This Empty Water guy sure was a clever man, Adrie thought while he was staring at his ink well. To think of it, actually, what this Empty Water guy had done, he could do too, if not better. His inkwell was the Haarlemmer Lake that he was going to drain and make fertile fields with grain and pastures with cows, come hell or high water! He could drain this lake in a heck of a hurry with his blotting paper from his exercise book. All he had to do was roll it up and stick it in his inkwell and the Haarlemmer Lake would be dry in no time.

Boy, did that water of the Haarlemmer Lake go down fast, it was an improvement on what this Empty Water guy had accomplished. In no time at all the Haarlemmer Lake was drained and he was ready for the bows. He could bet on it that he could teach this hydraulic engineer a lesson in hydraulics. What had taken him years to accomplish, he had done in seconds. This was not just a stride forward in science; this was a giant step for mankind in the future. While he was dreaming away, he could see in his mind the cows grazing in the pastures and the stooks of grain standing in the fertile fields. This was hydraulics at its best! He was sure to get the Nobel Prize for his accomplishment to save thousands of people from starvation.

While he was admiring his masterpiece, he was suddenly interrupted by his mad teacher who didn't seem to share his view on ingenuity in draining this little miniature Haarlemmer Lake. As a token of appreciation for his contribution in hydraulics, he didn't win the Nobel Prize. No, he got a spanking with the stick which came out of the corner of the classroom for this special occasion.

It seemed that a prophet is never honored in his own country and neither is a scientist. In this strange world appreciation was totally lacking; he was a scientist who was going to make this world a better place to live in but listening to his teacher he was a bellwether full of wantonness who did everything out of pure mischief. She concluded her praise about this young scientist by stating that he never had learned anything; he was like a fox that loses his hair but not his tricks.

Well, what do you know? The problem with his teacher was, she tried to fight progress and didn't have the foggiest idea about the life of an inventor. In order to be an inventor, you had to be curious and try to find out what makes the thing tick. Needless to say that he possessed all those qualities and talents but they had done him no good. This dumbbell of a teacher thought that everything had already been invented by Thomas Alpha Edison but she had it all wrong. This was just the beginning of a new era.

There was a report card three times a year which showed how well the students were doing or how bad they were doing. The report card was marked with marks from one to ten with ten representing one hundred percent and it came in three colors; white, black and red. As long as there was only black and white on the report card it was alright. If there was also red, Adrie was in trouble. All marks from six and higher were written in black ink and marks under six, including five and a half were written in red. That probably meant that you were in the red. The parents only had to open the report card to see if it was any good and if there were red marks on the report card there was hell to pay and instant doom followed automatically.

In spite that Adrie was the top student of the class, he had significant trouble keeping the red marks out of his report card. The report card gave marks for all the subjects that were taught but also included marks for Neatness, Industriousness, Behavior and Writing.

Industriousness was not a problem; Adrie was always finished first with his tasks. The teacher couldn't deny that and after he had finished his task he did a lot of extra work like blowing in the inkwell and sucking the ink out of the inkwell with his blotting paper. He was so industrious that his teacher had to become industrious herself to fill his inkwell. If that wasn't industrious, what is? The teacher had no problem with that and gave him a seven or an eight. Actually, that was a low mark for somebody that was that industrious. Ten was the highest mark she could give but even that didn't do him any justice; it was too low for his industriousness.

However, neatness attracted quite often a five. The trouble was that he wrote too fast which gave him a bad mark for writing but his poor writing didn't translate into neatness in his exercise books either so he could end up with two bad marks for his poor writing. It was a double whammy.

When he got a red mark for writing, his parents gave him extra work in writing at home. He learned to write slower and his mark improved dramatically. His behaviour mark was quite often a five and he could end up with three red marks. Luckily, Adrie had never more than two red marks on his report card or else he might have failed a grade. More than two red marks was usually an indication of not passing your grade. They could have made an exception for Adrie; it would be stupid to fail him a grade because of his bad behavior. If they had given marks for bad behaviour he would have had a good mark too.

Only once did he get a red mark for one of the subjects; it was for Dutch language. He seldom made a mistake in the spelling of words without even trying. He should never have had a red mark for Dutch language but he did. Whenever there was a mistake made in the spelling, the teacher underlined it with red ink and the students had to write the words she had underlined underneath the exercise the proper way. That way the students should get the hang of the correct spelling.

That took up some room in the exercise book and that's what Adrie wanted. When the exercise book was full he could take it home and he needed that book for the dry flower collection that he had started. The sooner the book was full, the sooner would he have the book to put the dried flowers in. On purpose he made mistakes that he had to re-write because he needed that book desperately.

Everything worked exactly as expected; the book was full much sooner than under normal circumstances. When his book was full, he took it home to put his flowers in. Once he had the book home, he didn't have to make any more mistakes and went back to normal. Unfortunately, it was too late and he got a red five on his report card for Dutch language. He had been so smart that he outsmarted himself.

Adrie's father and mother were not impressed and thought that he had a problem with the spelling so they gave him extra work at night in spelling exercises. His next report card showed a significant improvement in Dutch Language, he had a nine. That made his father and mother think that the extra work they had given him in spelling really had helped a lot.

The three tone report card, which showed red marks, was a disaster for the pupils who got their knuckles rapped by their parents. No matter how bad your report card was, you had to show it to your parents. When the teachers handed the report card over to the students, they had to take it home to be signed by their father to indicate that he had seen it.

(Johnnie came home and asked his father: "Dad, can you write your signature with your eyes closed?" When his father indicated that he could, Johnnie said: "O.K. then, could you put your signature on my report card with your eyes closed?")

(It was no problem to get a good mark for arithmetic, that was his best subject but some kids had a bad mark. When Peter had a bad mark for arithmetic, his father raised hell. Peter said indignantly: "I don't understand that you of all people has to raise hell about my mark for arithmetic. You can't even pick the six winning numbers of the 6/49 lottery.")

(Dick had a problem with his home work when his dad was watching his favorite T.V. program. "Dad where are the Alps?" Dick asked his father.

"Ask your mother she puts everything away," was the answer Dick received.)

(A little boy asked the teacher scepticaly,"Do you get paid for teaching us?" The teacher answered with a smile, "Yes." The boy said: "What a world this is! We do all the work and you get paid. That's ridiculous."

The report card came three times a year. At the end of a Grade there was always Parents Night to give the teachers the opportunity to belly ache about Adrie's behavior. A person might encounter a sore head the morning after the ball if he had been drinking too much Seven Up. The morning after Parents Night could give Adrie a sore behind if the teacher had told his parents that he was misbehaving at school. It was like a suspense movie, he could figure that the teacher had blabbered about him; the big question was how much?

Very carefully, he took his seat at the table to eat breakfast. He sure didn't want to draw attention before the lecture of his parents which was coming up fast. Of course, he was kind of curious what the teacher had said about him. From past experience, he could figure that it wasn't very good and he wasn't about to ask. Sooner or later, it would be revealed to him, probably sooner. Whenever his father or mother opened their mouth or coughed by accident, he was alert, instantly on guard and prepared to be struck by lightning.

In spite that Adrie had the best marks of the class for Arithmetic, Dutch language, History and Geography, the teacher had talked about him and it wasn't favorable. For punishment he had to go to bed at night one hour earlier as usual to smarten him up.

It just wasn't fair; he already had been punished by the teacher and after parents night, he was punished once more after his good deeds had been revealed to his parents. To top it off, the Reverend said that God would punish your sins in the hereafter. No wonder they were saying that crime didn't pay; they hit you over the head three times.

In order to improve on this hopeless situation between student and teacher, he could have tried behaving. He wasn't unwilling to do just that but there was a problem, he was a Homo sapiens which made it hard to denounce his descendants. That was next to impossible. I am who I am, so willy nilly he had to experiment whether it was appreciated or not, with dire consequences.

Adrie didn't pray for a better relationship with his teacher but miracles do happen. Something happened to his teacher that made her change her view about him. She probably had been on the Road to Damascus.

Since the children received their preliminary education in a Christian school, the children had to listen to a Bible story every morning. One time after she had ended her Bible story, she scanned the class and asked: "Does anyone of you know a fitting hymn to this Bible story, which we can sing together?"

Most of the kids looked dumbfounded at her but nobody raised his or her hand. Adrie knew about 90% of all the hymns and had no problem to think of a fitting hymn that would hit the nail right on the head so proudly he raised his hand. When he told her the hymn that would compliment her Bible story, she was amazed about his brightness. He had gained instant admiration from her.

From there on, she would ask every morning after her Bible story for a fitting hymn that they could sing. He became her official hymn advisor. At last she saw the light after a long dark tunnel. Hopefully the light she saw was not from an oncoming train.

Adrie could see a vast difference; she even started to favor him. For the first time since she had become his teacher, she started to appreciate his talents. It was a blooming pity that she hadn't discovered his talents sooner so he would have had more mileage out of it. However, better late than never, he was thinking. If she had seen the genius in him sooner, she would certainly have learned to appreciate his inventions, especially the one with the storm at sea in his inkwell and the one of the Haarlemmer Lake, also in his inkwell.

(Why are you shaking your head in disbelief? If you believe that dinosaurs can be re-created from D.N.A. you should have no problem believing in this philosophy.)

With less than three months before the end of Grade Two this miracle happened. It makes this story more or less like another Hollywood movie with a happy ending. However, the story is not finished yet, it's only starting.

GLEANING WHEAT

Once Adrie had reached the critical age when he was old enough to go to school, he was also old enough to put his two cents worth into the egg production and to do some wheat gleaning. Was he ever proud that he was at last good for something! At night he wasn't that proud anymore, it had been a long day and he was tired.

Since Willie and Adrie had to go to school, they could only help when they had their holidays. With Adrie joining the forces to combat the Depression, the egg production had become a family enterprise. Ko was the hardest worker of the family; she got up with the chickens so she could pick up chicken feed on the wheat land but first of all she had to make breakfast for the family.

Making breakfast wasn't the only thing she had to do; they had to take along a warm lunch. She had to boil potatoes and vegetables that were mashed together. In order to keep the food piping hot, the pan with hot mashed food was wrapped in several layers of newspapers. Next, an old coat and a woolen blanket were wrapped around this package to enhance the insulation. The blankets that were used in winter on the beds to keep them warm served well in summer to keep the food warm. In spite of the primitive methods, the food was piping hot at noon; you could easily burn your tongue on it.

There was an urgent need for transportation of the supplies and also to transport the picked up wheat and straw back home. Arie knew also a way to solve that problem. The Arabs carry their babies on their back but Ko wasn't an Arab and had bought a second hand baby carriage that was used first for Willie and later for Adrie. Ko had also transported whole car loads of flowers that Adrie had picked with the carriage.

The baby carriage had been retired and was standing in a corner of the bike shed but the baby carriage came out of retirement and had to serve them for a long time yet. It didn't owe them any money but Arie wasn't finished with it. He stripped the baby carriage until the under frame with the wheels was left and mounted a big wooden box on top of it. All of a sudden it wasn't a baby carriage anymore; it was now a hand pushed cart that could be used for transportation. They had instant transportation and it had cost nothing to make it. The very first car that the family had was a baby car.... (carriage).

Adrie learned a lot in those hard times, he learned to survive and improvise. With little you could do a lot; everything had a double or triple function and everything was recycled once or twice. They were so inventive that if Thomas Alva Edison hadn't invented the electric light, they would have invented it. Edison beat them to it. Besides, all important inventions had been made by U.S. bike repair men Graham Bell, Thomas Alva Edison and the Wright Brothers. That left them out.

Well prepared, they went to the wheat land with a carpenter's apron to put the loose wheat heads in. The heads that had some straw on it were picked up and held in the hand as a bouquet of flowers. As soon as somebody had a hand full of wheat, Arie would come with a gunny bag and his pocket knife to cut the heads off the straw. The heads went in the gunny bag and even the straw was taken home. They had a use for everything. That straw was thrown in the chicken coup for the chickens to lie in. Everything possible was done to please the chickens because they were the egg suppliers.

With the four of them they covered a swath and when they came to the end of the land, they turned around to do another swath. When they were finished with the land there were very few wheat heads left, if any.

The daily program was very strenuous, especially for Adrie who was the youngest. At one time he wanted to help desperately and now he had to help, he wished he was too young again to do anything. The daily schedule was as follows.

7.00 A.M. Rise and shine for breakfast.

7.30 A.M. Load up the cart and walk to the wheat land.

8.00 A.M. Start of the daily task, gleaning.

8.40 A.M. Arie had to leave to go stamping because he had to get a stamp on his relief card in order to qualify for relief. He was back in a little over an hour to resume his work.

10.00 A.M. Coffee break with a sandwich.

12.00 Noon. Till 1.00 P.M. Lunch time.

This was the time that the hot meal was consumed and KO would read a chapter from the Bible that was always taken along every day.

3.00 P.M. Coffee break again. They always took lots of coffee along because it was a long day. Coffee was kept warm in crocks, the same way as the food was kept warm with layers of newspapers and old coats and blankets. The coffee was still warm in the afternoon thanks to the well-working primitive method.

(The thermos bottle hadn't been invented yet and even if it had been invented

it wouldn't have made any difference. They wouldn't have been able to buy it anyway. A thermos bottle is a remarkable thing; it can keep things warm but also cold. The question is, "How does a bottle know whether you want it hot or cold?")

6.00 P.M. Loading up wheat and straw and walking home.

7.00 P.M. Supper, usually five slices of bread with a fried egg, thanks to the chickens.

8.00 P.M. Children's bed time.

(A daily program like this looks worse than a sweatshop. If you would show this work roster to the authorities today, they would step in and call it child abuse. If parents today made their children of six and nine work like this, the children would be taken away from them. During the Depression, everything was geared for survival, the children had to roll up their sleeves and their help was needed. They had to pitch in to get food on the table.)

Taking the coffee breaks into consideration, they worked nine hours per day and on Saturday they only worked eight hours. So there was a total work week of 53 hours for which they were rewarded 10 cents per week and a one cent ice cream cone. It meant that they were working 5.3 hours for one penny. (Anybody interested in a job like this?)

That didn't mean that they had every week 10 cents to spend because that money had to go into their piggy bank. The only direct reward was the ice cream cone. When it was hot on the land the children would think about the once a week ice cream they would consume on Saturday night. Arie and Ko found that the children should be rewarded somehow for all the hard work they did. Actually, the ice cream cone was a pretty good incentive; normally they never would get an ice cream cone.

Besides those rewards they had fringe benefits. Two coffee breaks and an hour dinner time with Bible reading as entertainment. The family Bible was always taken along wherever they went. That might sound crazy but in those pitiful times people needed guidance to strengthen their faith. Christian families read a chapter out of the Bible every day and that way it took three and a half years to finish the Holy Book.

Besides the ice cream cone that was consumed on Saturday, they also quit an hour earlier and called it quits at five o' clock. The kids had to have time to eat their ice cream cone because they had to go to bed at eight o'clock.

To work nine hours per day was a long time for children but they had to beat the plow. After the harvest, the farmer was anxious to get his land ready for winter and would plough his land as soon as possible. They had about six weeks to pick up the wheat for the chickens to feed them an entire year.

Most farmers seeded before winter; it was called winter wheat which was favored by the farmers. It gave bigger heads and kernels which translated into more wheat production and that translated to more money in the farmer's pocket. The land had to be ploughed, manured and seeded before the night frosts came. In spite of all his effort, if there was a bad winter, the wheat would freeze and in spring he had to re-seed again. That was called summer wheat which yielded less wheat.

A lot of times the wheat was wet so it had to be dried first before it could be stored. If you didn't do that, the wheat kernels would sprout and start to grow. When it is wet it can also brood and get quite hot so that a spontaneous fire starts.

Once the wheat was dry, it was stored on the loft floor on a pile. It was feed for the chickens, but there were other hungry creatures that didn't see it that way. The wheat was also good food for rats and mice. However, nobody was interested in protecting those critters from extinction. The chickens supplied the eggs and the rats and mice were only harmful; they only supplied little turds, so they had to be caught.

Actually, in spite of the fact that it was a horrible time with degradation of the people, it still was a time that had certain enchantment. The whole family worked together the entire week with one common goal, to make ends meet and to get food on the table. It was a family enterprise, the whole family toiled all week together to keep their heads above water.

After the wheat gleaning was finished, Arie went to do some potato gleaning. There were lots of fields where they had been growing potatoes and the potato harvesters left quite a few potatoes in the field. Arie would dig around the hills and get quite a few potatoes. He was growing some potatoes himself which was not sufficient to see him through the winter until the new harvest. With the extra potatoes he dug up, he had lots of potatoes. Actually he had way too many potatoes and sold some of the surplus.

In spite that Willie and Adrie worked hard with wheat gleaning, there were strict rules at home. This was alright but what wasn't alright was that Adrie's father couldn't stand much from the children. In fact he couldn't stand anything from his children. The terrible time with its disillusionment and disappointments had probably a lot to do with it. It is hard to take that when you are forty years old, they shove you to the side like an old suit, because you are too old. That doesn't improve your humour.

The house in which they lived was a free standing house. You could walk around it or rather you could run around it, in the kids' case. They were tearing around the house like a pony running the fence in a new pasture. Only if papa wasn't home could they run around the house. If their father was home at night, he was reading the newspaper and if the kids were flying around the house, as he put it, he couldn't concentrate on his newspaper. Sometimes the kids got a warning but more often he would come outside to send them to bed. It was a long standing rule that they couldn't run around the house so it didn't come as a surprise if angry papa sent them to bed.

Willie and Adrie had smart ideas when they were playing games. They were young and not even an angry dad could stop them. Whenever they were running around the house they would bend over when they passed the window so their father wouldn't see them. In most of those cases their smart ideas back-fired. One night they were playing hide and seek, Adrie had figured out a way that his sister couldn't find him. All what he did was stand at a corner and when he heard his sister walking through the gravel; he knew what way she was coming. Before she could see him, he disappeared around the corner, walked to the next corner and played cat and mouse with her. Finally, his sister had figured him out and after walking to the corner; she double-backed tippy toe. That way she came from the opposite direction and Adrie ran right into her. Jubilantly she shouted: "I got you."

Her shout was followed by another shout, this time from their angry father who was fed up with all the shouting and before they knew it they were in their beds. Their father said he was tired and couldn't stand it that they were flying around the house. Adrie didn't understand this bologna, if he was tired how come that he and his sister had to go to bed? He should go to bed himself.

In the morning it wasn't much better. They had to go to bed early because children have to sleep the clock around, they have to grow. (Good excuse.) There were all kinds of slogans and proverbs to tell the kids how good it was to go early to bed and also to rise early.

The early bird catches the worm.

Early to bed and early to rise
Makes you healthy and wise.

Don't you believe it! The children went early to bed and indeed they woke up early, but that didn't mean that they could rise early. Their parents had a different life style and went late to bed and late to rise, which meant that the children had to stay in bed till their parents were ready to get out of bed.

No problem, they could play in their bedroom they thought. The way it turned out, there was a problem since their bedroom was adjacent to their parent's bedroom and the walls were thin. How do you play quietly when you are young and full of pep?

Their father woke up and he wasn't a bit amused to rise early to catch the famous worm. He came to the children's bedroom, gave them a spanking and sent them back into their beds. And so in spite of the proverb, the early worm got away because the early birds were sent back to bed, with hot buttocks from the spanking they had received.

"Proverbs, my foot!" Willie said quite cheesed off. "They preach them to you as Gospel but everybody takes them for granted. A good one is "Reap the day." 'When we try that, all we ever reap is an angry father and a spanking for a starter.'"

At school they had good slogans. An etching on the wall stated "Water is the healthiest drink." A smart Alec had scratched, with pencil, underneath; "But beer tastes better." The Principal wasn't amused at all. With the terrible pollution in The Netherlands it became more and more evident that beer tasted better than water. In order to make the water potable they put a lot of chlorine in it. When you made tea you could taste the chlorine. Even the water from the rain barrel wasn't what it used to be. In a lot of cases, it came as acid rain.

Yes, children had to sleep the clock around for the simple reason that it was good for them. It happened to be that what was good for the children was also good for the parents. When they were sent to bed early their parents were rid of them and had rest.

During the Depression there was very little affordable entertainment, if it cost more than nothing it was too much. One of the entertainments was singing hymns. Arie's step father, called Father Penning, had an old pedal organ. You had to pedal to get the air needed to make the music. Whenever the family came together, they would all sit around the organ and sing when Father Penning played the organ. Father Penning had trouble playing sharps and flats, so the singing didn't go all that smoothly. People didn't mind, they were entertaining themselves with what they had, even if it was far from perfect.

Father Penning repaired clocks, he wasn't a professional but he managed to fix most of them. At one time he had a clock that struck thirteen times after he had fixed it, everybody had a good laugh about that one. He had about fifteen clocks hanging on the wall in his house. Not all clocks were striking at the same time and especially when it was twelve o' clock the noise was a five minute ordeal.

Times were changing and some people now had a piano in the house to replace the organ but what really replaced the organ was the radio. More and more people had a radio except the unemployed and other poor people. The Demerwes were among the ones who didn't have a radio which didn't mean that they couldn't listen to the radio.

On Tuesday night when there was a good radio show called Snip and Snap, they went to Aunt Pietje's house to listen. It was a rather comical show with two guys who played two old ladies. For Willie and Adrie it didn't mean a thing that they didn't have a radio; they weren't allowed to stay up to listen anyway.

Their parents solved their problem and went to listen at Aunt Pietje's place, which was only a ten minute walk. Every Tuesday night, Willie and Adrie's parents went to their aunt to listen to the revue. They put the kids to bed at 7.45 and walked over to their aunt, just in time for the show. As soon as the cat leaves the house, one can expect that the mice are dancing. With their father and mother gone, the kids were dancing too. Their father and mother had a good night and so did the kids. As soon as their parents had left, they came out of bed to play cards or aggravation.

Everything went just fine until one night, after they had left and Willie and Adrie were already playing their games at the table, their father and mother had come to the discovery that they had forgotten to take something along. They came back to pick it up. Their parents sure had a surprise that five minutes after their mother had tucked them in; they were already out of bed again.

Willie and Adrie also had a surprise, because they hadn't expected that their parents would return and of course they received their scolding. There was also the threat that from now on, they would check up on the kids to see if they would stay in bed. Willie and Adrie took this threat with a grain of salt because once they were listening to the radio, they wouldn't return to see if the kids were still in bed. However, they had learned from this incident; they were more careful and waited a little longer to get out of bed, just in case those dumb people returned to pick something up they had forgotten. They also kept an eye on the street; they had trusted those people that when they said they went out to listen to the radio, they weren't supposed to return till a few hours later.

Just in case their father and mother made good on their threat to check up on them, they were prepared to slip back into bed in seconds before they entered the house. They never had baby sitters, their parents couldn't afford it. Besides Willie and Adrie were alright by themselves, except they didn't go to sleep but played games instead. That way everybody had a good Tuesday night.

Adrie and his sister would fight each other all day about whose turn it was to lick out the porridge pan. Even the film on the milk caused an argument; they took turns for that as well. The old cheese rind was a delicacy after you put it on the stove to bake. They watched each other like hawks to see if the pieces were the same size and would scream murder if they thought they weren't. Amazingly, on Tuesday night they were such good friends. Ten minutes after their father and mother left, they would be contemplating if the coast was clear to get out of bed to play their games.

There was only one house key which had to be used by four people. The only way that would work was if they had a hiding place. Arie had an idea; he put the key on the ground, put a small can over it, and put a bigger can over the small can, next a pot over the big can and a big pan over the pot. To finish it off, he put a small pail over the pan and a bigger pail over the small pail. He thought that if people would look underneath the pail, to find another pail and a pan and a pot. Before they would see the can, they would think it was just a bunch of old pots and pans, give up and quit turning over utensils.

Not so; he had under-estimated the curiosity of boys. One day, Adrie had some friends playing with him at the back of the house, when one of the boys wondered what was underneath the pail; he lifted the pail and saw another pail. He lifted the next pail, the pan and the pot and was down to the big can. He thought this was a big joke, put all the utensils back in place and called the other boys to show them. When Adrie found out that the secret hiding place was just about to be discovered, he prevented him from turning over the last can. At night he told his parents that the hiding place wasn't safe, so they had to find a better one.

There was a little shelf for the pee pot and it was close to the little bathroom window. That was an excellent place to hide the key. The little window was left ajar so you could open it from the outside to reach the key. Adrie was too short to reach the key, but an old pail turned over did fine to make the key come within his reach. Actually, he didn't need a key to get into the house; he could stand on the pail, jump up into the window opening and wiggle through it. Nobody ever found out about the new hiding place and nobody figured that there was a little shelf with a key.

A SCANDAL IN THE FAMILY

There was a song in the Bahamas which was called "A shame in the family." According to the song there was a young boy who fell in love with a girl and he wanted to marry her. He told his father about his plans and asked his dad what he thought about it. When his father heard the name of the girl, he had the shock of his life. This girl was his illegitimate child with another woman. He told his son: "You can't marry this girl because she is your sister! Don't tell anybody what I told you because that would be a shame in the family."

The boy was devastated and his mother asked what his problem was. At first he didn't want to tell her but he finally caved in. He told his mother that he had fallen in love with a girl but he couldn't marry her because she was his sister and begged his mother not to tell anybody because it would be a shame in the family.

His mother said: "Listen boy, go and marry this girl; this old fool of a husband of mine thinks he is your father but he is not and this girl is not your sister. However, don't tell anybody about it because it would be a shame in the family."

In the best of families there is a shame or a scandal. Ko's family wasn't an exception to the rule. Ploon was Ko's younger sister and when she was finished with elementary school, it meant the end of her education. There was no money for further education so she had to go to work. In those days there were few factories in which girls were employed and moreover, in little towns there weren't even factories. Without any further education, household work was the only work she could tackle.

There was a farm on the Hordyk, about a ten minute walk from where Ko and Arie lived. The owner was Jan Lems. After his father died he had run the farm with his mother, who cooked, cleaned house and did all kinds of chores. She was as strong as a horse and pulled even farm wagons by hand. When Jan Lems was 66 years old, his mother was almost ninety years old and she was in senile decay. Jan Lems needed a housekeeper who also would look after his aging mother.

Ploon got the job; she lived in at the farm so she could look after the old mother. Ko often stopped in at the farm to have a cup of coffee with her sister and since Adrie didn't go to school yet, his mother took him along. That was alright with Adrie, he loved playing at the farm; there was so much to see; all those cows, pigs, chickens and horses. Another attraction of the farm was his aunt Ploon, who gave him cookies and candies. There was also Jan Lems who was the boss and owner of the farm. To Adrie, he was Jan Lems but that was just about to change.

Ploon worked hard at the farm; she cleaned the house, prepared the meals, looked after the old mother, milked the cows and went to bed with the boss. Of course, this was a secret because for sure, it would be a shame in the family.

According to the Reverend, your secret sins will always be discovered. In those days it was considered sin, especially by the church, when you had premarital sex. Why did this stupid Reverend have to be right about the discovery of secret sins? The one that gave the secret away was the baby, who was the result of sleeping together. Apparently that's not all what they did; they must have done more than sleeping in bed.

One night, Adrie was only five years old, Jan Lems came to see Ko and said to her: "Ko, can you come over to have a look at Ploon? She acts so crazy."

Ko took Adrie with her to the farm and indeed when Ko came at the farm, Ploon was in bed screaming with pain. Ko asked what the problem was and Ploon said that she had terrible cramps. Indeed she had terrible cramps; she was pregnant and was in the process of delivering her baby. To her this was not a happy occasion, to deliver a baby when she wasn't even married. It was more than a shame in the family, it was a scandal and illegitimate babies were marked as bastard on the birth certificate.

Nobody knew she was pregnant, Ko, her own sister didn't even know. Ploon had been wearing wide clothes in order to conceal her growing tummy. She hadn't even told Jan Lems who was the father of the baby and had fooled everybody except the baby. Babies are well known not to be fooled with, they come whether they are welcome or not.

If this incident had happened forty years later, nobody would have given it much thought but in that time a baby out of wedlock was a terrible thing with nasty consequences. When the baby announced it was coming, Ploon got panicky and tried to prevent the baby from coming. When her cramps came, she folded her legs to prevent the baby from entering this so hostile world. She had initially fooled her sister, but Ko had already brought three children into the world, and knew the symptoms. Ko wasn't fooled any longer; she knew all about the birds and the bees and told Jan Lems: "Get the doctor immediately and tell him that he has to deliver a baby."

It meant that Jan Lems had to jump on the bike, pedal to the doctor's house and verbally give him the message. In those days, you couldn't dial 9-11, worse, there were very few telephones. Consequently, there was about a twenty minute wait before the doctor arrived. In the meantime, Ko took care of her sister and if it hadn't been for Ploon who had been trying to prevent the baby from coming, Ko would have delivered the baby long before the doctor arrived. However, when the doctor arrived the problems were soon resolved and Ploon delivered a healthy baby girl. The baby was kind of blue when it was born because of the forced delay in being born. They called the baby girl Aplonia (calling name Plonie) after her mother.

Of course, the first question was, "Who is the father?" Jan Lems said it wasn't his baby; he was a respectable farmer and also an elder in the church and feared a scandal. Although it was obvious that Jan Lems was the father, she could have been dating another man. Ploon admitted that she had gone to bed with her boss which was good enough.

Arie Cornelis, Ploon's father, had a job to do; he had to go to tell Jan

Lems, who was a year older than he was, to become his son in law. Jan Lems asked: "What makes you think that I'm the father of that baby?"

"If you aren't the father who is?" Arie Cornelis asked. "Or do you think that the baby is from the Holy Ghost?"

"Of course not," Jan Lems replied.

(According to the Bible, Marie was conceived by the Holy Ghost and Jesus was born from the Virgin Marie. Even in her own country Palestine they didn't believe that and Marie had to go to the Temple for a candlelight ceremony for cleansing purposes. Whenever a girl was pregnant and didn't want to admit that she had had sex, her father would say: "It probably is from the Holy Ghost."

Much later the Pope declared in a Papal Bull that though Marie was conceived the normal way, she was free of sin because of the conception.)

Arie Cornelis continued: "Ploon says that you are the only one that she had sex with which means that you are the father."

Finally, Jan Lems admitted that he had had sex with Ploon and took the responsibility for the baby. He added to his confession that he would marry her. The problem of the out of wedlock baby birth was history, but more problems were waiting and it wasn't the announcement. News of the unannounced birth spread like wildfire through the family.

One of the first priorities was that the happy couple had to get married. This event could be described as putting the horse behind the carriage. Ploon had always had great dreams and expectations about her wedding day. In her dreams she had seen herself in a beautiful white wedding dress symbolizing innocence and chastity, a nice bouquet of red roses, sitting in a coach drawn by two beautiful white horses and a barn burner of a wedding party.

Well, her wedding day didn't go quite according to her dreams. Her dreams had little chance to become reality. In the first place; she was poor and couldn't afford it. However, Jan Lems had enough money to pay for a wedding party like that but things had changed. The premature baby had buggered it all up. A white wedding dress was out of the question; that would have been a big laugh, for virgins only. Of course, lots of couples had sex before marriage and quite often the bride in white (virgin) had quite a big tummy. When the bride entered the church the organ would be playing:

Here comes the bride,
Big, fat and wide.

Most of the couples tried to stay ahead of the stork. If the girl became pregnant, they got married in a hurry and got off with a whole skin. When the baby was born within seven months of their wedding day, they simply said that the baby was premature a couple of months. It was an 8 lbs. 3 oz. baby but it was premature. Yes, those premature babies were heavy in those days.

This worked both ways; even when a girl got pregnant after they got married and the baby was premature, evil tongues had it that it was a forced marriage. Forced; because of the girl being impregnated before they got married. Hypocritical people would always count the months after the wedding to determine if the baby was conceived within wedlock, even if it was born within wedlock.

Ploon didn't have a white wedding dress. It was worse; she didn't have a wedding dress at all. There wasn't a bride's wedding bouquet, no horse drawn coaches and no wedding party. When the great day of the wedding arrived, Ploon put on the best dress she had and Jan Lems put on the best suit he had, they jumped on their rusty old bikes and pedalled to Town Hall where the wedding took place. After the ceremony, they pedalled back home to have a cup of coffee with a cookie.

While they were getting married, Ko was baby sitting the premature baby, who was so premature that she came ahead of the wedding. How about that? Of course, Adrie was with his mother while she was baby sitting and when the unhappy couple returned from the wedding ceremony, Adrie was bluntly told that Jan Lems was now Uncle Jan because he had married Adrie's aunt. What do you know? In spite that there was no barn-burner of a wedding party, people talked for a long time about this wedding.

This too-late marriage wasn't the end of the degrading ceremonies that they had to put up with. The church had also something to say about the sin of premarital sex which they had committed. Normally when it was established that premarital sex had taken place, the couple had to make a confession of guilt for the Church Council because they had sinned against Article 45 of the dogma of the church. After their confession there would be an announcement in the church that Brother Sex and Sister Love had confessed their sins against Article 45. The only time that people confessed to have sinned against Article 45 was when the stork was coming while they weren't married yet. All people who had premarital sex said nothing and got away with it unless a baby spoiled their fun.

Making a confession of sinning against Article 45 for the Church Council was alright for Ploon but there was a problem for Jan Lems. He was a farmer and in those rural communities farmers were running the church. As soon as he had become an elder of the church, he was part of the church council. If you were a member of the church council you couldn't confess your guilt in front of yourself. In that case he had to confess his terrible sin of premarital sex before the whole congregation.

One Sunday morning during the regular church service, he had to kneel down in front of the church and say that he had sinned against Article 45. He also had to repent and ask the Lord for forgiveness for sinning against this famous article.

Then, the Reverend stated: "Brother Jan Lems has confessed to having sinned against Article 45 because of weakness of the flesh, and has shown real remorse. The Lord being strong himself, understands our weaknesses and is forgiving this brother because Jesus has paid for all our sins on the cross."

The word sex or premarital sex was never used; it was always sin against this dumb article. Everybody knew what it meant. The Lord had forgiven brother Jan Lems alright but people never do. Even if they forgive, they never forget what they forgave; their memory lasts a life time.

Among the so called real Christians, a girl who was engaged in pre-marital sex was considered to be a whore because she was immoral and idolatrous. All according to the Bible. According to most of the people, a whore is a woman who is engaged in promiscuous sexual intercourse for pay, but those hypocrites took it a step further. The Reverend had explained it on one occasion that, "A person who worships idols, in this case sex, instead of the Lord is idolatrous. They do not obey the Ten Commandments so they commit idolatry."

(That was quite a sermon and it wasn't on the mountain. It makes me think of the joke when Moses came down from the mountain with ten stone tablets under his arm. He said to the Israelites: "I got some good news and I got some bad news. For the good news, I got it down to only ten commandments. For the bad news, adultery is still sin.")

All this had a disastrous effect in small towns where everybody talked about it. People went by the Bible that states: "Flee from fornication," meaning "No sex before marriage." Everybody shied away from a woman like that; it was almost as bad as contacting leprosy; everybody left when they saw a woman like that coming.

It wasn't only the woman that suffered because she had an illegitimate child, illegitimate children were called bastards and mothers told their children not to play with bastards. On the birth certificate, the name of the parents weren't given; the birth certificate would say "Bastard." Christian people they are, the illegitimate child has done nothing wrong and yet he or she is an outcast. Those people that know their Bible so well are unforgiving while the Bible teaches us to forgive.

With Ploon and Jan Lems, it wasn't much better; even the family was rude and unforgiving. When Jan Lems married Ploon, he was 68 years old but Ploon's father was only 67 years old. The joke went around that the son was older than the father.

Jaap Dalm had worked for farmers when he was growing up; they had given him a raw deal. As a matter of fact, they had run him out of town. He was glad the way his life had turned around for him but he still hated farmers. He hated farmer Beet who had fired him but he tarred all farmers with the same brush, he hated them all. That included Jan Lems and Ploon, they never had done him any wrong but he hated them any way. According to him there are no good farmers, the only good farmer is a dead farmer.

On one occasion when Ko had a birthday, Ploon was present and when Jaap Dalm arrived a little later, he announced: "When I came past the farm, I saw that cholera farmer in the yard." That was Jan Lems, Ploon's husband. Ploon never moved a muscle in her face, she had heard more abusive language during her life. She was like everybody else; she absorbed it but never forgot.

Ploon left and Jaap Dalm stayed for supper which was a good opportunity to bring it up again and do some real gossiping. He said: "In the church he had to confess his sin of having sex before marriage and the Reverend had said that the Lord forgave his weakness of the flesh."

He took another sip of his coffee and continued: "The Lord forgave the weakness of the flesh alright, because he understood that even an old buck likes a green leaf." (Jan Lems was 68 and Ploon 23 when this happened.) He added: "You can believe that old cholera farmer had a whale of a good time jumping every night on his young domestic servant. This baby was certainly not the result of one time sex."

(In The Netherlands they use few four letter words but instead they use real rough language in which they wish a person all kinds of horrible diseases to describe a person they hate. Cholera farmer, typhus farmer, or pest farmer is used in the daily language. Of course, it doesn't necessarily have to be a farmer; it could be a cholera baker or a typhus blacksmith.)

Another example about sex in the thirties was about a couple, Mr. and Mrs. Verhoog who lived a few houses away from the Demerwes. Mrs. Verhoog had been married before, and when her husband died she received a substantial pension from her husband. The only problem was that if she married again she would lose the pension of her late husband. There was a way out; they decided to go to Scotland to be married by the blacksmith. In Scotland this is a tradition; they say the blacksmith welds the iron together so he can also weld (unite) people together. At the ceremony, the blacksmith seals the deal with a big bang with his hammer on the anvil.

In spite that the marriage was sealed with a big bang, this marriage wasn't recognized in The Netherlands and that way she kept her pension. It was a miserable time and Mr.Verhoog was without work but with the pension of his wife they still had a good income. They thought this was alright, but the people didn't. If the Dutch Government didn't recognize the marriage, they didn't either. One day Mrs. Verhoog had a squabble with the neighbor lady and they started to call one another names. The neighbor lady said: "If I were you I wouldn't say anything; you aren't even married; you are just a whore."

Mrs. Verhoog was so upset about this incident that she moved to the city where nobody knew her and very wisely she didn't tell anybody that she was married by a blacksmith.

THE KICK UNDER THE TABLE

After all the degrading ceremonies the newly married couple carried on with life on the farm. In the meantime Adrie went to school and was already in Grade 2. During the harvest Adrie's Aunt Ploon and his new Uncle Jan were plenty busy at the farm. Aunt Ploon helped out a lot and they asked Adrie's mother to do the housekeeping for a few weeks. When that happened, Adrie had to go to the farm for lunch. It was ten minutes farther from school than his own house but he loved it. The food at the farm was a lot better than at his own home, there was always meat and bacon with the meal and his aunt always gave him a banana and an orange.

After lunch, they always read a chapter from the Bible and since Adrie could read very well, his uncle asked him to read it aloud. Everybody was full of praise that he was only in the second grade and could read even difficult words without a problem. His younger cousins admired him because he could read from the Bible; they thought that was really smart.

In spite of all the admiration Adrie had, he also received quite often a kick under the table from his mother, when they were eating. Uncle Jan's mother was pushing ninety and was in senile decay but she had still a healthy appetite. She was a fat heavy woman who could eat like a boat worker. Unfortunately, she was a danger to herself, and didn't know what she was doing. For safety's sake Aunt Ploon had her tied down in an armchair. Since she couldn't control her potties anymore, she had cut out the bottom of the chair and had tied a big peepot under it. Whenever she had to go, she could just let go without dirtying herself.

When they were all eating lunch, that big woman was tied down in her chair and was eating her lunch as well. Aunt Ploon had to keep an eye on her all the time; you never could tell what she would do next. Whenever her plate was empty, she would throw it to Aunt Ploon shouting: "Here Ploon, it's empty."

The plate would fall in smithereens on the floor which caused a burst of laughter from Adrie's side. He never had seen anything like that in his life; it was really funny he thought. Adrie's mother didn't think it was funny and gave him a kick under the table, plus a meaningful glance crossed the table. Of course, she was right; it's sad enough that people end up that way but tell that to a seven year old boy, he doesn't understand what's going on.

The craziest thing Adrie saw was real gross. When they were eating, it could happen that the old lady did her big job on the potty. If aunt Ploon realized it, she would empty the potty and nothing further happened. However, his aunt was quite busy and she sometimes missed it and before she knew it, the old lady would grab a hand of her poop out of the potty to smear it into her hair. Adrie couldn't believe his eyes; never had he seen anything gross like that before. Yes a seven-year old boy laughs about things like that in spite of a kick under the table and sore shins.

The kick under the table was a standard way of communication between mother and son. One day when it was raining cats and dogs, Adrie's mother wanted him to stay inside because she wanted neither cats nor dogs. She already had one cat and she certainly didn't want a dog. Adrie had other ideas; he wanted to play outside and walk through deep puddles so that the water ran into his boots. Of course, you had to know where to find those places but Adrie knew them all. He could find almost anything, including trouble.

There were some indoor games to play, like dominoes, and there was a deck of cards. They even had the game "Aggravation" which was a nice game for the unemployed to play. This way the unemployed who were aggravated already could be aggravated some more.

Adrie knew a few very simple card games but he had often watched when his parents were playing Joker and wanted to learn that game more than anything else. His mother knew a trick to keep him inside the house and said: "If you stay inside the house I'll teach you and your sister how to play Joker."

It was a deal; Adrie was happy to learn playing Joker because it was an adult game and not those simple kid games. Adrie caught on pretty fast and couldn't get enough of it. At night they went to Aunt Pietje for a visit and Adrie was still full of playing Joker. He started to talk about it and got a kick under the table from his mother. His mother put her finger on her mouth indicating that he had to shut up. Adrie didn't understand why he couldn't talk about playing Joker but he got the message on their way back home. His mother said: "Never talk at Aunt Pietje's place about any card game because she thinks that playing cards is sin."

Aunt Pietje went to the same church as the Demerwes and she thought it was sin that Adrie was allowed to play cards. Adrie didn't understand it at all especially the part that playing cards was sin.

Aunt Pietje was married into the family by marrying Henk, (Ko's brother.) Henk was a loner like his father and it was a miracle that he got married. One day he came to Ko's birthday in the morning to wish her a Happy Birthday. He came early in the morning so there wouldn't be any other visitors. That back fired, while he was drinking his coffee he saw Aunt Ploon coming who was also his sister. In a hurry, he gulped up his coffee, looked at his watch and said: "I better get home to feed the chickens."

To him two was company and three was a crowd. Henk was in the Dutch Navy and served in the Dutch East Indies. He was there for two years at a stretch. It took over six weeks to sail to the Indies so the Government had decided to keep their people there for two years before giving them two months leave.

Consequently, all his children were born two years apart. Henk just went home on leave to make another baby. When he came home he saw for the first time his baby who was almost two years old and put another baby in the oven. There was enough proof that her children were not from the milk man. She had two daughters and two sons and was mostly alone by herself to raise her family. Actually Henk was doing alright for himself in spite of the long stretches away from home. The years that he served in the Tropics counted for double which gave him a very good pension when he retired.

To Adrie, the woman who Uncle Henk had married was known as Aunt Pietje but her children called her "Pietje Poker." Whenever her children misbehaved, she gave them a spanking with the poker. She sure deserved her nick name and her excuse to use the poker was that it was the only way to beat some sense into the children if that was possible.

By the rest of the family she was known as "The Complainer." She was always complaining about her aches and pains and about the big house she had to clean. It was too much work to keep it clean. Actually Uncle Henk and Aunt Pietje were a well matched couple. She could talk and gossip to no end and he would seldom say anything. When she was talking it probably went into one ear and got out of the other ear. If she had handed him a note that said: "I lost my voice," he would have been quite happy.

Adrie knew somebody he could talk to about playing cards, it was his Uncle Jaap Dalm. He loved to play Joker and came over quite frequently to play cards. The only thing that he didn't like was when the women were talking during the game. That was holding up the card game and he would always say: "I can peel the potatoes before it's my turn again the way you women play!"

When Adrie told him that Aunt Pietje thought that playing cards was sin; his Uncle Jaap said: "That dumb woman doesn't know what sin is. If you are putting butter on your butt while you are eating dry bread; that is sin!"

Adrie had to think about this statement for a while but after due consideration he thought that it was funny and he laughed about it. His Uncle Jaap could make the craziest remarks and Adrie liked it. It occurred to Adrie that they would never commit that sin because they had never butter in the house. Butter cost too much money so margarine replaced the butter.

Arie and Ko had numerous fruit trees in their garden and one was a plum tree with delicious plums. When the plums were ripe, Uncle Jaap would never miss coming a few times to eat some of those delicious plums. One time when he came, he was kind of late and it was already dark which meant that they had to get their plums in the dark. There had been a storm and quite a few ripe plums had dropped on the ground which made it easy; all they had to do was pick them off the ground.

Adrie had followed his father and Uncle Jaap, if they were going to eat plums, so was he. Putting a few delicious plums behind his teeth was his favourite pastime. After swallowing a few plums, Uncle Jaap asked: "Say Arie, are there plums that don't have a stone?"

Arie answered: "No, all plums have a stone in them."

"In that case, I must have swallowed a slug," was Uncle Jaap's reply.

There were lots of slugs in the garden that were as large as a plum but if he had swallowed a slug he would have tasted it. He probably had swallowed the stone and thought there was no stone in it. However, after this incident he became known as the slug eating uncle.

THE COMPLAINT DEPARTMENT

The complaint department was manned by Adrie's father and mother. If Adrie had caused damage, he had to pay for that out of his piggybank. Other complaints attracted a licking or early to bed or both. It seemed to Adrie that whenever there was a complaint, those people were always right and he was always wrong.

In spite of the strictness of his parents, people didn't have to come with childish or silly complaints, his parents didn't appreciate that. One of those silly complaints came in when he had made a go cart from the old baby carriage. The go cart lacked an engine, you had to push it, but for the rest it had everything. It had a real steering wheel with two strings which made the cart change direction when you turned the steering wheel. There was even a horn in the car; they just shouted beep-beep or toot-toot. Another needed feature was a brake and Adrie had made it. One could say that the brake was primitive and that it malfunctioned. They actually should have recalled that model race wagon for brake defects but unfortunately it was already too late.

This brake was Adrie's personal invention and he was mighty proud of it. One could say that it was the last great invention in modern brake technique. It was also very simple, so that spare parts were always readily available. All what was required to brake the cart was a stick that you could stick between the spokes of the wheel. The wheel wouldn't turn anymore and drag over the road which slowed the cart down in a hurry. It was magnificent and it worked like a charm. He should have patented his invention and sold it for big bucks to General Motors.

Wout Koekoek, a boy of Adrie's age, lived across the street and he was very interested in this great invention. Wout asked if he could have a ride in Adrie's cart, which also meant that Adrie had to push him. Why not; Adrie didn't mind to push his admirers, that way they could see for themselves what a great inventor he was.

In order to make the cart go faster, Adrie pushed him down the hill. By the time they came to the bottom of the hill, the cart had quite a speed so it was time to test the brakes. Wout Koekoek took the stick and pushed it between the spokes the same way as he had seen Adrie do it. The brakes worked perfect alright, too perfect. The wheel came to an abrupt halt and because it was blocked, the car turned sideways and toppled over. Of course, there had to be a brick wall and of course Wout Koekoek had to fall with his head against it. Blood was flowing through the arena and Wout Koekoek was squealing like a pig which they are about to butcher. Wout ran home screaming for his mother and Adrie decided to go home as well. He had to check the braking system of the car and start all over again from square one.

At night, Adrie didn't think about the incident anymore but he was unpleasantly reminded of the accident. There was a knock on the door and his father answered the door. Adrie looked around the corner to see who was at the door. When he saw Wout Koekoek's father, he could figure that he wasn't about to praise Adrie for the king size hole in his son's head. He thought it better not to show himself and stayed out of sight but curiosity will kill the cat, so he stayed to listen.

The old Koekoek said to Adrie's father: "I came here to complain about your son!"

Adrie's dad asked: "What has he done this time?"

"Your son is a rough devil and a danger to society; thanks to him, my son has a nasty hole in his head!"

"How did this all happen?"

"It happened with that stupid cart your son has made. They are flying like idiots through the street with that car, so you can expect nothing but accidents as you can see!"

To Adrie's great surprise, he heard his father say: "Well, why are you coming to tell me all this, I can't fix the hole in your son's head. You should go to a doctor instead, he can fix it. If my son had thrown a stone against his head, you have the right to complain but when your son by accident falls out of the cart, nobody can help that and it's silly to blame my son for it."

The complaining Koekoek hit the road and Adrie's father came back in the living room. His mother had heard part of the discussion and asked: "What was that all about?"

After Adrie's father told his mother about the complaint, his mother said: "That stupid guy has always something to bitch about; he probably thinks that his son is a Saint!"

Adrie's mother said to Adrie: "You are better off not to play with that boy anymore, those people are so childish!"

Adrie couldn't agree more; he had been good enough to give him a ride in his brand new cart with the latest inventions and what did he get for thanks? A silly complaint! That was the first time that complaints were not taken seriously, and for a change his parents were on his side. However, there was another incident where the complaints were rejected by the complaint department.

When Adrie and his friends were growing up they were playing most of the time in the polder. (A polder is a low lying area between rivers with a lot of ditches that surround the fields.) You could say that the kids were growing up in the polder; they were always jumping ditches and playing games. Of course, it happened that nature called while they were playing and when you got to go, you got to go. They did the same as the farmers who worked the field, they didn't go home to extend their back bone; they just dropped their pants at the side of the ditch to do their business. Since there was no roll of toilet paper hanging at the ditch side, they just took a handful of grass to polish their bum. That was the natural way and rural people never gave it a thought.

However, there was a man with the very long name Piet Put, who had a son with a long name as well, Dick Put. Piet Put was born in the city and in the city there are no fields with ditches to relieve yourself. However, people in the city don't dirty their pants either when they got to go.

In those days there were no service stations, there were only gas pumps and you couldn't use the bathroom of a service station. In order to help people out in the busy part of the city, they had placed urinals where you could have a leak only. Those urinals didn't have white stone fixtures, they simply had a hole in the ground which was connected to the sewer, similar to a drain in your basement floor and it looked identical too. People who were in need of a bathroom to do their big job would pretend they were going in for a leak, but instead they would drop their pants and let go.

Some people didn't aim too well and didn't deliver their droppings in the vicinity of the hole. It didn't take long for the urinals to become full of messy piles. If you went in for a pee, you had to watch not to step in those piles, especially when it was dark because the urinals weren't illuminated.

If you were a woman you had to sweat it out; it was a man's world and nobody gave it a thought that women had need for a bathroom as well. Of course, a hole in the ground as urinal is all right for men but women have a problem with it and need better facilities.

Actually, to relieve yourself at the ditch side was a lot better than doing it in the urinals but not according to Piet Put, who called Adrie and his friends dirty pigs who dropped their pants outside instead of in the bathroom! He had a little book store with very little business so he had all the time to spy on the kids. His favorite past time was standing on his balcony, with his binoculars, to find out what the boys were doing in the polder. That way he had found out that they did their business at the side of the ditch.

Apparently he didn't like it a bit. "Only savages do their big business in the field," he said. "Everybody else goes on the toilet." Consequently, he ordered his son not to play with Adrie and his friends anymore because they were a bad influence on him. Piet Put must have spent a lot of time spying on the boys because they weren't relieving themselves all day and every day. It was only sporadically that the need was high and they resorted to the fields.

Dick Put told Adrie and his friend Jaap what his father had said. Jaap didn't understand a bit of the whole thing and said: "What kind of an idiot is that father of yours? You have to drop your pants or else you dirty yourself."

Dick Put didn't take his father's orders too seriously and kept playing with Adrie and Jaap in the polder, to the dismay of his father. He had no other friends and liked jumping ditches.

Adrie and Jaap never gave this incident much thought and had figured that if Piet Put saw Dick in the polder with them, he probably would give him a spanking when he came home. They had never figured that Piet Put would hold them responsible for what his son did.

However, one time when they came out of the polder, they were walking home through the street and saw Piet Put in front of the house. It was obvious that he had been spying on them again and had seen his son in the polder with Adrie and Jaap. As soon as he saw the three boys, he came running towards them, gave Dick Put a kick in his behind while he was shouting: "Go to your nest you disobedient S.O.B." (In The Netherlands a bed is called quite often a nest in rude language.)

When he was finished with his son he came after Adrie and Jaap. As far as they knew, they hadn't done him any harm but judging by his angry face and the speed with which he came after them, they weren't so sure. For safety's sake they were going to get pretty fast out of there without asking any questions. They ran home as fast as their legs would carry them with the angry man close on their heels. Out of breath Adrie stormed into his house, scaring his mother with his sudden wild appearance. She asked: "What's the matter now?"

Adrie didn't even have to answer his mother's question because Piet Put was already at the door. He was breathing like a post horse and started to tell Adrie's mother that Adrie did indecent things in the polder. According to him Adrie and his friend had their pants down all the time and he kept repeating that to Adrie's mother, it was just horrible in his eyes. Since it wasn't warm at all outside, they didn't drop their pants to cool down; they only dropped them if they had to make a dropping.

Piet Put went on very excitedly and shouted: "This is no jungle, when you have to go you do those things on the toilet at home."

Adrie's mother replied: "Do you like it better that your son does it in his pants when he is far away from home?"

"I don't like it that boys drop their pants outside, it's immoral!"

"Man, don't get so excited about immorality, those boys are only eight years old and all what they do is jump ditches in the polder but when nature calls they've got to go!"

"You better stop your son from doing those immoral things because I will keep an eye on him. Those immoral things cannot be tolerated in a decent society."

The angry man left and Adrie's mother said: "Don't play with kids that have a stupid father like that. Stay away from them."

That was kid number two Adrie shouldn't play with according to his wise mother. That wasn't an order but Adrie didn't need an order, he wasn't that happy to be chased by an angry Piet Put. It seemed that Piet Put had punished his son pretty good because Dick Put stayed very wisely out of the vicinity of Adrie and Jaap, the immoral kids. Adrie and Jaap didn't care at all; they didn't need Dick Put or Piet Put to entertain themselves. They were much better off without childish people like that.

Piet Put should have seen when Gerard Ploeg was busy extending his back bone when the farmer came into the pasture. Gerard was bending as close to the ground as possible so the farmer wouldn't see him. Tough luck, the farmer spotted him and came in his direction. He was kind of caught with his pants down, as they say. However, Gerard wasn't caught that easy, not even with his pants down, he was going to take a run for it. With the farmer that close, there wasn't time to wipe his butt and he wasn't going to dirty his pants so he ran away while he had his pants down. Adrie and Jaap were standing at a safe distance to watch this comical sight. The farmer must have enjoyed it as well; at least he didn't chase Gerard.

It was a hilarious sight and they were laughing to their heart's content in spite of the immorality of the scene. Where were your binoculars Piet Put? If he had seen it, he would have sent the morality police after Gerard Ploeg if his heart hadn't stopped beating because of shock.

THE CAT CAME BACK

Of course, the children were getting all the regular children's sicknesses like measles, scarlet fever and whooping cough. When Willie went to school, she contracted all of those and after she got better Adrie got sick. This was an advantage because when Adrie went to school he already had had all those childhood sicknesses. Half the class was sick at home but Adrie was immune.

There was one sickness that Willie had that she didn't pass to Adrie. It was called "Nettle Rose," because it looked as if you had slept in the nettles. Willie's body was covered with large, itchy blisters. She had to rub a raw onion on the blisters to get some relief. In spite of the raw onion, she didn't sleep a wink. Ko figured that Adrie would get it too but luckily that didn't happen. He had fallen in the nettles before and might have been immune, though that was not how the sickness came.

Usually, if Willie had something that Adrie didn't get he would scream murder. When he missed out on getting Nettle Rose, not a squeak was heard from Adrie. All of a sudden there was something that his sister had that he didn't care for.

With all those children's sicknesses, it was very important that a proper diagnosis was made by the doctor. Ko had a problem with that; she had a very old doctor, Doctor Moll. He had been a good doctor and had done yeoman service for the people of Yselmonde. His business was booming when the sprawling town was building more and more houses. With more and more people settling on the dykes, a young doctor by the name of Dr. Meerkerk moved in.

People now had a choice of two doctors, some stayed with Dr. Moll and others took the young Dr. Meerkerk. Ko had stayed with Dr. Moll because he had more experience than a young doctor. That was smart thinking, but when Dr. Moll got older he became as deaf as a stone which made it difficult to practice medicine. The only hearing aid there was in those days was to shout in the deaf man's ear.

At one occasion when Willie had a problem, Dr. Moll was called in. He examined her and asked Ko if she had pain. Ko said: "Yes, she has a terrible head ache."

Dr. Moll replied: "Oh yes, a little belly ache." He prescribed some medicine and left.

Ko wasn't satisfied at all and wondered about his diagnosis. She now was getting belly ache medicine for a head ache. That was it; Dr. Moll was a nice man alright but he had to go. Right after Dr. Moll had left, Ko called Dr. Meerkerk and told him what had happened. From there on Dr. Meerkerk was the doctor in charge.

(Ko wasn't the only one who wasn't satisfied with the services of her doctor. An elderly gentleman wasn't feeling well and became irritated with his doctor because he wasn't getting better after five visits. "Look," said the doctor, " I'm doing all I can to help you. I can't make you any younger!"

"I wasn't particularly interested in getting younger," said the man, "I just want to continue to grow older.")

Some people wondered if this young Dr. Meerkerk was on the ball and knew his stuff. A kind of smart guy was going to find out. When he had to bring back a urine sample so the doctor could determine what his problem was, he filled the bottle with horse piss. When he made his visit to find out what the doctor had found that caused his problem, Dr. Meerkerk said: "From your urine sample I found that you should give that horse more oats." Indeed Dr. Meerkerk knew his stuff and wasn't going to be fooled.

In those days if you needed a doctor there was no phone to call him, so somebody had to jump on his bike to deliver a verbal message to the doctor. In the waiting room there was no bell or telephone to ask for the next patient.

When the doctor was finished with a patient, he would just say to the leaving patient: "On your way out ask the next patient to come in."

In the early Depression years, Willie and Adrie didn't own a cat, yet they had a cat in their house. It was the cat of the neighbors which came as a regular beggar to their home for hand outs. The cat knew exactly when they were eating; she never missed a meal. As faithful as a dog she came to the house, day after day, for favours. She could always count on Adrie to give up a small piece of cheese, from the small piece of cheese which he had on his bread. A cat is just like God; she never looks if you give her a big piece of cheese, even a small piece is welcome. The cat looks into your heart, if you can share with her.

The cat was Adrie's pet and in return the cat made Adrie her pet. This resulted in getting all the kittens in his bed when she had a litter. For the cat, the timing was right, just when Adrie had one of his children's sicknesses, she had her litter and as a concerned mother she was looking for a good place for her young.

To make it easier for Adrie's mother and more pleasant for Adrie, his mother had put his bed in the living room. When the cat came for her piece of cheese, she saw a good place for her litter and went back right away to get her young kittens. She was as busy as a working bee to drag all her kittens into Adrie's bed. According to her knowledge this was the best place in the world for her kittens.

Was Adrie ever excited to get all those kittens in his bed; all of a sudden he wasn't bored anymore. Somebody else was also excited. The neighbor boy came out of school and saw that the kittens were gone. Where did they go? When he found out where the kittens were he came right away to get them.

A cat can be stubborn; as soon as the neighbor boy left for school, the cat was busy taking her litter back to the best place in the world. You couldn't tell that cat anything; she knew a good place when she saw it.

Adrie's aunt had also a cat and when her cat had a litter, she gave one of the kittens to Willie and Adrie. They called their cat "Meepee." It was only a little kitten but in spite of that, the neighbor's cat never showed up again. Territorial rights are respected in nature.

Meepee never went hungry; she ate the table scraps and what ever she could beg from Willie and Adrie. Ko used to cook a couple of extra potatoes, mashed them, put some watery gravy on it and there was the cat's meal. For breakfast she crumbled some bread in a dish, poured a little bit of skim milk on it and breakfast was ready. Everybody survived on those skimpy meals and so did the cat. They had low-quality food, so the cat only saw a little piece of cheese, meat, fish or egg at a time.

One day there was a surprise for Meepee. With the few chickens they were keeping, it was possible to have an egg for breakfast. Ko would beat up a couple of eggs and fry them for breakfast. She would also beat up an egg for Arie and mix it with sugar. Arie had asthma and the doctor had ordered every morning an egg mixed with sugar. One morning Ko bungled, she had beaten up the eggs they were going to eat in a big mug. She also beat up an egg for Arie and put some sugar in it. Ko was in a hurry and put by mistake the beat-up egg with sugar in the frying pan. They tried to eat it on their bread but a fried egg with sugar tastes terrible. Ko said: "I'll fry another egg; fried egg with sugar doesn't taste good at all. The cat can eat the fried egg with sugar; she doesn't mind an egg with sugar."

Ko put the egg with sugar on a plate and put it on the floor for the cat. The cat dashed away from the plate with the egg, she never got a whole egg in her life so this couldn't be right. Whenever the cat ate egg, it would be just a little piece Willie or Adrie gave her. The cat was used to get hell even if she looked at a fried egg.

It took some coaxing to persuade the cat to eat the egg. They had to break it up into little pieces and give her a little piece at a time. An animal isn't dumb; they know their stuff. You teach the cat to stay away from the food you are preparing and give her a whack if she doesn't. Don't try to give her a whole egg because she just won't take it.

When they ate fish, the centre bone and the head was for the cat. They never fried the fish head, the cat ate it raw. The cat almost had competition for the fish heads. There was this Prime Minister by the name of Colyn who wanted to give the fish heads to the unemployed people. He said there was a lot of good food in fish heads. In spite of all the good food in fish heads, he ate steak himself.

In spite of the food she was given and the mice and birds she caught, Meepee didn't live very long. She got pregnant and didn't survive the ordeal. One night, the family came home and the cat was crying at the other side of the fence. She always jumped on the fence but this time she couldn't. Adrie went to get her and everything seemed to be normal when everybody went to bed.

The next day, Adrie went to school in the morning and when he came home for lunch, he wondered where the cat was. His father already knew that the cat was dead; he probably should have told him. Instead he said: "The cat is sleeping in front of the wheat pile."

That was her favourite spot. There was a pile of wheat dumped in the loft; that was chicken feed. Of course, it was also mice feed which attracted mice and this in turn attracted the cat. When Adrie went upstairs, the cat was indeed lying in front of her favourite wheat pile, but she was dead. A couple of feet away from her was a dead kitten she had delivered. Usually a cat delivers more than one kitten, so the rest must have succumbed when the delivery got into trouble. It's not often that cats have trouble with delivering a litter because the kittens are very small but it probably was an internal bleeding.

It was the first time in Adrie's life that he was confronted with death and it hit him pretty hard that his pet was gone. He was inconsolable; his mother didn't even manage to comfort him. Adrie didn't even want to go to school, what was the use? Luckily, his friend came calling on him to walk to school together. To his mother it was a God-sent help.

The nine lives of the cat are legendary but when Meepee died she didn't return to live her next life. However, after Adrie came out of school there was another consolation. They just started dinner and guess who came for dinner? It was the neighbor's cat! As soon as Meepee was buried, she came back to reclaim her rightful place. The cat knew when there was another cat and she also knew when the cat was gone. She probably thought: "A house without a cat is not a house. Those people need a cat." So the cat came back and Adrie had a cat again.

(What is an octopus? Answer: A cat with one life left.)

There was another illness which was not restricted to children, it was tuberculosis. However, quite a few children contracted tuberculosis because they were underfed and had very little resistance against diseases.

Tuberculosis of the lungs is called consumption because it consumes your body; it makes you skinnier and skinnier and wastes away your entire body. It was a very contagious disease; people who had contracted it had to be quarantined. They built a little shed at an outer corner of the pasture, surrounded it with barbed wire and put a sign on it that the shed was occupied by a person who had consumption. People wouldn't even come close to the barbed wire lest they would get consumption as well.

The family of the person that had consumption would bring food to the victim through a small window. Once you were lying in a little shed like that, the only way you would get out was dead in a pine box. Never alive! Several people, who were diagnosed as having consumption, just slit their wrist to get it over with.

The battle against tuberculosis started with the invention of the X Ray or Roentgen photo. X Rays are capable of penetrating body tissue which makes it possible to obtain a photo of the lungs to study if tuberculosis is present. Early detection was crucial to have success with the treatment. Many sanatoriums were built to nurse the victims back to health if possible.

A truck with an X ray machine came through the street once per year. It was compulsory to have your lungs X rayed. If anything was wrong, your doctor was notified and the doctor would take the necessary steps to get you in a sanatorium for a rest cure.

In the sanatorium they tried to make you as fat as the fattened calf so your body had ammunition to fight off the dreadful disease. They bombarded you with glasses of milk and eggs to fatten you up because that was good for you. Treating consumption is similar to treating cancer; the earlier it is detected the better the chance of survival. Many people were infected by cows which had tuberculosis. Drinking milk from those cows could easily infect you. In most of the deadly diseases of that time, the major cause of death was lack of breath. The same as today.

Cattle had as much trouble staying in good health as the people. There are as many diseases for cattle as there are for humans. Tuberculosis was very common among cows in those years and people were getting tuberculosis from the cows. The milk was pasteurised which killed the tuberculosis bacillus but the trouble was that the milk maids were in direct contact with the cows and other people were involved in getting the milk to the plant.

Tuberculosis is a very infectious and contagious disease. If the cows had it, humans were infected very easily. The Government had a great plan to get all the cows tuberculosis free. This was easier said than done because the dairy farmers were not impressed. It wasn't that they didn't want a herd free of disease; the problem was that cows with tuberculosis had to be destroyed without compensation. Most of the best milk cows had tuberculosis because the lean cows were the best milk givers. The fat cows stored more fat in their body and those cows could fight off tuberculosis easier than the scrawny cows. Tell the farmer to destroy his best milk cows without compensation and you'll see a stubborn farmer.

The Government stuck to their guns and ordered all T.B. cows destroyed. There were government inspectors to test the cows and if even one cow was found to have tuberculosis, they were not allowed to deliver milk to the milk plant. It was a financial disaster for the farmers; the cows couldn't even be used for beef, they had to be destroyed. In this unpopular and expensive way to the farmer, the cattle became tuberculosis free.

This was not the end of the farmers' nightmares and monetary problems. Hardly had he recovered from the financial disaster to make his herd T.B. free when another epidemic broke out among his cattle. This time it was hoof and mouth disease which is the most wide-spread and contagious sickness among cattle. Large blisters on the hoofs and mouth of the infected cow appear and in no time at all the cow can't eat anymore and dies. The disease is spread fast through the milk and urine and the cow has to be destroyed immediately in order to prevent the disease from spreading to other animals of the herd.

Almost all farms were posted with signs, stating: "Hoof and mouth disease. Infected area." In spite of the precautions which were taken to prevent the disease from spreading, all of The Netherlands was infected. In 1938 and

1939 the farmers lost more than half of all their cattle to the disease. Luckily, today's cattle can be vaccinated against this so costly disease of hoof and mouth disease, which is a good thing with a world cattle population of over one billion.

TAKING CARE OF DRUNKEN CHICKENS

With all the hardships that were experienced and all the emergency steps that had been taken, the Depression became a way of life with no end in sight. Everybody had multiple chores to fulfil and did his job. Two grown up people and two children were battling to keep food on the table and a roof over their head.

Children had no time to be bored; they had a host of chores to do. Some jobs were specifically done by girls and others by boys. The girls had to help their mother to peel the potatoes, clean the vegetables, make the beds and dust the furniture. They also had to do the unattractive jobs like cleaning the bathroom and emptying and cleaning the pee pots. When the girls were peeling the potatoes and could peel a potato without breaking the peel, the parents said: "You can get married when you can do that!"

Filling the wood box, fetching water from the rain barrel, keeping the weeds out of the garden and digging up the potatoes were chores the boys did. Some chores were done by boys and girls, shelling peas and cutting beans were such jobs. They also grew a lot of French beans which had to be sliced very thin. That used to be done with a very sharp knife which could easily result in injuries. When the bean slicer was invented, all you had to do was feed the beans into the slicer and turn the wheel. It remained a dangerous job; the bean slicer had two holes and you had to push the beans into the holes. The problem with this new invention was that the slicer didn't know where the bean ended and your finger started. If one wasn't careful, a little flesh of your fingers could be sliced by the mill to compliment your meal with meat.

It never had occurred to Arie and Ko that it would be worse when he went back to work. The Government had dreamed up a money making scheme at the expense of the unemployed. They had established the Crisis Committee a long time ago and they had made it possible for the unemployed to pick up meat and margarine for half the price.

That was appreciated but the next step they took was far from appreciated. There was a lot of heath and bush land in the Province of North Brabant that could be turned into wheat producing land. The Netherlands imported a lot of wheat from abroad and that would help the Dutch economy. Way back, the Government had looked at the viability of such a project but they had decided that it wasn't economical.

When the Crisis Committee had a good look at the project, they came to the conclusion that it wouldn't cost much money at all if they used the thousands of unemployed people to do the labor. They were now on relief and they could be made to work for a little bit more than their relief money. And so it was decided to make wheat land out of the beautiful Province of North Brabant. There were many beautiful trees and there was a lot of heather growing. A lot of wild life inhabited the area but it had all to go in order to get more wheat and keep the unemployed busy. The project was called "Relief Work Program." By producing more wheat of their own, it got the U.S. economy even in more trouble when The Netherlands didn't import that much wheat any more. Who cared, it was a matter of survival.

First of all, they established the Heath Exploration Company. (Unpopular called by the unemployed the "Heath Exploitation Company.") They made some movable work camps and hired some busses to transport the unemployed people to their place of employment. Dr. Colein, the Prime Minister, had said that The Netherlands weren't little Russia but with establishing work camps, he came one step closer to making it Russia.

The unemployed were paid the same money as they received on relief but there was an incentive, if they did more than their minimum task they could make one or two guilders more. Most of the times with unfavourable weather they couldn't even do their minimum set task but if they were lucky that it didn't rain too much, they sometimes managed to get a couple of extra guilders.

Even if this happened it didn't improve anything. When Arie was on relief he was home and could go gleaning to get chicken food and potatoes. The only thing that helped a little bit was that when he was in a work camp, he didn't eat at home so there was more for his family. Unfortunately, the disadvantages outweighed the advantages, there was less chicken feed and when they ran short, additional food had to be bought.

"Morning Chicken Feed" was for sale; it was flour mixed with ground fish heads. It was served first thing in the morning and only had to be mixed with a very little bit of water. The chickens were crazy about it and it was said that it improved their egg laying capacity.

All unemployed people were forced to work in labor camps or they wouldn't get relief money anymore. They went for two weeks at a stretch and left Sunday night at 8.00. It was a few hours driving and they had to start work on Monday morning at 7.30. They had to put in a nine hour working day every day and Saturday they worked five hours which gave them a total of 50 hours per week. After two weeks they would come home on Friday night after a full day's work and since they didn't work on Saturday, they only worked 45 hours that week. They came home about 10.00 p.m. which left them very little time with their family. Arie had little more time then to do some of the heavy work around the house, take a bath and go twice on Sunday to church. At night he had to leave again for another two weeks in order to participate in the rat race.

Life had changed drastically with Arie away from home. The duty of raising the kids became the sole responsibility of Ko and the workload changed as well with one man gone. Adrie was promoted immediately to chicken feeder, egg collector, rat catcher and gardener. Promotion came fast in those days.

It was almost like in the army with fast promotion. During the war a soldier can be promoted to be a Corporal when the Corporal dies and when the Sergeant dies he is immediately promoted to Sergeant. In no time at all he can become the General. When people go they have to be replaced.

In the meantime, Ko was doing some work for rich women and wasn't home in time to cook supper. Willie would have been able to do that but she also was doing some chores after school for which she got paid a little. Everything was geared to make some money to keep the wolves away from the door.

The job to cook supper went to Adrie. Ko figured that he could easily do it because he knew how to light the stove and she would peel the potatoes and cook the vegetables the night before. There was no meat so she didn't have to worry about it.

When Adrie came home from school, he lit the stove right away. First some paper with fine wood, then some coarser wood and finally coal. When the coal was burning it was time to put the potatoes on the fire. He watched the potatoes constantly so they wouldn't cook dry and burn. In no way would he let his mother down, she depended on his help and he was very proud that he could cook the supper when he was only six years old. About ten minutes before five Adrie put the vegetables on the stove so they would be hot. At five o clock everybody came home for supper, the potatoes were ready and the vegetables were hot so supper could be eaten.

Adrie had become a busy body with all his chores. The very first thing he had to do in the morning was to check the rat traps. It wasn't only the chickens that were interested in the food that was thrown in the chicken pen. There were also the uninvited rats. Jaap Dalm had thought that the chicken coop was strong enough to keep lions and tigers in it. Indeed the coop was strong enough that you could keep a lion in it and it would be difficult for the lion to get out. If the lions and tigers would encounter difficulty in breaking out of the hen house, the rats had no difficulty to get in. With all kinds of chicken food in the hen house, a lot of rats were attracted that were free loading at the chicken owner's expense.

Rats didn't just eat the chicken food that the family had obtained by the sweat of their brow; they also had a liking for the eggs. The rats would make a little hole in the egg and suck it empty. It hadn't been in the planning to feed the rats to keep them alive. They were not living in India where the rat is considered to be holy. In India, Buddhist priests feed pastry to the rats while more than a hundred thousands people starve every year.

Since there was competition for the eggs, Arie went into the rat catching business. He couldn't put poison in the chicken coup because it would kill the rats and the chickens as well. That would be like throwing the baby away with the bath water. Calling the rat catcher of Hamelin to do the job for him wasn't a good idea either because that man wants to get paid for his services and since he had no money there could be trouble.

According to legend: Once upon a time, in 1284, there was a severe rat plague in the German town of Hamelin. The rats did a lot of damage to the crop and chewed holes in the houses of the people. A Piper that strolled through the town told the people that he had a way to get rid of the rats. Of course, he didn't do it for free; they had to pay him for his services. He started to play on his pipe and led the rats to the river where they drowned. That was a job well done but when the Piper went to collect the money for services rendered, they told him that his check was in the mail. Oops, wrong again, in 1284 the checks hadn't been invented yet! Any way, the Piper was told to go to hell; he didn't get his money and was laughed at. That made the piper very angry and since there was no collection agency in those days, he took revenge by taking the children to the mountains, with his piping, where they disappeared.

Arie had no money to pay a Piper and to avoid the problem of having a mad Piper on his hand, he decided to buy rat traps and catch his own. There were different kinds of rat traps, the cage type in which the rat enters and closes the trap door, has the disadvantage that the rat is caught alive and you have to kill it yourself. Arie preferred the killing type of trap so all you have to do is throw the dead rat away.

When Adrie's father went to work in a work camp, Adrie was only six years old when he was promoted to be the official rat catcher and he wasn't even a Piper. At night, after he had put the chickens in their night coop, he set out some rat traps with cheese and a piece of bacon hide. That way the rats had a choice of menu. In the morning, before he let the chickens out of their night coop, he first checked the rat traps. The dead rats were removed and the traps were taken out of the chicken coop so that he didn't catch chickens instead of rats. He also had to feed the chickens and all that work he had to do before he went to school.

One morning, when Adrie checked the rat traps, one trap had gone off but there was no rat in it. That was no surprise; it happened more that the rat didn't get caught. He was just about to let the chickens out of their night coup when he heard a noise in the corner. It was a big rat which probably had triggered the rat trap but had escaped the deadly blow. The rat seemed to have received part of the blow, he was dazed with fright and tried to make his get-away. That Adrie had come into the chicken coop was no help to the rat and frantically he tried to escape.

Adrie wasn't just about to let him get away so he could suck some more of the precious eggs. He grabbed the rat by the tail and ran to the kitchen where his mother was, shouting: "Look Ma, what I got!"

His mother had the shock of her life when she saw the rat trying to curl up, so he could bite Adrie's hand, in order to obtain his release. She shouted: "Drop the rat because he tries to bite you." Adrie dropped the rat and his mother grabbed the coal shovel to hit him over the head. Guess who won the battle? Of course, Adrie's mother.

The chickens played a very important part in the lives of the Demerwes. Thanks to the chickens, they saw eggs on their table and sometimes they ate chicken and chicken soup. In spite that they were good to their chickens, the chickens all ended up on the chop block.

(Of course, there is the chicken's side of this story about their treatment. At the poultry farm, the chickens are lining up to have their fortune told by a gypsy chicken. The gypsy chicken looks into the crystal ball and says to the chicken: "I see a bad future for you, your chopped off head will be lying in the blood stained earth and I can see a surprised expression in your lifeless eyes.")

Anyway, love can't come from one side, so for services rendered beyond the call of duty, the chickens had a party once a year. There was even a dram to make the chickens tipsy. Who is there to say that a hard working chicken can't have a drink?

Adrie's mother made every year five bottles of black berry gin. She put the black berries into a bottle with water and sugar and let it yeast in the sun. Because of the pressure that is released when the yeasting process takes place, she couldn't put a cork on the bottles. The cork would pop long before the champagne was ready, so she put a white cloth on the bottle. Pressure would drench the cloth with gin that was being made and the cloth would become red.

This attracted dozens of beautiful butterflies that came also for a nip, they thought it was nectar. They sucked up the juice and became tipsy so that they fell off the bottle on the ground. That was a good time for Adrie to arrive because he had a butterfly collection. All he had to do was pick up the drunken butterflies which couldn't even fly away.

In Fall when the black berry gin was ready, Adrie's mother pressed the juice out of the berries. The juice gave her gin and the pulp went to the chickens. There was enough alcohol in the pulp to make the chickens drunk when they pecked up the pulp. They sure must have appreciated a nip because they finished the pulp in no time at all. Nice place to be for the chickens; where else could a chicken get a drink during the Depression?

In no time at all the chickens got drunk as a skunk and fell over. They couldn't even walk to their night coop any more so Adrie picked up the drunken chickens and put them in their coop to sleep it off. It was a funny sight to see the chickens with their head falling over to the side, staring with their glassy eyes at Adrie.

It wasn't hard at all to organize a free Happy Hour for the chickens. Nobody ate the pulp anyway, so it cost actually nothing to give the chickens a good time. They tittle tattled a bit before they were in Morpheus' arms and the next day it was business as usual.

Alcohol destroys brain cells but that didn't bother the chickens because they don't have any brains. Alcohol is also bad for the liver but since they had the chickens only for three years, they had at the best of times three parties during their short life. The chickens died long before their liver gave up. Whenever people get drunk they have the usual hang over the next day. Chickens don't seem to have that trouble, they don't even have a head ache, at least they never asked for an aspirin.

With that much gin in the chickens, they had hoped that the eggs would contain eggnog the next day instead of a plain yoke. The chickens were good but unfortunately they weren't that good.

When you keep chickens for eggs you need some new chickens every year. Some farmers were brooding some eggs, with the help of the chickens of course, because if the farmer himself would sit on the eggs with his fat behind he would break them all. Arie never went into the egg brooding business because first of all, you have to keep a rooster to fertilize the eggs. A rooster eats a lot because he has to work over all the chickens and that's hard work.

Even when you get a nest with chicks, about half of them are roosters which don't produce eggs. Arie was thinking like the big chicken farmer, he wanted to see eggs for giving the chickens food. You can keep one or two roosters for future use if you are brooding the eggs, and the rest of the roosters you can keep until they have some meat on their butts so they are ripe for the butcher block.

If you don't want roosters at all, you'll have to separate the roosters from the chicks because you don't want to feed unprofitable roosters. That sounds easy but it's not! Adrie looked under a little chick's tail. He wasn't exactly stupid but he couldn't see the difference, to him it were all little chicks. Adrie could sex an elephant because the sex organs are substantial but under the tail of a chick between all those feathers, he couldn't see bugger all. He might as well look at an ant's rear end, nothing to see either.

Adrie didn't think that he was stupid for not being able to tell the difference between a hen and a rooster. When the chicks come just out of the eggs, the roosters' antenna is still built-in and with maturing the comb and antenna develop which is a sure sign that you are looking at a rooster.

There was a hatchery in the neighborhood from which they bought their young chickens. They employed a Chinese who selected the chicks right after they came out of the eggs. He was about 95% correct with his selection.

With Adrie's father working in work camps, it was now Adrie's duty to get some little chicks in a box. This was a rare opportunity to gain some knowledge and he asked the Chinese how he could tell which chick was a rooster. The Chinese looked very professionally as if he had the selection of chicks boiled down to a science and said: "Well you have to know what to look for."

Well, Adrie knew what to look for but his problem was he couldn't see what he was looking for. Perhaps he needed a microscope to see it. It seemed that the Chinese wasn't just about to give up the knowledge, which probably had been passed on from father to son for many generations. This dumbkopf of a Dutchman wanted to know things that made him a living; why should he tell Adrie or anybody else?

When Adrie talked to his Uncle Jaap Dalm about the Chinese that didn't want to tell him the sexing secret of the chickens, his uncle said: "When you go out dining Chinese and look at the menu, you find that you can order chicken balls. In my school book it said that it is the rooster that has the balls. I've looked often enough under a chicken's tail but never did I see balls. It could be that I'm short sighted and need glasses or binoculars to see those things that Chinese can see. Maybe the chicken balls are from the roosters that they missed when selecting the chicks. Maybe, just maybe, they are not as smart as they think they are and just try to cover up their mistakes by telling us that chickens have balls."

THE DEVIL MADE HIM DO IT

Most of the time they say: "A penny saved is a penny earned." In Adrie's book it was different; it was more like "A penny earned is a penny earned." Adrie managed to earn a penny and not save it, which was quite something at his home. Two houses away from Adrie lived Mrs. Willemstein. She was an old woman who had trouble walking and was depending on others to do her errands. Whenever she needed something from the grocery store she tried to find somebody to get it for her. One day she needed a couple of items and was looking in the street where Adrie was playing. She knocked against the window and asked if Adrie could go to the store for her. When he returned she gave him a whole penny as reward. "Wow!" you say.

A penny was a lot of money in those days. You could buy an ice cream cone, liquorice or other candy for it. That penny was earned and it didn't go into his savings bank. His father and mother didn't know he had made a penny so he got away with it. He was a big spender and invested that entire penny in candies.

After his candies were finished, he was looking for Mrs. Willemstein to see if he could go to the store for her and walked frequently passed her window. She never had to knock twice against the window. In fact, she didn't have to knock at all. She only had to nod her head or beckon with her hand and Adrie came to the window. He understood that language as well as a knock against the window. Adrie had to because it was his livelihood or actually his candyhood.

A few houses away from school was the candy store. That was a good location; if the school kids had a penny they would spend it there. They sold all kinds of candies, liquorice, gum, mints etc. Anything a kid could desire was sold in the candy store and everything cost one penny. The price was geared for kids who had a penny to spend.

In spite that a penny was the smallest unit of money, it was very seldom that Adrie went to the candy store. Whenever he received money for his birthday or when he received ten cents for gleaning all week, he had to put that money in his piggy bank so he could pay for the windows he broke, he guessed. Occasionally he broke a window when he threw a stone through it or kicked a football through the window instead of through the goal. Actually, his parents said that he had to save money for his future. He didn't know that he had a future but he had to save for it anyway. And so all his money went into his piggy bank except the few times he ran an errand for Mrs. Willemstein. That money was the only time he could buy candy.

Sometimes his friend gave him a piece of liquorice or a candy. In spite that he was Adrie's friend there was a catch to it. His friend was poor in the Dutch language and if he didn't know how to spell a word, he tried to peek at Adrie's paper who was pretty good in spelling.

If Adrie was in a good mood he would turn his paper to give him a chance to copy the words he couldn't spell. To make sure that he would be in a good mood when he wanted to peek at his paper, his friend gave him candy from time to time.

Adrie wasn't blessed with material things, he was poor but what he lacked in materialism he made up with his mental capacity. In his life he wasn't dealt a very good hand, but he had one trump called intellect and he played his trump well. The early stages of his life had taught him that there were no freebies, only the sun comes up free; for the rest you have to pay one way or another.

Even his friends were smart; they knew that everything was for sale if the price is right, and in Adrie's case a couple of candies or a piece of liquorice could create a miracle. All of a sudden he removed his arm and turned his paper so they could read it and copy what they needed.

In spite of his trump card which he played so well to obtain candies, there always remained the wish to have money of his own which he could spend on candy. Well, he had money in his piggy bank and of course he knew that money was for his future. Maybe there was a future and may be there wasn't; to Adrie the future was only an illusive dream. It really didn't matter; he was seven years old and living today.

Yesterday is dead and gone
And tomorrow is out of sight.

To him it was today that counted. What do you buy when you leave your money in your piggy bank? A piggy bank only encourages kids to become misers and it turns parents into bank robbers.

On a beautiful summer day, he took a handful of money out of his piggy bank. There were pennies, nickels and even a couple of dimes, perhaps there was eighty cents. He didn't have time to count it because he was in a hurry. He knew what he wanted and he also knew where to get it. For his purchases he wasn't going to the candy store, there was a lot better place. Downtown where his mother did her shopping there were lots of stores where they sold candy. His mother had taken him along one time when she did her shopping so he knew how to get there. It was about a forty minutes walk which was no problem for his young legs.

The only shops that were of interest to him were candy stores and grocery stores which sold candy. He bought a lot of different things; liquorice, gum, honey drops, a couple of sticks of sweet wood which you could chew, chocolates and peppermints. Since he hadn't taken a shopping bag with him, all his purchases had to go into his pockets. After a while his pockets were bulging so he decided to go home. He hadn't finished all his money yet but that didn't matter, he was in no hurry. After all they didn't build San Francisco and Los Angeles in one day either, that took time, too.

Home he went, he thought! However, in the heat of buying candies, he had walked farther than he thought and hadn't really watched where he was going. He had had only eye for candy and candy stores and that had caught up with him. Since he wasn't sure about the way home, he decided to ask somebody. All he had to do was to look for an intelligent person, who could tell him the way to go home. There was a gentleman with a hat, he looked kind of bright. However, when he asked him if he knew how to get to the Hordyk, he didn't know. That showed Adrie that he wasn't the only stupid person in the world.

In spite that the man didn't know where the Hordyk was, he was very helpful. Too helpful for Adrie's taste! They happened to be almost in front of the police station; the man grabbed his hand and pulled him into the police station. He told a policeman that Adrie was lost and disappeared. So much for intelligent people; he didn't even know where the Hordyk was, worse, he never had heard about the Hordyk and to make up for his ignorance, he put him in the police station to let them figure it out.

There he was right in front of the policeman with his pockets full of candies. The policeman wondered what he had in his bulging pockets. It was none of his business; Adrie didn't ask him what he had in his pockets, so why should he tell him what he had in his pockets! For all he knew he might be after his candy; he had to be careful. Adrie told the policeman that he had nothing in his pockets but the police man didn't believe that and he had to empty his pockets so he could verify that.

Next, he asked a stupid question: "Where did you get all that money?" There was a slight problem to answer that question! Of course he knew where the money came from but he couldn't tell him that. He could figure out on his ten fingers that the cop would tell his parents and then there would be hell to pay. The consequences could be devastating; if he told him the truth, he could be charged for stealing his own money.

To be on the safe side, he told him that his neighbor boy had given him the money. The problem was that this cop was some kind of a disbelieving Thomas and he didn't believe a word of his story. Could he help that the kid from next door was that nice!

The next question was: "What is the name of the boy who gave you the money?" Yep, he knew it, the cop wanted to know the name of the boy who gave money away so he could get some too. This darned cop wanted to know everything and said he was getting to the bottom of this! Adrie could sense major trouble!

His parents were informed about his wild adventures and his dad came to pick him up from the police station. Of course, the cop told his father everything and also said that his father should check out the story about the money-giving neighbor kid.

Before they went home, they stopped at the nice neighbor boy who had given money away. The way it turned out, he wasn't a nice kid at all! He said he never gave Adrie any money. What a rotten kid that was, he certainly was no help. How was that again? They always say: "Don't lend money to your friends because it will bugger up their memory, especially when you ask the money back at a later date." In this case it was kind of reversed; he hadn't borrowed money from him, he had given money to him, but all the same he had lost his memory, that poor kid.

There they were; Adrie stated that he gave him the money and the kid said he never gave him any money. The boy's father and Adrie's father agreed to go back to the police station and let them figure out the truth and nothing but the truth. It was as if he was having a nightmare, he had been very glad to get away from the police station in the afternoon and now they were heading back to the police station.

At the police station, they were both questioned. The same question was repeated over and over again: "Where did the money come from?" It started to look like an interrogation by the Gestapo. The cop said: "Somebody is lying and I'm going to find out who the liar is; I'm going to throw you both in jail until you tell me the truth."

He opened a door of a complete dark room which was supposed to be jail. Of course, he had turned off the light before hand to make the room dark when they entered. After they had entered, the cop left and from the other side of the door he asked the neighbour kid and Adrie: "Is it dark in there?" What an idiot, he probably didn't know that you can see as much in the dark as without light!

The neighbor boy started to cry and though Adrie didn't cry he had nothing to laugh about either, this was serious business. When the cop opened the door again he said: "This is your last chance, if I don't hear the truth right now you'll both be sleeping in jail tonight!"

They went to a room with light and the same question was asked again. Slowly but surely it started to dawn to him that he was in a hell of a mess. How did he get into this mess anyway? How was that rhyme again?

Oh what a tangled web we weave,
Once we have started to deceive.

Maybe he could tell the cop that he had found the money but that would never do, he wouldn't believe that anyway. The cop asked again: "Where did you get the money?" Since he didn't know anymore lies he told him the truth and said: "I took the money from my piggy bank." That changed the picture; suddenly the cop believed him. It probably had been written on his forehead all the time "Liar, liar, your pants are afire." Relieved that they finally believed him, he wondered what would happen next.

The fathers were called in and told that Adrie had robbed his own piggybank. All could go home now and nobody had to sleep in jail. They only had locked them up for a couple of minutes to scare them and flush the truth out of them and it had worked.

Finally they went back home which was better than in jail. Of course, he could expect to be punished for his evil deed of disobedience but fortunately his punishment wasn't bad at all. Naturally his parents were very disappointed in him that he had done the forbidden thing. He felt kind of like Adam, who ate from the forbidden apple. Fortunately it wasn't his fault at all!

His mother said: "You see it's the devil that makes you do wrong things and he leads you into temptation. The devil shows you nice things like candies and puts greed into your heart so you want to have them. See, deep in your heart is a little voice, called conscience, which warns you if you want to do wrong things. However, the devil tries to subdue your conscience that you don't hear that little voice anymore and that's the way you fall into sin."

"I'll be damned," Adrie thought. "I thought I was a rotten kid to steal my own money but luckily there is nothing wrong with me, it was that damned devil. First he cheated Adam and Eve when he peddled apples in Paradise from the forbidden tree, so that they lost Paradise. And now this dirty devil made me do it to get me into trouble. From now on I should be more on the qui vive because once a devil, always a devil. A kid my age could get into severe difficulties as I have already found out."

Fortunately his parents knew all about the devil and his dirty tricks. He had thought of all kinds of excuses to tell his parents why he had disobeyed them but he never had thought in his life that he could blame the devil for the wrong things he'd done.

There was a song that must have been made with him in mind:

The heaven is in your eyes,
But the devil is in your heart.

There you are, the devil is everywhere with his dirty tricks; it is just terrible what a devil with his pitchfork can do! In order to prevent him from taking money out of his piggybank again, his parents gave him an exercise book to keep track of how much money there was in his piggybank. Every time he received money, he had to enter it in his book and add it. Thanks to the devil his first lesson in bookkeeping started at the early age of six. So you see that even a dirty devil is good for something. As they are saying there is some good in everyone!

THE NAKED LADY OF BAGDAD

Bad times bring out bad things in people. The people who didn't make illegal money had no way to make ends meet. Especially young people went over to theft since relief wasn't adequate to sustain a family and theft was increasing with so many people unemployed. People were desperate and they would even steal the nails of the cross of Christ to feed their family.

One day when Adrie was playing in the street, he saw his father biking with bare feet. He always had socks and shoes on but since it had been a sweltering hot day that even made the Devil sweat, he probably had taken off his socks and shoes to get relief from the heat.

Arie had taken off his socks and shoes alright to combat the heat wave, but that was way back. When he passed the harbor of Rotterdam he saw some kids wading in the refreshing waters of the shallows. That looked cool to him and he decided to join them to get some relief from the heat. He wasn't only relieved of the heat but of his socks and shoes as well. When he went for his refreshing walk in the water, he left his socks and shoes on the side and when he returned his socks and shoes were gone. Arie had no alternative but to bike home with bare feet. Cool man!

It was a good thing that he couldn't swim and had decided to go skinny dipping. In that case he could have lost not only his shirt but his pants as well. That wouldn't have gone over at all to have a naked man biking home. In The Netherlands the people were so prudish at the time that ladies who were bathing at the beach rented a bathing coach when they were bathing in the sea. The coach was pushed a bit away from the beach allowing the lady to take a dip in the refreshing sea water without being seen by other people. Even without a coach there wasn't much to see when a lady was wearing a bathing suit. Bathing suits of that time covered everything except the ankles of the lady. Wow! The bathing suits of that time covered more than the pyjamas of today. Alas, that was a long time before the string bikinis appeared on the beach.

(There is this joke about pyjamas:

A farmer came into the city and for the first time in his life he saw pyjamas in a department store. He asked the sales clerk: "What are those crazy suits with the big stripes for?"

The sales clerk answered: "You wear those suits during the night, sir."

"Oh, in that case I don't need any because I never go out at night," the farmer replied.)

The Netherlands wasn't the only backward country that was very prudish. In Spain you weren't allowed naked in the street either. That became known when one of two Dutch guys who were vacationing in Spain was arrested for walking naked in the street. This is a real story and not a joke.

Two Duch guys were on vacation in Spain. They had a car which was pulling a camper and had been taking turns with driving during the night. When one guy was driving the other one would have a nap in the camper.

Early in the morning, the man in the camper woke up and decided that it was time to take his turn to drive the car. He had been sleeping naked because of the heat and decided to have a shave first before dressing himself. While he was shaving, the car stopped for a red traffic light and when it pulled away all of a sudden, the man lost his balance and fell against the door which opened and he fell stark naked into the street. He didn't get very far because he was arrested by the Spanish police for immoral conduct.

His friend, who had been driving, decided to wake up his friend so he could do some driving. He stopped the car and camper on a quiet spot and opened the camper door. To his surprise there was nobody in the camper. What had happened to his friend? All he could do was to report the mysterious disappearance of his friend to the police.

When the police checked with the other police posts, the mystery was soon solved. His friend was sitting in the city jail and had some explaining to do as to why he wasn't properly dressed when he had his walk.

Actually, they were pretty unlucky that this incident happened in Spain, which is mainly a Roman Catholic country. Had it happened in Bagdad there would have been no problem at all. At least according to a popular song in The Netherlands:

I saw a lady in Bagdad,
Who walked naked in the street and I saw that.
I called a cop and asked: "Hey man what is that."
The cop said: "Be quiet, in Bagdad you can do that."

This was just a song because the reality is that Bagdad is mainly Muslim where the ladies walk underneath a veil rather than stark naked. Nudity isn't only frowned upon; any exposure of flesh can be deadly. In Muslim countries they are not interested in seeing Adam before the fig leaf. They would have stoned the lady who did such a thing.

If the two Dutch guys had been in Bagdad; they would have found out that the police weren't understanding at all. On one occasion, a visitor in Bagdad was arrested because he hadn't obeyed a traffic sign that was written in the local language. That he couldn't read the sign wasn't taken as an excuse, he was tossed in jail where he received ten lashes with the cat o' nine tails before they let him go.

A lot of people who couldn't buy meat were keeping rabbits so they would have some meat on the table. Other people who liked rabbit too, but didn't like to take care of rabbits were stealing rabbits. At night, people had rabbits in their shed and the next morning they were gone. There were a lot of thieves around.

(On a dark windy night, there was suddenly a bolt of lightning. When Mary looked at the window, she saw a burglar who was trying to get in through the window. Hysterically she screamed: "Bill, Bill, there is a burglar coming through the window."

Bill looked with sleepy eyes at the burglar and said: "Be quiet, don't scare him. Maybe he can get the window open. It's the window we couldn't open after the painters left.")

In spite of the fact that the Government insisted that prosperity was just around the corner, that's where it stayed, "Around the corner." The tens of thousands of unemployed people never got to go around the corner and got poorer all the time. At the best of times prosperity is usually the period from Friday's pay check to Saturday's shopping.

Whenever the Government came up with a new budget, there were always more cuts to the unemployed. In every budget, the thumbscrews were turned on a little more. The magical word in the budget was always "Economizing." As soon as the Government started to economize at the expense of the unemployed, they had no choice but follow suit.

The Government had done almost nothing to combat the Depression. They only combated the consequences of the Depression and not the cause. All the wrong steps were taken with their economizing. Their opinion was that in a bad economic time, the wages had to be lowered and the prices of goods would automatically go down. With lower prices more goods would be sold and business activity would increase. That was the most stupid policy ever, where did the Government think that people would get the money to buy cheaper goods when their wages have been lowered?

Another ignorant plan to get the economy going was to destroy a lot of cars, trucks, ships and buildings. If that was done the country would be busy with replacing the destroyed things which would decrease unemployment. Nobody seemed to think of the right solution of paying the workers more in which case they would have more money to buy the produced goods and business activity would increase. That but only that would decrease unemployment.

Finally Minister President Colein saw that his economizing didn't work and looked at President Roosevelt in the U.S. who had massive work programs in place to get the people working. Roosevelt had the right attitude to pump money into the economy instead of economizing. Colein decided to have work programs too as long as they didn't cost too much money. He allotted $60 million to make a bush in Amsterdam and a Maas tunnel in Rotterdam. Those were the only projects the Government came up with. It had as much effect as a wet fire cracker to get the economy going.

The plight of the unemployed was far from pleasant and every time that the deficit had to be reduced, the unemployed got it in the neck. After Colein was spending $60 million on work projects his budget was not balanced which made him resort to some more economizing. Like before, he was economizing at the expense of the unemployed by lowering their benefit payment. A reporter asked him how those people could survive. They barely had dry bread on the table so how could they survive with less.

If a fish keeps his mouth shut, he can't get into trouble and Dr. Colein would have been well advised to keep his trap shut as well. Instead, he opened his mouth and said: "We have to economize in order to have a balanced budget and everybody has to take his share. It would be unfair to have only the working people pay for it. The unemployed will have to tighten their belt like everybody else. Besides, the unemployed don't contribute to the wealth of the country, they only consume the wealth. Yet they expect to eat every day steak and lobster, there is also a lot of nourishment in fish heads."

He surely had opened a can of worms that got away on him. All newspapers carried front page articles that Dr. Colein had stated that the unemployed were good enough to eat fish heads. After the damage was done to his Christian image and leadership, he had a speech on the radio stating that he merely meant that there were a lot of vitamins in fish heads. It was only an illustration and it had never entered his mind that the unemployed should eat them. Why then would he even have mentioned it? Some people are hypocrites and he was one of them.

Hein Colein had a one track mind and that was economizing. With his plan to cut the payments to the unemployed, he had the entire country in uproar. On July 3rd 1934, the Communist Party organized a protest meeting in Amsterdam. During the meeting people got so furious that they went out on a rampage after the meeting. They barricaded the main arteries of the city, broke up the streets and threw the cobble stones at the police.

Mayor de Vlugt asked the Government to send military troops to subdue the uprising. Tanks and machine guns eventually restored order after six civilians were killed and another thirty were wounded. The only thing that was accomplished was that the city of Amsterdam removed the cobble stones from the streets and put asphalt streets in place. This was as a precaution that if there was another rebellion the people couldn't throw cobble stones at the police. They took their ammunition away.

Another incident happened on the Cruiser, "The Seven Provinces." After lowering their wages three consecutive times, the crew mutinied. The answer to that problem by Hein Colein was to have everybody sign a document that they would respect the legal Government and obey orders. If they didn't they were dismissed. All other Navy personnel had to sign this document as well.

With all the incidents that had come because of his economizing policy, Colein became unpopular and especially insulting the unemployed did him in. There were many unemployed and a lot of votes were lost. In the next election he was defeated by a land slide.

TREASURE BIKE SHED

There are hundreds of books and movies with all kinds of attractive stories about hidden treasures. Those stories are all too familiar; it was usually pirates who had buried their booty on an uninhabited island. As the story goes, the only man who knew where the treasure was buried; died. Of course, there was a map with unclear directions. Many parties went out to look for the treasure but it was never found. It's still there for you to find.

There were also lost gold mines and there was the story of "Old Jake," who gave instructions on his death bed where he had buried his gold. The result was always the same, the gold was never found. There are lots of treasures to be found but you still have to find them. Good luck, you'll need it!

There is one treasure story you probably never heard of, it is called "Treasure Bike Shed." It could be a lack of your education so let me tell you about it. In spite of the Great Depression and the terrible bad time which had dumped Arie and Ko into poverty, they had buried a treasure in the bike shed. The treasure was a glass jar with 10 guilder bank notes. This sounds incredible in a time they were struggling to survive and were eating dry bread that they would have such a treasure. There were only four people in the whole wide world that knew where the treasure was buried and there was no secret map to reveal the location.

It was the crazy circumstances in which they lived that made it necessary for them to bury that money. The money lender had given Arie grace to pay off the loan but he had to make interest payments of 195 guilders per year, at the end of the year. Of course, Arie had to save every week for the interest which came to 3.75 guilders per week.

Normally, Arie would have put that money in the bank every week so he would get interest on it. Unfortunately, this was not normal anymore. When things were still normal before the Depression started, there was the bank secret, so nobody but nobody, not even the Government could get information from the bank.

The difficulty came when the Government started to talk in the House of Commons to abolish the Bank Secret. According to the Government there were many people on relief that had money in the bank. In that case, they would be required to finish that money first before they would get relief payments.

Arie had money in the bank to make it possible to pay the interest at the end of the year. The Government didn't care for what reason people had money in the bank, money in the bank was money in the bank and people wouldn't get relief until they had used up that money. For Arie it meant that he wouldn't qualify for twenty weeks for relief payments and it would also mean that he didn't have the money to make his interest payment at the end of the year. Veldhoen, the mortgage lender, had made an agreement that as long as Arie paid the interest he was satisfied but if he didn't have the interest payment he could figure that Veldhoen would kick him out of the house. There was no pity for defaulters; you had to fulfill your commitments or else!

People who were on relief with money in the bank withdrew their money and put it in an old sock or in the old mattress. The old rascal of a Prime Minister hadn't figured that the unemployed people would beat him to it before he could get his dirty hands on their money.

After the horses had escaped he was closing the barn door. In a daring radio speech, he announced that the Bank Secret would never be abolished. Only in Russia under Communism where the State controlled everything could that happen. The Netherlands was no Russia and the Bank Secret would stay.

Arie had his reasons not to trust that Christian Reformed Prime Minister, he went to the bank and withdrew his money. He was rather safe than sorry. The bank manager asked him if he was taking his money out because of the possible abolishing of the Bank Secret. It was none of his business, it was Arie's money so he could withdraw it whenever he liked. He told the banker that he needed the money to pay his bills.

No, you could never trust that Christian Prime Minister who was a blatant liar. Twice before he had told a bunch of lies and people had not forgotten. The first time when there was pressure on the Dutch currency, rumors had it that the Dutch currency would devaluate. "Not so," said Colein, "The Dutch currency will not be devalued." Only three days later the Dutch currency had been devalued by 10% in spite of his promise.

He had his reasons to lie because first of all he had to make a lot of money before the Dutch currency could devalue. He had all kinds of money that he wanted to convert into English pounds. In those days the English pound was the safest currency in the world. "As sound as the pound," was the slogan. By changing his Dutch money into English pounds he made a mint after the Dutch money had devalued. After the Dutch money had devalued it was worth 10% less than before on the world market. All he had to do was convert his English pounds back into Dutch Guilders and he had made himself 10% on his money in three days. That was unheard of in those days when the interest rates were only 2.75% per year. It was a gold mine.

Lie two came about after England had gone off the Gold Standard. The word was out that the Dutch Government contemplated to follow suit. When the Dutch currency wasn't backed up by gold anymore, it dropped in value on the international market. Again, Doctor Colein had told the Dutch people that this would never happen. For the same reason, he lied because he had to manipulate his money first and made another 8% on it.

Yes, this hypocrite Christian Reformed Prime Minister could lie like a conjurer. He was one of the leaders who told the people that they shouldn't lie because hell fire would be waiting for them if they did. Apparently, the leaders didn't believe in God or the Ten Commandments. They probably figured: "Listen to my words but don't look at my deeds." Alas, even a Christian leader could go wrong if the devil made him do it. Actually he didn't need the devil to make him do it; he was the devil himself according to the unemployed.

Unemployed people were gullible; they couldn't win for losing when their leaders took advantage of them. The Prime Minister made 10% on his money in three days but the unemployed couldn't keep their money in the bank to get 2.75% per year, lest the Prime Minister would take it away.

It says in the Good Book: "The one who has shall be given but the one who has not, from him shall be taken whatever he's got." Right on!

Instead of having their money unsafely in the bank, they put it in an old mattress which was a lot safer they thought. It didn't take long for the thieves to catch on and when they burglarized a house they would cut open the old mattresses to find the money.

The little bit of money that Arie had was sure giving him trouble, it was safe nowhere. First he had to take it out of the bank to prevent the Prime Minister from taking it and now he had to take it out of the old mattress so the thieves wouldn't' get it. However, he knew a way to have his money in a safe place where the evil Prime Minister and the thieves couldn't get it. Every thief and his brother knew about the old mattress but they didn't know anything about hidden treasure. There was an indoor bike shed in the house with a dirt floor. He could bury his money there safely until he needed it to make his interest payment.

He had a glass jar with a screw on lid which would keep his money safely underground. It was water tight so no water could get in it. The kids were also in on the deal, they were told and shown where the money was buried, just in case Arie and Ko would die. Then there would have been another story about a hidden treasure that never had been found because he didn't make a map.

Arie started out by putting twelve banknotes of ten in the jar and after three months he had another three banknotes which he was going to put in the jar as well. When he opened the jar, he had the surprise of his life; the money was gone! Fortunately it wasn't that bad because it would have been another mystery to be solved. The money was still there but it was spoiled. He thought that his jar was waterproof but moisture had been able to get in the jar and the colors of the banknotes had run together quite a bit.

The money he had never quit giving him problems. He could go to the bank to get new banknotes. As long as they could see the watermark and the number on the bill they would exchange it for a new one. It had happened that a goat ate a ten guilder bill. The owner of the ten guilder bill had butchered the goat instantly, took the pieces of the bank note out of the goat's stomach and got a brand new bank note at the bank.

In Arie's case, the watermark and number were still in tact so he should have no problem to get new bank notes. He could bet his boots that there was going to be a problem when a man on relief comes to the bank with 12 discolored banknotes. The question would be: "Where did you get all that money while you are on relief?" and the next thing he would know was that the Government would have the money and he would be holding the bag with the consequence that he couldn't pay the rent to Veldhoen.

Spending the discolored money and saving the new money that was coming in was the only way out of this predicament. Ko bought for a couple of guilders groceries, paid with a discolored ten guilder bill and she got normal change back which was not discolored. That way they would slowly get rid of the discolored banknotes. The problem didn't go away because not everybody accepted the discolored money. There were a few refusals of people who didn't trust that discolored money. It looked like bogus money that they had made themselves.

One of the suppliers gave Ko an idea. A couple of times he had already accepted a discolored banknote and he told Ko: "I had at one time a couple of discolored banknotes like this when I had my wallet with ten guilder bills in my raincoat and got drenched. I forgot to take my wallet out of my pocket when I came home and my ten guilder bills looked exactly the same as yours."

Now here was an idea! In order to speed up the exchange of bad looking money for good looking money, Arie went to the bank with three discolored banknotes and told them the story about his wet raincoat. You weren't supposed to lie, but what the Prime Minister could do, he could do just as good if not better. At the bank they checked the watermarks and the numbers and gave him three brand new bills in exchange. After all, the money had to go back in the old mattress where it would stay dry unless they pissed their bed.

BREAD WITH SOAP AND NAILS

Willie and Adrie were born and reared in the long extension of the Victoria Era in which the siblings were raised the Puritan way. When they were young, they had absolutely nothing to say; they had to listen to their elders which included their parents, teachers, the Reverend, uncles, aunts and even the neighbors. The law stipulated that only when you were of age, that was when you were 21 years old, could you go your own way.

Your father and mother were responsible for you till you were 21 years old, and your father was the head of the family; he made all the decisions and whenever he said: "No," it was no. All documents had to be signed by your father, even when you registered for a course. Your father had to sign, because the signature of a minor wasn't valid. There was such a provision made that your mother could be the head of the family in case your father had died or was in prison. Even that was possible in those days.

Your parents brought you up with the assistance of the school and church and if deemed necessary, with the help of the police. Your parents picked the school and the church for you. They sent you to school and took you to church, twice every Sunday, plus on that same Sunday you had to go to Sunday school.

As children from Christian parents, they were raised the Christian way, which included a lot of prayers. For a starter, when the children went to bed they had to sit on their knees and pray to the Lord to keep them safely through the night. When they got up in the morning they had to get on their knees again to thank the Lord for keeping them safe.

Right after was breakfast with saying Grace and thanking the Lord for the food they were about to receive. When breakfast was finished they had to say thank you again to the Lord for the food they had received. The same happened with lunch and supper. Moreover, before the classes started at school there was a prayer furnished by the teacher and another prayer when the kids went home. That was in the morning and afternoon.

That was six prayers each day for eating and two for sleeping plus four prayers at school which amounted to twelve prayers a day. On Sunday there was the same number of prayers except there was no school but with going twice to church on a Sunday, the Reverend took over where the teacher left off. The children that went to Sunday School had two extra prayers on Sunday.

With all those prayers, Adrie could pray as well as the Reverend. When he was playing with his friends, they were playing house, school and church. One time when they were playing church, the parents were listening behind the door and heard Adrie play Reverend. They were astonished how well he could pray and thought that he should become a Reverend.

Every day, the head of the family read a chapter from the Bible, usually with supper. The children were supposed to listen and were checked whether they did or not. After the reading stopped, the children were supposed to say the last word that was read.

(A man who was walking through the forest came suddenly eye to eye with a Grizzly Bear. The man ran away as fast as he could but the Grizzly was gaining on him. In his desperation he started to pray and said: "Dear Lord let this bear take up religion."

When the man looked back, the bear was standing with his paws folded and said: "Thank you Lord for the food I'm about to receive.")

Some Roman Catholic children said Grace with their meal as follows:

In the name of the Father, the Son and the Holy Ghost,

> The one who eats fastest gets the most.
>
> Lord bless this meat,
> Let's open our kisser and eat.

That made a lot of sense but an Arab prayer makes sense as well.

> May the fleas of a thousand camels infest the crotch of the person who screws me up and may their arms be too short to scratch. Amen.

One time when his mother was saying Grace, Adrie was kind of absent minded and had his eyes open. His father said right away: "When saying Grace you have to close your eyes."

Adrie countered: "How come I have to close my eyes while you have yours open? If you had your eyes closed as you should, you could not possibly see that I have mine open."

"I can have my eyes open when we say Grace," Adrie's father replied, "Because I have to check to see if you do things properly. I have to supervise this house."

"And who made you supervisor?" Adrie wanted to know, "I could have had my eyes open to check if you had your eyes closed."

"You just keep your disrespectful mouth closed and if you don't close your eyes I'll close them for you," Adrie's father shouted.

It was wiser not to say anything anymore, Adrie thought. He wondered why he had a mouth and eyes if he had to close them. It made him also wonder why a person has to fold his hands and close his eyes when you are praying or say Grace. What were they not supposed to see? His dad only told him to close his eyes and didn't give any explanation, why? At an opportune time he asked the Reverend that question.

The Reverend had his answer ready: "When you pray, you have to have all your attention on your prayer and think about God. If you look around while you are praying you see things and your attention is distracted. The same counts for your hands, if you fold them, they are at rest and they stay where they are."

(Closing your eyes while you are praying has another advantage. When the missionaries came to Hawaii, they were preaching to the Hawaiians that they had to close their eyes and pray to the Lord. The Hawaiians had obeyed and they said: "When we opened our eyes again our land was gone.")

While he had the Reverend explaining all kinds of riddles, Adrie had one more question. "What does the word Amen mean; other than that you can open your eyes again?"

The Reverend answered: "The word Amen is a Hebrew word and it means 'So be it.'"

Twelve prayers a day and proper decorum were the compulsory things the kids had to do, and to top it off, their parents expected them to be obedient, well mannered and well behaved. Unorthodox language wasn't tolerated.

A penis was called "A little thing" and others called it "A pisser" suggesting that's all you could do with it. You were not supposed to have sex or talk about it because sex was a dirty word.

In spite that kids weren't supposed to talk about sex, they did the opposite. They got away with it as long as their parents or teachers didn't hear it. There were a lot of taboos in those days. The kids weren't allowed to smoke, swear or bet. As an answer to all those forbidden things, they said jokingly: "Damned, let's bet a cigarette." That was a way to do all your sins at once.

(Johnny said to his mother: "My brother is a stupid idiot."

His mother replied: "Johnny you aren't allowed to use such vulgar language."

"But mother," Johnny said, "William Shakespeare said that there are no dirty words, there are only dirty minds."

"If that little boy says such crazy things," his mother replied, "I don't want you to play with him anymore.")

Maybe it's kind of dumb that some people have never heard about William Shakespeare. Even today there are people who haven't heard about "The Walls of Jericho."

(The teacher asked Randy: "Who destroyed the walls of Jericho?"

"I didn't do it," Randy said.

That answer was way off base as far as the teacher was concerned and she wondered what kind of a home he came from so she visited his mother. "I asked Randy who destroyed the walls of Jericho," the teacher said to Randy's mother, "And he said that he didn't do it."

"If Randy says that he didn't do it, he didn't do it," the mother lashed out at the teacher.

As a last resort the teacher went looking for Randy's father and found him finally in the pub where he was looking for work. The teacher said to Randy's father: "I asked your son who destroyed the walls of Jericho and Randy said he didn't do it. Next I went to his mother and told her that Randy said he didn't do it. His mother got mad and said: 'If Randy says he didn't do it, he didn't do it.'"

Randy's father replied: "Listen, I don't want to cause any problems and difficulties, maybe I can help. How much do those walls of Jericho cost?")

William Shakespear was often taken as the one who wrote perfect English in his plays and books. A defence lawyer tried to discredit a witness and told the court that the witness was totally unreliable and he was a real asshole. The judge ruled him out of order because of his unparliamentary language. The lawyer objected to this decision arguing that in William Shakespear's famous works, the word asshole appeared three times. The judge adjourned the court until the next day and told the lawyer to prove that to him. The next day, the lawyer brought the required documents from Shakespear and indeed the word asshole appeared in them three times. Therefore the judge ruled that the word asshole was a parliamentary word after all. Who is going to argue with Shakespear?

Furthermore, the kids weren't allowed to make a fire in the street, steal apples or pears and they weren't even allowed to make faces in the mirror. They warned you that behind the mirror there was a black man, with a black hand, who didn't like it if you made faces in the mirror and he would give you a slap in the face. The result of this would be that the black of the black hand would rub off on your face, and once the black was on your face, it would stay there for the rest of your life. In that case you were doomed as a cursed Flying Dutchman to run around with a black face.

Adrie couldn't help but thinking that the Negroes were probably people who made faces in the mirror and were slapped in the face with a black hand from a black man. Negroes were actually ordinary white people, who used to have a white face but became black after making faces in the mirror.

The mirror in Adrie's house had a black corner, it wasn't really black but it looked that way after some of the silver from the back had come off. It was an old mirror, which had served rich people till the back coating started to come off a bit so they gave the mirror to Ko. Well, the price was right and it also confirmed the story of the black man who had been peeking around that corner and in doing so had dirtied the mirror. Yep, that was living proof that the black man was indeed there.

It was all sheer nonsense, but children believe all kinds of bull because the people who take care of them tell them. When Willie and Adrie were growing up, they couldn't even stand in front of the mirror like Snow White's stepmother did and say: "Mirror, mirror on the wall, who is the prettiest of all?" Such pride would have had a fall for sure and you would have been punished with a black face.

Besides the story of the black man in the mirror, there was also a Sand Man who came to throw sand in your eyes so you would fall asleep. There was also living proof that this was so because in the morning you woke up with sleepers in your eyes that you had to wash out.

When the parents gave the children a licking they said with a painful face: "It hurts me more than it does you."

Even when his parents were hurt more than he was, Adrie wouldn't mind trading places to give his parents a licking. That way they didn't have to suffer that much and Adrie didn't mind to be hurt more. Of course, that was out of the question, he had better not think about such a drastic change.

At Sunday School; the teacher told the kids that they always had to tell the truth and nothing but the truth, or else they would be punished by the Lord. Of course, the kids were sinners and didn't always comply with their education and why should they? Their parents could tell a bunch of lies, so why should the kids be any better?

There was a newspaper in Holland that was called: "The Truth." Nobody would speak the truth in Holland, the parents told all kinds of lies and the children followed suit.

In order to keep the children in line, the school and parents used a lot of scare tactics. First of all they were taught how God would punish them if they sinned. Even the parents believed it; they were told by their favorite Reverend and passed the message to the children.

If this wasn't bad enough, the children had to satisfy another authority on good behavior who wasn't kidding. It was St. Nicholas who came every year on his birthday from Spain to The Netherlands in a steam ship. St. Nicholas came to celebrate his birthday, which was on December 5th, with the good kids who were obedient and did everything they were told by their parents and teachers.

(St.Nicholas was on his way from Spain to The Netherlands again. Suddenly the boat hit a rock and a lot of water entered the ship. Black Peter, his helper, started right away to make another hole in the boat. St. Nicholas asked him what the hell he thought he was doing. Black Peter answered: "That way, the water that enters the boat has a way to run out.")

St. Nicholas loved good kids and brought presents for them but he hated bad, disobedient kids, for them he had a special treatment which was delivered by his helper Black Peter who would put them in his bag and take them back to Spain for some smartening up lessons.

They were locked up in Spain and got nothing to eat but dry bread with water. Only on Sundays would they get bread with soap and nails. That was quite a change of the regular menu. The soap served to clean your soul and the nails you were eating were supposed to give you iron will power to get back on the right track when you returned from Spain. Rehabilitation of the knave was secured that way; children who returned from Spain were reborn and would look like a new kid in the block.

For the Dutch children there was a catch to it; they only would receive presents if they had been good all year. That was of course a tall order, too tall for most of the kids. When St. Nick's birthday came near, they started to scramble to be good for a while. It was a nice try which didn't help at all because St. Nick knew everything. His spies were as good as the K.G.B. in Russia. If you had been good only the last couple of weeks, it wouldn't satisfy St. Nick, he demanded good kids all year around.

If you had been naughty or disobedient, you had it coming. And it wasn't candy what you had coming, instead of getting presents and candy you would get punished with a double whammy. For a starter you wouldn't get any presents and to top it off, the Holy Saint brought his helper "Black Peter," who was as black as soot, along to flog the naughty children with a bunch of willow twigs. While Peter was flogging the bad kids he was singing:

"Nice kids get candies.
Bad kids get spanked on their panties."

That wouldn't be that bad if you could get out of your panties before the spanking started. Actually, that St. Nicholas – Black Peter team did the work of the police. The police would lock you up in jail and St. Nick would lock you up in Spain. What's the difference?

When St. Nick visited the children at home or school, Black Peter would throw some gingerbread nuts and candies in the room for the children. That made the children scramble for the candies.

On the eve of St. Nick's birthday, the children put their wooden shoe underneath the chimney with some carrots and sugar lumps. Those treats were for the White Horse that the Saint was riding over the steep roofs of The Netherlands. Now, that was very thoughtful of the kids, that horse had to do a lot of work in a short time and it was very dangerous work because the roofs were pretty slippery during the winter months. The carrot would improve the eyesight of the horse and the sugar lumps would bugger up his teeth so that he couldn't chew his carrot anymore. Kids never gave those complex problems a thought. That was Santa's problem; the kids did the best they could.

Together with the treats for the horse, the children wrote a letter to Saint Nick to tell him all about the presents they would like and seldom got them. In turn Santa would write letters to the kids to be good which would never happen. That was a short order for the Saint when he was sitting on his white horse on the roof to read the wishes from the kids but the Saint managed as long as the wishes of the kids weren't off limits because of his near empty purse.

Adrie couldn't get the hang of St. Nick who brought presents to the kids because it was his birthday. Santa Claus in England was different, he brought the kids presents because it was Christmas. If Adrie had a birthday he was expecting to get presents and not give them away. After he had thought about this, he thought he saw the light and decided that Saint Nick was a Holy man and Holy people don't receive presents or they wouldn't be Holy. It sure doesn't pay to be Holy because you get nothing and everything is a give away. The Saint must have figured that there had to be presents on a birthday and since he couldn't receive any he gave them away.

A youngster wrote a letter to St. Nick: "Santa, I've been half bad and half good, so I'd be happy if I got half of what I'm asking for."

With the venture to bring presents to the kids, St. Nick was accompanied by his all time obedient servant Black Peter. Black Peter's task was to climb through the chimney to get the carrots and sugar lumps for the horse and exchange them for presents. He also took the letters the kids had written to Saint Nick and exchanged those letters for a letter from the Saint.

The letters from St. Nick looked more like a moralizing sermon. Adrie was always surprised how detailed St. Nick could sum up the bad things he had done. He raised supreme hell and told him that he only had one more chance to behave in the coming year or the next year he would take him to Spain. When next year came Adrie got a very last chance and luckily he never ran out of chances.

After delivering all the presents, the bag of Black Peter was empty which came in handy because now there was room to put the bad kids in to take them to Spain. It was some kind of a re-cycling program, when the bag had served its purpose there was another purpose to use it again.

* * * *

How did we arrive at all this nonsense about St. Nick coming with a steamboat from Spain to The Netherlands to give the good children presents and to have Black Peter beat the crap out of the naughty children with a bunch of willow twigs? St. Nick was also supposed to ride on a white horse over the steep roofs of the houses to deliver the presents and Black Peter crawled through the chimney to put the presents in the boots of the children that they had put underneath the chimney. While Black Peter was busy doing his job, St. Nick was yawning on his horse. Visiting all those children, made it a long day, there was no doubt about it.

It took some doing before the St. Nicholas story was in place. As a matter of fact, it took well over a thousand years to get the celebrations going in The Netherlands. However, all the things that were done during the celebrations make sense if you read the history about St. Nicholas.

It all started in Myra (Turkey) in the year A.D. 300 when Nicholas became Bishop. Nicholas was already famous before he became Bishop. He had inherited a lot of money from his parents which he was going to use to help the poor people. Nicholas looked at the terrible things that were going on in Turkey and figured that he could help the people.

There was this real rich man who ran out of luck and had become poor. He had no money for his three daughters' doweries and figured that they would become ladies of the night. Bishop Nicholas heard about this terrible prospect and went to the man's home to throw some golden coins through the open window to pay for the doweries of his daughters. The man's boots were standing in front of the open window and the golden coins landed in the man's boots. That's why the children put their boots underneath the chimney to catch the goodies that St. Nicholas would throw through the chimney. Throwing of gingerbread nuts and candies also reflects that St. Nicholas was throwing golden coins into the room of the poor man for the doweries of his daughters.

This throwing of gold coins had its repercussions. A greedy man had heard about the good Nicholas who threw golden coins through the window of poor people. He was interested to get his share of the golden coins and faked poverty. Nicholas figured the man out and instead of golden coins he threw a parcel with lead through his window with the message that the man had to fill it with gold and give it to the poor people. In case that he was not doing what he was told Nicholas threatened him that he would be beat up with a bunch of willow twigs. The willow twig weapon of Black Peter was derived of this incident and so was the spanking of bad people or kids.

Nicholas was well known by the Pope and when the old Bishop of Myra died, the Pope appointed him to be the Bishop of Myra. It's hard to picture St. Nicholas in jail but in A.D. 303 the new Roman Emperor Diocletian who was persecuting Christians threw a lot of Christians in jail, among them was Nicholas.

Many Christians were thrown to the lions and others had to fight gladiators for their life or were burned at the stake. Other Christians succumbed in Roman torture chambers. By a decree of the new Emperor Constantine all prisoners were set free and Bishop Nicholas returned to Myra to do his Bishop duties again. All prisoners who had survived the ordeal were declared Holy by the Pope.

There were some incredible stories about Bishop St. Nicholas; he was even credited with bringing back to life three boys who had died from starvation. Many people in need received help from Bishop St. Nicholas. He loved good children and always told them to be obedient to their parents. More and more people admired St. Nicholas and even sailors and prisoners adopted him to be their patron.

After Bishop St. Nicholas died, people in Turkey couldn't forget him and kept celebrating his birthday on December 5th. They told their children that they would receive presents from St. Nicholas if they behaved. If they were naughty he would beat them up with a bunch of willow twigs to punish them.

The parents also told the kids that St. Nicholas had a helper called Clampus who had horns, a forked tongue and red eyes. The children were terrified of him which was the idea to make them behave.

People in Italy were also worshipping St. Nicholas and brought his bones to Italy. The bones were said to have healing power which attracted a lot of sick people with arthritis and other illnesses to view the bones in order to be healed.

St. Nicholas was heralded over all of Europe even in Russia. Whenever there was a new church built, the name of the church was St. Nicholas Church. England alone had over 400 St. Nicholas churches.

When St. Nicholas came to The Netherlands, the story was kind of modified. That Saint Nick came by steamboat from Spain happened because Saint Nick was the Patron of Sailors. Whenever there was a severe storm that got the sailors in trouble they prayed to St. Nicholas to make them survive the storm.

The story that St. Nick was riding on a white horse; over the steep roofs in The Netherlands came about because of their God Wodan who was riding on a horse through the Heavens.

In spite of all the good qualities of St. Nick, he was disrespectfully called by the big kids "Stinking Claus." Now, that wasn't nice at all since the good man brought presents to the kids. However, the Dutch saying is that you get shit instead of thanks. That's people for you.

Though the bigger kids were very disrespectful, St. Nick was met with great fanfare in the harbor of Rotterdam. When the steamboat arrived, St. Nick was already sitting on his white horse on the deck of the steamboat. He was waiting impatiently for the mooring of the boat; it was a busy time for him and he wanted to get his work done as fast as possible.

As soon as the ship was moored, St. Nick would ride on his white horse through the centre of Rotterdam, for his triumphant entrance in The Netherlands. He was smartly dressed in a red robe and had a red miter on his head, because he was a bishop. With all the red in his dress he looked like a Communist on the May Day parade on the Red Square in Moscow but he looked good and he brought the presents and that's all that counted.

Instead of Clampus who accompanied St. Nicholas in Turkey and Italy, the Dutch had St. Nicholas accompanied by Black Peter, his helper, who was the Bogy Man who put the bad children in his bag to take them to Spain. He was also the unfortunate fellow who had to climb through the chimney to put the presents in the shoes that the children put underneath the chimney.

Everybody celebrated his birthday and he was honored everywhere. Originally, St. Nicholas was a feast for the children but the older people got into the celebrations as well by giving each other presents. Within no time, St. Nicholas became the most popular feast of The Netherlands.

Unfortunately, politics and religion were interfering. It was a Roman Catholic feast and the Protestant clergy didn't like it a bit that St. Nicholas celebrations were so popular. They criticized the honoring of St. Nick who was just a Roman Catholic Bishop who amounted to nothing. He had never done anything worthwhile and had never performed miracles; he certainly didn't deserve to be honored. The Protestants demanded that the feast should be outlawed.

However, the Dutch people kept celebrating and the Dutch Government didn't manage to get rid of St. Nicholas. The Dutch people had a good time and were not about to have the Government take it away from them. When the Protestants saw that they were losing the battle, they gave in that St. Nicholas was a good man who gave to good people but he wasn't holy. They didn't want to call him St. Nicholas so they called him Sinterklaas. That's why in The Netherlands there are two names, St. Nicholas by the Roman Catholics and Sinterklaas by the Protestants.

The celebration of St. Nicholas was not all that popular with the bad children who feared to be punished by St. Nicholas. Older children didn't necessarily believe in Saint Nick any more but the parents told them that if they didn't believe in Saint Nick any more they wouldn't get any presents.

Some younger children like Adrie didn't believe in Saint Nick anymore either. His sister was three years older than he was and of course she was proud to announce that Saint Nicholas didn't really exist. She had a good tip for Adrie, she said: "Don't tell our parents that you don't believe anymore in Saint Nick, just pretend that you believe or they won't give you anymore presents." That was real smart of his sister Adrie thought, what would he ever do without his sister?

The rumor that Saint Nick was a fake and the parents only told the story to keep the kids in line spread like wild fire. However, the bad kids weren't so sure when St. Nicholas Day came near. Their bad conscience was bothering them and they didn't feel so good when they were facing St. Nick.

Adrie's parents had noticed that Willie and Adrie weren't that impressed with St. Nick anymore. They figured that they had to do something about it to reinforce the respect for him. Just after St. Nicholas birthday, Adrie's father had visited Uncle Jaap and came back with the sob story that Adrie's cousin Corrie had been taken to Spain by Black Peter. Adrie wasn't that easily convinced but his father was hell bent to prove it to him.

The next morning Adrie received a picture postcard from Corrie in Spain. She had written on the back: "Greetings from Corrie in Spain, I was a naughty kid last year and Black Peter took me in his bag to Spain."

"Now do you believe there is a Saint Nicholas?" his father asked.

It was convincing alright but Adrie wasn't completely satisfied. Upon a thorough inspection of the postcard, he came to the conclusion that there was a Dutch postage stamp on it. Actually, he was very disappointed because he collected postage stamps and a stamp from Spain would have been welcome in his collection. How could it happen that a postcard that came from Spain had a Dutch postage stamp on it? When he told his father and mother that the card didn't come from Spain, they asked: "Why not?"

When Adrie told them that a postcard from Spain should have a Spanish postage stamp on it, Adrie's father had an explanation: "St. Nick must have had some postage stamps left from The Netherlands when he got back to Spain. He couldn't waste postage stamps and finished them up first."

Nice try! Even Adrie could see that St. Nick couldn't waste any postage stamps but he couldn't see that the post in Spain would let him do it. On further inspection of the card, he found out that the postcard stamp had been stamped on the post office of Bolnes, the town where Corrie lived. Now wasn't that a coincidence, those people sure tried hard to prove the existence of St. Nick. Adrie could smell a rat and told his father and mother that he didn't believe their story. "It just couldn't be," he said.

His father and mother looked meaningfully at each other signifying that they had bungled it. You just couldn't sell those kids apples and tell them that they were oranges. In a last ditch effort to save their scam his father said: "Your Uncle Jaap is coming on the weekend, so ask him if Corrie is in Spain."

When his Uncle Jaap came on the weekend, Adrie's father had briefed him on the gross bungling with the stamp. He had time to think about an explanation before he saw Adrie. As soon as he saw Adrie he said: "I received a picture postcard from Corrie yesterday. As you know St. Nick took her to Spain because she had misbehaved."

"I received a picture postcard from Corrie too," Adrie replied, "but it didn't come from Spain, it came from Bolnes. The post office stamped it Bolnes. You can't send postcards from Spain with a Dutch stamp on it; the post office won't allow it."

His uncle glanced at him as if he was testing his intelligence and thought: "What a smart Alec!"

He must have weighed his answer before his explanation came. He said calmly: "Oh no, the postcard was mailed in The Netherlands in Bolnes.

The captain of the steamboat came back to Bolnes after he had dropped off St. Nick in Spain. Santa's mail is always taken back to The Netherlands by the captain and the captain lives in Bolnes, that's why the postage stamp is stamped with Bolnes. All the Dutch children who were taken to Spain by St. Nick sent their mail back with the steamship. If Corrie behaves well, Black Peter might release her in a couple of weeks."

Nice try! Adrie could see it all; Corrie was going to be released just before he was going to visit his uncle. To him, the case was closed; he didn't even have to hire Perry Mason to solve the mystery of how a Dutch postage stamp happened to be on a picture postcard that came from Spain. It saved him a lot of money that he had figured it all out by himself.

After Willie heard this nonsense about Corrie who was supposed to be in Spain, she told Adrie: "Those people are pulling the wool over your eyes; there is enough evidence to prove that St. Nick does not exist."

If you don't believe in Santa you don't get presents, the parents told the kids. "Tough," said the older kids. "We never get much from Santa anyway."

It was very noticeable that St. Nick and the Devil had a lot in common; they were always shitting on the same pile. When the rich children got presents from Santa, he gave them out of the horn of plenty and as soon as he started to hand out presents to the poor kids they were very skimpy.

Sometimes there were rebellious kids who didn't take flack from anybody, not even from St. Nick. A boy, who was scolded by St. Nick for being naughty all the time, had the hang of the bogus Santa and told him off. He sputtered: "Why do I have to be such a good boy? That rotten kid across the street is a real pain and what do you do? You give him the nicest presents and I get all the crap. You can keep your presents; it's not worth my while to be good for a bunch of trash!"

Old St. Nick could put that in his pipe and smoke it.

Adrie didn't get all that much from Santa either, a few candies and perhaps a sweater that he desperately needed and that was all. There was a lot of room left in his shoes. The only toys he had was a cloth rabbit and a wooden duck. But one year Santa had outdone himself, probably Adrie's mother had made some extra money that she used for some toys.

Santa brought a toy car in a box. The box had a picture on it of how the car was supposed to look when it was assembled. When his mother looked at the box, she thought that the car was assembled but when Adrie unwrapped it; it wasn't. Ko had no connections with Detroit to get the car assembled so she had to find a friend who could do it.

Unfortunately, the parts must have been made by an unemployed Japanese laborer. The car was a lemon; it made exactly two trips from one wall to the other. Then the winding spring broke and the car was ready for the junk yard. To Adrie it didn't matter that the car didn't go by itself anymore, he just pushed it across the floor and that way the car went where he wanted it to go.

(The real problem is that we can't have a "Next Generation of St. Nick." There was a movie "Star Trek" which went over pretty good. After they had exhausted all possible angles of "Outer Space," they brought in The Next Generation. In St. Nick's case this is impossible because St. Nick can't get any children! Did I hear you ask "Why?" The answer is "Black Peter is carrying his bag." Ha, Ha, Ha and not Ho, Ho, Ho.)

Besides, the vulgar language kids used they had some beautiful songs. Most of them were disrespectful songs about St. Nick that aren't even suited for this realistic book. The children were singing a song:

See the moon is shitting brown beans,
On the rascal's balding head.

The rascal was St. Nick and the song was derived from a decent song. For the next song, "Parental guidance and viewer discretion is advised since it is uncensored."

Sinter Klaas was hoping and wishing,
To catch a big one when he was fishing,
His hook got caught in his own ass,
Ouch, ouch that was a nasty gash.

A visit from Saint Nick was always the highlight of Saint Nicholas Day and most of the kids were looking forward for it, except the real naughty ones. They had it coming. Uncles or neighbors would dress up as Saint Nicholas and Black Peter to make that visit to the kids. At school, two teachers would dress up and receive the kids for an audience.

Saint Nicholas Day wasn't a day free from school. The children didn't do much studying that day, all they did was singing nice songs about St. Nick to butter him up to give them presents. Most of the day was spent on singing and waiting the arrival of St. Nick.

St. Nick would see a class at a time and a messenger came to tell the class that his Sainthood was on his way over to Grade Four. Right away, the teacher would get the class to sing the Saint Nicholas songs they had practiced for weeks. That did St. Nick's old heart a lot of good. With proper decorum the good old Saint was seated, so that he wouldn't keel over during his stay. Black

Peter threw some ginger nuts and other candies on the floor to show that St. Nick was indeed the good Saint. That's the part the kids liked most, when they were scrambling for the candies.

Finally came the moment that all the students had to answer for all the bad things they had done in the past year. One by one, the students had to face St. Nick either to be praised or to be scolded. The good students were praised and told to keep up the good work. They were even sitting on his knee. The bad students didn't sit on his knee; they were standing shivering in front of St. Nick wondering what this Saint was going to do with them. They got a firm warning: "Shape up or I'll ship you to Spain." Most of the students were told that there was room for improvement except some favorites of the teacher who got nothing but praise.

Before Adrie was in Grade Four; he was always black listed by Saint Nick as well. He always received some kind of a scolding for his disobedience to the teacher. This time he wasn't even mentioned, the Saint had probably given up on him, which was an indication that his teacher had nothing to complain about him.

Most of the time, St. Nick did a lot of threatening which seldom materialized into anything. However, there came a time that St. Nick had to show who was boss and had to put up an example. He had to show the kids that he meant business, that he wasn't kidding and that it wasn't an idle threat to take naughty kids to Spain. After Black Peter had unloaded the presents and candies there was lots of room in his bag.

The worst student, Piet van der Velde, was at the end of the line; he needed special treatment and was singled out to show the kids what St. Nick did to bad kids. Piet had stolen all the erasers and pencils from the class storage room, and to top it off, he had also stolen his grandfather's golden watch. He was a boy with long fingers who stole like a raven. Of course, St. Nick knew all about his evil deeds and was going to deal with this bad kid once and for all.

When Piet appeared in front of St. Nick, Black Peter read from the "Book of Sins" about all the bad things he had done the past year. Judging by his face, St. Nick got real mad and said: "Say Black Peter, this boy doesn't listen at all, he is on the wrong track, we cannot condone such a misbehaviour; we have to teach this boy a lesson and smarten him up in Spain. You better put him in your bag."

Piet Van der Velde was always a real bully and bold as brass, but when St. Nick lashed out at him, he didn't look good at all. He was trembling on his legs and shivering all over; you could hear his teeth chatter when Black Peter took a step forward in his direction. Black Peter turned to St. Nick and said: "Yes, St. Nick, I agree, the best thing to do is smarten him up in Spain."

Black Peter grabbed Piet van der Velde and put the screaming kid into his bag. Piet was struggling to get free, but Black Peter was a robust guy; he was a guy that you rather have as a friend instead of an enemy. Besides those black guys were good in boxing and Piet van der Velde was not about to be "The Last White Hope." He was in the bag and stayed in the bag. Piet started to howl like a wolf in a snowstorm on the Siberian tundra and yelled: "Oh sweet dear St. Nick; please let me out of the bag and don't take me to Spain. I'll never do it again and I'll be a good well behaved boy all year and I promise to be obedient."

When St. Nick heard the plea of the little bandit with the words good, well behaved and obedient, it worked as oil on the waves and melted St. Nick's old heart. The old Saint straightened his back in spite of his age. In the sagas of the "Arabian Nights" the magic words were: "Sesame Selassimi Open Up" and the door of solid rock opened. In dealing with St. Nick the magic words were "Good, Well behaved and Obedient."

When St. Nick heard those magic words he said to Black Peter: "Say, Black Peter, do you hear that? This boy promises to be good, well behaved and obedient, all year. What do you think? Maybe we should give him one more last chance."

Black Peter said: "If he promises all those things St. Nick, I agree we should try it one more time; I'll let him out of the bag."

St. Nick wasn't finished with Piet who stood now shaking in front of him. St. Nick wanted to cash in while the going was good and give him a last reprimand. Piet was quite shaken by the turn of events and shuddered at the thought of being taken to Spain in a bag. He looked as white as a ghost when he listened to the conditions he had to meet to regain his freedom.

St. Nick shook his threatening finger in front of Piet's face and said: "You better remember, all year, what you have promised me. If you break your promise only once, next year you won't be so lucky to get out of the bag."

Piet replied: "Oh, yes, my dearest Saint Nicholas, I'll keep my promise all year; you can count on it that I'll be good." Still relatively shaken, Piet returned to his seat and uttered not even one word for the rest of the afternoon. He was certainly impressed.

All of the kids had followed this spectacle of a kid being bagged by Black Peter with visible interest. Nobody had ever witnessed St. Nick that mad before. However, St. Nick had to show the school kids who was boss.

St. Nick was the Good Nick and some kind of a Boogy Man when you misbehaved. When the children grew up and dumped St. Nick as a hot potato, the parents and teacher changed tactics. They preached that there was God who would punish you and there was the police who would put you in jail and the Reform School. To Adrie this looked like a double whammy, first the police would get you and in the hereafter God would punish you again. It sure showed everybody that crime didn't pay.

If you play Monopoly and you have to draw a Chance Card, you might draw a card telling you: "Go direct to jail, don't go through Go and don't collect $200." This might sound terrible, this kind of treatment when you have to go to jail, but it's nothing compared to the jail Adrie's parents were picturing.

According to his parents if you had to go direct to jail, the police would throw you in jail, you had to eat dry bread and you had to sit all day in the dark. Of course, there was electric light in jail but you had to sit in the dark so that you could think about your sins. If there is light, your mind is distracted because you see things. The truth was that if you were in jail, they put you to work. In The Netherlands you had to glue paper bags for the grocery stores. They had a job for you when you were in jail and sitting in the dark was out of the question.

Of course that was the jail from yesterday; nowadays the jail birds are certainly not eating dry bread in the dark. They are eating steak and are watching T.V. It's in the planning to purchase some trailers, in order that the people in jail have their wife or girl friend coming for the weekend so they can have sex.

The gay community is already shouting "discrimination" and want their gay partner to have the same rights. In the States, this sex on the weekend business for the inmates is already in full swing. Watson, a serial killer, has made good use out of those romantic weekends; he fathered three children while in jail. His nincompoop girlfriend, with her three children, is on welfare at the tax payer's expense.

Where is punishment? The tax payer always pays for this kind of nonsense. Even when there is an election there are ballot boxes in jail so the poor prisoner can vote because it is his constitutional right. It used to be that when you had jail time you automatically lost those rights, it was part of your punishment.

No the convict of today is not sitting in the dark thinking about his sins. It's very likely that some of the inmnates are holding hands with their gay partner on the weekends. If they think about anything at all, they probably think about the next heist after they come out of jail and are thinking about a better way to pull it off so that they don't get caught.

The jail birds used to make the license plates for the cars in Saskatchewan, that was in the time that you got a new license plate every year. Nowadays, we have to economize and get a new license plate every five years. Consequently we have a nice new shiny car with a crumbled up license plate.

When growing up kids trespassed on the laws, they had to answer to the Children's Judge in Juvenile Court. Instead of sending them to jail, he sent them to Reform School. If you had done something wrong, you were always threatened with Reform School. Only if you had gone too far would they send juvenile delinquents to Reform School. Even if you had stolen something valuable such as money or jewellery, they would give you a firm warning and some kind of a second chance. When you stole apples or pears from the neighbour's yard they might threaten to send you to Reform School but that was just an idle threat. If they had to put all the kids that stole apples or pears to Reform School, most of the boys would have been there.

Murder meant automatically Reform School and you wouldn't be released till your 21st birthday. At the Princess Juliana School it happened twice that a boy was sent to Reform school. The first case was Piet van der Velde versus the people. In spite that he was once put in the bag of Black Peter, he ran into trouble after trouble. He had stolen and sold a golden watch and got a second chance from St. Nicholas and the police. St. Nicholas had warned him that any more wrong doing would get him into Spain and the police had warned him that he would go to Reform School.

Not long after, he got a licking from the Principal after misbehaving in the classroom. He threw a tantrum and shouted at the Principal that he would kill him. After school, he told the other kids that he would bring a knife to school in the afternoon and he would stick the knife in that bald-headed Principal's heart.

Indeed in the afternoon, he brought a knife to school; it was only a little box cut knife but it was sharp. Piet was very proud of himself and showed the knife to everybody. He stated: "That bastard of a Principal is as good as dead; I'll finish him for good."

A couple of tell tales were so friendly to inform the Principal of his pending death. The Principal went up to Piet and demanded that he surrender the knife. Piet got very angry and shouted: "The only way you'll get my knife is in your heart!"

The Principal managed to get a hold of the knife blade but Piet pulled it through his hand and the Principal ended up with all his fingers severely cut. The police picked Piet up the same afternoon and when he appeared in Juvenile Court, the Judge said that he was a very dangerous boy and had to learn obedience and manners. He was sentenced to one year in Reform School.

The second case which resulted in Reform School was "The people versus Joe." This case was of quite a different nature. Actually, one could say that it was all about nature. When Joe was already in the seventh grade and was about 13 years old; he became sexually active which was a "no, no."

It started when he walked through the pasture that there were some cows in heat and for lack of a bull the cows jumped on each other. At that stage the cows are dry; (that is, if it doesn't rain) and don't give milk anymore. A visit to the bull produces a calf and the cow gives milk again so she can feed her calf.

When Joe saw that the cows needed a bull, he got the wrong idea; he beat the bull to it, jumped on the cows and acted as a bull. Adrie was still a few years younger than Joe, he had seen a bull jump on a cow but never had he seen a boy jump on a cow. The other kids tried to tell him not to do that because the farmer wouldn't like it if he saw it. Maybe the farmer wouldn't have liked it but the cows didn't seem to mind it at all. Whenever Joe walked through the pasture the cows were following him close as if they were begging him: "Joe, come back, let's do it again." For lack of a bull in the pasture the cows liked Joe for an amorous affair.

It wouldn't have been so bad if he had stuck with the cows but when the amorist expanded his horizons and tackled a girl, he was finished. One day he grabbed a thirteen-year old girl, threw her on the ground, tore her panties down and jumped on top of her. The cows had been very cooperative but the girl started to scream: "Mother, mother, the boy is doing it to me."

Joe knew how to fix that problem; he stuffed a handkerchief in her mouth and continued. There was only one problem, the girl acted differently from the cows. Had the cows walked behind him to get more, the girl ran straight to her mother and told her all about Joe. Her mother went to the Principal and the Principal questioned Joe.

The Principal scolded him severely and called him a dirty boy to have sex. Joe's defence was: "What's so dirty about sex, if it wasn't for people having sex nobody of us would be here, unless the Lord made us all from dust and blew life into our nostrils like he did with Adam."

That statement didn't go over at all at a Christian school, the Principal called the police and Joe was promptly arrested. When he got in Court the Judge didn't give him a Stud of the Year Award. The Judge didn't give him a warning either; he called it rape, sent him straight to Reform School for two years and stated that he had to learn proper morals and ethics at the Reform School.

It's very doubtful that two years at the Reform School makes a kid demure. Some kids went from the frying pan into the fire when they went to Reform School as is illustrated in the next joke.

(A boy who had sexually assaulted a couple of girls was sent to Reform School like Joe, to be reformed to a decent citizen. After half a year at the Reform School, he was allowed to stay with his family for a weekend. His father picked him up and when they were sitting in the bus, on their way home, the father thought: "I just wonder if he improved after half a year at the Reform School."

He decided to test his son and said: "Look at the nice girl in front of the bus, nice legs, nice boobs, nice..."

At this stage his son interrupted his dad and said: "That's nothing dad, look what a nice behind that male bus driver has."

Yes, you could see that he really had improved at the Reform School.)

Most of the punishment the children had to endure was to be sent to bed without food. It's a punishment that is hard to understand how that it will accomplish anything. Send a child to bed but feed it first; a growing child needs good food so the body can develop properly. This was sure bad parenting but many kids faced this punishment.

Whenever Adrie's parents sent him to bed without food, he didn't care at all if they were eating Brussels sprouts because that was the only thing he just couldn't swallow. It made him keck at it so he was toying with his food. His parents didn't believe in rejecting good food, not wanting Brussels sprouts was bologna. (Nice try, all of a sudden Brussels sprouts were bologna.) When the Brussels sprouts were cooking on the stove, it already made him sick to the stomach. He just couldn't stand the sight, smell or taste of Brussels sprouts.

When they put Brussels sprouts on his plate underneath his very nose, he started to heave which made his father mad. He sent him to his bedroom with his plate with Brussels sprouts and potatoes, with the message not to come out of his bedroom until such a time that his plate was empty. With a sigh of relief he did what he was told, for a change, and disappeared into his bedroom because in his bedroom he could handle Brussels sprouts. He ate the potatoes and the Brussels sprouts went into his pocket, to be discarded outside at an appropriate time. All of a sudden his plate was empty and he could return to the table for his porridge.

Adrie's parents loved Brussels sprouts and therefore they ate them every Sunday during the winter months, when Brussels sprouts were available. No, there was no understanding for his problem at all because fresh vegetables were good for you. He couldn't agree with them more; as long as they were talking about cooked pears or apple sauce but in his humble opinion, Brussels sprouts were good for nothing, they only made him sick.

Of course, children weren't supposed to swear or use four letter words; if they did, their mother washed out their mouth with water and soap and then all of a sudden lovely words would come out of their mouth. At school when the teacher heard one of the boys use four letter words, he said: "Did your mother never wash out your mouth with water and soap when you were swearing?" The boy answered: "Yes, she did, but it didn't help bugger all."

(Joke time! A little boy had lost his parents in an accident. The boy was Roman Catholic and instead of sending him to an orphanage, the priest decided to take care of the orphan. However, there was one problem; the boy had been raised in the slums and was swearing like a trooper, he could sing the swear words and curse all angels out of heaven. That didn't go over very well with the priest so he decided to teach the boy not to swear anymore. He said to the boy: "It's sin to use the name of the Lord in vain, God will punish you for this!"

The boy replied: "That's all very nice and dandy but when I'm mad I have to swear."

The priest said: "It's all in your head, if you get mad you can just as well say: 'Hooray' instead of all the terrible swear words you are using."

Every time the boy was swearing, the priest reminded him to say: "Hooray" instead. At last the boy didn't swear at all anymore and the priest was very happy with the result. He turned out to be a nice boy after all, the priest thought.

One day when the priest and the boy were walking in the woods, the boy had to go to the bathroom for a big job. The priest said: "Go and do it behind that bush there where nobody can see you."

The boy disappeared behind the bush and after a few minutes the priest heard loud swearing. When the priest went to investigate what the problem was he said to the boy: "I thought we had an agreement that you would say: 'Hooray' instead of swearing."

The boy said: "Go to hell, I'm not going to shout "hooray" when I'm hanging with my behind in the barbed wire.")

When the kids were growing up they could get a licking any place. One time Adrie was running behind the bus and got his ears boxed by a man from the neighborhood who said: "You can't run behind a bus, it's dangerous."

Very wisely, Adrie didn't say anything at home about the incident. His parents would have said: "The man is right," and they would have given him an additional licking.

THE STINKER AND THE GIRL CRAZY BOY

Going to school when your father was unemployed caused some harassment by the other kids who were fortunate enough that their father was working. They stated that your father was a lazy bum who did absolutely nothing.

There were other degrading encounters for the children of the unemployed. Once a year the school went on a day's outing by buses to children's entertainment parks and did some sight seeing. Every week the children had to bring ten cents to pay for this day's outing. Of course, with the desperate money situation at home, Adrie couldn't participate and didn't go out on that day.

There was also provision for the children to get milk at school for five cents. Again it was something only the rich kids could enjoy because Adrie's parents were poor. The rich kids would get milk at school, went on a day's outing, had better education, better health and had more fun. (Except the blondes who have always more fun according to the advertising.)

Adrie had all kinds of encounters with his teachers. When his report card said: "Advanced to Grade Three," it meant that he finally was rid of Miss Kouwenhoven, the sour puss. She had made his life sour although the final couple of months there had been a turn around when she wasn't picking on him anymore. In spite of that, he couldn't love her but at least he could stomach her.

For the first time that he went to school, Adrie was facing a male teacher. The first two grades were taught by female teachers and from the Third Grade on there were male teachers. Probably, the school board had figured that the first two grades wouldn't pose a problem for female teachers but when the kids got bigger masculinity was needed.

Adrie wasn't all that impressed with Mr. Kerselen who was teaching the Third Grade. It could very well be that he had landed from the frying pan in the fire the way it looked. The problem was that Mr. Kerselen loved the girls and had very little use for the boys, if any. He and Miss Kouwenhoven could have been great contenders for the Nobel Prize in discrimination.

The main reason that Adrie couldn't get along with him was because of the sick jokes that Mr. Kerselen thought were funny but Adrie thought they were not. Whenever he thought the joke was funny he would laugh and if it was just another sick joke he wouldn't laugh. What's wrong with that?

Everything was wrong with that. When you are working and the boss tells a sick joke, everybody laughs or you don't get a raise. Worse yet, you might be without a job. Mr. Kerselen couldn't fire his students when they weren't laughing about his jokes but he could be plenty miserable to them.

A head on collision was in the offing and it happened when Mr. Kerselen was teaching Dutch language. He was trying to explain that "less" means without. He mentioned a few examples such as "Fatherless children are children without a father" and "Motherless children are children without a mother." The class was asked to mention some more. One kid said: "Childless people are people without children." Another kid said: "If something is harmless it is without harm."

"Very good," said the teacher.

"What the other kids can do, I can do too, if not better," Adrie thought. Unfortunately it didn't turn quite out for the better.

In The Netherlands there was a big transportation company with two owners "Lawrence and Les.". On all the big trucks that they owned, the name of the company was painted in big letters, "Lawrence and Les." Everybody knew the name of that company; it was like Mercedes and Benz. Why did Adrie think of something stupid? He was going to participate in providing words with "less" and raised his hand. Once he had the floor he said: "Lawrence and Les."

Everybody understood that this was bull and laughed, except one person who didn't laugh. It was the teacher. He probably wanted to get even, Adrie thought; if he didn't laugh about his jokes he wouldn't laugh about my jokes. To top it off, he started to raise the roof and said very uncomplimentary things to him. He said: "You probably think you are the comedian here but I won't condone such behavior in my classroom! You come here to study and not to poke fun at everything I try to teach you! You probably think you are the funniest at home but here at school this is not appreciated. Go and stand in the hall until you get serious with studying!"

When the teacher said that he thought he was the funniest at home it occurred to him to say: "I'm not the funniest at home; the doorknob is the funniest because he shakes hands with everybody who enters the house." That was some kind of a sick joke in those days. However, on second thought he decided it was smarter to shut up and stand in the hall until this sourpuss got over his disappointment that the class had laughed so spontaneously about what he had said.

The next incident didn't end with standing in the hall. There was some kind of a stupid riddle. "It's green and it flies through the sky. What is it?" The answer was "A Brussels Sprout behind a flying machine."

When Mr. Kerselen told his stupid joke riddle, nobody in the class knew the answer but Adrie did. Proudly he put his finger in the air. The teacher responded: "So you think you know what's green and flies through the sky."

Adrie said: "Yes Sir, it's the spit of a pilot!"

Everybody laughed except the teacher and Adrie. After Mr. Kerselen was through with him he had nothing to laugh about.

There was another incident in the classroom but this time Adrie played no role in it. One of the boys had to write something on the blackboard and while he was writing he scratched his behind with his other hand. The teacher said: "Don't you stand there scratching your tart."

"I have ants in my pants," the boy replied.

The teacher didn't understand what the boy said and asked him to repeat and the boy said: "I said I have beetles on my butt." Of course the teacher didn't like this vulgar language and the teacher sent him to the hall.

Of course, there was the unnecessary graffiti on the bathroom walls. One time when Adrie went to the bathroom he admired a master piece.

I am the Angel Gabriel,
I shit sausages very well.

The lyrics were so good that he had to repeat that in the classroom to the other boys. They all liked it, but the teacher who overheard it was a rotten spoiler. He shouted at Adrie: "Vulgar language like that is not acceptable in the classroom; I will not condone it. Do you understand that?" Adrie replied: "Hear! Hear!"

The teacher didn't like that answer and said: "Go and stand in the hallway!"

Adrie could tell that the teacher meant business and hurried to the safety of the hallway before the teacher decided to give him a spanking. The hallway wasn't as safe as Adrie had thought it to be. It wasn't all that bad to stand there away from the fury of the angry teacher. Unfortunately, he had come from purgatory into hell. After standing in the hall for a few minutes, the Principal walked through the hall. He was really interested as to why Adrie was standing in the hallway. It was very nice of the Principal to show interest in him, but he could figure that this whole thing was going to have serious repercussions.

He asked: "What are you doing in the hallway?"

His honest answer was: "Nothing!" That was the truth and nothing but the truth. That answer didn't satisfy the Principal and he wanted to know what he had done to deserve this. Adrie's answer was again: "Nothing!"

For a while it looked as if the Principal was mad that Adrie was sent to the hallway for nothing because he walked madly into the classroom. He was probably going to straighten out Adrie's teacher. Of course, he had that wrong again and when the Principal returned he hadn't straightened out

Adrie's teacher, he straightened Adrie out instead. When Adrie was reading the graffiti on the toilet wall and also when he repeated it in the classroom, he had been laughing. At this crucial moment in his life, there wasn't a smile left on his face. Why did this Principal have to poke his nose into everything? It was bad enough to be punished by the teacher. Looking at the cheerful face of the Principal could mean a calamity for Adrie.

It turned out worse than he had expected. The Principal thought that Adrie had written the poem on the wall and apparently he didn't like the lyrics. That he didn't like the poem wasn't Adrie's fault. He wasn't as good as Robert Burns yet but give him time, he was still young. For the next three minutes, Adrie had to listen to a moralizing sermon. The Principal said: "You always seem to think that you are funny, but those vulgar rhymes aren't funny at all, they are disgraceful. You can't keep going on like this because you are a bad example for the rest of the class. If you keep doing those evil things you'll be heading straight for the gallows."

At least Adrie had his future forecast free; that was a bargain. If he had to go to the gypsy to have his future told it would cost him a buck. The Principal did it for free and he didn't even have to ask. After all, Adrie had to clean all the smear and grime from the entire toilet door. He hadn't even written anything on that door and really got undeserved credit.

For poetry, the toilet door is a winner everywhere in the world. People become instant poets when they are sitting on the biffy for some reason. There was another poem on the toilet door what made Adrie smile but he had learned his lesson and said nothing in the class room. He certainly didn't need another job of cleaning the toilet door.

There was another red mark for behaviour on Adrie's report card. That was no surprise at all with a teacher who doesn't understand students who don't laugh at his sick jokes. In his book that meant bad behaviour and in Adrie's book it meant a red five on his report card.

(In spite that Mr. Kerselen didn't like Adrie's jokes, there are a few good ones about teachers who ask questions in order to get some stupid answer.

One day the teacher said: "We know that heat causes an object to expand and cold causes it to contract. Now, can any one give me a good example?"

Billy: "Well, in summer the days are long and in winter the days are short."

Teacher: "What does it mean when the barometer is falling?"

Student: "It means that the guy who nailed it up did a lousy job!"

The teacher said: "Everyone who thinks that he or she is stupid, stands up."

After a minute had gone by, a little boy stood up. The teacher asked: "Do you think that you are stupid?"

The boy answered: "No I don't but I hate to see you standing there by yourself."

The father tests his six year old son in arithmetic to find out how well he could do division. He asked: "If you have four pears to divide with two. How many pears does each one get."

Johnny answered: "I don't know."

The father: "Why not?"

Johnny: "Because at school we always divide with apples."

(Of course when you are dividing pears, it depends with whom you are dividing. If you divide four pears with my brother, he gets three and I get one.)

The teacher said to Robby's mother: "Your son has a thirst for learning, does that come from you or your husband?"

"From both of us," answered the proud mother. "He got the learning from me and the thirst from his father.")

The kids at school made crazy drawings that weren't appreciated by the teacher. Kids pictured everything the way they saw it. When they were making drawings, in their expression of art, they didn't leave anything out. They drew animals in full detail and nothing was missing. Whenever they entered a horse or cow stable, there was always a pile of shit behind the animals and when the kids were drawing animals, the pile of shit was never missing.

The teachers at school didn't really appreciate that kind of drawing, especially when they drew them on the blackboard. They probably never had been in a horse stable which explains why they didn't know anything about it.

There are a lot of abbreviations with letters meaning something. The class got a special assignment to jot down all abbreviations with four letters. As for example "G.D.F.C." which means "General Dutch Football Club." And "R.D.A.C." which means "Royal Dutch Auto Club." The abbreviation "U.S.A." wouldn't qualify because it only has three letters. You also had to know the meaning of the letters.

When the students brought their homework back to school, they took turns announcing their abbreviations. Everything went right until one of the pupils came up with "S.D.A.P." which means "Social Democratic Arbeits (Labor) Party." It was a qualifying abbreviation but the teacher didn't want to hear what the letters meant. When the student wanted to mention what the letters meant, the teacher cut him off and said: "We all know that it means 'Support the Darned Absent Peanut man.'"

In the Netherlands, the Socialist Party was the S.D.A.P. and since the education was biased, Socialism didn't suit the purpose of the Christian school.

Consequently Socialism was outlawed in the curriculum and you weren't supposed to talk about it. Christian Churches and schools alike had the policy that Socialists were rebels. In many countries, when Socialism started, the church lost its power in government. "Ostrich Policy," was followed by the churches. If you don't like it you pretend it doesn't exist and stick your head in the sand. "If you hear no evil and see no evil then there is no evil."

(U.S.S.R. meaning United Socialist Soviet Republics would have qualified as a four letter abbreviation. Only in Canada and other English speaking countries would it have qualified. In The Netherlands the U.S.S.R. was known as Russia. Just as well; nobody wanted to hear the explanation of the teacher what those letters meant anyway.

The U.S.A. is by no means the only United States in the world, among the United States are the U.S.S.R. Yes, they were forcibly united but so was the U.S.A. during the Civil war.)

Education at the Princess Juliana School was biased, prejudiced and racist. It was so bad that when a Negro kid came to the school, the children were keeping their distance and were very careful not to touch the black kid lest they would become black themselves. They probably thought that it was contagious. When one of the kids accidently touched the black kid, he looked fearfully at his hand, afraid that some of the black had rubbed off on his hand.

On the positive side of the education, the school had some guests coming in to demonstrate different things. At one time they had a potter with a potter's wheel who demonstrated how pottery was made. Everybody had a kick at the cat and could try for a few minutes to make an earthen bowl on the potter's wheel.

There was also a Negro from Surinam, a Dutch colony, who paid a visit to the school. The reason that they allowed a black man to visit the school was that he was a teacher in Surinam. They didn't see him as a Negro but as a teacher. He showed different things from Surinam, among them a coconut. Nobody had ever seen a coconut before and everybody had thought that the only trees in the world were apple and pear trees. The Negro told them that in the Tropics there were Palm Trees. That was educational.

What was even more educational was that the Negro was walking with an earthen crock with water on his head without holding it with his hands. Adrie was amazed and was going to try that as soon as he was home. He didn't have an earthen crock so he took a pail of water instead. When the pail with water crashed on the floor, his mother came to have a look what was going on and when she saw all the water on the floor she still wondered what was going on. She got the hang of the picture when Adrie announced that he wasn't going to Surinam after all because he couldn't carry a pail with water on his head.

Despite that Adrie was fired as the comedian of the classroom, the year went by pretty fast. However, there was no happy ending to this story since reconciliation between teacher and student did not occur. The teacher disliked him and the dislike was mutual. In spite that Adrie didn't laugh at his jokes, he moved on and was advanced to Grade Four. Mr. Kerselen couldn't have failed him in Grade Three, he was the top student of the class and moreover he wanted to get rid of the competition in telling jokes.

From past experience Adrie knew that it was better not to be noticed very much. It was no good to be in the foreground so he decided to try for the background. In plain English this means that he was trying to sit in the back of the class, rather than in front where the teacher could see him. That was a brilliant idea, so why did it backfire?

When the students entered the Fourth Grade classroom for the first time, Adrie tried very desperately to sit in the very back of the classroom, preferably behind a couple of tall guys to hide a bit, in order not to be noticed. To be noticed had turned out to be very hard on his behind, which took the brunt of the outburst of his furious teachers.

Mr. Sybrandy didn't look too bad but that could be deceptive, his experience told him. He was only eight years old but he had already had a lot of experience and he learned fast, especially when he got a spanking. For a starter, the teacher let the students select their seats to enable them to sit beside their favorite friend. He could always correct the seating, if in his opinion this was needed. Adrie was heading for the rear of the class but somehow all the seats in the back of the class had been taken. There were probably more boys who had the same idea of sitting in the rear and had secured a seat already. He should have patented his brilliant idea.

Too late now; so he decided to take a seat anywhere. However, all the seats were taken except two. The Principal had counted the number of students who were registered for the class and had made sure there were enough seats. There were going to be 11 girls and 12 boys in the class. Twelve benches would be just right since there were two children to a bench. According to the Principal's calculation there should be one vacant seat. That's exactly the way it worked out, if Adrie had taken a seat there would have been only one vacant seat.

Adrie had a problem with that because they had a stinker in the class. Piet Vandervelde pissed his pants a couple of times a day and also pooped his pants. Boys were all wearing shorts and at a couple of occasions there had been a hunk of poop lying underneath his bench that had dropped from his shorts. He stank an hour in the wind and of course nobody wanted to sit beside him. Therefore the teacher had put him in the very last bench of the classroom. That way the smell wouldn't bother the other students as much.

The teacher had received a report about the behavior of his new students from the teacher in Grade 3 and knew that he had to put up with a stinker and of course a comedian. He had been waiting to intercept Piet Vandervelde to put him right away in the last bench. Nobody was going to sit beside him, yet that was the only place left, except there was another seat vacant beside Mary Thunderman. That was Adrie's second problem because boys didn't sit next to girls at school, so that was out.

Actually, Adrie had his wish, he could sit in the back of the class without the competition of his classmates; the very thing he always wanted. However, his desire to sit in the rear of the class had completely disappeared. He would rather sit in front of the classroom than beside the stinker. It seemed that he had fixed his own wagon but good and was just standing in the back of the class not knowing what to do.

Mr. Sybrandy overlooked the classroom as a general overlooks his troops. He turned to Adrie and said: "Be seated. There are still seats left."

Oh yes, he knew there were seats left but come hell, high water or an angry teacher, nobody in this whole wide world could make him sit beside the stinker. No way Jose!

The teacher asked: "What seems to be the problem? There are two seats left."

That was a stupid question, if Adrie had ever heard one. If Mr. Sybrandy didn't know what the problem was, he surely was going to tell him all about it. Adrie said: "I'm not going to sit beside Piet Vandervelde because he shits his pants."

The teacher hadn't thought there was going to be a problem to seat the students. He said: "There is one more seat left beside a girl, so if you don't want to sit beside Piet Vandervelde, you'll have to sit beside a girl."

Probably, the teacher had figured by giving him an option that he would elect to sit beside Piet Vandervelde instead of sitting next to a girl. He sure had that wrongly figured. The choice was easy for Adrie; he didn't mind sitting beside a girl, she didn't poop her pants and smelled a lot better than the stinker.

It was with the blessing of the teacher that he stepped to the bench where Mary Thunderman was sitting by her lonesome self. He seated himself next to her on the same bench and thought that she would be happy to have a new neighbor. On the contrary, as soon as he sat down, she jumped out of the bench as if she had been stung by a whole swarm of bees. She announced to the teacher that she wasn't going to sit beside a boy. Marie probably thought that boys had leprosy.

Seating the class was a problem that didn't seem to go away. Mr. Sybrandy frowned meaningfully at the class as if he was praying for wisdom to solve this hostile situation of girls versus boys. The class was in suspense wondering what the teacher was going to do next. Personally, Adrie wouldn't care less; it was not his problem anymore, he had a seat and that's all that counted.

If the teacher would have had the wisdom of Solomon, he would probably have sawn the bench into two halves. That would have solved the problem. Actually, the teacher was better than Solomon, he asked: "Who of the girls doesn't mind sitting beside a boy?"

Stientje Louter raised her hand and the teacher said: "O.K. go and sit beside Adrie!"

Stientje Louter sat down beside Adrie and Mary Thunderman occupied the vacant seat of Stientje Louter. At that stage a movie could have been made and called "The battle of the sexes." Unfortunately, Adrie missed the boat which meant that the world had to wait for fifty years before somebody else thought of it.

The teacher was obviously happy the seating problem had been resolved and carried on with teaching the class. When the Principal saw that there was a mixed bench in Grade Four, he said: "I'll see if I can find another bench somewhere."

Stientje Louter replied: "What for, I have no problem sitting beside a boy. At home I'm sitting beside my brother and he happens to be a boy, too."

The Principal seemed amazed with this so true statement and said: "Very well then, that saves me a lot of trouble."

The mixed bench got along pretty well. However, the other boys of the class had to say something about this arrangement and called Adrie a sissy and a girl crazy boy. They said: "If you are a boy at all you wouldn't sit beside a girl. That is never done at school!"

It didn't matter to Adrie what they said, they probably were jealous that he had such a pretty neighbor. He just pretended that he didn't hear the comments and since they didn't get him mad, the name calling was finished in a couple of days.

For several months there was a mixed bench in Grade Four. The situation changed when one of the boys moved away and another seat became available. It was strange to sit next to a boy again, and actually he missed that bright girl who had shared a bench with him for that long.

Most of the teachers of the Princess Juliana School were very strict and dictatorial but Mr. Sybrandy, the teacher of the Fourth Grade, seemed to be different. He had a little understanding for youngsters who were growing up. There was one thing Adrie never ran out of, it was fantasy. He always thought of something stupid which got him into trouble several times.

There was a hymn that they were singing with a line in it "The Lord cleanses sinners." When people were taking a bath and put clean underwear on, they would say: "I'm going to cleanse myself." When they were singing the hymn and came to the line, "The Lord cleanses sinners," Adrie mumbled to himself: "He must have given them a bath and put clean underwear on them."

The two boys who were sitting in front of him heard that and started to laugh. When the teacher heard that Adrie said something that made the boys laugh, he said to him: "If you have something funny to say, come to the front of the class to tell it, then we all can laugh."

There he was in front of the class with his mouthful of teeth, almost peeing his pants from anxiety, because of the dire consequences which were in store for him. Why couldn't he control his lips and shut up for a change? He had buggered up before and had obviously learned nothing.

The teacher waited patiently for a minute or so. You could hear a pin drop which wasn't there; it probably was the sweat running off his face hitting the floor that you could hear. After the teacher had been patient, he became impatient and said: "Well?"

That gave Adrie another bright idea. However, from unpleasant experiences, he knew that his bright ideas weren't very well received at school. In spite of that, he was going to give it his best shot and said: "A well is a hole in the ground; if the hole is horizontal it's a tunnel."

The teacher probably knew that already and said: "Very good but that's not what you said back in your bench. Tell us what's so funny!"

Adrie was on pins and needles but no way was he going to repeat what he had said. Making fun of a hymn was certainly intolerable, he could sense that. It would be better to be punished for his refusal to repeat what he had said than to be punished for the stupid thing he had said.

The teacher knew a better way to get results. He said to the two boys who had been laughing: "You two boys come to the front of the class and tell us this funny thing so we can laugh, too."

One of the boys was friendly enough to tell the whole story in full detail. The class roared with laughter, there were only two persons in the classroom who weren't laughing; the teacher and Adrie. All of a sudden he didn't see the fun of it anymore; there was nothing to laugh about. Without a doubt, the teacher who wasn't laughing was going to punish him for his evil deeds. He was standing in front of his teacher as dumb as a sheep stands in front of his shearer. He was always talkative but now he was tongue tied and had nothing to say.

According to the Bible "Miracles Happen" and the Bible was right. The teacher said: "Go back to your seat and commence your arithmetic exercise."

Adrie couldn't believe his ears that he got away with all this. The teacher probably had thought it was funny too that his student had seen it that way but you couldn't see that on his straight face. As a teacher he probably wasn't supposed to laugh, at least not at school. He probably told all those funny things to his wife so they could laugh together.

Adrie could consider himself very fortunate that he was a fast learner. On the other hand he also seemed to be a slow learner; he never learned how to stay out of trouble. The stupid songs they were singing got to him again. This time it wasn't a hymn, it was a spring song that went as follows:

The cold harsh winter is at bay,
Now laughs the lovely May.

When they were singing "Now laughs the lovely May," Adrie thought it right to add the laughter to the song and said: "Ha, ha, ha!" A burst of laughter of the class followed. It looked as if he was a born entertainer, he got everybody laughing again.

The teacher stopped the rest of the song and said to Adrie: "If you know the lyrics of the song better, why don't you come in front of the class to demonstrate how they should be."

The way this Grade Four was going, he was standing in front of the class more than the teacher. Adrie thought that the teacher had it in mind to let him sing the song by himself in front of the class. When he was standing in front of the class, the teacher said: "So you think that you are the lovely May that's laughing?"

As usual, whenever he was standing in front of the class, his speech had disappeared and he had nothing to say. He didn't know whether he should say yes or no. The teacher knew how to handle a silent treatment and said: "Let's try that song again, the class will do the singing but you shut up because you are the lovely May, so you get to do the laughing. Got the picture?"

Adrie didn't particularly like it but he got the picture. The teacher started the singing by the class. As a real conductor he was swinging his conductor stick up and down as a yo-yo. After the class had sung, "Now laughs the lovely May," the teacher stopped the singing of the class and turned to Adrie for the laughing part. Modestly he said: "Ha, ha, ha."

The teacher said: "That's not much laughter for a lovely May after a cold harsh winter. Can't you do any better representing the lovely May?"

To make the teacher happy, he added to his part, "Ha, ha, ha, ha."

The roar of laughter that followed was tumultuous. Adrie had never heard the class laugh that loud, it was almost like a riot. Even the teacher seemed to enjoy it and wasn't going to stop the fun, he just let it go. When the laughter finally subsided and calm had returned to the classroom, the teacher said to

Adrie: "I hope you got it out of your system. This time I want the song perfect without the laughing part."

It never happened again that the class sang that good, they sang like Carusos. At last they had a teacher who appreciated humour and liked a joke. It improved the morale, teaching and learning considerably in the classroom. Teachers come in all shapes and sizes, all with their own idea how to keep order in the classroom. This Mr. Sybrandy gave the students the opportunity to get the crazy things out of their head. He had a little understanding.

ORANGE FOREVER

The Royals in The Netherlands were from the Orange Dynasty that went back all the way to 1568 when Willem of Orange, a German Principality, came to The Netherlands to help the Dutch to battle the Spanish that ruled The Netherlands. His nick name was "William the Silent." That nick name wasn't bestowed on him because he talked the ears off your head. On the contrary, when they tried to get some information from him, he asked: "Can you keep a secret?" The answer was "Yes." He promptly said: "Me too."

His motto was: "Speaking is silver but being silent is gold."

It was a religious struggle. After Marten Luther had established the Protestant Church, the Spanish Roman Catholics burned the Protestants at the stake. It only took Willem of Orange and his successors 80 years to get the Spanish out of The Netherlands.

However, after the Spanish were sent home, Willem I became Governor of The Netherlands. After Willem I died, his son Willem took over and they called him Willem II. The son of Willem II became Willem III and so on till there was a Willem V.

Willem V was far from popular in The Netherlands after losing most of the colonies to England. He made a pact with France and France became a Dutch ally. At that time France and England were constantly at war about the colonies so The Netherlands and France were now battling the English together. This venture backfired when Napoleon came to power. Napoleon was much obliged and made a French province out of The Netherlands. After Napoleon was defeated, Willem V returned from exile to The Netherlands and assumed the position of Governor again. In 1815 when Napoleon escaped from Elba, the Dutch people were scared they would be occupied by France again.

After the French occupation, Willem V had gained popularity and the Dutch people appreciated the Prince of Orange again. Willem V saw his chance; he grabbed the bull by the horns and declared that from now on The Netherlands would be a kingdom.

Nice guy, this Willem V to make a Kingdom out of The Netherlands. The trouble with a Kingdom is that you need a King but in The Netherlands they were very fortunate because they had a volunteer for the job. If you guessed that Willem V was the volunteer, you are right.

Since this was the beginning of the "Kingdom of The Netherlands," they made Governor Willem V, King Willem I because he was the first King of The Netherlands. This was quite a promotion for the new king to move up four Willems; from Willem V to Willem I.

The successors to the Dutch throne were Willem II and Willem III. Willem III married Emma who became automatically Queen. So The Netherlands had a King and a Queen. King Willem III died suddenly in 1890; which ended the Willem story because no more royal Willems were born. For the next three generations, the succession to the Dutch throne went through the female line. Queen Wilhelmina had only one daughter Juliana and Juliana had four daughters but no sons.

When King Willem III died, his only child Wilhelmina was only ten years old and too young to ascend the throne. Upon the death of her husband, Emma was not Queen anymore; she only had been Queen as long as her husband lived. All she was was the mother of the future Queen Wilhelmina. The Dutch Government appointed Emma to be the Regent until Wilhelmina was old enough to be the Queen.

In 1898 Wilhelmina was old enough and according to the history books she was installed as Queen because she was the rightful heir to the throne. All what was needed was the formality. After the installing of Queen Wilhelmina, she had a ride in the Golden Coach through De Hague so the people could see their brand new Queen. When the very naive Wilhelmina saw all the shouting flag waving people, she asked her mother: "Are all those people mine?"

Her mother answered: "No my dear, they are not yours, you are theirs!" (Historic revelation.)

As time went by, Wilhelmina married Hendrik who became Prince of the Netherlands but not the King. Only when a legal King marries, his wife becomes Queen. Not the other way around.

Prince Hendrik was a womanizer and his behaviour left much to be desired for a Prince of The Netherlands. Beside all his amorous adventures he must have hopped in bed with his own wife as well because they had a daughter called Juliana in 1909. For 29 years there hadn't been a Royal birth and for some time it had looked as though the Orange Dynasty would come to an end. Prince Hendrik died young but he had lived long enough to make an heir to the Dutch throne and Juliana was the legal heir to that throne.

For the children of the Princess Juliana School, it was an exciting time in 1937 and 1938. There were a lot of celebrations that had to do with Royalty. The School Board of the Christian Schools was more Royal than the Royals themselves and whenever they could, they arranged all kinds of celebrations for the school kids.

Princess Juliana was the only child of Queen Wilhelmina and was destined to be the Dutch Queen in the future. Of course, the Dutch Government was hoping that Princess Juliana would marry and have some children so that there would be successors to the Dutch throne. There was some kind of a problem that royalty had to marry royalty. To find a suitable husband for Juliana was no problem at all. All of a sudden the Dutch Government announced the engagement of Princess Juliana to German Prince Bernhard of Lieperbiesterfeld. Nobody had ever heard about a Prince Bernhard and neither had they heard about Lieperbiesterfeld so it must be in the booneys.

Most of the starving Dutch people would have nothing to do with Royalty; they made all kinds of jokes and gossiped about this Prince Bernhard. They said that Prince Bernhard's pig's father was a boar (male pig). That wasn't all that insulting because his father could have kept a pig, they didn't say that he was a pig. Moreover, Prince Bernhard had to say: "Aunt" to the Rhine Bridge because it was all in his family. This of course was pure nonsense.

Other jokes weren't that kind; they suggested that Princess Juliana must have kissed a lot of frogs to find herself a handsome Prince. It could very well be that an evil witch had cast a spell on Prince Bernhard to make him a frog. This spell could only be broken if a pretty Princess would kiss him. Luckily for Prince Bernhard he was in the right place at the right time and there he was. The people lost a frog and gained a Prince.

(There was an old guy who walked through the field. A frog said to him: "If you kiss me I'll become a beautiful Princess and I'll do anything you desire."

When the old man picked up the frog and put it into his pocket, the frog said: "You forgot to kiss me; if you don't kiss me I can't become a beautiful Princess."

The man said: "At my age what in the world do I want a beautiful Princess for? I rather have a talking frog.")

Actually, it wasn't all that hard to find a Prince in those days. Before 1870 Germany consisted of several German states of which Prussia was the biggest and most powerful. Those Principalities were ruled by Princes. After the unification of Germany those Princes still inherited the title of Prince but were unknown to the world. However, for a Princess it sounds great when you can say that you are going to marry a German Prince.

It really paid off for Prince Bernhard to marry the gold mine Princess Juliana. As soon as he was married he became Prince of the Netherlands which gave him a handsome income of 1 million guilders per year. Plus he also got a dozen or so very important jobs for which he had to do little more than make a speech off and on, sign a few papers and cash his big honorarium checks. Only people on top of the ladder qualify for jobs like that because you have to be a person with an important name and that he had, "Prince Bernhard of the Netherlands."

Most of the Dutch people had no use for their new Prince who made that kind of money while they were starving. They weren't even invited to the plush wedding to which all the important people of the world were invited because they were only 10 million guilders short in their bank account.

When Princess Juliana and Prince Bernhard were getting married, the School Board provided a fund for big celebrations. The children sang a Patriotic Song which had been especially composed for the event by a famous Dutch poet and at night there were several torch light parades in which all school kids participated with a burning lampion. *(Across the border in Germany they had many spectacular torch light parades by the Nazis. They were the foreplay of the Second World War.)*

Adrie's mother had made an orange blouse for him and he was real proud to wear it. Other kids were wearing an orange sash and the girls had orange ribbons in their hair. Even though Adrie's parents didn't care for the Royals, Adrie loved them; it was the only time that he was treated in his unexciting life.

The same year yielded another great event in The Netherlands; it was the World Jamboree for the Boy Scouts that was held in Vogelesang. There was also a song about that great event and the children were singing it, too.

The Jamboree wasn't even finished yet when the school children were introduced to another great song. This song had a lot to do with the bees and the birds. It was about Juliana who was expecting the stork with a bundle of joy by the end of January 1938. This Prince Bernhard was a fast worker in spite that he had been a frog and he took all the credit.

People were crazy with joy. Before Princess Beatrix was born, people weren't quite normal, but with the royal birth, people became crazy. Whenever Prince Bernhard was released from the lunatic asylum they could lock up the rest of the population.

(As the joke goes: Prince Bernhard visited a lunatic asylum. The manager gave him a tour of the institution and was leading him around. Prince

Bernhard asked: "Are some of those people cured and do they get back to normal again?"

The manager answered: "Yes, most of the people here are nursed back to a healthy normal life. Look at that man on that bench there, he used to be very disoriented but he goes home next week. If you like, go and chat with him and judge for yourself!"

Prince Bernhard seated himself beside the man and started a conversation. After a while, he was really impressed and asked the man: "Do you know who I am?"

The man said: "No I don't, I've never seen you before."

Then Prince Bernhard said: "I'm Prince Bernhard!"

The man looked at him, tapped him on the shoulder and said: "When I came for the first time to this institution, I thought I was Napoleon but it doesn't take them long here to get those crazy ideas out of your head.")

When the day came close that the stork was going to deliver the baby to Princess Juliana, the whole country was waiting for the signal whether it was a girl or a boy. If it was a boy they would shoot the cannon 101 times and if it was a girl they would shoot 51 times. That was an old custom held over from the time that there was no communication other than messengers, mouth to mouth, smoke, light or a noise signal. All the people had to do was count the shots and they would know what gender the baby was. When the baby was born there were basically three methods of communication, by telegraph, telephone or tell a woman. Especially the last one was most effective. In spite of the good communication means they decided to do it the old way.

When Princess Beatrix was born in 1938, they fired 51 cannon shots and they all missed. That was another thing Adrie didn't understand at all; why didn't they fire exactly 50 or 100 shots? The explanation they gave him was that it was meant to be 50 and 100 shots but the gunners were usually quite drunk and didn't count too well. In case they miscounted there was this extra shot to make sure that the royal baby wasn't short-changed from the onset. The baby would be really cheesed off if that had happened.

(It was a good thing that Women's Lib hadn't been invented yet. If this had happened today it could have caused a riot. Why did a Prince get twice as many shots as a Princess?)

Anyway, there was a reason to celebrate and at school there was a great feast. The children sang all kinds of patriotic songs, got a cup of coco and a rusk with orange hail. As a highlight they saw a Mickey Mouse cartoon. Yes, this was a real barn burner; the children were talking about it for months. Walt Disney was the first one to make cartoons and came up with Mickey Mouse cartoons as early as 1928. They were the only movies the Church and the School Board would allow. Apparently Mickey Mouse was an innocent character.

While Adrie was drinking his coco he wondered why this baby already was announced as "Her Royal Highness Princess Beatrix?" Her Royal Highness Princess Beatrix was born in 1938. That was eight years after his Commoner Lowness Adrie was born. Yet, she took priority as the heir to the Dutch throne.

The Dutch people were hardly sobered up from the celebrations (i.e. the big shots only, others didn't get drunk on a cup of coco) when the School Board was preparing for another barn burner. (With all those barn burning parties the Dutch barn became a disappearing landmark in The Netherlands.)

This time Queen Wilhelmina had been on the Dutch throne for forty years, which must have been pretty hard on her hemorrhoids. It was another reason to paint the town red. Those festivities took place on August 31st so it was still summer which meant a lot of outdoor activity.

Actually it had been touch and go for Queen Wilhelmina that she was still the Queen. The 1930's were turbulent times and being King or Queen was a high risk profession in those days. Everywhere in the world they did away with royalty, which often meant that the King or Queen was killed. King Farouk of Egypt said: "In another ten years the only King around will be the King in the card game."

In France Louis XIV lost his head on the guillotine, which was a French specialty; especially invented to make sure that there was no counter revolution after the revolution.

In Russia, the whole family of Tsar Nicholas was shot and the corpses were thrown in a lime pit to avoid people burying the remains and worshipping them as martyrs.

In Spain, the King was luckier, he was a Communist and when Franco took over, the King was told to buzz off. He was lucky to keep his head in the right place and survive the anger of the people.

In The Netherlands, in spite of the sad times during the Depression with all the poverty, there were all kinds of celebrations and all of them were because of the royal family. While people were starving, millions of guilders were spent on fireworks and other festivities. The schools cashed in on this festive mood and made Patriots out of the school children, teaching them love for the Fatherland and the Queen. Children were taught that the Orange Dynasty was the best thing that ever had happened to The Netherlands and they had done a lot for the Dutch people.

Before the Queen stepped down, she was going to visit the City of Rotterdam. For this occasion the children at school were going to see the Queen. As if there is anything to see on a Queen especially if you end up seeing only her hand. Months before the occasion, the school children were taught to sing all kinds of Patriotic songs that were made up for this great day to tout the greatness of the Queen and the House of Orange. They heralded the Queen as the Promised Messiah and included in the songs, of course, the National Anthem.

The Dutch National Anthem is the longest National Anthem in the world, it has 18 stanzas and it was composed by Wilhelmus van Nassau. To satisfy his ego, he had a stanza for all the letters of his name. The first stanza started with a W and the next one with an I and so on. It was easy to start the first stanza with a W because he started it with his own name.

Wilhelmus van Nassau,
I am of German blood.

The closing of the first stanza states that he always honoured the king of Spain, which is very unlikely because he was wrestling away The Netherlands from Spain, and the King of Spain had Wilhelmus van Nassau killed by Balthazar Gerards, a worker at the Spanish Palace. Balthazar Gerards was killed by the Dutch for the shooting of Wilhelmus and the Spanish King elevated Balthazar's family to nobility. Luckily, the school kids had only to learn the first stanza and the sixth stanza.

After months of preparation, especially the singing of the songs, which was considered to be very important, the big day was there. Hours before the arrival of Her Majesty, the kids of all schools were already lined up along the parade route.

Traffic had come to a halt and the motor police were checking out the parade route for safety. The motor police were riding 500 c.c. B.M.W.'s, with an attached side carrier wherein another cop was seated. The motor bikes travelled at high speed close to the sidewalk where the people were standing. Everybody was well advised to keep his or her nose over the sidewalk lest it would be cut off by a passing motorbike.

There was lots of time for a repetition of all the beautiful songs the school children had learned. They weren't supposed to slip up on the right words; it would have been a blooming pity if the Queen had heard a wrong word in her closed limousine, which travelled at high speed as if it had to keep up with the motor police. When the Royal limo passed, the window was down a few inches which gave the Queen a chance to wave to all her loyal subjects with a lame hand. Now wasn't that nice! Yes, the school children and other people were pretty lucky there, they saw the Queen's hand in a white glove and you don't see that every day. The school teachers encouraged the children to shout:

"Long live the Queen" and "Orange forever" and the children waved their flags frantically as if they were the ones to guide the motorcade.

For a variation, they were shouting: "Hip, hip, hooray." That word "Hooray," had blown across the English Channel from England. It was an English invention and was used for the very first time when Lady Godiva rode stark naked on horse back through the county. She did this in order to protest the high taxes of the Count who was her husband. According to her, she had nothing to wear and she couldn't buy any clothes because of the high taxes her husband assessed. Anyway, when she was riding naked through the county, the people weren't shielding their eyes; they had a good look at her and were shouting: "Whore A."

(One time that the Queen was visiting a city, a man was shouting: "Whore, whore!" The police arrested the man promptly and when he appeared in court, the judge said: "You have insulted the Queen by calling her a prostitute."

The man said: "N-n-no judge, I w-was o-o-only t-trying to say, hoor, hoor, hooray.")

Visits of heads of state or other dignatories always attract a lot of people. A lot of people are standing hours in the rain to get a glimpse of them. The Pope is one of them, when he visited there were all kinds of relics for sale. There was bathroom soap for sale portraying the Pope on a rope. It was advertised as "Pope soap on a rope." It sold like hotcakes; you don't get a chance that often to wash yourself with the Pope.

One of the spectators who had been chosen to say a few words to the Pope said: "It was like talking to God." Usually when the Pope arrives in a foreign country, he falls flat on his nose. That's the way it looked to Adrie but he had that wrong. The pope kissed the earth of that country. Adrie thought that this was very gross; a dog could have pissed on the ground before the Pope arrived.

Prince Bernhard himself supplied enough gossip to fill a book. Evil tongues had it that he had a daughter in Paris which was never proven. What was really proven was that he was a lousy pilot. He had a little airplane at the Airport of Iepenburgh where he wasn't known for his good flying. Whenever he came in for a landing everybody got out of his way. Even after the landing when he taxied off the runway, nobody was safe. He taxied like a maniac and his plane was turned upside down by a wind gust on one occasion. Another time there was a wind gust that slammed him into a hangar.

There was always something that went wrong. In a few years time he had half a dozen of accidents. Unfortunately they couldn't take away his flying license; he was the Prince of the Netherlands. How can you tell a Prince that he doesn't know bugger all about flying. So everybody shut up, nobody was ready for his head to be chopped off.

With driving his car he didn't do any better, he had several accidents and totalled two cars in the span of five years. He was lucky to be alive and made headlines in the newspapers several times. In the mishaps that he had, he sustained only minor injuries. Prince Bernhard was as hardy as the weeds, he couldn't perish.

The Government wanted to give him a chauffeur but Prince Bernhard didn't want to burden the Dutch taxpayer and rejected the offer. No, that would be a waste of money; he was a very good chauffeur himself. The reason that he had that many accidents was because the other people couldn't drive a car. It had never been his fault, the police could verify that. (The police knew better than to give Prince Bernhard a ticket.)

In spite that the Dutch people were negative about Prince Bernhard, he wasn't all bad; there is some good in everybody, even if it's hard to find. Prince Bernhard was very talented; he was some kind of an ambassador and was well known the world all over, even in Argentina.

His best friend was President Peron of Argentina. Prince Bernhard went frequently to visit his friend Peron. No, it didn't cost the Dutch tax payers any money. Prince Bernhard was some kind of a good-will ambassador for The Netherlands and he did a lot of business while in Argentina. He sold Dutch locomotives and in exchange he bought canned Argentinean beef. This canned beef was sold to the unemployed for half price; that was the only way unemployed people had a small piece of meat on the table on Sundays, all thanks to the Prince!

Whenever Prince Bernhard arrived in Argentina, his friend President Peron arranged a welcome party, presented and paid for by the friendly people of Argentina. And as soon as Prince Bernhard had finished his business in Argentina, he presented a farewell dinner to President Peron, his ministers and other poor people from the slums of Argentina. This dinner was of course paid for by the friendly taxpayers of The Netherlands.

After all his hard work in Argentina, the poor Prince came back to the Netherlands. He was over-tired and over-worked, which made it necessary to see his personal doctor. His doctor ordered a rest period in the Swiss Mountains which was of course paid for by the Dutch tax payers. Yes, this Prince Bernhard had a good job with very good fringe benefits. To think that this poor Prince had to go all the way to Switzerland, far from his beloved wife Queen Juliana, to regain his strength. Poor fellow!

Love can't always go one way in a good relationship. Prince Bernhard had worn out the threshold of Peron's Palace in Argentina and to give the people in Argentina time to put in a new threshold, Prince Bernhard invited President Peron for a state visit to The Netherlands. Prince Bernhard's invitation came on behalf of the Dutch Government. The Dutch Government didn't know anything about it, but they were briefed on the return of the hard working Prince.

Of course this was an offer President Peron couldn't refuse, so he accepted. Yes, that was a great event when President Peron came to The Netherlands. The Dutch Government assembled a royal train, to make it easy for Prince Bernhard with his important guest to travel all over The Netherlands.

Prince Bernhard wanted to show off for President Peron and stated that he would drive the royal train himself. The Dutch Government had the shock of their lives; they had figured it out so well, to keep the Prince off the road with his car and out of the air with his airplane and now this Prince was going to throw the rail traffic in disarray. Yes, the Dutch Government always wanted a Prince but this wasn't exactly what they had been looking for.

The Dutch Government suggested making up a program for the visit. When Prince Bernhard brought it up again that he personally would drive the train, the Minister of External Affairs suggested that it would be better for Prince Bernhard to entertain President Peron. Entertaining was the magic word; he was very good at that and certainly the right man for the job, so he abandoned the idea of steering the train. What a blessing!

This royal train went all over The Netherlands. When the train came into Rotterdam, the school kids were allowed to see the train. The railway was half a dozen of blocks from the school but they had a clear view. Half an hour before the train came by, they were already outside. It didn't matter to the kids that they had to wait because it was during school time anyway. Finally the train steamed passed, on one side of the locomotive was the Argentinean flag and on the other side was the Dutch flag, really impressive. There was only one thing lacking, the kids didn't see Prince Bernhard shovelling coal on the fire to get steam, but then Prince Bernhard had more important things to do, like toasting President Peron with some Dutch gin.

A POOR FAMILY

Millions of people were dumped into poverty with the Great Depression and one of those families was the Demerwes. They were so poor that they couldn't even pay attention. Poverty had become a way of life and everybody tried very hard to put some fun into life in spite of the poverty. Other people of the middle and upper class didn't have the foggiest idea what it was to be poor.

At an English private school where the children of the well-to-do people were educated, the teacher wondered how much the children knew about different classes of the society. All his students had been brought up with the silver spoon and he gave them the task of writing a story about a poor family.

One of his ignorant students wrote the following story. "Once upon a time there was a real poor family; the father and mother were poor, the children were poor, and even the butler and the chauffeur were very poor."

The Demerwes were a lot poorer than the family which was described by the bright student. Adrie's father and mother were poor and so were he and his sister. That's all there was. If they had had a poor butler and a poor chauffeur, they wouldn't have been so poor. Good for the butler and the chauffeur that they didn't work for the Demerwes because those guys would have been poor as well. One could say that they were as poor as Job except they didn't use a piece of broken pottery to scratch their behind. *(According to the Good Book; Job was so poor that he didn't have nails to scratch his behind and used a piece of broken pottery. Why do I have to tell you what the Good Book says?)*

Rich people have no idea what it is like to be poor. Marie Antoinette was a French Queen in the 1700's. When she was told by her advisers that the French country people had no bread to eat, she replied: "Then let them eat cake."

The attitude of rich people towards the poor is quite often terrible. In Charles Dickens play "A Christmas Carol," the stingy Scrooge was asked for a donation for the poor. His reply was: "Why should I give to the poor. If I give to the poor, soon there will be no poor people which would be terrible because it would put you guys that do charitable work out of business."

If Scrooge had looked at the Demerwes he wouldn't have to worry that after giving them money that they wouldn't be poor anymore. They were a bottomless pit in which you could throw all kinds of money and you never would hit the bottom.

How do rich people like to be poor? Well ask the Queen, she is the richest woman in the world. You don't have to ask the Queen anymore because some bright reporter already did ask her if she wanted to be a pauper. Her reply was loud and clear: "I certainly don't want to be a pauper."

Nobody ever asked Adrie if he wanted to be poor. For no amount of money in the world did he want to be poor but his father and mother were poor so automatically, he was poor too. It was some kind of an inheritance of poverty. Joe Louis, champion heavy weight boxing said: "In my life I've been poor and I've been rich, but I like being rich better." Adrie too, except he hadn't been rich yet.

Being poor made a lasting impression on him and whenever he made plans for the future, it didn't include being poor. On the contrary, he hated the thought that his chauffeur and butler would be poor and he wanted to be so rich that his chauffeur had a chauffeur and his butler had a butler.

They weren't the only people in the world who were poor but that is a cold comfort when you know that there are more poor people in the world. The same can be said of starvation; if you have no food, the knowledge that two thirds of the world population is insufficiently fed doesn't make your hunger go away.

It was hard to believe that once Adrie was glad to be poor. One night that he had to sleep at his aunt's place, his cousins had to take a spoonful of cod liver oil when bedtime came. They were saying that cod liver oil was made from whales. That might have happened at one time but nowadays it's made from cod fish. It contains vitamin D and is used especially in winter time when there is less sunlight that also contains vitamin D.

To his annoyance, they included Adrie in this blessing. When he tasted the spoonful of crapiola he wanted to spit it out but his aunt prevented him from doing so, she said: "It tastes bad but it's good for you!"

Adrie didn't buy it and said to his aunt: "How can anything that tastes that terrible be good for you?" Of course, his aunt was bigger and older so she won the argument.

Actually, Adrie didn't care that those terrible tasting things were good for him, he liked chewing on a piece of tar to get white teeth or butter cane from a dirty ditch a lot better, at least that was tasty. In a way he was glad that they were poor and had no money to buy trash like that. Even medicines were usually tasting awfully and bitter. His parents said: "That's good; bitter in the mouth makes the heart healthy."

His parents believed that and didn't care that Adrie believed that all those terrible tasting things wouldn't do him any good. He was only a kid and had to swallow bitter pills because the doctor and his parents said so.

In spite that they were as poor as a church mouse there were also nice things. Ko had very few luxuries but she had a peacock feather in her Bible which served as book mark. There was a ticking clock hanging on the wall that would strike every hour and half an hour. The clock had to be wound once per week which was a job Arie did on Saturday afternoon after he had taken a bath.

After that was done it was supper time and after supper came the enjoyment. Arie would read the paper and when he was finished with the paper he would smoke a cigar in his easy chair. If it was not raining he would go to the street to get some fresh air. There were always groups of men in the street who were telling their big stories. If you didn't have a story to tell you were welcome to listen. Some people came to tell stories and others came to listen, there was a place for everybody in that society.

Birthdays were highlights, the whole family that lived within travelling distance came together to gossip. One of the reasons that nobody missed those family gatherings was that nobody could afford not to be there. If you were not present you could become easily the target of the gossip.

The second reason was that the proverbial bottle always came on the table with a birthday; there was always a drink to cheer everybody up. Only on special occasions like birthdays came the bottle on the table. That was all people could afford because of chronic lack of money. Nobody wanted to miss that drink; it was an opportunity not to be missed. Homemade gin was the drink that was being served; it was made from black berries. It was good especially when you don't drink more than a dozen of drinks per year. Those birthday parties were by no means a big drunk. There were usually twelve people present at a birthday and there was only one one-litre bottle.

Miraculously, the people were allowed to have a drink. The Reverend imposed all kinds of restrictions on the church going people but he probably liked the stuff himself and then it was alright. Moreover it's hard to tell a Dutchman that he can't have a drink. The pattern of the gin drinking Dutchman was set during colonial times and was there to stay.

Even the children like Willie and Adrie got a little drink; they were also Dutchmen and belonged. A Dutchman is a Dutchman even if he or she is still little. The children shared all the miseries and poverties but if there was anything at all they shared, they belonged.

Ko was already busy early in the afternoon when she had to host a birthday. She had to polish the copper tea light that burned on spirits. After the lamp was lit you could smell it through the entire house. Coffee or tea was served in a Chinese porcelain tea set that she had received from her brother Henk as a present on her birthday. Henk was in the Navy in Indonesia and had bought the tea set there.

Willie and Adrie were also busy when there was a birthday; they decorated the chair for the person who had a birthday. Everybody got into the act on occasions like that and of course they took their turn as well. If there were presents, they were always cheap and small but no matter how small they were they were always wrapped up.

THE HOUSEHOLD WORK ROSTER

In the Good Old Time everything was done by hand and most of the household chores were back-breaking work. The women were the ones who were designated to do the housework, which included cooking, cleaning and raising the children. All women had a work roster that wasn't hanging on the wall; it was an unwritten law which everybody knew.

Monday, laundry day.

On laundry day, oceans of water had to be carried from the rain barrel into the house. In winter it was even worse when the rain barrel was solidly frozen. Ko couldn't afford to use water from the tap so she shovelled lots of snow in pails the day before laundry day and put them in the house to melt. Besides, rain water was a lot better for the laundry, it was softer than tap water and saved a lot of soap.

In those days there was also a water stoker who provided hot water at the price of two pennies per pail. A lot of people got a couple of pails of hot water for the laundry or bathing in the laundry tub. Ko couldn't afford to pay two pennies for a pail of hot water so she made her own in kettles and pans on the stove and was busy for hours to get enough hot water for the laundry.

Washing clothes more than once a week was unheard of. There were three loads of laundry; one load was designated for the white laundry such as bed sheets, shirts, blouses etc. The second load had colored blouses, handkerchiefs etc. and the last load was for work clothes, socks etc.

Today, even a child can do the laundry but in the old days it took a lot of hard work and knowledge which was passed on from mother to daughter. That's why the girls had to help in the household so they could learn the ropes. When Adrie was still too little to carry pails with water for his mother, he wanted to help, too. His sister was helping and though he wasn't a girl that didn't mean that Adrie couldn't help. First the laundry had to be sorted out and the white laundry was first. Adrie got the hang of sorting out the laundry pretty fast and putting the laundry from one tub into the next one was a piece of cake.

There was also a mysterious pail with a lid on it. Adrie's mother had put it in the corner behind the laundry tubs so Adrie couldn't reach it. When his mother went into the house to get some more hot water, he was going to have a peak to find out about the contents of the secret pail. As soon as he opened the lid, he saw that the pail was full of white rags soiled with a lot of blood. Holy cow, Adrie didn't know what he saw. The only other time that he had seen such a thing was after a baby was born. There was no new baby which made him wonder who had cut his finger. All of a sudden, he heard his mother yelling at him: "Keep your damned fingers off that pail!"

He never had heard his mother swear before; maybe she was just trying to teach him a few valuable words for his vocabulary. In those days there was no Kotex so people made their own bandages from old bed sheets and they laundered them.

There was a lot of manual labor to do. For a start, the water had to be heated on the stove because there was only one cold water tap in the entire house. There was the washboard to rub the clothes against and a brush to brush the dirty spots in the clothes. Ko didn't have money to buy a wringer so she had to wring the clothes by hand. If you had arthritis in your hands you could forget about doing the laundry.

White bed sheets, blouses and shirts had to be blue rinsed after they had been washed in Sunlight Soap and put on the bleach field in the sun to bleach. There was no soap powder so people made it themselves; they shredded a bar of Sunlight soap. The white wash we do today, with all the special bleaching soap powder, which washes the whites whiter and the blacks blacker, can't stand in the shadow with the wash Ko did with her Sunlight soap and blue rinse. Her white wash was as immaculate as the Holy Virgin and it smelled nice and fresh like the outside air. There was a lot of white laundry in those days; underwear was always white. You never saw a guy with little flowers on his underwear and sheets with rose patterns were never heard of.

Bed sheets with roses were advertised for quite a while; they were supposed to give you a better sleep which made you perform better. They used John Belleveau, a good hockey player who played for Montreal, in the advertising. He said that it was because he slept under rose pattern bed sheets which gave him a better slap shot than anybody else. When he was questioned on Front Page Challenge if he really slept underneath rose pattern bed sheets he said that he did.

There was also Gordy Howe another hockey player who played for Detroit and he played such good hockey because he ate a certain kind of chocolate bar because it gave him a lift. If you believe what the commercials tell you, you have been snowed.

Actually, John Belleveau and Gordy How both missed the boat, they could have done much better if they had slept underneath sheets that had been washed by Ko. John Belleveau would have scored three times as many goals as he ever did and Gordy How would have played a lot better hockey too without a lift that he got from eating those lousy chocolate bars.

People had only one suit in those days. When a young man married, he bought himself a black cloth suit with a black high hat for that special occasion. He would wear that suit his whole life for special occasions such as weddings and funerals. The last special occasion that he wore that suit would be on his own funeral. He got married and buried in the same suit. Quality of clothes was very good in those days.

With work clothes it wasn't much better, if you had two corduroy pants and two chequered work shirts, you were rich. Most people had one pair of work pants, one work shirt and one set of underwear.

(Anecdote: One evening there was a knock on the door and a little boy went to see who was at the door. A man at the door asked: "Is your father home?"

The boy said: "Yes, my dad is home."

"Can I see him for a minute?" the man asked.

The boy replied: "That's impossible because my dad is in bed."

"Oh, is your father sick?" the man asked.

"No my father isn't sick", the boy answered, "but my mother is washing his underwear so he has to stay in bed!")

Luckily, everybody in the Demerwes' family had two sets of underwear so nobody had to go to bed when the underwear was washed.

((Time for a fitting joke. A Customs officer was checking the suitcases of arriving travellers. He came across a suitcase of an English girl and found seven pairs of panties in her suitcase, so he said: "What in the world are you doing with seven pairs of panties in your suitcase?" The girl said: "I have a pair of panties for every day of the week!"

"Well, that made sense," thought the Customs officer and he let her go.

Next there was a French girl and he wondered if she had seven pairs of panties in her suitcase. However, he counted only six pairs of panties so he said: "How come you have only six pairs of panties in your suitcase?"

She replied: "I need a pair of panties for every day of the week but on Sunday I don't wear any panties."

"All right!" thought the officer. A little later, he checked the suitcase of a Ukrainian lady. By that time, he had already a panty complex and looked feverishly for her panties. He counted twelve pairs of panties, so he said: "Can you tell me what you are doing with twelve pairs of panties in your suitcase?"

The Ukrainian lady said: "Sure, one for January, one for February...")

Good thing he didn't check suitcases during the Depression because he would have found no panties at all. Looking at the number of panties people have today, this must be a bountiful time with lots of panties.

There is a song where a girl sings:

You can kiss me on a Monday, on a Tuesday etc.
But never on a Sunday,
Because that's my day of rest.

It's very clear that Sunday is her day of rest; she doesn't even bother to put on a pair of panties. At least the Ukrainian lady had a pair of panties for every month. And remember the poor guy who had to go to bed when his wife washed his underwear.

Tuesday: Ironing day. That was a big day, too, because everything had to be ironed, including bed sheets. The only thing that wasn't ironed were the work socks. All this ironing depended on the cooperation of the weather. If it was nice and sunny there was no problem but if it was raining, the laundry had to be dried on clothes racks in the loft.

Sometimes there was a dust storm right after you put your laundry on the clothes line and you had to take your clothes inside in a hurry or the clothes would be dirtier than before they were laundered. In winter the clothes would freeze to the clothes line. A lot of times some of the heavy clothes weren't dry yet to be ironed on Tuesday.

The ironing was done with irons that were heated on the stove. Most of the women had at least three irons that they used in turns to give them an opportunity to heat up again. To check if an iron was hot enough for ironing, Ko would spit on the iron; if it sizzled the iron was hot enough. Nothing was simple and yet it was simple, a little spit did the trick, but you had to know about those little tricks. There was an advantage to the old fashioned irons compared to the electric iron we have today. The old irons were made of cast iron and they always worked, even if you dropped them on the floor they wouldn't break. Your toes were the only things that could break if you dropped your iron.

Wednesday; was the day that those darned socks had to be darned. Darning socks has become a lost art; nobody darns socks anymore, if there is a hole in the sock you throw it away. In the old days, socks were darned so much that there was little left of the original sock. Even if there was a hole in the sock as big as a fist, Ko would mend the sock. She had no money to buy new socks so she fixed them. Old socks that were beyond repair were used to darn the other socks. Even if the sole of the sock was all hole; the top part of the sock was still good enough to darn the other socks.

Everything that had a little life left in it was used again; it was recycling at its best. Old sweaters and socks were unravelled and the wool was used to knit gloves. Ko was always darning socks, repairing clothes, knitting socks, gloves or a sweater, her hands were always busy.

Thursday was heralded as the most wonderful day of the week. In the morning when you got up there was half a week to go and at night when you went to bed there were only two days left. It was also a very important day which was used to fix all other clothes. Buttons were sewed on and if there was a hole in your pants, a patch was put on it. Quite often there was a hole in a patch which made it necessary to put a patch on a patch and even if that patch got a hole in it there was some more repair. There was no money to buy new clothes so they had to be repaired even if they were totally worn out. All other necessary repairs were done on that day as well.

Friday was Working Day. All the other days people were just horsing around and now they had to do some work. The house was cleaned thoroughly, all by hand. There were no vacuum cleaners to do that job. Carpets and floor mats were taken outside, put on the fence and with a rug beater the dust came out.

Willie was more involved in the house cleaning to help her mother. One day, Adrie thought that his sister was crazy; she was dumping old tea leaves on the floor. She moved them across the floor and swept them up again. He couldn't believe his eyes; that was absolutely crazy. At first he thought that if she dumped tea leaves on the floor it would be more worth her while to sweep the floor. Like always, he had that wrong again. The old tea leaves were actually forerunners of carpet shampoo because they had cleaning qualities. It did a good job and it was dirt cheap; people drank tea every day and therefore they had lots of used tea leaves and consequently lots of shampoo to clean the carpet.

If you saw somebody throw tea leaves on the carpet today and sweep them up again, you would think that this person was one brick short of a load. In the Good Old Time this was normal; everybody did it and it wasn't crazy at all. Only if you deviate from what everybody else is doing, are you crazy.

Saturday was the day of car accidents with the few cars that were around in those days. A car seemed to be driving peacefully on the dyke and all of a sudden it crashed into the back of another car. What had happened?

The Netherlands was a very clean country in those days. After working all week to clean the clothes and inside of the house, on Saturday the outside of the house had to be cleaned. The door knobs and bell pulls were all made from copper. They had to be cleaned and with copper polish they were made shining as if they were brand new. There was another big outside job to be done. The outside door steps had to be scrubbed with water and soap.

That job was usually designated for young girls with short skirts. When the girls were bending over to clean the steps, they showed a lot of bare skin which made man look at the legs of the girls instead of at the traffic on the street. All of a sudden the car in front of them stopped and the following car crashed right into it. That job of scrubbing the front steps should have been designated for grandmothers with skirts that covered their heels to make it safe on the road.

(Things have changed in The Netherlands, with a lot of people from Turkey and Morocco moving in, the Dutch girls are not seen cleaning the outside steps anymore. They find that they have better things to do than showing their legs to dirty old men and consequently the steps stay dirty. There is also an advantage to that. It's much safer on the road with less accidents. People now can look at the traffic. Nothing else to see.)

After the house was cleaned inside and outside, there was one more thing to clean. It was the people. Clean underwear was put on Saturday afternoon after taking a bath. There was only one bath per week and one time per week clean underwear. That's all they could afford and that's the way it was.

The bathtub was invented in 1850 and the telephone in 1875. If you had been living in 1850 you could have sat in the tub for 25 years without the phone ringing once. In the 1930's, eighty years after the invention of the bathtub, ninety nine percent of the people didn't have a bathtub and very few people had a telephone.

In summer, the laundry tub substituted for a bath tub. To take a bath was a job and a half in those days. First Adrie had to fetch some water out of the rain barrel and his mother put the regular kettle and all kinds of pans and pots on the stove to heat. When the water was hot, it was dumped in a large laundry tub that was so big that an adult could sit in it comfortably. The entire Saturday was spent heating water and everybody taking a bath.

In winter when it was freezing the balls off brass monkeys in the back room, it was too cold to sit in the laundry tub. Taking a bath was suspended till spring and everybody got a pail with hot water in front of the stove to do a cat wash when it was his turn.

It was almost as bad as Roman bathing, the Romans were only having a bath once a year during the Middle Ages. This was brought on by the belief that nudity was sinful and subjected the body to evil spirits. The Dutch people didn't share the Romans belief but they did believe that a bath with freezing temperatures was subjecting the body to unnecessary strain.

Sunday was Lord's Day and you had to rest, according to the Bible. When Adrie did just that when he went to church twice on Sunday, he wasn't allowed to rest. As soon as the Reverend started to preach Adrie got quite sleepy. When he took forty winks, he was resting he thought. All of a sudden he got poked in the ribs by his father who said: "You don't come to church to sleep, you have to listen to the sermon. That's the word of the Lord."

Adrie didn't see it that way; it said in the Bible that the Lord made heaven and earth in six days and he rested on the seventh day. How could he rest when he had to listen to a boring sermon? He had to listen to everybody and his brother all week and on Sunday he should be able to rest.

This household schedule was pretty well kept up by everyone. Every house had its laundry hanging on the clothes line on Monday and on Saturday you could see everybody cleaning outside.

In some ridiculous towns it wasn't allowed to hang the underwear of women next to men's underwear on the clothes line. The bylaw read that it would create dirty minds among the people and therefore it was forbidden.

(When a man came in town, he said to the waitres: "There must be an awful lot of Roman Catholics in this town."

"What makes you think that?" asked the waitress.

"I saw a lot of underwear with crosses in it," the man replied.)

With all the manual work that had to be done, women didn't have much time to take a coffee break. They made coffee alright but had hardly any time to drink it. Women sipped coffee and tea from their saucers so they wouldn't burn their snout. The women of that time didn't have time to wait till their coffee was cold enough to drink, so they poured a little bit at a time on their saucer, to cool it down faster. According to an old grandmother people didn't even have time for sex, let alone drinking hot coffee or tea. When the world was speeding up, drinking coffee or tea from a saucer became uncivilized and unlady like.

(The young granddaughter asked her grandmother: "Say grandma, did you also have sex when you were young?"

The old grandmother replied: "No my child, we were way too busy for that.")

When Willie and Adrie got older they had to get out of their parents bedroom. Arie made a little bedroom in the loft for Willie. The rest of the loft was Adrie's bedroom; he could sleep there and store his precious few possessions.

Willie washed herself in her bedroom; she had a little wash basin with a water can. She filled the water can at night and took it to her room. When she got up in the morning, she could wash up. Adrie preferred the cold water tap; horsing around with a washing basin and a can with water was way too complicated for him. He didn't like those cat washes; he liked lots of water.

The loft wasn't very cold because the chimney went through it. It was a brick chimney so the bricks got a little warm and radiated some heat to the cold loft. When it was freezing fifteen below, they used some old coats to supplement the blankets. They didn't have that many blankets but old coats kept them warm too.

The kitchen had a stove with an oven. Wood was dried in the oven and on a cold day, you could open the oven doors and stick your feet into the oven to warm them up. It was also possible to bake bread in the oven, but the only time Ko baked bread was during the war. Normally the oven doors would be open and the heat from the oven would spread through the room.

There were some real cold winters when it was hard to keep warm. It was so cold in the house that when they were eating breakfast, everybody was sitting around the pot belly stove which was red hot. You could burn your front while your back was freezing. If you were sitting around the table your fingers would get numb. The house didn't have a basement, which made the floors cold during winter. Everybody used slippers all the time but when it was freezing it was hard to keep your feet warm. When it was that cold they used foot warmers which were actually foot stools with a pot of burning briquettes.

At one time when it was very cold, Adrie had been playing indoors for quite a while. When his mother came in, he wanted to show her something and got up from the table. He didn't make it, he collapsed and fainted. His mother didn't know what had happened to him but she got him out of the living room into the cold kitchen and tried to revive him with a towel of cold water and smelling salts.

He came too again and Adrie's mother got the doctor right away to see what had caused Adrie's fainting. The doctor's diagnoses was carbon monoxide poisoning caused by the foot warmer. Luckily, Adrie's mother had been working in the cold kitchen and wasn't affected by the poisonous gas at the same level as Adrie was. If they had been both constantly in the living room they could have both collapsed at the same time and been killed.

The doctor ordered the entire house to be well ventilated. Apparently, the briquettes that had been started in the stove before they were put in the foot warmer; weren't burning too well and had developed carbon monoxide. After that incident the foot warmers weren't used anymore. Instead they used hot tiles; the tiles were just put on the stove and whenever you had cold feet, you took a hot tile from the stove and put your feet on it.

Carbon monoxide is colorless and odorless; you can't see it and you can't smell it, but it's deadly. Many people have been killed in a closed garage when they had their car running. Some of those incidents were suicides; people tired of life and problems choosing a painless death to find a long time solution to a short time problem. They lock the garage, start the engine and sleep away. When we get electric cars, people will have to think of another way to kill themselves. Many people have been killed by carbon monoxide when they were stuck in a snowstorm. They let their engine run to stay warm but deadly carbon monoxide penetrates their car and by the time their rescue arrives, they are dead.

Smelling salts were used a lot whenever people fainted, but you had to use them the right way. One time when Arie was soaking his infected finger in hot soda water, he fainted. Ko knew how to handle that problem; she got the smelling salts and put the bottle right underneath his nose. It didn't help because she had forgotten to take the cap off the bottle.

Other people used a method to revive people in a more pleasurable way; they used a little brandy. At one occasion when a guy had fainted, a lady was wetting his lips with brandy. Apparently it helped and the man shouted, "Pour!"

A CHURCH FOR THE RICH

More and more houses were built on the Hordyk. First of all there had to be a school to educate the kids of all those people who occupied those houses. After the school was built, people realized that they also had to have a place to worship. It took a 40 minute walk to go to the closest church and older people couldn't walk that far.

The new church was a small church, seating about 400 people and it was a Christian Reformed Church. Adrie's parents were Christian Reformed and were happy with a church they could reach with a ten minute walk.

In most of the churches, the members had to lease their seats for a year. It was a money making business which gave the rich people the best seats. The seats in the front of the church were the most expensive seats and the further the seats were to the back of the church, the cheaper they were. Most of the churches had a so-called "goat gallery" for the extremely poor people who couldn't afford to pay for their seats. Those seats were free but it also marked the poor people from the rich who were sitting in the front of the church. Teenagers who were sitting in the goat gallery were dismayed that they were called goats and therefore they began to bleat like a goat, before the church started, to the dismay of the executive. If they were goats they were going to act like goats.

The church on the Hordyk had a different approach. They had three collections; one for the church, one for the poor and one for the organ fund. That organ fund was necessary to pay off the electric organ which they had bought on credit and with a collection for the church; they didn't have to lease the seats to the members. Everybody was happy with that arrangement.

If the poor people ever thought to get a good seat, come again. When the church was finished, all the prospective members came to register. They also came to select seats. That way, they had the same seat every week and could leave their Bibles in the church. Everybody had their preference where they wanted to sit, but most people wanted to sit in the center and not in the back of the church. The church was divided in three parts and the middle part could seat ten people. On each side of the middle row was a row of benches with seating for six persons and there were two aisles, one on each side of the center row.

Of course, somebody has to decide where everybody is going to sit. Some people have to sit in the front and others will have to sit in the back. Adrie's father and mother wanted to sit in the center at the sixth or seventh row from the front. The administration of the church turned that request down. They said: "The center is reserved for large families. That way they can sit all together."

That didn't sound too unreasonable and very handsomely, they were seated in the side row. One of the four seats they had was behind a pillar. It was Adrie who was put behind the pillar. He was only five years old and didn't care that he couldn't see the Reverend. There wasn't much to see on a Reverend at the best of times.

When the first church service was held, it was very obvious that the rich people were sitting in the center in the front, and the poor people were sitting at the sides. The very poor people like the Demerwes had also a seat behind a pillar or were seated at the very back of the church.

There were house visitations to all members of the Church. Two elders or one elder with the Reverend visited the members during the winter. On those visitations the members were criticized if they didn't come to church regularly and it was also a draft to get the young people to the Girls Club, Boys Club, etc. if they didn't join voluntarily. The Reverend and elders were always asking the question: "Are you people praying to the Lord every day?" It gave them an indication if people were slipping up on their religion. And of course if the answer was negative, they resorted in additional preaching which included the threat of hell fire.

On the very first house visitation, Ko had something to say about the seating selections. She said: "You told us that the center row was reserved for large families. How come that Disco and Vaandrager are sitting in the front of the church and in the center row? They are both man and wife and have each only two seats. We are with four people and we are sitting at the side and we have also a seat behind a pillar."

Mr. Ouwens, one of the elders, who were visiting answered: "It was very difficult to seat everybody and naturally there are quite a few people who are not completely satisfied. As for Disco and Vaandrager who are only occupying two seats each, they are filling up a couple of seats that were left after we had seated the large families."

"How come then," Ko argued, "that Goudriaan, with a family of eight, is sitting on the side and they are not sitting together?"

Ouwens replied: "Goudriaan registered very late when all seats in the center were gone and they had to be happy with the leftovers."

Actually Goudriaan had never gone to church until he became unemployed. He was only a goods and money Christian who had joined so he would receive aid for his large family. There were many people like that; they went to church as long as they were on the receiving end.

Ko didn't buy that excuse and quite cheesed off she said: "It seems to me that if you are rich enough, you can sit on the Reverend's lap and if you are poor, you are pushed behind a pillar."

Ouwens was very well aware about the truth he had been told but wouldn't admit it, he said: "We did the best we could and no matter how we had done it, there would always be people who are unhappy with the arrangements."

It became very clear that the Demerwes were never counted in the church. After the war was finished they had more unpleasant experiences. During the war there had been plenty of work for everybody but the postwar years needed skilled people in trades. Arie was a ground worker for which there was no demand at all.

One of the people on the Hordyk was working by Boele's dockyard in Bolnes. When he heard that he was unemployed he said: "They are asking for laborers at Boele, why don't you apply for a job?"

He was lucky that they hired him in the parts magazine, so he always worked in a nice warm place. That did him a lot of good with his asthma. When he was just starting there, they didn't pay him much but a raise in the future might improve that. In the meantime he tried to make some money on the side with jobs that he could handle.

For many years the church on the Hordyk had a verger, whose duty was caretaking of the church and on Sundays he was an usher. Caretaking meant to clean every week the church and keep things in shape. Mr.Vat was retired and had done this job for many years. When he got older he became sick a few times and had asked Ko if she could clean the church. That worked out fine and usher duties were performed by an elder. When Vat's health was failing, he threw in the towel and called it quits. Now the Church Counsel was looking for another verger.

When Arie and Ko heard about this part time job that was available, they applied for it. Ko could do most of the cleaning and Arie could play for usher on Sundays. After a few weeks, they had found a new verger but it wasn't Arie. Mr. Byl was the new verger. He was kind of an old tall guy that almost stumbled over his own long legs. He walked straight up in the church and looked only straight ahead, as if he was scared that people would look at him. He never did much of ushering and seemed very shy and not on the ball at all. Moreover, he didn't do much on cleaning the church either. There was a layer of dust lying on all the benches and it didn't look that anything was ever done on the floors either. It looked that he did little more than collecting his paycheck.

There were visitations again and this time, the elders who came to visit the Demerwes had it coming. Mr. Disco and Mr. Nieuwkerk were the elders who were doing the visitation. Mr. Disco was an older retired man who was an experienced elder. He had white hair as an albino and could walk with his Bible under his arm as if he was the Reverend himself. Mr. Nieuwkerk was a newcomer as an elder, he was only recently elected. Those newcomers were always put with a long experienced elder to learn the ropes. After the usual beating around the bush, about the rainy weather that had lasted for over three days, the conversation became more casual. Ko said: "I have a question. How come we didn't qualify for the job of verger?"

Disco scraped his throat to answer the question: "When we were looking for a capable man, we had to look at it the business way. We had to be sure that the position would be satisfactorily filled. In a case like that we can't let our feelings decide what to do, that would be defeating the purpose. It was not my decision only, the committee made the selection."

It was very obvious that this hypocrite was full of lies and excuses and Ko said annoyed: "What do you mean that we were not good for the job; we have kept the church clean for several months when Vat was sick and the church was a lot cleaner than it is now. The way the church now looks is a disgrace and you are really telling me that he does a satisfactory job?"

There was more throat scraping followed by Disco's reply: "If he doesn't fulfill the obligations that his job demands, we will take the appropriate steps to remove him. So far we haven't received any complaints about his functioning."

Ko said: "Well, I have a complaint; the benches have a layer of dust on them, they are never dusted and the floor looks disgraceful."

Disco wrapped himself in a cloak of Christian hypocracy and replied hypocritical: "That's the first time that we hear a complaint but as you yourself are interested in the job, we can not consider it a well founded complaint. You will have to learn to see the good in the man and not condemn him because he took the job you wanted. That's what the Lord demands of us."

Adrie had never heard so much bull in his life; the lies and cover-ups were numerous. In spite of the insults and the discrimination against the poor that they had experienced, the Demerwes stayed with the church but they remembered. About a couple of months later, Disco came to see Arie. He said: "We have started a special program to get more members in our church. We need canvassers to go from door to door to tell the people about Jesus, how he died for our sins on the cross and how he can save us."

"Well go ahead," Arie replied, "I'm not a Reverend."

"Jesus said to go out to all creatures of the entire earth and tell them about the Redeemer Jesus. And he didn't say that to Reverends only," Disco preached.

"I don't know why you are coming to me to ask me to preach the Gospel; I wasn't even good enough to be the verger in the church. You thought that I couldn't even clean the church, so what makes you think that I can preach," Arie countered and added, "Why don't you do that yourself, you are retired and I am working."

About half a year later, Disco made headlines in the church. Willie Sintmaartensdyk was the domestic servant for the Reverend. She was eighteen years old and had a boyfriend. Disco came quite frequently to the rectory to discuss church business with the Reverend and Willie knew him pretty good. One afternoon, he rang the doorbell and when Willie answered the door, she said: "The Reverend isn't home."

"That doesn't matter," said Disco, "I only want to check a book in the Reverend's study."

She didn't see anything wrong with that and let him in. About five minutes later he told her: "I found what I was looking for and now I'm ready to go to bed with you."

"You ought to be kidding," Willie said, "go with your own wife to bed but not with me."

Apparently Disco didn't take no for an answer, he grabbed her, tore the panties off her behind and tried to throw her on the floor. Willie fought back, gave him a black eye and threw him out of the door. Had the Reverend a surprise coming when he heard that his top elder had tried to rape his servant.

Disco tried to sweep this incident underneath the carpet. When a normal member of the church commits such a sin, he or she has to appear before the Church Counsel and confess the sins committed. When an elder who is in the Church Counsel commits such a crime, he cannot appear before the Church Counsel because he is part of the counsel. In that case he has to confess his sins to the entire congregation and ask the Lord for forgiveness with everybody present. In order to prevent this degrading ceremony to take place, he wanted to resign so he wasn't in the counsel anymore and could just come for the counsel, instead of the entire congregation. The Reverend, however, refused to accept his resignation before he had confessed his sins in front of the congregation. He said: "You committed this sin when you were a member of the Church Counsel and you have to be dealt with accordingly."

That Sunday, the white haired hypocrite Disco was sitting on his knees in front of the entire congregation to confess his sins. After that the Reverend said: "I will accept your resignation right now."

Very timid and with a weak voice so that hardly anybody heard it, he said: "I hand in my resignation."

The Reverend said: "I accept your resignation."

That was the end of hypocrite elder Disco. He was still attending church services, with his Bible under his arm, but never was allowed to be in any executive position.

A little announcement appeared in the church news paper, which was distributed to the church members. It said: "Due to ill health and family reasons, Mr. Disco has resigned from the post as elder in the church."

Everybody knew what the family reasons were and as for the health reasons, people were joking about it. They said: "The ill health is probably caused by his wife who hit him with the rolling pin over his head; otherwise Disco is in a reasonable shape. An old geezer who tries to rape eighteen year old girls is not that sick."

With the growing population, the membership of the church kept increasing which gave the unnecessary arguments and even fights. Five minutes before the service started, a little red light was switched on. It didn't mean that the ladies of ill repute could sit down; it meant that all the seats were up for grabs. In the front of the church there were some reserved seats with a metal plate "Reserved." Those seats were for people with a wooden leg, hard of hearing or with another severe handicap, but when the red light came on all seats including the reserved seats were up for grabs. If you didn't have a seat in the church, you waited till the red light came on to sit down.

The Verger was in charge to put the red light on and on one fatal Sunday morning, his watch was probably out of wack which made him switch the light on ten minutes before the service started. Some of the reserved places were taken by other people when the reservists came to claim their seats. However, the red light was on and the people didn't want to move which made the people of the reserved seats very angry. They started to use rough language like: "Get off my seat you stupid bugger!"

This resulted in a reply by the seated people: "Don't you see the red light is on, you asshole!"

Even the Elders didn't manage to stop the argument, they said: "This is the House of the Lord where peace and tranquility should reign instead of hostility."

Finally the Reverend came to settle the argument; he really had to say something about the people: "I can't believe that Christian Brothers and Sisters behave like heathens. There are enough places to seat everybody and if there are not we'll bring in some chairs. Only where love is, will the Lord bestow his blessings. We can't worship unless you people make up. Everybody who was involved in this brawl should shake hands with each other and say: 'I'm sorry.'"

About five minutes late, the Reverend could start the Service, more than a bit disappointed about the attitude of his flock. Luckily nobody had been swearing, that was done by an Elder who had a business. He was the worst example of Brotherly Love and was always swearing at his workers. After several complaints had been made, he was removed from office.

Of course, the Reverend made unannounced visits to check up on certain things. He was sure not much help to the desperate unemployed people. On the contrary, he criticized the people that were trying to save themselves some money. Reading the newspaper was almost a luxury that they couldn't afford. However, they needed the newspaper because they needed toilet paper. In those days rolls of toilet paper hadn't been invented yet, so in Canada they took Eatons catalogues. In The Netherlands there were no Eaton's catalogues so they used the newspaper instead. In a Royal order of the Royal Palace, the Queen ordered that the newspapers had to be cut in squares and put in the bathroom. Even a Queen has to wipe herself.

There were different newspapers that cost five cents per week in those days but there was a Christian newspaper, called "The Rotterdammer" that cost one penny per week more which amounted to four pennies per month. It was a foregone conclusion that the Demerwes were going to read the cheaper newspaper.

One time that the Reverend visited, the newspaper was on the table. The Reverend picked it up and asked: "Why are you Christian people not reading the Christian newspaper and read a heathen newspaper instead?"

Ko asked: "Why is our newspaper a heathen newspaper?"

The Reverend replied: "The paper you are reading publishes sport events that are going on on Sunday. On Sunday you'll have to be in the House of the Lord instead of attending sports events. Besides, only The Rotterdammer writes our point of view, that's why it's a Christian newspaper."

Ko replied: "We can't afford to read the Christian newspaper, the other newspapers cost one penny less per week than the Christian newspaper. We have to save money wherever we can."

The Reverend was going to sit good for this one and a sermon that equalled the Sermon on the Mountain was in the offing. The Reverend started: "We are privileged people that can read a Christian newspaper; the people in Russia can only read "The Prawda which is a Communist paper. Just think what the Lord will say on Judgement Day that you read a heathen newspaper instead of a Christian newspaper just to save one penny per week. Just think about it what Jesus did for you, he gave his life for you. If this is not worth one penny per week, how can you expect to be saved by Jesus? All those things will be taken into account on Judgement Day and your chances to go to Heaven will be very slim. If you want to enter the Kingdom of Heaven you have to be a Christian even if it costs more money!"

Ko asked: "Do you really think that we are going to hell because we didn't read a Christian newspaper?"

The Reverend replied: "I'm not going to be the judge on Judgement Day."

"Lucky," Ko replied, "because if you were, we certainly would end up in hell because we read the wrong newspaper."

Ko and Arie were Christian Reformed but didn't believe that kind of nonsense. To them the Christian newspaper should be competitive with the other newspapers but they figured that the Christian people would buy their paper anyway and if they didn't the Reverend would tell them.

Well, it hadn't worked for Ko and Arie who read the cheaper newspaper. They didn't want to argue about the issue with the Reverend or Elders and told the Reverend that they couldn't afford to read an expensive paper so they had to quit reading the paper all together. "Will that be alright?" Ko asked, "if we quit reading the paper or is that sin too?"

Not reading a newspaper was alright so from there on, if somebody knocked on the door, the first thing they would do was hide the newspaper. It was very easy with cupboard beds, all they had to do was open the doors of the cupboard bed, throw the newspaper on the bed, close the doors and all was well. If by accident the Reverend or Elders would ask which newspaper they were reading, they could always say that they couldn't afford to read a newspaper. That would be lying, which they figured was alright. In their mind: "A little lie for the better is no lie."

One night there was a knock on the door and luckily it wasn't the K.G.B.

in Russia that came to round up the people to transport them to Siberia. It was the second worst thing that could happen; it was the Reverend who made a visit for obvious reasons to keep control of the unhappy unemployed people. As soon as there was the knock on the door, the newspaper had been thrown safely on the bed and the doors were closed. When he asked how everybody was doing Ko answered: "Not very good with being on relief. All we experiencing are poverty and hardships. Why are we the ones who are being abused by the Government?"

Like always, the Reverend used his favorite line: "There are no simple answers to complex questions but you never should lose your faith. I know you people have a hard life, but God has a special meaning with this and don't forget that you also receive many blessings from the Lord. You should count your blessings instead of complaining. Don't forget that Jesus was born poor, too, and he was the son of God. You have to be satisfied with your lot."

The next song seemed to be special made for them.

If you are worried and you can't sleep.
Count your blessings instead of sheep.

The blessings, during the Depression years, could be counted on one hand. The Reverend summed them all up:

Blessing one: "You are still alive!"
Blessing two: "There is still food on your table even if its dry bread!"
Blessing three: "Jesus loves you; that should be a consolation to you!"
Blessing four: "The Lord takes care of you!"
Blessing five: "There are people who are worse off than you!"

WHEN I GROW UP I'M GOING TO EAT PASTRY EVERY DAY

One day, the teacher asked the students at school what they wanted to be when they were grown up. A growing up boy is easily impressed with the things he sees. Some boys who had seen an airplane wanted to soar like eagles and become a pilot. Other boys wanted to be a doctor so they could hear the patients say "Ah" when they would have a sore throat.

Adrie's uncle had a little farm and whenever he visited the farm his uncle took him along when he went to milk the cows. It was about a five minute ride with horse and wagon to the pasture and Adrie thought that this was swell. Of course, he wanted to be a farmer.

A woman can change her mind and so can a growing up boy. All of a sudden he wanted to be a bus chauffeur. Why this sudden change? Well, he saw other things that were more attractive, and a bus goes faster than a horse and wagon.

Adrie's grandmother was already old and she had trouble keeping her house clean. Every two weeks, Ko went to help her to clean her house and took Adrie along. His grandmother lived in Rysoord which was about 10 kilometres from where they lived. During the Depression, his mother didn't have a bike which meant that they had to go by bus. Travelling by bus was right up Adrie's alley, he loved it! They had to walk about ten minutes to catch the bus on the Dortse Streetroad and had to pay for the distance they travelled. The shorter the distance the less you paid which gave Ko an opportunity to save money. If they walked to the next bus stop, they saved themselves two pennies, so that's what they did. A penny saved was a penny earned and two pennies saved was two pennies earned.

His grandmother gave Ko some money for helping her because she needed money to raise her kids and his grandmother needed help to clean her house. Everybody helped everybody in those days. In spite of the money Ko made, she still had to count her pennies because she had to make ends meet.

Up to the age of five, you went free on the bus and when you were five years old you had to pay half the fare. Even when Adrie was six years old his mother never paid for him; he was just a little fart and the bus driver hardly saw him. As soon as the bus stopped, he got in and ran straight to the back of the bus. That way he could look out of the rear window and see a lot of the world. At that age, he hadn't seen a heck of a lot of the world and he was going to change that. Maybe the bus driver questioned his age but he probably knew that his mother was poor and let her get away with it.

After he had looked out of the rear window for a long time, he knew all the houses in the streets and his interest changed. With his big blue eyes he watched the bus driver. Wow! that was great, driving a bus!

When they went to Rotterdam downtown by bus it was even more interesting. The bus drove over the Hordyk which was a narrow street with many sharp curves. There was no power steering and no automatic transmission in those days, which made driving a bus quite a chore. With quite a speed, the bus negotiated the sharp curves in the road which made the bus driver yank constantly on the steering wheel. In the same time he had to shift the gears back and forward, and was moving the stick shift as vigorously as a violin player.

This was all very interesting but there was one more thing that made the job of bus driver very attractive in his eyes. The bus driver had a book with tickets for the fare, and a leather bag for the money. When he had to give change, he would stick his hand in the leather bag and he would have a handful of dimes and quarters. Yes that was impressive; he never had seen that much money in his entire life. That bus driver was rich, just to think what he could do with all that money.

This was it; now he really knew what he wanted to be, he wanted to be a bus driver with a lot of money. No, he didn't want to be a farmer anymore; being a bus driver was a heck of a lot more fun and he would also have a lot more money than if he was a farmer.

Thus he knew very well what he wanted to be but he knew quite a lot more than that! He even knew what he was going to eat every day and it certainly wasn't shoving cheese. No, that wasn't on his program at all.

Whenever there was a birthday party in their house in those meagre times, his mother would bake pancakes. There was an extra cookie with the coffee and a glass of lemonade. That's all they could afford.

When his Aunt Ploon had a birthday, they would get a piece of cream pastry, she could afford a lot more than his mother could. That was good stuff, he thought, and his whole face showed that he loved it. His aunt had usually a couple of extra pieces of pastry and she would give an extra piece to Adrie. He could eat pastry every day instead of once in a blue moon and told everybody: "When I grow up I'm going to eat pastry every day."

The people who heard him say that smiled and said: "If you want to eat pastry every day, you better find a heck of a well-paying job."

Adrie didn't share their concern as to where the money would come from. He had it all figured out; he was going to be rich because he was going to be a bus chauffeur. A bus chauffeur has lots of money; he had seen with his own eyes that he had a leather bag full of dimes and quarters. It never occurred to him that it wasn't his money, he wasn't that well informed.

Actually, he wasn't informed at all. He only saw the nice things, like a bag full of money and driving a nice bus. Little did he know that being a bus driver wasn't fun at all; as a matter of fact, the bus driver had a hard time to complete his route in time because he had a tight schedule. Sometimes there were a lot of passengers to whom he had to give a ticket and change. There was also a level crossing of the railway with a barrier. It was a busy railway between two cities and it could easily happen that the bus had to wait seven to ten minutes when a freight train and two passenger trains had to get through. People waiting for the bus would say: "That darned bus is late again."

The bus route on the Hordyk with the railway crossing was a bad route but it wasn't the worst one. There was one bus route between Rotterdam and Ridderkerk which was a ten kilometre trip but 3 kilometres were on a high narrow dyke. If busses would meet or a bus met a truck, the bus had to go quite close to the edge of the dyke. There was no protective rail and in winter when it was slippery it was dangerous to drive on that high dyke. The dyke was about thirty feet high and at the bottom of the dyke was a narrow road serving some houses, but the road wasn't a through road so the bus had to drive on top of the dyke.

Sooner or later an accident was in the offing. It was sooner. After a freezing rain, a bus slid off the high dyke which could have been a real disaster. The bus driver could see it coming, the bus would roll over and the bus would be flattened, passengers included. As a last resort, the bus driver took a drastic action; he stepped on his gas pedal to make the bus accelerate fast. Because of the speed the bus didn't roll over but drove off the steep dyke with a speed of about forty kilometres per hour. When the bus hit the road below, quite a few windows broke and quite a few people had glass cuts but luckily nobody was seriously injured.

That was a narrow escape and a good bus driver; the passengers were quite happy and everybody considered himself lucky. Only one man was very mad; it happened to be the boss of the bus company. He called the bus driver in his office, called him an idiot and fired him. According to the manager, it was irresponsible to drive off the high dyke with a speed of 40 kilometres per hour. The bus could have hit the bottom road and collapsed like a harmonica. It showed that being a bus driver wasn't that great a job but a kid wouldn't know about all those things.

There was severe competition among the bus companies; they even went to court to settle their arguments. One of the big bus companies was in Ridderkerk and was called R.A.G.O.M. which meant Ridderkerk Auto Garage Onderneming (Enterprize) Maatschappy (Company). They had busses going every where; even to Rotterdam. The City of Rotterdam had electric trams and also busses. They didn't like the competition and passed a bylaw that busses from out of town couldn't enter Rotterdam.

Unhappy with this by law, the R.A.G.O.M. bus company didn't take that and went to court. In court it was decided that busses from out of town couldn't transport passengers within the city limits but they could drop off people from out of town anywhere in Rotterdam. They also could pick up people in Rotterdam and transport them to any destination out of town.

This time, the city of Rotterdam wasn't very happy with the court decision and the executive of Rotterdam Bus had a brilliant plan to drive R.A.G.O.M. Bus into bankruptcy. R.A.G.O.M. Bus had a very lucrative bus route from Rotterdam to Dordrecht, it was a trip that took one hour and busses went every hour. There were also many passengers which made the route very profitable.

Rotterdam Bus decided to serve the same route and had busses driving five minutes ahead of the R.A.G.O.M. Bus. They figured that most of the people were waiting at least five minutes at the bus stop and that they would take most of the business away from the R.A.G.O.M. Bus. Consequently, their busses would be almost empty and they would lose a lot of money. The sooner R.A.G.O.M. Bus was bankrupt the better, at least they would be rid of the competition.

Rotterdam Bus had calculated this venture wrong and it was they that had empty busses. Most of the people were mad at Rotterdam Bus because of all the hassle, and were boycotting their busses. Many times when they were waiting for the bus, people would wait for the R.A.G.O.M. Bus and let the Rotterdam Bus go by empty. Adrie and his mother didn't join the boycott because the Rotterdam Bus was two pennies cheaper and that was all what counted. Transportation war or not, they had to save money.

(Yes, dreams come true in Blue Hawaii, according to a song Elvis Presley used to sing. In reality not too many dreams come true. When Adrie was dreaming about becoming a bus driver, he was serious about it. In spite of his eagerness, he managed never to drive a bus in his entire life. Several times he drove a semi but never a bus.

One of the popular songs in The Netherlands was about a boy who was standing on the beach staring and listening at the sea. He was intrigued by the dashing waves on the beach and the song of the sea. He vowed that he would become a sea captain on an ocean going ship and guess what? He accomplished exactly what he had planned.

This must have been a lucky coincidence. A lot of plans are made by growing up kids which are only an illusion and never materialize. It looked like the singing of the sea and the dashing of the waves on the beach were more attractive than the tooting auto bus.

Even if he had managed to become a bus driver, something would have been missing. The bus driver of today has no leather bag in which he can stick his hand to display a lot of money. The leather bag with money was replaced by a plastic see through coffee grinder without coffee, in which you have to deposit your money for the bus fare. The bus driver is merely watching that you pay your fare and if you over pay he won't give you change.)

There was another teacher who asked if the students were going to learn foreign languages. A few students said that they wanted to learn English because it was the most important language in the world. Others wanted to learn German because they spoke it across the border and others wanted to learn French. There was even a student who wanted to learn Esperanto.

Esperanto was a man made language which everybody in the world was supposed to speak so that you didn't have to learn different languages. The language was invented by a Russian physician in 1887. Esperanto means "One who hopes." It was based on words used in the most important languages and was simple to learn, to speak and to write for everybody. All nouns ended with the letter O, all adjectives ended with an A and there were a lot more things to make the language easy.

(Esperanto worked quite well before the war, a lot of people spoke it. After the Second World War, English took over to become the main language in trade and commerce.)

Adrie wanted to learn English, French and German, but English first of all. The teacher said: "If you want to learn different languages don't forget to learn Spanish; they speak it in Spain and pretty near in all of South America and Central America."

There were other things that had to be learned and Adrie learned them the hard way. Growing up kids play a lot of jokes, usually at the expense of the smaller kids. A lot of times Adrie was the prey of the older kids who knew it all and Adrie felt as if he had been born stupid and had never learned anything.

One day a big boy came up to him and stated that he could smoke through his eyes. That Adrie didn't believe; he had seen people smoke through their nose but smoking through your eyes sounded incredible. The big boy was willing to demonstrate it and said: "When I inhale smoke you have to press hard with your hand on my chest and in the same time you have to look at my eyes and you'll see smoke coming out of them."

Adrie did what he was told; he pressed his hand against his chest and looked at his eyes. The boy pressed the burning cigarette butt against Adrie's hand which made Adrie scream from pain and he said some unfriendly four letter words to the boy. Everybody was laughing and thought this was a good joke. The only one that wasn't laughing was Adrie who couldn't see the fun of it. Instead of smoke coming out of the boy's eyes the tears of pain had come out of his own eyes. That was no fun; that was bull as far as he was concerned.

Then one day, a lad asked Adrie if he had a pocket knife in his pocket. When Adrie told him he didn't have a pocket knife, the lad asked: "How then did you get that crack in your butt?"

Adrie could handle that joke, that was funny and he wouldn't mind being funny, too. Everybody around him seemed to be a joker so why couldn't he be a joker as well. What everybody else could do he could do too. The next boy he met was going to be the first victim of his joke. He asked the boy: "Do you have a pocket knife?"

The boy said: "No, I don't have a pocket knife."

Everything went beautiful Adrie thought, and asked the boy proudly: "How then did you get that crack in your butt?"

When Adrie was asked that question, he didn't have an answer, but this boy had an answer, he answered: "I cut that crack open on the barbed wire."

It looked to Adrie that he couldn't win this drollery of playing jokes, it was beyond his comprehension. Another wise crack was when you told somebody something and he asked: "Why?"

The response was: "Why are bananas crooked?"

Adrie learned also the answer to that question: "Because they grow crooked. If they would be straight, they wouldn't be bananas." Ha, Ha.

It seemed that all the other kids were smart, they had one up on him and Adrie was born stupid and cradled dumb. However, he was taking it all in for an appropriate time when he would call the shots.

Sticks and stones,
Will break your bones.
But calling names won't hurt any.

Everybody knew that and believed it. (Much later we found out that name calling did hurt mentally.) That's probably why name calling was very popular. If you had red hair, they would call you a red fire torch, or a carrot head.

If you had freckles, they would ask if you had been walking in the rain because you had started to rust.

If you were squint-eyed, they would ask if you had been crossed with a Japanese.

If you were fat you were a fatso and if you were skinny you were the runt of the litter.

If you were old the youth would call you an old dingbat.

When you were short you were shortie and when you were tall you were a long end.

With all the name-calling that was going on, they called a person with glasses a four eyed monster. In those days if you needed glasses the glasses were paid by the Government Health Insurance. You would get the glasses you needed but they would put them in the cheapest frame possible. If you wanted to have a different frame you had to pay extra. Consequently the poor people were recognizable by their cheap health insurance glasses.

One day, Adrie was working with a guy who wore glasses. After a while another guy with glasses arrived and they started to ride one another about their glasses. The one guy said: "Hi there, you four eyed monster." The other guy replied: "Hi too, with your cheap health insurance spectacles." They were both laughing because they both had glasses. Adrie missed that part and thought it was kind of funny.

A couple of days later he saw one of the guys with his glasses and greeted him as follows: "Hi there, with your cheap pair of health insurance glasses."

Adrie had seen this chap laughing about this remark when the other guy with glasses said it but this time he wasn't laughing. He was madder than a participant of the "Mad Hatter's Tea Party." He jumped up, grabbed Adrie, threw him on the floor, jumped right on top of him, punched him in the nose and screamed at Adrie: "You damned pest, I hope you will become blind as a bat, so you would appreciate it if you could see through a pair of cheap insurance glasses."

Gee, Adrie had thought that he would laugh but he really seemed to be cheesed off with him. This guy didn't even seem to know that calling names didn't hurt any. This saying was complete debunk because calling names hurt Adrie when the guy with glasses became as mad as a hornet and beat him up.

There was another popular saying in those days; they would say: "When I see glasses, I have to go to the bathroom." Of course this is all very stupid and ignorant but that's the way it was, they said those things. It's a good thing that Adrie didn't say that to this mad guy. He probably would have beaten the crap out of him, stating: "Now you can do it in your pants instead of going to the bathroom!"

(There was an important dinner and an important guest would be attending. Mother felt a little uneasy about her important guest since he had a long pointed nose. She knew her son Johnny too well and expected that he would make a smart remark about the gentleman's nose. In order to avoid unpleasant complications, she took Johnny aside before dinner and instructed him not to talk about the man's nose. After the important guest had arrived, mother saw to her consternation how Johnny was observing the long pointed nose. She got real nervous and upset and after she had poured the tea, she asked her important guest: "Do you take sugar in your nose?")

THE COLORFUL HORDYK

There were about 400 houses on the Hordyk and Adrie knew all the people who were living there. People seldom moved during the Depression time and the war years. When you went to school you made friends and enemies and you knew all of them including their parents.

One could write a book about the colorful Hordyk; it brought forth a lot of colorful people who tried to make a living during miserable times. Everybody contributed to make it colorful and each acted in their individual way. Merchants and beggars took the lion's share of the colorful parade from day to day. The Hordyk was certainly not a quiet place, merchants delivered goods and services from door to door. They didn't come with a van to deliver the goods; they came with horse and wagon, or in most cases with a hand wagon or tri-cycle. Hand wagons had a dog underneath to help pull the heavy loads.

Anyway, all the noise in the street didn't come from neighing horses and barking dogs. It was the merchants themselves who were responsible for making all the noise. As soon as they arrived in the street, they made their presence known by shouting with a loud voice to praise the merchandise they were selling.

For beginners, there was the vegetable man who shouted: "I got delicious juicy pears and snow white cauliflower!" When he shouted his face became as red as the red beets he was selling. He was also some kind of a joker, when people asked him: "What are you selling today?" His answer was: "A little sunshine."

There was also a fish man whose presence became known by the smell of fish and his loud voice which you could hear three blocks away. He shouted that he had salted new herring and smoked eel. The fish man didn't only draw the attention of the people, cats and dogs loved the fish man as well. Most of the fish was cleaned on his tricycle which he used to deliver his merchandise and whenever he cut a head off a fish, he threw it to the animals that surrounded his tricycle. A fierce battle was the result and the strongest animal usually got the fish head.

This might have been contradictory to the policies of Dr. Hein Colein, the Prime Minister who had suggested giving the fish heads to the unemployed people. That way he could save himself a lot of money and pocket that money with his buddies.

People had very little to eat and when they had cats or dogs, the animals fended a lot for themselves. There was no cat or dog food and no vet for the household pets. If the animals got sick they just died. Dogs even had rabies. It was called dog madness. When that happened, the owner usually clubbed the animal to death. Nobody had a firearm to shoot it and the lethal needle to put an animal to sleep hadn't been invented yet. What else could they do?

Next came the flower man who had beautiful roses and gladiolus. No sooner had this man left when the cheese man started to shout about his finest Edam and Gouda cheese which was the finest cheese in the world.

There was one man who did very well in attracting customers; he came with a horse and wagon loaded with pots and pans, dishes, pails, rug beaters and a host of other household utensils. With a very loud voice he announced his wares with a rhyme.

Pots, pans and dishes; All to your wishes.
A knife and a fork to cut and eat your pork.
My bargain prices are the best,
From North to South and from East to West.

At one time Ko wanted to buy a pee pot for Willie. It was an article which was well hidden behind tons of other merchandise and it took some doing to produce the wanted article. The neighbors who were standing around the wagon told Willie to try the pot to see if it was the right size. "Alright," she said and disappeared with the pot inside the house.

Jan Veer was the petroleum man who supplied the people with oil for their cooking stoves and oil burning lamps. Other merchants like bakers and milkmen had their steady customers and didn't shout other than to their horse when it had to go or stop.

The baker had a story of his own. Why is the moon so pale? Answer: "Because of the sleepless nights." Ha, ha, stupid joke.

Next question: "Why is the baker so pale?" Same answer: "Because of his sleepless nights." Some more Ha, ha, for another stupid joke.

Who needs a baker anyway? All you have to do is pour hot water into a rabbit hole and you get hot cross bunnies. The independent baker from before the war has disappeared from the stage. You might find some remnants of his kind in third world countries, but in today's society we find giant bakeries where thousands of loaves are baked every hour. The Hordyk also had an independent baker. Baker Timmers had a little shop beside his bakery. He baked some cookies and pastry and you could buy bread in the store. His wife ran the store because Baker Timmers was busy enough with baking and delivering bread.

He had to get up at 3.00 every morning except Sunday. That explains why he was so pale because he didn't get much sleep during the night. At

3.30 a.m. he started to work. First of all, he had to light his oven in which he burned coal. Next, he had to mix the flour and knead the dough. There were machines for that but the machines didn't run on an electric motor, he had to turn them by hand. He also had to check the temperature of the oven all the time; it wasn't done automatically with thermostats. If the oven was too hot, the loaves of bread would have a burned crust. People didn't like that so instead of selling the loaves for five cents, he sold them for four cents, which cost him money.

By 8.00 a.m., the bread came out of the oven; he loaded it in his hand wagon and started the delivery right away. People had fresh bread every day except on Sunday. That's one of the things we miss today; we go to the super market, buy ten loaves of bread, throw them in the deep freeze and we have bread for the entire month. Only one problem; it's not fresh. Bread gets stale pretty fast but when you freeze it, getting stale stops. With a deepfreeze, you can keep bread good for a long time.

At 8.00 a.m., the baker had already done half a day's work, but he had to deliver the bread to his customers. By 4.00 p.m., he was finished with his bread route and went to bed for a late afternoon nap. There was really nothing to laugh about Baker Timmers' sleepless nights, it showed. He was as skinny as a rail and as pale as the moon.

Ko's neighbor was always joking about the skinny baker. Whenever he saw baker Timmers in the street, he would say: "I see that fatso is delivering bread again." If it was windy he would add: "He'd better hang onto his wagon else the wind might blow him away."

Baker Timmers had a son who followed in the footsteps of his father. He looked as if he was the runt of the litter, just skin over bone and no color in his face. To tell them apart, his son was called "Fatso Junior." The bakery went from father to son. If a baker was rich he would deliver his bread with horse and wagon, but the poor baker had only a hand wagon.

In those days there was no sliced bread and it wasn't wrapped in plastic bags. The baker had to be clean as a whistle, because he handled the loaves with his hands. In the city, there were urinals at the corners of the busy streets. One time a customer saw the baker go into the urinal who never washed his hands, there was no opportunity. When he came out of the urinal, he grabbed a few loaves, put them in his basket and came to her to deliver the loaves. She refused the bread because he hadn't washed his hands and also took another baker, who went to a little shop to throw away some water but he always washed his hands.

The Demerwes lived next door to a blacksmith who had four different bakers to deliver bread. He didn't have an orphanage to feed; he only had four sons and four daughters. The reason that he had so many different bakers delivering bread was, those bakers delivered bread with horse and wagon. Horses needed horse shoes, so if the bakers could supply him with bread, they would take him to put shoes on the horses. The four bakers took turns for one week to deliver his bread. Baker Timmers never delivered bread to the blacksmith because he didn't have a horse.

The loaves were notched in the centre, so that you could break the loaves in two halves. That was done on purpose to make it possible to sell half loaves because "Half a loaf is better than no bread." It was practical; there was fresh bread delivery every day and it was possible that you only needed one and a half loaves. If you would take two loaves, you would have half a loaf left which would get stale.

If you took half a loaf, the other half was sold to the next customer. There was a problem though! A loaf of bread cost five cents and therefore half a loaf cost two and a half cents. The problem was that there were no half cent coins. You couldn't break a penny in two like you did with the loaf of bread; there was no notch in the penny.

The baker couldn't charge three cents for half a loaf of bread; his friendly customers would have called him a swindler who was operating a gold mine. There was lots of competition so he charged two cents for half a loaf, that was good business practise, he thought. His customers were pretty happy with this arrangement; he never sold that many half loaves before. If a customer needed two loaves of bread per day, he would take two and a half loaves. The next day he had half a loaf left and bought one and a half loaves. That way he saved one penny every two days.

That might sound pretty stupid but everybody counted pennies during the Depression. It went beyond all bounds and those transactions cost him eighty cents per week because he delivered one hundred and sixty half loaves of bread. He took the necessary steps to cut his losses. If you bought half a loaf of bread, he would charge you two cents like before. The only difference was, you owed him half a penny. He wrote it in his pocket book and the next time you bought half a loaf of bread, he would look first in his little book and if you still owed him half a penny, he would charge you three pennies for that half a loaf. Now he was even again.

This clumsy situation was caused by a hefty deflation which made the purchasing power of money go up. A penny was too big a unit in some cases. The Government corrected this problem by issuing half penny coins and two and a half penny coins. The two and a half penny coin was just right to buy half a loaf of bread. In case people paid him with three pennies, he had a whole pocket full of half penny coins so he could give change.

(After the war, the situation was reversed; there was a hefty inflation and there was no use for half pennies anymore. Consequently, the Government took

the half penny and the two and a half penny coin out of circulation. Eventually, the penny became worthless because of more and more inflation and the penny disappeared as well. The nickel was the smallest coin and if it didn't come out even to a nickel, the amount was rounded up or down to the nearest nickel. The Dutch Government was contemplating taking the nickel out of circulation as well when more inflation occurred. That didn't happen because with a United Europe they now have Euro Dollars.)

One man came with a tricycle in the street; he didn't have to shout to his horse because there was no horse. In spite of that, he made a lot of noise. He had a large bell on his tricycle to draw attention and to top it off; he screamed his lungs out of his throat shouting "Raggabino." It was probably the Latin word for rags because he came to buy your rags. He paid a couple of pennies for your old rags and he sold the rags to the newspaper printer who made paper out of them. He paid more for woollen rags than for linen and cotton because he sold those to the garage for the motor mechanics who had dirty hands. To make sure that people would distinguish him as the rag man, he was walking around in rags himself so there could be no mistake.

One day, this raggabino man came to Ko dressed in a nice suit and wearing a neck tie. At first, Ko didn't recognize him because he looked a different man. He said: "I am selling Singer sewing machines now."

Ko couldn't get over it that this ragman had changed so much for the better. She said: "Oh my, how nice for you that you have such a good job that you can walk around in a nice suit!"

The former ragman replied: "They can shove that nice job and that good suit; I made four times as much money in the rag business than by selling sewing machines."

Ko asked: "Why then did you quit the rag business if you made so much money with it?"

"I did it all for my kids," he answered. "At school my kids received all kinds of nick names; they were called 'Mary Rag' and 'Johnnie Rag.' Because of that, my kids hated the rag business."

Yes, this Singer sewing machine salesman had a good job and walked around in a fine suit. At school, the children could now be called "Marie Singer" and "Johnnie Singer" which should make them very happy. Only one thing was wrong, his nice job didn't put bread and butter on the table and neither did it keep the wolves away from the door. He was more or less starving just to walk around in a nice suit.

Some people sold services from door to door. One of them was a man who came with a wheelbarrow on which he had a grinding stone and a little anvil. The grinding stone was a sand stone which ran through a trough of water. It was a wet grinder and this man came to sharpen your blunt knives and scissors. Ko did a lot of sewing so she needed a good pair of scissors. From time to time she had her scissors sharpened but the knives were sharpened by themselves on a plank with fine sand.

In spite that it was a self done job, the knives were as sharp as a razor blade. Nick, Adrie's cousin, could vouch for that, he had the unfortunate experience to find out the hard way. His father was slicing bread with a knife that was so dull that you could sit on it with your bare behind to ride to Cologne and it wouldn't hurt a bit. Nobody ever sharpened the knife which made it difficult to cut bread.

One day, his father decided to sharpen the knife to make the job of slicing bread easier. He did a very good job as Nick found out when he came home unaware of the improvement which had taken place. Nick was hungry and decided to cut a piece of cheese; he pressed hard because the knife was blunt, he thought. Unfortunately, the knife was very sharp; cutting cheese was a piece of cake. The knife sliced the cheese very well and almost cut the thumb off his hand.

Nick was bleeding like a pig and was holding his hand underneath the cold water tap when his sister Marie came home. She wrapped a bandage around his wounded hand and took him to the doctor. It took several stitches but after the wound had healed, he could hardly move his thumb. Apparently, some of the nerves had been cut and he had to go to the hospital for a repair job.

Besides the noisy merchants there were also lots of noisy musicians that came through the street every day. There was the organ grinder who came with his huge barrel organ. In those days the organ had to be turned by hand which made the job of organ grinder a hard job. Later on, turning the organ was done with a little motor.

There were all kinds of musicians in those days. Two guys playing an accordion and a fiddle were among the musicians. Somebody else played a guitar and was singing "Oh Solomio." There was even a guy who was playing a mouth organ and also a guy who was whistling a tune on his fingers.

Another guy was called "Crazy Dirk" who was pan handling. He was just shouting and acting crazy. Everybody thought he was crazy, they were sorry for him and gave him some money, food or old clothes. Even the police never touched him because he was harmless and they were convinced that he was crazy. He lived in a basement room with his relatives for free. He wouldn't live in a room for which he had to pay, he wasn't that crazy. When Crazy Dirk died, they went through his room and found well over $10,000 hidden between his raggedy clothes.

It didn't matter whether the musicians were noisy or not, there was one thing you could count on. It wasn't the word of the sponsor; that came much later. But there was always a man going around with his hat asking for money for the unemployed musicians.

The noisiest group were three musicians with copper blowing instruments. When those guys came into the street it sounded as if they had come to blow down the walls of Jericho. It was a miniature brass band which wanted to be heard. Next door to Adrie lived an old blacksmith who was very sick and needed rest. Whenever his daughter heard the musicians come; she ran to the street to meet them. She gave them a dime and asked if they wouldn't blow their musical instruments too close to their house because her father was very ill. No problem, a dime was a lot of money in those days; a guy would pick the sun out of the sky for that kind of money. Most of the people donated a penny or even half a penny.

Jaap Kraak had no musical talents at all; he couldn't even whistle a tune but that didn't deter him from bringing music to the people. He had an old hand wagon, put a gramophone with a big copper horn on it and he was in business. It wasn't beautiful but it was loud and that's all that counted.

There was also a Potato Peel Man who came once per week to your door to take your potato peels off your hand. You didn't get any money for your potato peels so Potato Peel Man was a lucrative business. He had a good business with no overhead and could afford a horse and wagon. The horse was fed potato peels so it didn't cost him anything to feed his horse and the remaining potato peels were sold to the farmers who fed them to the cows, horses and pigs.

Even his wife contributed to the colourful Hordyk. The potato peel man was married to some kind of a nincompoop that didn't contribute anything to the marriage but having five children. The house was always a mess and the children were running around in rags worse than the rag man. She didn't even have potato peels for her husband because she didn't cook potatoes. Making a warm meal was never done in her household; she always gave the children bread.

With that many horses on the street there were also piles of horse manure. That created another job "The shit shoveler." A man with a tricycle with garbage cans came through the street to shovel all the horse manure into the cans. A more modern, more civilized word for such a person is a "pooper scooper."

Of course, there were many panhandlers who didn't contribute in sound to the colorful Hordyk. All they did was collect alms from door to door. Ko had no money to give away because she was poor herself. However, there was a very old man with a beard and in those days there were no pensions for John Blow. When you are old it doesn't mean that you don't eat anymore and this old man took anything he could get to make a living. Adrie's mother couldn't spare money but she gave him a cup of coffee. The next door neighbor might give him a penny or a sandwich and that's how he stayed alive.

A few weeks before Christmas, the noise on the Hordyk extended to late at night. In The Netherlands, people didn't eat turkeys for Christmas dinner, nobody could afford that. Instead, most people raised rabbits for their Christmas dinner. Those rabbits had to be skinned and those skins could be used for fur coats. This brought out a lot of peddlers who wanted to buy your rabbit skins. They would walk through the street shouting: "Hare and rabbit skins."

Other vendors would try to sell a rabbit to people who weren't raising their own. Beware if you were buying a rabbit because you could very well eat your neighbor's cat. When you skin a cat it looks identical to a rabbit and therefore the honest merchants left a piece of skin on the leg for station identification.

Charitable organizations tried to cash in on the Christmas spirit as well. They were selling tickets for a rabbit, a goose or a duck from door to door. There was even a lottery for a turkey which was rare for The Netherlands. People couldn't afford turkeys, but of course if you were lucky in the lottery, you didn't mind. The way the lottery worked, it actually was a double lottery. First of all you had to draw your ticket from a box and the number you would draw was the amount of money you paid for your ticket. If you drew number 1 you would pay one penny for your ticket. There were 35 numbers in the lottery, so you could end up paying 35 cent for your ticket.

That was too rich for Arie and Ko, and it counted them out. It was a sure thing that Arie and Ko weren't going to eat turkey for Christmas. When the draw was made number one was the winner and the winner was Farmer Hoving who had bought his ticket for one penny. He was raising turkeys himself and sure didn't need another turkey. It looked as if the infamous Devil was shitting on the same pile again.

Some of the merchants weren't exactly honest, as Aunt Pietje found out. She had a Christian Reformed milkman because she was Christian Reformed and she said that you had to support the people of your church. She would live to regret it.

Ko was Christian Reformed too but she bought milk from a milkman closer to her home. This Christian Reformed milkman was sitting in the front row of the church singing hymns with his hypocritical face. He probably was contemplating on Sunday who he could swindle come Monday.

Aunt Pietje had four children and bought two litres of milk every day, which were measured into her big milk pan. That milk pan held exactly two litres of milk, she thought. She only had one big pan so she cleaned the pan every day to have it ready for the milkman, when he came to the door.

When the Christian Reformed milkman got sick, he hired somebody to take his place as long as he was sick. His replacement came to Aunt Pietje's door; she gave him the same pan and asked for two litres of milk. A little later, the milkman came back with the pan full of milk and asked for another little container because he couldn't get two litres of milk in the pan.

Aunt Pietje was perplexed; for years the pan had been big enough to hold two litres of milk and suddenly it was too small. The pan couldn't have shrunk; the only explanation was that the milkman had swindled her for many years. She got about one fifth of a litre in the second container. This amounts to about 75 litres per year that the milkman ripped off. It's hard to believe that she was the only customer he cheated; he must have made a mint in a dishonest way for many years.

Did she have a bone to pick with this cheat of a milkman! The first day he resumed his duties, as a dishonest milkman, he had it coming. With a happy face he said to Aunt Pietje: "Good morning madam, nice day, isn't it?"

When he heard what Aunt Pietje had to say, he almost got sick again. She said: "No, it isn't a nice day, you cheater; for years you have stolen about one fifth of a litre of milk, every day. You are a thief!"

He was looking at Aunt Pietje as if she just had taken away his candy and stuttered: "Please forgive me; I'm really sorry, this will never happen again; you can count on it."

Aunt Pietje was furious and said: "You are darned right it will never happen again; you don't have to come to my door anymore; I'll find an honest milkman. Good bye."

The milkman was short of saying that the devil made him do it, but he had probably thought that if he asked for forgiveness, she would forgive him because she was Christian Reformed as well. Aunt Pietje was unforgiving in spite of her religion. Honesty is the best policy, they say. The milkman lost one customer but it could snowball. When the word went around, more people might be looking for a different milkman.

At school with arithmetic, there were problems to be solved, such as: "A grocer buys 100 pounds of sugar for 10 cents per pound. With over-weighing he loses 5% of his sugar. When he sells the sugar for 17 cents per pound, how much profit does he make?"

An owner of a grocery store could easily lose pounds because of over-weighing. In the middle of the counter were his weighing scales, so the customer could see if he was receiving the correct weight. The grocer would make sure that the customer didn't feel cheated; he always gave a little more when he was weighing. This was good for business.

In the case of the dishonest milkman, he was under-measuring which was bad for business. Not all Christian Reformed businessmen are cheats; the only thing is that you don't expect it from them and that's why those cheats are called hypocrites.

Ko's milkman wasn't Christian Reformed, he never went to church but he was honest and helpful. In the old days it was a problem to keep milk good for longer than a day. There were no preservatives and no refrigerators; only the rich had an ice box. The ice box was something similar to the cooler we take to the lake. It was a well insulated box with chunks of ice in it and between the chunks of ice you put your milk or beer to keep it cool.

To make the ice box work, an ice man was needed. Actually, there were two kinds of ice men coming through the street. One was selling ice cream cones to the kids, and the other one was selling blocks of ice to the rich people who had an ice box. Neither one of the two icemen had the Demerwes as a customer; they didn't have an icebox and neither did they have the money to buy ice cream cones. The only thing Ko had to keep her milk good was a concrete floor in one of the cupboards. She put her pan with milk on the concrete floor to keep it as cold as possible.

The major problem was to prevent the milk from getting sour on Sundays. For that purpose the milk man came twice on Saturday because he wasn't allowed to peddle milk on the Lord's Day. Late Saturday afternoon or at night the milkman would come to deliver the milk which was needed for Sunday. It worked alright, but when the temperature went up to 40 degrees Celsius in Summer, the milk spoiled on Ko. On a hot Sunday afternoon, the milk had gone sour and Ko said to Adrie: "Let's go to the milkman to see if he has some milk left."

The milkman lived only a block away from Ko, which made it easy enough to get some milk. Ko said to the milkman: "Can I buy some milk from you, all my milk is sour?"

"No I can't sell you milk on the Lord's Day," the milkman replied. "That would be asking for trouble; if they catch me, they'll take my license away. But I can give you some milk; it says in the Sunday's Act that I can't sell milk on a Sunday but it doesn't say that I can't give milk away."

Ko had no objection getting free milk; money was hard to come by and that way she could use her money for other things. The milkman had a deep well in which he lowered his milk cans. That way, the milk cans would be standing in the ice cold water and he could keep his milk good for a couple of days. When Ko left with ice cold milk, the milkman said: "Whenever you have sour milk on Sunday, come to me and I'll give you some."

Aunt Pietje had a different milkman after she had disposed the dishonest milkman but she wasn't particularly fond of him. When it became winter, the milkman had a dripping nose and she saw that a drip from the milkman's nose fell into her milk pan. When she shouted at the milkman: "I don't want that milk because a drip of your nose fell in it," the milkman replied: "Never mind I'll give you some other milk."

Resolutely he emptied her milk can with the nose drip in the big container on his wagon and started to measure the milk again. Aunt Pietje couldn't believe it, she said: "You just emptied the can with your nose drip in your container and now you are giving me milk from that container. I don't want milk from you because you are a dirty milkman."

The milkman was looking sheepishly at her as if he was thinking: "What a stupid woman, one drop out of my nose in a full milk pan; you never taste the difference."

Finally, she asked Ko if she wanted to send her milkman to her so she could buy milk from him. It wasn't a Christian Reformed milkman but she had changed her mind about that.

The farmers delivered their milk to a milk plant called "Sterovita" which was always advertising that their milk was safe because it was checked seven times for bacteria. It didn't impress the poor unemployed people who were drinking blue skim milk. They said: "Yeah, Sterovita milk, seven times controlled means seven times skimmed to get whipping cream to export to England." In those days a lot of whipping cream was shipped to England so the rich people could drink coffee with whipping cream. To pay for the whipping cream, the English sent tennis balls to The Netherlands. They were urgently needed so that Prince Bernhard and his buddies could play tennis.

(When the cows were watching the advertising of Sterovita milk that said it was checked seven times for bacteria, one cow said to the other cow: "It makes you feel sort of inadequate, doesn't it?")

There was only one grocery store on the Hordyk which contributed greatly to making the Hordyk colorful. Nobody could have ever foreseen the tremendous change in grocery shopping. It's hard to picture the old grocery store and it's also hard to explain. The best thing is to hop on my time machine to move back in time.

Going back in time can be a very dangerous proposition because you could get killed easily by things beyond your control but that's the chance you have to take. It's even possible to prevent your own birth if you kill your grandfather before he made your father.

All aboard for the adventure of a life time. Everything moves fast in reverse but we notice two huge buildings that are collapsing. It are the Twin Towers of the Trade Centre in New York that came down when jets flew into them.

We see two more great explosions which were caused by the two atomic bombs that were dropped on Hiroshima and Nagasaky at the conclusion of World War II. Moving back farther means venturing through World War II and the time machine could be taken for a plane with bombs on its way to a target. Luckily we aren't noticed and arrive safely in the year 1936.

Get moving because we are going to do some grocery shopping. Grab your shopping bag because there are no plastic shopping bags. As a matter of fact, plastic hasn't been invented yet. We don't have a car; we don't even have a bike; we are poor which means we have to walk. It's only a five minute walk and it's nice weather; some fresh air will do you a lot of good.

Today, the average super market sells about 30,000 different products, compared to the old grocery store which sold perhaps 30 different items. We have arrived at the grocery store of Fleurtje Groenenboom. Actually, it is not a store, it is a big house. The big living room has been changed into a store and Fleurtje and his wife live in the back of the house. If there is nobody in the store, they are usually in the back in their living quarters.

We open the door and a little, non-electric, copper bell starts tingling. Fleurtje hears the sound of the bell, and he comes right away to the front to serve his customers. It's a little store; if there are 10 people in it, it's crowded. You don't help yourself because everything has to be weighed into paper bags.

There is a counter with a weighing scale. It's a comparing weighing scales; you put a one pound-weight on one side and the bag with sugar or salt on the other side. If there is a pound of sugar in your bag, the needle of the weighing scale is in the middle. Beside the weighing scales are the copper weights; there are weights of half an ounce, one ounce, two ounces, half a pound, one pound and one kilo which is two pounds.

When more people enter the store, Fleurtje shouts to the back of the store for his wife to give him a hand. If there are people ahead of you, you wait patiently until it's your turn. In the meantime you talk to the other customers; everybody knows everybody.

Behind the counter there are half a dozen bins; they contain sugar, brown sugar, salt, soda, flour, and coffee beans. You have to grind your own coffee at home with a coffee grinder. There is also a pail with syrup. Everybody has a syrup can at home, and when it's empty, you go to the store to have it filled.

A big tub with green soap is behind the counter. You bring your own container to get it filled. On the shelf are glass jars which contain cookies, candies, salted liquorice, peppermints, and chocolates. Only a few items come packaged; including tea, Sunlight soap, jars of jam and bottles of lemonade. There is not much choice with only two different kinds of lemonade, usually orange and carbonated lemonade. You also have a choice of strawberry jam or raspberry jam. For bottles and jars you have to pay a ten cents holding deposit, which is a lot of money for those days, in which you make twenty guilders per week.

When it's your turn you say: "One pound of sugar." Fleurtje grabs a bag and weighs a pound of sugar for you. He puts it on the counter and looks at you. You say: "One pound of salt." The same procedure is repeated until everything you want is on the counter. Fleurtje grabs his eternal pencil from behind his ear and adds everything on a piece of paper. You pay and hand him your grocery bag. He puts everything in your bag and away you go.

When you come home, you put everything in your own containers and you are all set for a week. There are only a few articles in the store, which makes grocery shopping easy; even a kid can do it. That's what the neighbor lady across the street thought when she was home late to cook her husband's lunch. Her husband had only one hour lunch time so everything had to be ready when he came home. She peeled the potatoes fast and put them on the stove, but by Jove, she had run out of salt. It was impossible to go away while the potatoes were cooking; if the water evaporated, the potatoes would burn to a crisp and that would be worse.

Little William was only four years old, but on the other hand, she had taken him often enough to the grocery store. He was smart for his age, and should be able to run an errand for her. She said to William: "Go to Fleurtje Groenenboom and get me one pound of salt. Let me hear if you can say it." Little William said: "Salte." That was great, she thought, Fleurtje would understand that for sure. She could have written it on a piece of paper, but William had to take money along too. If he had to carry too many things he would lose either his note or his money. No, this was better.

William went to the store and Fleurtje asked: "What do you want William?"

William looked eagerly at the glass bottles with candies and said: "Salte."

Fleurtje looked where William was looking and thought, "Of course, the kid wants salted liquorice." He looked in William's hand and saw two pennies thus he gave him two pennies worth of salted liquorice.

William went home happily, he was sure his mother would give him some of that delicious liquorice. His mother wasn't as happy as William when she saw what he had brought home. "Holy smokes," she said and looked desperately out of the window as if the solution to her problem was outside. Indeed, the solution to her problem was outside; it was Adrie, who just came home from school. She ran outside and asked if Adrie could run to the store for salt and gave him a penny for his trouble to buy some candy for himself. For a penny Adrie would run like a race horse because he seldom had a penny to buy candies. Everything turned out alright, except to get one pound of salt she had spent five cents instead of two.

Even during the Depression, most people had some kind of a home library. Most of the books were obtained from the kids that went to Sunday School and got a book for Christmas. Another way to get books was on coupons from Van Nelle Coffee and Tea. When you bought a pack of coffee or tea there would be a coupon in the package. The coupon was good to obtain books. Five coupons would give you a thin book and if you wanted a thicker book you had to have more coupons.

One of the books was called: "How Piggelmee got big."

Piggelmee and his wife were dwarfs; they lived in a stone pot. One day in a storm, a tree fell on the pot and broke it in two. Piggelmee's wife was crying while Piggelmee was reading the newspaper. He said to his wife: "It says in the paper that the Miracle Silver Fish is in the river, I'm going to the river and see if I can find that Miracle Silver Fish and ask him for another house, this time a real house."

Piggelmee went to the river and shouted: "Dear Miracle Silver Fish, please come up, I want to talk to you." There was a ripple in the water and the Miracle Silver Fish appeared.

Piggelmee said: "Dear Miracle Silver Fish, we are living in a stone pot. A tree fell on the stone pot and the stone pot is broken, could you give us a real house to live in."

The Miracle Silver Fish said: "Go home; your real house is already there."

When he went home, he found his wife in a real big house but she wasn't all that happy. She said: "Go back to that Miracle Fish and ask him to make us big now we are living in a big house." Piggelmee went back to the river and called for the Miracle Fish again. When the Miracle Fish surfaced, Piggelmee said: "Now we are living in a big house, we would like to be big."

The Miracle Fish said: "Go home Piggelmee and you both will be big."

When Piggelmee entered his home, he and his wife became instantly big. Unfortunately, his wife wasn't very happy. She said to Piggelmee: "Go back to that Miracle Fish and ask him for food to eat and drink."

Piggelmee returned to the river and asked the Miracle fish for food to eat and drink. The Miracle Fish said: "Go home Piggelmee, all the food that you possibly can eat and drink is already there."

When Piggelmee returned home he found the kitchen loaded with all kinds of food to eat and drink. His wife wasn't happy at all and told him to go back to ask the Miracle Fish for furniture.

Again, the Miracle Fish gave Piggelmee what he asked for but his wife was really nagging. She said: "All what we have to drink is Van Nelle Coffee and I'm getting sick and tired of it, go back and ask that Miracle Fish for something better to drink than Van Nelle Coffee."

Reluctantly, Piggelmee went back to the Miracle Fish and said: "My wife doesn't like to drink Van Nelle Coffee all the time, she wants something better to drink."

The Miracle Fish got really angry this time when he heard the request from Piggelmee and said: "There is nothing better to drink than Van Nelle Coffee. I'm sorry for you Piggelmee but because you want better than the best, I'll punish you and take back everything that I gave you."

When Piggelmee arrived back home, he found everything gone and his wife was sitting in front of the broken stone pot and they were dwarfs again. His wife said: "This is terrible that we lost everything but the worst is that we have nothing to drink anymore. Please go back to the Miracle Fish and ask him if he can give us back our Van Nelle Coffee to drink."

Piggelmee returned to the Miracle Fish and asked: "Please Miracle Fish could you please return our Van Nelle Coffee of all the things we have lost, so we have something good to drink."

The Miracle Fish was sorry for Piggelmee and said: "I do this only for you Pigelmee, you can't help that your wife is always bitching. Without Van Nelle's coffee and tea, life is not worth living. Therefore I'll grant you this wish, so you can drink Van Nelle's coffee and tea for the rest of your life. You cannot come back to me because I'm leaving."

There was a final ripple in the water when the Miracle Fish disappeared forever. When Piggelmee came home his wife was already pouring a delicious cup of Van Nelle Coffee for him and they lived very happily ever after, enjoying there Van Nelle Coffee.

This is just a saga teaching us that we appreciate the good things of life after we lose them. In Canada they never heard about Van Nelle Coffee. They have plenty of advertising about Columbia Coffee which is picked by Fernando one bean at a time because the beans have to ripen on the tree.

After take off of a D.C.8. the stewardess tells the captain that they forgot the Columbia Coffee. Abruptly, the captain makes a 180 degree turn to get the coffee. On another occasion when Columbia Coffee is served on a ship, the ship almost capsizes because all people run to one side of the ship. The Miracle Fish wouldn't be very happy if he heard about all this.

The Christian Reformed milkman wasn't the only merchant that swindled people by under-measuring milk. Even Fleurtje Groenenboom who was a grocer thought that people wanted to be cheated.

Fleurtje Groenenboom had a son, Mels Groenenboom who went to the same school as Adrie. One time Mels made a statement which Adrie didn't quite understand. He said: "There are a lot of people who want to be cheated."

After the war it was a chaos with almost everything. Society stepped back at least a decade. To get supplies was all that counted; they usually came in bulk. Coffee came in 100 pound bags, so the old bins came in handy.

Fleurtje Groenenboom had three bins of coffee, he filled all three bins from the same bags but he priced them differently. The selling price of coffee was 30 cents per pound. He had one bin at that price, the next bin was 34 cents per pound and the third bin was priced at 38 cents per pound. It was all the same coffee but most people bought the medium priced coffee, they didn't want that cheap coffee and the expensive coffee they couldn't afford. People swore that if you paid four cents per pound more for the coffee, you had much better coffee and it was worth every cent. They sure could taste the difference. Who were they fooling? It was all the same coffee. Apparently it was all in their head.

It showed again that if people wanted better coffee, they get it but at a higher price. If the Miracle Silver Fish would have heard about it, he would have been very angry.

Granted that people are stupid but Adrie didn't think that a grocer would rip off his customers like that. Where do they learn those things? When Mels told Adrie what his father did, he was flabbergasted. If his father had known that he told Adrie all about his obscure practices, he wouldn't have been very happy.

(On the other hand there were a lot of honest merchants. It was the proverbial one bad apple in the basket which made all those people look bad.)

Everything in the grocery store has changed especially the products for sale. Most of today's products hadn't been invented yet. The old grocery store had no split peas, plastic diapers or Kotex for women. Minute rice wasn't heard of and neither was Uncle Ben's instant rice that is done as soon as it hits the water. Even the pencil behind Fleurtje's ear has disappeared but so have the brains of the sales clerks.

Going to McDonald's for a hamburger. One hamburger costs $2.95 and three of those hamburgers cost $12.85 according to the girl. Adrie knew that it was wrong; it should be less than $10.00. The girl went to the cash register again and said that it was this time $7.15. That was not right either but he could live with that outcome since it was less than it really was.

There was another daily appearance on the Hordyk. It was the postman. Jobs like postman were restricted to men. The postman of yesterday was courteous, neatly dressed with a crease in his pants which was as sharp as a shaving blade and he was accurate. He was always in uniform and in The Netherlands he also wore a cap to protect his valuable head. On his cap were three large letters "P.T.T." which meant Post, Telegraph, Telephone. The post office was actually the headquarters of all communication systems except radio and television.

In those days of yesterday, you could see the postman from afar; there was no doubt that it was the postman. His uniform showed it and the postman was proud to wear his uniform; it was the symbol of authority and dignity. He would never shed his uniform even if it was hot in summer. When it was so hot that the sparrows dropped dead from the roof because of heat exhaustion, he kept going. The postman was accurate; he always came at 10.00 a.m. in the street, you could put your watch right with it.

When the Hordyk started to expand rapidly; there was a problem. In the beginning there was a house here and there and the houses were numbered accordingly. However, when you start building houses between number 1 and number 3, all you can do is number them 1A and 1B. After a while it became quite messy and Town Hall decided to solve the problem. They renumbered all the houses, which made quite a change.

The house of the Demerwes used to be number 33 but the new number was 121. Of course, a change of address notice was sent to the family but some people don't make the change in their address book and keep using the old address. It didn't make any difference to the postman what number was on the envelope; as long as he saw the name Demerwe on it, he would deliver it. He knew where everybody lived; that was his business, and he would have been ashamed if he hadn't been able to deliver a letter in his district.

The postman was not only accurate, he was also scrupulous. At one time there came a change of address notice from one of the relatives. Ko put the card on the chimney mantle; she would put the new address in her address book at night. A little later she discovered that she had to write a postcard. After she had done that, she put the postcard on the chimney mantle so she could mail it at night.

That evening Ko mailed the postcard. About an hour after she had returned, she looked at the chimney mantle and there was the postcard that she had mailed. It just couldn't be; she didn't imagine things so there must be an explanation. By accident she had mailed the address change card instead of the postcard. She knew the time the mailman came to empty the mail box and she walked back to the mail box. When the mailman came, she told him what had happened and asked if she could get the address change card back. The postman said: "I have to deliver all the mail that's in this post box; you can't ask anything back once it's in the mail box. But don't worry, if your address is on the card we will deliver it again tomorrow."

Indeed, the next day the card was delivered for the second time. The mailman of those days was scrupulous; you couldn't talk him into anything that was against the regulations.

The Hordyk was colourful in more than one way. There were also a bunch of gossiping old ladies who had a color of their own. It was probably yellow.

Their only problem was that they weren't curious but they wanted to know everything and were forever spying on everybody. Most of those old goats had a spying rear view mirror mounted in their window. That way they could view both sides of the street without turning around.

To make it even more interesting there was a dirty old man on the colorful Hordyk. It was the bike repair man Wim Kramer who lived with his sister. He had a work bench that he never cleaned up, he never threw away a broken old part that he had replaced; he just put it on his overfull work bench. Most of the time when he put something on his bench, it fell on the floor because there wasn't any room to put it.

Wim Kramer was very good at bike repairing, but his specialty was to put the saddle on the right height and pitch for young girls. He had a special stand made for the bikes so that a person could sit on his or her bike and paddle. That way he could see if the saddle was too high or too low. The girls could stay in the saddle while he made his adjustments and by planned accidents he would touch and brush the thighs of the girls with his hand.

The only time that the Hordyk became sombre instead of colourful was when somebody had died. When that happened the whole neighbourhood put white sheets in front of the windows that stayed until after the funeral. People going to the funeral were all in black, the women wore a black veil in front of their face and the men wore a black suit and a high black hat on their head. That was quite expensive but the black suit and high hat went from father to son and if you didn't have a black suit or a black high hat, you borrowed one.

Mourning was also in black; a widow or widower would mourn for a year wearing black clothes. When your father or mother died you would wear a black band around your arm for a year indicating that you were in mourning. Funeral announcements were on black cards with white letters. Most of those customs have died.

At that time there were no Funeral Parlors in The Netherlands and corpses were not embalmed. When somebody died the mortician would come with a coffin to put the body into. The coffin with the body stayed in the house until the burial took place and the burial was done with black coaches drawn by black horses, everything was black.

The funeral director was very versatile, he said: "The way the wind blows, blows my coat."

What he meant was that he would go any way to please his customers. If the family of the deceased person was Protestant, he would pray on the grave, if they were Roman Catholic, he would make a cross when praying and if they were Atheists, he would uncork a bottle on the grave. He did everything to make a buck.

People were buried, only a very few people were cremated. It was against the law that states that people have to be buried within three days after they die. There was a reason that cremation wasn't allowed in The Netherlands. It was a Christian nation that believed in eternal life. When you are dead you are supposed to wait in your grave for the arrival of the Angel Gabriel who will blow his trumpet to awake the dead. Burning corpses was seen as a Devilish practise, only the Devil ran an eternal fire called "Hell." People in The Netherlands were mainly Christians who believed that they had to be buried facing East because Christ would come from the East.

Most people want the congregation to sing: "How Great Thou Art", "Whispering Hope" or "The Old Rugged Cross" but there was one old lady who was different and wanted the people to sing "It's a long way to Tipperary" when she was buried.

Actually, it doesn't make much difference to the person that's being buried what they sing, he or she doesn't hear it anyway. History has proven that statement wrong. King Charles V had ordered a certain ceremony upon his death and he wondered if they would do it. He organized with his body guard to pretend that he was dead so there was his funeral. After the ceremony he came out of his coffin and was satisfied that everything would be done as ordered.

People had found a way to sail around the law that people couldn't be cremated. They had established a Cremation Organization. Only if you were a member of such an organization could you be cremated. After the cremation of a member had taken place, the crematorium was fined one hundred guilders for defying the law. Of course, that one hundred guilders was charged to the family.

(It might look like a stupid law that forbids cremation but it was even more stupid that in a town where the people who lived East of the railroad couldn't be buried at the local Grave Yard.

If you wonder why? The answer is, only the dead people can be buried and the statement was that people who are living East of the railroad couldn't be buried there.)

(Many years later when the shoe was on the other foot, most of the people got cremated as there was not enough room to bury everybody. Competition among the Funeral Homes was severe and a cut rate Funeral Home offered cremations for $535.00. When one of the employees was fired there were some sour grapes and he told about the practices of the Funeral Home. He claimed that animal ashes were mixed with ashes from humans to save time and money. When the family received their ashes, there was no way of telling whether they had received the ashes of their spouse or the ashes of a German Shepherd.)

THE SCAVENGERS

Adrie and his sister Willie were real collectors; they could teach a packrat a valuable lesson or two. Whenever they had to go somewhere, they had to walk since there was no money for the bus fare. They didn't mind walking at all; his sister would walk on one side of the road and Adrie would walk on the other side. No, they weren't mad at each other, they were only scavengers. Anything that somebody else had discarded, Willie and Adrie had good use for. After they had gone through the street, it was clean. The street sweeper had good help on those two.

They found cigar bands, empty match boxes, silver paper and empty cigarette packages because there were no full ones. Their parents didn't allow them to pick up cigarette and cigar butts but other people did that. It was Depression time and many unemployed people had no money to buy cigarettes so they made them out of butts they found. When Adrie and Willie were a little bit older, they collected the butts as well because they wanted to smoke. At that stage they didn't think about their parents who had said no to smoking and collecting butts.

The Netherlands was the country of cigars and there were quite a few different makes with different bands. They glued the bands in an old exercise book and they had about a hundred different ones.

The empty cigarette packages provided them with playing cards. They cut the front and back off the package, which provided them with two different cards from one package. There were about eight different brands of cigarettes which provided them with sixteen different cards. The art was to get as many cards as possible when you were playing cards.

Each player would have his stack of cards, shuffle them and put the stack in front of him on the table, face down. You couldn't see which cards there were. The first player would play the top card and turn it over so you could see the card. The next player would take his top card of his deck and put it on top of the played card. Whenever the card played matched the card on top of the pile, the player would get the whole pile of played cards.

If you were unlucky enough, you could lose all of your cards in a hurry, in which case you had to head for the streets to do some more scavenging. On the other hand if you were lucky you could win a lot of cards, sometimes Adrie had over a hundred cards in his box. Of course, it didn't take long to lose them all if he was unlucky the next day.

The silver paper they collected, they gave to the teacher at school. When the school had a lot of silver paper, they took it to a depot where they melted it to get tin. That's all that silver paper is, tin rolled out to very thin sheets.

Silver paper proceeds were used to finance missionary work. Churches were sending missionaries out to all parts of the world to convert heathens to Christians. Jesus said; when he founded the church: "Go and preach the Gospel to all people of the world!"

Of course, if Jesus said it, you have to do it, though Adrie and Willie were only the financiers. They helped to finance the missionary work of the churches, in order to save the souls of many heathens. Because of their contribution, the heathens would go to heaven instead of hell. That was really nice of them and they were glad to be of service. Sometimes, they wondered how many heathens they really saved.

In spite of the hard scavenger work that Willie and Adrie did, the Missionaries weren't all that great and made one boo boo after another. Of course, people didn't know about the failures, they heard only about the accomplishments. The Pope believed that it was impossible that there ever could be too many Roman Catholics in the world. He sent his missionaries everywhere to build churches for the converted pagans.

However, there were also Protestant churches who wanted to have a stake in developing countries. If they left missionary work to the Catholics, the Catholic Church would become too powerful for their liking. They also went into the business of converting pagans and building churches.

Business in religion became competitive and real dirty. Slanderous charges were often used to show the heathens that this was the only right church in the whole wide world. The heathens who were converted to Roman Catholics were told by the Protestant Ministers that Roman Catholics never could go to heaven. Roman Catholics were sinning because they were worshipping idols. They pray to Holy Mary Mother of God and that is contradictory to the teachings of the Bible. You are only allowed to pray to God and Jesus. Also statues of Mary and Joseph were idols according to the Protestant missionaries.

The Catholics fired back with their ammunition and stated that Christ had established one General Catholic Church and the Protestants were just a bunch of rebels on which God will look unfavorably on Doomsday.

In the cross-fire were the converted heathens who didn't understand any of this and got confused. For the simple minded pagans, preaching left much to be desired. "When you pray to God he can give you anything you desire," they were told by the missionaries. The pagans were impressed with the ships the missionaries came in and admired the clocks, watches and jewels of the white man. In their simple mind, they were under the impression that if they asked God for those things, he certainly would give them. The natives became cargo Christians; they wanted to share in the goodies of the missionaries and prayed for the stuff that had come in the cargo of the white man. When God didn't deliver, they were cheesed off, dumped Christianity and turned back to Pagan worship.

On another occasion, the missionary had told the pagans the story about the Israelites in the desert and how God fed them with Manna from Heaven. When the natives were hungry, they were holding up blankets to catch the Manna from Heaven. Again, the Lord didn't provide them with what they expected and many souls were lost.

In spite of the gross bungling of the missionaries with the silver paper money that Willie and Adrie collected, they managed to get more than a foothold among the heathens. The trump of the missionaries was that they out-smarted the medicine man of the natives, and seeing is believing, the heathens figured.

Not always was the White Man's doctor superior to the Medicine Man. A scientific expedition in Brazil's Amazon had a problem when one man of the party had an infected foot. When gangrene set in, the doctor of the party feared the worst. To save the man's life his foot had to be amputated which was impossible outside a hospital.They were in the middle of nowhere and they decided to see if they could get help from an Indian tribe in the vicinity, to transport the sick man.

When they asked for help, the Medicine Man came out to have a look at their problem. He looked at the infected foot and said: "Me heal foot."

Everybody of the party rejected his offer except the sick man who said: "It's my foot which is at stake so it's my decision. I want the medicine man to heal it; the way my foot is now I will lose it for sure so I have nothing to lose."

All the members of the party, including the doctor, were watching the Medicine Man how he treated the infected foot. Hygiene was totally lacking and the medicine he used was unheard of. A mixture of animal dung with herbs and fruit was put on the infected area. Next, by lack of gauze he covered the wound with cob webs. Finally he made a drink from roots and tree leaves which he gave to the sick man to get the fever down.

Nobody from the party thought that the infected foot would heal. To everybody's surprise, the next day showed a remarkable improvement, the swelling in the foot was gone and the patient's temperature was back to normal. After a week, the patient was completely recovered and they could continue their trip.

Even Ko had a problem with old folk medicine. At one time Adrie had an infection on his hand and when his Grandmother saw it she took a crust of molded cheese and rubbed it on the infected area. Ko had the shock of her life when she saw it but Adrie not only survived the ordeal, the infection cleared up within days. Old people knew their medicine as well as a medicine man in the wilderness.

Ko didn't believe in healing by herbs or other natural substances but seeing was believing. When she saw the result she had to admit that molded cheese was a better medicine than the ointment she had used to treat the infection. Molded cheese is actually nothing more than penicillin which is made from mold.

Often the missionaries built churches as a bastion for religion. On the negative side of this can be said that missionary work made Colonialism and Imperialism possible. Missionaries also allowed Fijians to be transported to the United States for display purposes. At circuses across the country, the Fijians were put into a cage with a poster stating: "Today we show you savages from the South Pacific." Of course, when Adrie was collecting silver paper, he didn't know about all those things. In his humble opinion he did a lot of good to finance missionary work.

Once you are a collector, it's inevitable to get collections. Adrie had collections of match boxes, cigar bands and dried flowers. Then one day, he was introduced to stamp collecting. When he was about six years old, he was at his friend's place. His father was cleaning up his office and with all the foreign correspondence he had, he received quite a few stamps from different countries. He always had saved the stamps and was planning to start a stamp collection. That idea had never materialized with his busy work schedule. When he came across the box with stamps, he decided to get rid of them. There was no time for this kind of hobby so why save them? He said to his son: "Here is a box with all kinds of stamps, you can have them and I'll buy you a stamp album to put them in."

Adrie's friend wasn't all that interested in a stamp collection and showed no interest. His father was determined to get rid of the stamps and asked Adrie if he wanted the stamps. That was a dumb question, Adrie was interested in everything and couldn't believe his ears that he was the recipient of a box with over a hundred stamps.

There were many German stamps from the inflationary period with denominations from one Mark to two billion Marks. At the beginning of the inflation, the stamps were worth less than one Mark but when the inflation went out of control it didn't take long before you needed a thousand Mark stamp to mail a letter. At the end of the inflationary period there were even stamps valued at 2 billion Marks. Imagine that you want to write a letter and you have to buy a two billion-dollar stamp to mail it.

While Adrie was admiring his newly acquired acquisition, his friend's father also gave him an envelope with bank notes from this same time when inflation was rampant in Germany. Adrie couldn't believe his eyes, there were all kinds of bank notes from 100,000 marks to 100 billion Marks. At one time, the 100 billion Mark banknote represented that much money and you would probably use it when you had to stock up on postage stamps at the post office. Today it was just a worthless piece of paper except for collectors like Adrie. A million Marks weren't even worth the paper it was written on.

For a starter, good old St. Nick brought Adrie a stamp collector's album to put his stamps in and for his birthday he would get an envelope with 25 different stamps from England, France or another country. Those envelopes cost only five cents. There were also envelopes with a hundred different stamps but of course they cost 25 cents which was too much for his parents to pay. His mother saved some of the money she made for birthday and St. Nicholas presents.

In those days when you had to mail a letter you had to put a penny stamp on it. There were even older stamps with a value of half a penny which were used before the First World War. There was a postage stamp collectors market where you could buy stamps for your collection or you could trade some of your doubles with other collectors. Adrie had no money to buy stamps but he had quite a few doubles. When he showed his doubles to other collectors he had no trouble trading them. Many of his doubles were stamps from the German inflation period with values of up to 2 billion marks. When he traded them he acquired quite a few more stamps for his collection.

One of his newly acquired stamps was a Mauritius stamp. They were always talking about the rare Mauritius stamp which was worth over a hundred thousand dollars. Unfortunately, the stamp Adrie had was a Mauritius stamp but not that Mauritius stamp. In the beginning of stamp making, the English colony Mauritius made some postage stamps. Mauritius was only a little island and there were only a few stamps made, that's why they became so valuable.

One of the more interesting things at the market was a collector who had a lecture about the history of the postage stamp. As late as 1840 the postal service in England was a losing proposition. There were no postage stamps because they hadn't been invented yet. If you sent a letter, the recipient had to pay for the delivery because nobody got paid before a service was provided. That was not a bad idea but it didn't work, mail service was quite expensive and the recipient of the mail quite often refused to pay for the mail service. This meant that the mail had to be returned to the sender. The sender didn't want his mail back so the mailman was stuck with mail that nobody wanted. Yet, the mail had gone back and forward through the postal system and nobody paid for it.

The Postmaster General appointed Mr. Hill to solve the problems of the post office. When Mr. Hill's report reached the Postmaster General's desk he wasn't amused at all. Mr. Hill suggested that the charges for a letter should be only one penny and the sender should pay up front for the delivery instead of the recipient paying on delivery.

Mr. Hill also recommended that the post office would sell envelopes with a stamp of the post office on it. Rich people who had their own envelopes could buy pieces of paper with the stamp of the post office on it so they could glue the little piece of paper with the stamp on their envelope.

The Postmaster General couldn't believe his eyes when he read the report; he moved his glasses to the point of his nose so he could look over them and told the Board of Directors: "This is the most stupid and ridiculous idea I've ever heard in my entire life. Selling pieces of paper with a stamp on it; how crazy can you get? It will never work. Mr. Hill is certainly not playing with a full deck. Moreover, his suggestion to charge one penny for a letter that goes through all of England and Ireland is crazy, we will lose an awful lot of money. It can't be done. The post office isn't a philanthropic institution which is subsidised by the English Government!"

In spite of the pessimistic forecast of the Postmaster General, Hill's recommendations were accepted and they were an immediate success. The one penny post was something the people could afford and many envelopes and also little pieces of paper with the postage stamp on it were sold. That's why a postage stamp is called a stamp because in the beginning that's all it was. The very first postage stamp would never mention the country where it was issued; it only would say: "City of London. One Penny" or any other city in the world. When they went through the post office the post man would cancel the stamp by putting another stamp on it.

After the postage stamp was invented, an old lady in London collected all those used postage stamps and glued them on her bedroom wall so she didn't have to buy wallpaper. She was the first postage stamp collector in the world and had over 15000 stamps on her wall. Of course, she had a lot of doubles but that didn't matter, it was cheap wall paper. At this stage, the early stamps already had a picture of the Queen on it which made some jokers suggest that this lady had saved more heads of English Queens than Henry VIII had chopped off.

That was a successful afternoon for Adrie, he had learned a lot and had also new stamps for his collection. Another great stamp for his collection was obtained when the Dutch Post celebrated 200 years of postage service in The Netherlands. The post office gave out a special commemoration stamp for this occasion. An unstamped postage stamp doesn't have any value so Adrie had to get it through the mail.

Adrie bought the stamp with an old post coach on it, stuck it on a picture post card that he sent to himself and waited patiently till the postman delivered it. After a few days the picture postcard was delivered and the stamp was very lightly stamped. The postman who had stamped the postage stamp was very courteous and had wanted to preserve its beauty. At that time all postage stamps were stamped by hand.

In The Netherlands they had also Children postage stamps with a surcharge, it wasn't G.S.T. or P.S.T. ,that surcharge went to invalid children care.

All beginning is difficult, they say. When you start from scratch there is a certain outlay of capital necessary. In the Good Old Time there was no capital for anything and certainly not for a hobby. When Adrie started to keep fish, he had two aquariums, the small aquarium was an old pan and the big one was an old pail. (Filled with water, of course.)

As for fish, he had no guppies, sword tails or other tropical fish. His fish supply came from the ditches in the polder; they were mainly stickle bass and salamanders. For his birthday he got a small aquarium. That way he could admire his beautiful salamanders. There were grey and brown ones, the brown ones were the females and the grey ones were the males, all according to the fish experts. Adrie had been looking underneath the salamanders' tail but to him, they all looked alike. He just had to take the expert's word for it. Some salamanders were spotted with green, blue and orange marks, they were called king salamanders because of their beautiful colors. It was doubtful they were kings among the salamanders.

Keeping salamanders in an aquarium is a job and a half. Salamanders are amphibian; they can live in water and for some time on land. As soon as Adrie had his aquarium, he put his salamanders in their new quarters and watched them for a while before he went to bed. The next morning he was going to feed his salamanders but where did they go? There wasn't even one salamander in his aquarium; they simply had crawled up the glass and out of the aquarium. Now he had to catch the salamanders for the second time; most of them he found but a few were gone. This meant that he had another job to do, making a wooden frame that covered most of the top.

Catching salamanders in the polder ditches was an art. Some people had a net to catch them but Adrie caught them with his fast hand and keen eye. He would lay flat on his belly, at the edge of the ditch, waiting for a salamander to come up for air. Once the salamander was near the surface, he could snatch it out of the water. No matter how fast you were, you would never grab a stickle bass out of the water; you didn't even have a chance with a net. However, Adrie had his own technique; all what it took was a rake. There were lots of weeds in the ditches where the stickle basses were hiding. With his rake he would throw a lot of those weeds on the shore and the stickle basses, still in the weeds, were now easy to catch.

It's nothing to keep fish, but fish have to eat and there was no money to buy fish food in the store. Nothing was a problem, the salamanders ate worms that were available in the gardens; all he had to do was dig them up. There was only one problem, salamanders don't hibernate during winter and the garden was solidly frozen. You can dry water lice but you can't dry worms for winter so there had to be an adequate supply of fresh worms during winter. Old pots and pans did the trick; Adrie filled them up with earth, dug up a lot of worms and put them in the shed where it didn't freeze. That took care of his winter supply.

A little later he caught some very little pikes about three inches long that had to go in a different aquarium. When they got bigger he had to catch little fish for them. It was a lot of work but work was never a problem in those days.

There were fruit and willow trees on the property where Adrie could find lady bugs and caterpillars. He took some old jam jars, made some holes in the cover so they wouldn't suffocate and he was in business. Those were nice for his collection, especially the caterpillars that spun a cocoon from which a beautiful butterfly appeared. Adrie didn't have a butterfly collection; strangely enough he never had thought that he could have one. He would just release the butterflies and watch them fly away. That was the way to do it, the butterfly would lay eggs on the leaves of the trees and after a while the eggs would be little caterpillars again. At that stage Adrie had some more work to collect the new generation of caterpillars. Thanks to his tireless work the caterpillars didn't become extinct like so many other species.

In his collection, he had a lot of lady bugs with black dots on their back. According to the people, each dot represented one year. If a lady bug had three dots, it was three years old. There were even lady bugs with six dots; they were old geysers of six years of age.

Everything crawling, walking, swimming or flying had Adrie's attention; he collected most of those creatures and the ones he didn't want to collect; he just would play with them like the flies and the spiders. The first time he observed a fly that flew in a spider's web, the spider came running out of breath to wrap the fly in its web, as if it was making a mummy of a deceased Egyptian Pharaoh, to have the fly ready for lunch. Adrie thought that this spider was a vicious murderer and he had to do something about that, he killed the spider and released the fly. This spider thought he could get away with murder but he couldn't if Adrie saw it. This was "Murder, She Wrote," he thought. He was full of sympathy for the unfortunate creature, the fly, which was getting the shitty end of the stick.

As a knight in shining armour, Adrie came to the rescue of the beautiful Princess and slew the fiery dragon. Oops, he got carried away there, all he really did was he came to the rescue of the fly. Immediately he got the spider out of its web, got it in a banana court, killed it and gave it a fair trial after. After the death sentence had been executed, he had to take care of the innocent victim the fly, which was lying in a dazed condition. The fly never knew what hit it so Adrie had to help it to survive the ordeal. He was short of giving the fly mouth to mouth resuscitation; instead he gave it some sugar to give it back its strength. That way it could safely land on his jam sandwich again. Those murderous spiders go about their business as if there was no tomorrow and before you knew it; the flies would belong to the extinct species. The fly couldn't agree more!

It took Adrie a while to realize that a spider doesn't kill for its pleasure and that its web is for its livelihood. When Willie told him that spiders are useful insects that catch the pesky flies and do the same work as the fly catchers in the kitchen that had sticky molasses mixed with glue on its surface, he studied his project some more. It took them longer to die than if you swatted them but no escape was possible. A fly catcher on the ceiling was a regular sight in all houses.

That was an eye opener to Adrie and he had something to think about. Whenever the flies came to feed on the molasses, they would get stuck and die. Here was the proof that flies were pests and spiders were useful. Immediately Adrie changed his policy, declared the spiders unsung heroes and condemned the flies.

If the spiders were that good, he could lend them a helping hand with some kind of a foreign aid policy. There were lots of flies around and they were rather easy to catch. After catching them, he threw them in a spider web and saw the spider wrap up the fly. What he first thought was a murderous spider, he now saw as a useful spider that relieved him of those darned flies. When he was throwing a little fly in a big spider web, it was like throwing Christians to the lions, it was no contest at all so he was looking for bigger flies that were harder to handle for the spider. Most of the time the spider managed but sometimes a real big fly, that was fighting for its life, buggered up the web and regained its freedom.

He wondered what would happen if he threw a big bumble bee in the web. Well, there was only one way to find out which was to try it. There were lots of bees around in the flower garden but he had to use caution not to be stung by a non cooperating bee for his experiments. He knew how to handle that problem, while the bee had its attention on the nectar he was gobbling up, Adrie would grab him from the back behind its wings so the bee couldn't sting him. To make it a fair fight, he looked for the biggest spider there was and watched the fight that developed.

There were some real big spiders with a cross on their back. Adrie called those Roman Catholic spiders and there were also spiders on high legs that elevated their body from the ground. Those were called "Hay Wagons" because they were high off the ground.

To see some more hostile fighting in nature, Adrie turned to the ants that have racial wars. He didn't particularly care that there were over five thousand different species of ants that have developed in the course of seventy million years on our planet. Ants are heat loving insects and thousands of species are found in the Tropics. The Netherlands are too cold but a few species are to be found and Adrie found them. It was the hostility that exists between red and black ants that interested Adrie. This hostility can easily lead to war, especially if there is a little boy that makes it happen.

Adrie dumped a shovel full of red ants on a black ant hill. Immediately, the sirens were going in the colony as a kind of early warning system that came too late. It was a total surprise because the black ants hadn't figured on airborne red ants. Before Adrie knew it there was some kind of a Battle of the Bulge on the go with many casualties. He was watching the battle very closely and in case the black ants were on the winning side, he could always call up some reservists as reinforcements. All he had to do was dump another shovel full of red ants on the heap of fighting ants and the fight could continue.

An ant racing contest was his next project. He took two ants out of an ant hill, put them down quite a distance from their nest, he then decided which ant was his and watched if his ant was going to be a winner.

A man who was imprisoned in a hostile country resorted to this game too. In order not to go insane from loneliness he took ant racing as entertainment. He took the ant racing one step farther and put bets on the ant racing. With a stick he would mark in the dirt how many millions of dollars he had won or lost. It was very exciting when you had nothing to do.

One Sunday, Adrie came to his uncle's farm after church. That was the Sunday routine, going to the farm for a cup of coffee. When he came to the ditch, he saw a dead chicken. He had seen other dead chickens in his life but this one drew his interest and he started his investigation immediately. No, he didn't investigate the cause of death of the chicken in order to play inspector Colombo. There was something weird with this chicken; it had hundreds of little critters crawling over it and come hell or high water, he was going to find out what made those critters tick.

A lot of flies had found the dead chicken, and had found it an attractive place to lay their eggs in the decaying flesh of the dead animal. The egg-laying female plans it right; laying her eggs where the larvae will be able to find food at hand as soon as the eggs are hatched. Never before in his life had he seen fly larvae so he was really interested. However, it was Sunday and it says in the Bible that you have to do all your work in six days but keep the Sabbath holy.

Therefore, he decided to explore the dead chicken on Monday. Actually, he didn't care about the Sabbath, he had gone to church and he was ready for adventure. However, the Sunday had a lot to do with it because he had just come out of church and had his good clothes on. Besides, he didn't have a container to put the critters in which meant that he had to come back on Monday. Then he would be better prepared with a container and reinforcement to catch all those critters.

The reinforcement he was thinking of was his friend Jaap Hoogland who was the lucky kid on the block to be selected for this honorable job. When he told Jaap about his all-important discovery, he was all game; he was as crazy as Adrie was or he wouldn't have been his friend.

They looked up an old can to put the critters in which made them ready for the scientific expedition of great discoveries. There was an unexpected hurdle to overcome, though. Jaap's mother was standing in the door and wanted to know where they were going and what they were up to. Jaap said: "We are going to catch critters on a dead chicken."

For some odd reason, she didn't seem to share his enthusiasm and said: "Yuk, that's dirty, you are not allowed to do that."

She might as well have talked to the door; their minds were made up; they were going to catch critters on a dead chicken, no matter what. This was a once in a life time opportunity and when opportunity knocks you have to go for it or be sorry for the rest of your life.

After arriving at the farm they had a disappointment to swallow, the dead chicken had mysteriously disappeared. Adrie's uncle probably had found it and cleaned up the mess. It was a thousand pities that they had missed a rare opportunity. That's what you get for postponing till tomorrow what you can do today, even if it's on a Sunday.

If their mission had been successful, the larvae would have become pupae and the pupae would have become flies. In that case there would have been a lot more flies around the house which suited Adrie fine, he could have caught a lot more flies to feed to the hungry spiders. Supply of meat for the spiders would have been secured for quite some time.

They didn't have the foggiest idea that those critters would become flies and they would have been really surprised to end up with a box of flies. Actually, it wasn't such a bad idea to catch larvae on a dead chicken because many a fisherman uses larvae for bait.

BANG YOU ARE DEAD.

Beside spider aid and ant war, there were games to be played in the street. When Adrie was in the First Grade at school, he played a lot with girls. The boys of his class said he was a sissy and a childish boy to play with girls. It didn't matter what they said, Adrie's philosophy was that a friend is a friend and you can never have too many friends.

One day there was a doll carriage on the sidewalk, which for some reason was in his way. He pushed it ahead a bit but unfortunately, there was some fresh dog poop on the sidewalk and of course the doll carriage had to go right through it. This didn't make the owner of the doll carriage very happy; she said: "I'm not going to play with you anymore because you drove my doll carriage through the dog poop."

That was fine with Adrie; maybe the other boys were right after all that girls were childish. The hell with the girls, the boys should stick together and play games. His first try to play with boys wasn't all that successful. A boy asked him if he wanted to play, "Bang, you are dead!" It sounded real interesting to Adrie so he went for it. If you wanted to play the game, you had to have a lot of fantasy but Adrie caught on pretty fast. All he really had to do was run after the other boy, point his finger at him pretending it was a gun and say: "Bang, you are dead!"

The trouble was that the other boy wasn't very honest; after Adrie shot him dead, he kept running. Adrie shouted behind him: "I shot you, you are dead."

The boy shouted back: "No, you missed me, I'm not dead."

Well, Adrie wasn't going to argue with him, whether he was dead or alive. Angrily, he yelled at him: "I'm not going to play with you anymore; you are cheating; after I shoot you, you can't run away."

It looked to Adrie as though you can't play with girls because they make a big issue out of it when you ride their doll carriage through the poop and you can't play with boys because they run away when they are dead. Wondering with whom he could play without having silly arguments, he went home.

After entering the house, he heard his sister coming down the stairs. Now here was his chance. He waited behind the corner and when she was really close, he jumped in front of her shouting: "Bang, you are dead!"

With a thud, she dropped to the floor instantly; she didn't move a muscle. All right! This was good playing; at least she played dead after he had shot her. On second thought it wasn't good playing at all; this was the real McCoy. He had startled her and she was so frightened that she had fainted. Helplessly he looked at his victim not knowing what to do. When his father came, she came to again and Adrie got a scolding. His dad said: "You'll scare somebody to death with your stupid games, go and play with your marbles!"

He got the message that those people didn't want to play "Bang you are dead." Miserably he left wondering why nobody wanted to play an honest game with him. Sure he could play with his marbles, he had marbles that were made from clay and glass marbles with stars in them. Besides those he had some home made steel marbles that were made from worn out ball bearings, the steel balls were excellent marbles, too.

There were some kids who had a little marmot in a cage. They went from door to door and asked the people if they wanted to see their marmot. Just to look at it would cost you one penny. Adrie didn't have money for this kind of enterprise. Worse, he didn't even have a penny to look at the beast. To participate in those kinds of enterprises, he had to come up with something else which didn't require money.

If there were people involved in recycling, it was Adrie and Willie. They took an old shoe box, cut some windows in it, glued some colored paper in the windows and cut out figures from old picture postcards, which they glued in the shoe box, and their show box was ready. All they had to do now was to find customers who were interested in paying a penny to peek in the box.

How can you play car without anything? If you have enough fantasy you can. Adrie and his friends would run through the street, make the sound of a car, pretended they were turning the steering wheel, shouted beep, beep and made the sound of squealing brakes. Here was a cheap car; all it took was some imagination.

Writing down license numbers of cars and motor cycles kept them busy too. There were not that many cars in the street where they were living, which meant they had to go to the highway between Rotterdam and Dordrecht to get a few license numbers.

Even the police was interested in the license numbers that they were writing down. The police asked Adrie if he could look at the license numbers. That was no problem because he was proud of the number of license numbers he had. The police took his book out of his pocket and wrote down one of the license numbers and asked Adrie what direction the car had been going. Luckily Adrie remembered and told the police. "Very good," the police said: "You are a big help." The police man left in a hurry, probably to get his man.

Kids in those days were experimenting with almost everything, the world was their playground. They burned old shoe laces and let them smoulder to make them stink. Burning the celluloid of the bike handle bars was also interesting. In those days there were no chrome bike handle bars and the handle bars were protected with a layer of celluloid to prevent them from rusting. The boys peeled off the celluloid from the handlebars and they had a fresh supply of celluloid to burn. They didn't care that the unprotected bike handle bars were rusting, they never thought of those things.

After obtaining the celluloid, they burnt it with a burning glass which was made out of an old lantern. A lens of an old lantern magnified the light in the lantern but it also magnified the rays of the sun and when focussed on the celluloid, it burnt.

Adrie and his friends were in a very good shape and were as fit as fiddles. No wonder that they were healthy; they took good care of themselves and spent a lot of time on their health. "An apple a day keeps the doctor away." Well, they ate more than an apple a day; quite often they ate half a dozen or more and their motto was "A dozen of apples a day; keeps a dozen doctors away."

Furthermore, they ate horse carrots that were as thick as their arms, they looked more like beets. Carrots are good for your eyes they say, so they took good care of their eyes. In order to get white teeth they chewed black tar. It was general knowledge that if you chewed black tar you would get white teeth. That way they didn't have to brush their teeth with Pepsident and make them wonder where the yellow went, as the advertising was suggesting.

The streets were paved with asphalt and when they were resurfacing the road deck, they had a tar melter which looked like a locomotive. They had piles of bags with pieces of tar which made it easy for the boys to get a good supply of tooth paste. Molten tar was spread on the road and sand and fine gravel was put on the tar to make an asphalt road. The boys made sure that they had their pockets full of pieces of tar to take care of their teeth.

Eating green apples that were as hard as a rock could give them a tummy ache but it also strengthened the stomach muscles. When they were eating green apples it made them shit like a sea gull, which was necessary to clean out their innards, and was therefore good for their intestines. A lot of people don't want to eat green apples but those poor creatures don't know what they are missing; neither do they know what's good for them.

When the boys had dripping noses, they took a deep breath through their nose to absorb the drip. You can't throw everything away if you haven't got a hanky. Some boys would move their tongue over the drip to get rid of it. Quite often they had a terrible taste in their mouth as if they had devoured the afterbirth of a cow. Instead of mint, they ate pieces of sugar beet. It's better than candies and you prevent rotten teeth.

In winter when they were thirsty, they ate snow and floating pieces of ice out of a dirty ditch and in summer they ate butter cane from a stinking muddy ditch. The cane was growing in the mud which made the bottom piece extremely soft like butter. Butter or cane, same difference; to the boys it tasted like caviar.

They took good care of their eyes, teeth, nose, intestines and stomach, all that was left to take care of was their lungs. Smoking like a chimney did that trick; all they had to do was look for cigarette butts in the street and roll them in a piece of newspaper. When they ran out of butts, they smoked dead sticks from an Elder bush. All they had to do was to peel off the outer core of the dead sticks and a nice piece of white soft wood was left. With a needle they poked a hole through the soft wood and their cigarette was ready. Fine wood aroma!

They also hardened their feet; they were always running barefoot and had lots of calluses. Even if they were running barefoot through a stubble field, they never felt pain. Only during the winter season would they wear more clothes than a pair of shorts. Consequently, their backs were dark brown, tanned by the sun. Mixed with the dirt of playing, they had a shining black color which could make a Negro jealous.

All they had left to do was increase their endurance so they could participate in the Olympics or the Marathon. In the polder was a large pasture with a wide channel on one end. You couldn't jump across the channel without a jumping pole. This was exactly what the doctor ordered for their training! The idea was to run ten times around the pasture, jump as far as you could into the channel and clamber against the high wall on the other side of the channel. If you were first on top of the high wall, you were the winner.

They were running nine and a half rounds together but the last half a round was a sprint. Just before reaching the channel, they kicked off their shorts and jumped into the ice cold water. After running ten rounds, they were perspiring heavily. The cold water would cool them down quite fast but it never bothered them a bit.

Next to the pasture was some land on which they were growing vegetables. Quite often there were some workers cultivating or harvesting their produce, which gave the boys an audience. The spectators never applauded when they were watching the performance but they were watching the boys with their mouths open. One could sense that they never had seen the likes of it before. Where else could you see ten boys running like crazy ten times around the pasture, kicking away their pants and jumping into the water?

Why didn't they get sick? The terrible time in which they lived had hardened them and their endurance tests had made them practically immune to colds, pneumonia etc. Only a bullet could have killed them at that time; they probably belonged to the Iron Race!

However, there was a more interesting game to play. They played with cheap hoops that originated from old bike wheels from which the spokes were removed. Usually they hit the hoop with a little stick to make it roll on the street. You could also apply pressure at the bottom with your little stick. That way, the hoop would roll for you without hitting it.

Daily hoop contests took place; the one first arriving at the end of the street with his hoop, was the winner. There were no prizes or medals since the organizers had no money. They were the organizers of course, but they were lacking safety precautions, such as closing the street for traffic. The cops wouldn't have allowed it anyway. Of course, it made it hard on the bikers who all of a sudden saw a dozen wild crazy kids, running through the street, beating the hell out of their hoops, and of course not watching the bikes or cars.

For the next invention they had a hurdle hoop contest, the hurdle being a barricade at the end of the street. The barricade was made out of sticks, stones and all kinds of debris they could get a hold of. It became a challenge to hoop right across the barricade. When the fast rolling hoops hit the barricade, they jumped six feet into the air which caused more casualties among the bikers.

Many complaints poured into the police department about the dangerous kids; the street wasn't safe at all anymore for bikers. Those complaints made the police come out for an investigation in the allegations of the angry citizens. Of course, like always the citizens won. The kids were told by the police that they were ignoring the safety of other citizens and from there on they couldn't hoop anymore in the streets. There were no playgrounds so the only place they could play was in the street. However, playing with hoops was out; that was way too dangerous according to the police.

Actually, it didn't bother them too much that they couldn't play with their hoops anymore; they were going to play a game called "Koten" which was played with bricks. For beginners they had to steal the needed bricks, everybody needed a brick. Next, they counted out to determine who was going to be the Koot Boy. The Koot Boy put his brick (called Koot) in a square and the other players threw their bricks trying to hit the Koot in the square. As long as the Koot wasn't standing up in the square the Koot Boy couldn't touch you. If the Koot was standing up and he touched you, you were the next Koot Boy.

It was a very interesting game; they all acquired skill in throwing bricks especially into the wheels of passing bikers. Those poor bikers were always the target of their games. They didn't like it a bit when the spokes of their bike wheel broke when the boys threw a brick against it.

The police department was flooded with complaints once more which made the police come out again to tell the kids that they were playing a dangerous game and they couldn't play it in the street anymore. Well, they couldn't play it in their living rooms either, their mothers would never have approved of that. Only the kids seemed to like the game; the brick layers didn't like it because they stole their bricks, the bikers didn't like it because it buggered up their bike wheels, and the police didn't like it because the citizens were complaining.

They had to play something and somewhere and the only way they could do it was by ignoring the police. When they were playing their Koot game they kept an eye on the street for a cop. Whenever they saw a cop coming in the street they would run away and hide. Sometimes they couldn't retrieve their bricks and the police confiscated them. They cared less; they would just steal some more bricks from the angry bricklayers.

Even playing hide and seek drew criticism from the property owners, who didn't like it a bit when they were running across their yard. The boys were inventive in their games; when they were playing hide and seek, the seeker had to call the right name of the person he had found. Well, they buggered him up. Adrie had a bright green sweater that you could see a mile away. He exchanged sweaters with his friend and when the seeker saw a bright green sweater, he was convinced that it was Adrie. He called Adrie's name and they jumped forward calling it a miss call.

The roughest game they played was "Thief with Liberation." They drew a chalk line in the middle of the school yard. There were two teams which tried to pull boys from the other side across the line into their territory. If successful, those boys were imprisoned in a prisoner-of-war camp. Strong guards had to keep the prisoners in, but a group of the other party tried to break through the lines in order to liberate the prisoners. Many punches were exchanged with bloody noses, black eyes and other serious injuries as result. This time it wasn't the police who came out to tell them they couldn't play it. It was the Principal who didn't like to bandage bleeding knees and arms every day.

Everything was forbidden, there were signs with "No Trespassing," everywhere. They couldn't do anything legally so they did it illegally. They weren't even allowed to steal apples and pears from the orchards, but they did it anyway.

Adrie's next door neighbor was a blacksmith, who was such a lucky guy to have a nice kid like Adrie as a neighbor. A blacksmith has many interesting things that boys like very much; the fire was especially quite an attraction. Actually, the fire was the main attraction of the smithy and the blacksmith didn't have a worry in the world that his fire would go out. The boys took care very well of that problem and made many visitations to his smithy.

The old blacksmith had two young sons working with him who didn't care if the boys played with the fire. When they entered the smithy the fire was usually low, but the boys were real worry warts, worrying that the fire would go out. In order to prevent that, they made the fire five times as big, which should have made the blacksmith very happy. On the contrary, the old man got mad, grabbed his hammer and threw it at the boys. He always missed; probably on purpose, but it scared the hell out of the boys.

This never deterred them; they always came back for more excitement. They always took chances and couldn't resist the thrill of having the blacksmith running after them with a hot piece of steel or a hammer. It was hard to let the old blacksmith down in spite of his temper. Who would look after his fire if the boys weren't around?

The boys loved to put an old piece of iron in the fire and make the fire really big to make the iron melt, which would make stars and sparkles. In their eyes this was beautiful, but the blacksmith didn't think so, which was just a difference of opinion.

In front of the smithy there was a big tree with many seeds. The seeds had a wing that made the seed turn around like a helicopter when it fell to the ground. "Ah, flying machines," the boys thought and were fascinated by the action of the seed. When the seeds didn't come down fast enough by themselves, the boys thought that the tree needed some help and threw stones into the tree. Throwing stones into the tree gave them many flying machines and one broken window. The house was pretty close to the tree and accidents do happen. In no time at all, the angry blacksmith came running out of his smithy to throw a white hot horseshoe between the fleeing boys which made them run for their lives. Those incidents of broken windows meant that they had to dig into their piggy banks to pay for the damage.

Summer time meant camping time for the boys. They liked camping very much and they loved to eat burned pancakes with soot and ashes. Their tent wasn't quite that good; it consisted of an old carpet and a few sticks from a tree which served as tent poles. It was very low so you couldn't walk in it; you had to crawl into it on all fours. The old carpet could soak up quite a bit of rain before it leaked through but even if the tent leaked, it didn't matter, everybody had fun and that's all that counted.

There was also need for a camp stove to bake the pancakes. Their camp stove consisted of bricks which they had to steal from the poor bricklayer. At the campsite they put the bricks in a square but left one brick out for air because a fire needs oxygen. They thought of everything.

Other preparations were needed to make the camping trip a success. All kids have a sweet tooth which can be satisfied with candies. And of course, the more candies they had the better it was for their camping trip. Many weeks before they went camping, they would save their church candies. When they went to church on Sundays, Adrie's mother gave him some candies to prevent him from getting a dry throat from the singing he had to do. Church candies were very important because only the Reverend had a glass of water on the pulpit to wet his whistle. The Reverend was drinking for all since he was the leader of the pack. When it was hot in summer, everybody saw the Reverend drink water, which made the whole congregation lick their lips. In order that they wouldn't cough and disturb the sermon, they had candies instead of water. It wasn't allowed to take a bottle of water or beer to the church but candies were all right with everybody.

Nobody had any money for the camping trip, and some kids used the church to provide money as well. When the collection bag was passed, they kept their money and dropped a button in the bag. Adrie wasn't easy to scare, but that he didn't dare, that was stealing from God. If he stole bricks from the bricklayer or apples and pears from an orchard it didn't bother his conscience, but stealing from God was sin, so he resisted the temptation. Of course, his parents and all other adults would see it differently, they saw stealing apples or bricks as stealing too.

After counting the days down, it was finally time to load up their little cart and march to the campground. It was a forty minutes walk to a grassy area with trees where they were allowed to put up their tent. They had two forked sticks which they had to put in the ground a bit because they were the pillars that had to hold up the tent. A longer stick went across, the carpet went over the long stick and the tent was finished. It looked like an Indian tepee, except it was much smaller and lower. There was work to do; they had to gather dead wood for the camp stove to bake their pancakes. It rains a lot in The Netherlands which makes the firewood wet and hard to light. For the first half an hour, the fire smoked a lot which made it possible for the kids to send their smoke signals to a distant tribe.

The best had yet to come; they had to make batter for their pancakes. All they had was water and flour, there was no milk or raisins to enhance the taste of the pancakes but the soot and ashes, which mixed unavoidably with the pancakes, improved them considerably. Finally the pan went on the fire and all they had to do now was waiting for the result and chew their church candies. When the wood was very wet, the pancakes were sometimes only half done, which was no problem at all; an extra spoon of sugar on the pancakes corrected that problem. The chef had an answer to all the problems that possibly could occur.

Rain or shine, soot or ashes, there was nothing that could dampen their camping spirit. They were experienced campers and nothing could spoil their camping trip. It was fun because they had a day out by themselves when they were only seven years old. Why shouldn't they be happy when they accomplished all that?

A farm is not the best place in the world to play, which Adrie found out the hard way. When you have an uncle with a farm, you want to visit your uncle so you can play at the farm. Nothing wrong with that! Adrie's uncle had about twelve cows, four work horses, chickens and a pig. He also had pastures for his dairy cattle and land on which he grew grains, potatoes and beets.

Once, one of the horses had an infected leg. As a work horse that was bad because the horse needs all four legs when working. His uncle knew a remedy to help the horse and himself at the same time. He took an old gunny bag and a pail with cow shit; he pasted the horse's leg elaborately with cow shit and wrapped the gunny bag around it. Adrie had been watching closely what his uncle was doing and said: "Yuk, cow shit, what good is that going to do to the horse's leg!"

His uncle explained that cow shit has medicinal value because it cleans out infections. Adrie didn't believe that shit would do that but when after a few days the horse's leg was healed, he could see it too.

Going with his uncle to the pasture to milk the cows was a real treat. First there was the ride with horse and wagon, and while his uncle was milking the cows he would play in the pasture. There were no snakes in the grass of the pasture but there was a lot of cow shit on which you could slip easily when you were running through the pasture. It was a fore-gone conclusion that Adrie would fall exactly at the place where the cow had dumped a fresh pile of shit. You could say that he was full of shit after playing at the farm, which his mother didn't appreciate at all. When he played in the polder he came home covered with mud. Playing at the farm didn't show any improvement to her, now his clothes were full of cow shit.

Adrie tried to explain to his mother that cow shit had medicinal value and it could even heal his sore knees. "Who told you that bull?" his mother asked.

"It's no bull," Adrie countered, "Cow shit healed the horse's leg so it could heel my knees as well."

"Well it won't heel your knees, I can guarantee you," his mother replied.

It wasn't much better in winter when the cows were in the stable. Behind the farm the farmyard was a quagmire. If he wanted to go to the horses to treat them to a sugar beet, he looked miry after walking through the mud.

The next time he went to the farm, there was a firm warning from his mother that he shouldn't walk in the mud. Adrie liked the horses and actually he didn't have to walk through the mud to reach them. There was a short cut; the horse stable was right behind the cow stable; you could reach it through the inside passage. The cows were tied down with ropes so they couldn't do you any harm.

Wrong assumption! Behind the cows there was a concrete floor to make it easy to clean up the cow shit. This was a smart idea, except that if a cow plopped her droppings on the concrete floor, the shit hit the fan blade. (Make this; that the shit splashed high up against the wall.) For a change Adrie was obedient; he didn't walk at the back of the farm through the mud and he was sure that he wouldn't look muddy when he came home. That was a smart idea but instead of muddy, he was going to come home looking shitty.

He took the necessary precautions before he crossed the concrete floor. As a general he overlooked the battleground. Everything was quiet on the Western front; it was going to be a piece of cake to keep him self clean in order not to get hell from his mother. In spite of his safety check, he didn't make it clean to the horse stable. As soon as he stepped on the concrete floor, a cow started to observe him from the corner of her eye, timing when to let go. When he was right behind the cow, the cow said: "Now." What else could she have said when she was lowing. She raised her tail and splash, splash. Adrie was disconsolate while this unworthy cow was staring at him with a false grin on her face, meaning, "Got You."

His mother didn't have a grin on her face at all when he came home. As soon as she saw Adrie she started to raise the roof, which wasn't very fair of her because he had enough trouble for one day. She said: "Look at you; you look like a piece of shit instead of a cuddly boy. I suppose you found some more medicine for your sore knees. I warned you, but you never listen!"

Adrie thought this was grossly unfair, he started to protest and said: "Yes you told me not to walk at the rear of the farm and I didn't do that at all; just look at my shoes and clothes; no mud at all."

Hopefully he looked at his mother's face to see if it impressed her that there was only shit on his clothes and no mud. Adrie could see that he was going to win this argument and had the gift of the gab in his closing argument. He told her how careful he had been in observing the cows before he crossed the floor and concluded his argument as a born toastmaster, putting some humor in it when he was saying: "Those cows do it on purpose. I can watch them for half an hour and nothing happens, but as soon as I take one step on the floor, some stupid cow has to shit. When I am under the shit from top to bottom, the cow is laughing for the next five minutes when she looks at me."

His mother replied: "And you believe all that about the laughing cow?" Luckily she had a smile on her face again and she said: "Take all those shitty clothes off and wash yourself well because I'm coming to check you over."

Adrie was pulled to the farm with an invisible magnet in spite of all those shitting cows which got him into trouble time after time. When he announced that he was going to the farm again, his mother wasn't all that enthusiastic about it, Adrie sensed. She let him go with a lengthy warning: "Don't come home under the mud and not under the shit either, for a change."

No problem, he had learned his lesson. This time he had great plans, he was going to surprise his mother by coming home as clean as a whistle. He would leave the horses alone so the cows couldn't shit on him and that way he would come home as immaculate as the Virgin Mary.

Beware of man traps when you are playing at the farm! There was a pitfall he didn't know existed. His uncle had a pulp pit full of beet pulp which was fodder for the farm animals. After a harsh winter and rain pouring on the pulp from time to time, the pulp becomes quite soggy and smelly. Adrie didn't know about a pulp pit; the wind had blown some dust and straw on it, so he couldn't see it either. It looked like a safe bet to walk across the farm yard; it was dry dirt and some straw, that way he didn't have to walk across the mud.

Wrong again! When he took one step, he sank into the pulp pit to his neck. It was the shock of his life; he never knew what hit him and he had significant trouble to get out of the stinking pit. There was no grinning cow this time but he was shaking on his legs, he could have drowned in the stinking pulp. It would have been better to have cow shit on his clothes, or mud. Unfortunately, he had to go home to tell his mother the good news, that he didn't have shit or mud on his clothes but for the bad news, he was covered to his neck with stinking pulp.

Arriving home, he wasn't that optimistic anymore about an excuse as to why he had bungled again. He stumbled into the back porch not knowing what to do. When his mother heard him come home, she came to the porch for a general inspection. His mother never seemed to be surprised about anything but Amazing Grace had just come home to give her the surprise of her life. She was speechless which Adrie never had thought was possible. The eerie silence that followed was the worst thing of all. If he was going to get a licking, she might as well get it over with. It looked like an hour before she opened her mouth when she said: "Holy cow, what happened to you?"

Usually, he made up all kind of stupid excuses before he came home, but this time he had failed miserably to come up with a satisfactory explanation. He was going to make an attempt to explain the ordeal he had gone through and started: "That damned pulp pit, I always have stupid accidents."

Adrie couldn't think of anything worth while to say anymore, he was feeling sorry for himself and started to sob. His sobbing could have broken Nero's heart thus it wasn't that hard to change his mother's opinion about her unlucky son. Immediately she got into action and told him to take off his stinking clothes. She made warm water for his bath and in no time at all, he was sitting comfortably, in clean clothes, sipping his hot cocoa.

Unfortunately, this wasn't the end of his farm accidents. He learned from those accidents alright and never made the same mistake twice. A donkey never gets hurt on the same stone twice and neither did Adrie. Of course, the donkey might find out that there are many stones to get hurt on. The same problem with Adrie; there were too many things that an inquisitive kid like him could get into trouble with. That's why there was always another accident.

In the stables, behind the cows and horses, was a little gutter to carry off the liquid manure to the liquid manure pit. The liquid manure pit was quite deep because it had to hold the liquid manure from the whole year. In spring when his uncle had to manure the land, he would drive the honey wagon close to the pit and scoop the contents of the pit into the wagon. Next, he spread it on his land. There were no pumps in those days to do this job. He used a pail on a long stick to dip in the pit and empty the pail in the honey wagon.

Old planks that had deteriorated through the many years of service, covered the pit. With the rotten planks, it wasn't safe to walk across the pit. Adrie's uncle knew this, but how was Adrie supposed to know? One day he took a short cut, by accident, right across the pit. The planks broke and he fell into the pit. Luckily, he could grab the edge of the concrete pit and also luckily, his uncle had emptied the pit not too long ago. With his bare knees he had to crawl up the concrete of the pit, which had the result that he was bleeding like a pig. For a change he was lucky; if he hadn't been able to pull himself out of the pit or even if the pit had been full, he would have been able to give his mother some more good news. He could have told her that he wasn't full of mud, shit or pulp but this time he was soaked in horse and cow piss.

Unfortunately, he still had to go to his mother to get his knees bandaged but that was no problem, his mother did this all the time. It was very seldom that he didn't have bandages on his knees. On all the photos from that time he always had bandages on his knees. Before one knee was healed, the other one was already bandaged.

When his mother found out what had happened to him, she told his uncle. He had the shock of his life and got new planks right away and repaired the damage. This is a classic example of: "After the calf has drowned, they fill in the pit." Or like in Adrie's case: "After the calf has bandaged knees, new planks are covering the pit."

Many accidents have happened at farms with wells and manure pits, which shows that a farm isn't a very safe place to play. Where could growing up boys play safely? It certainly wasn't at the railway. "The railway is no place to play for kids," Adrie's parents said.

Adrie and his friends didn't agree; there were lots of things you could play with at the railway. The Netherlands is a small country and train passenger service was quite developed before the war. Instead of steam engines pulling the trains between the big cities, there were electric trains. Over the railways there were electrical wires that work the same way as a trolley bus. In order to avoid a voltage drop, they had to have quite high voltage. At the level crossings there were signs in place to tell everybody about the danger. The signs said: "High Voltage! Touching of the wires can be deadly!"

That was plain and luckily Adrie and his friends believed it. There are those doubting Thomases, who have to try everything and test to see if they aren't just kidding on that sign. A boy had a long stick from a tree and touched the wires; the high voltage travelled through the green stick and killed the boy instantly. If it had been a dead stick, he probably would have gotten away with it, but a green stick contains a lot of water which is conductive to electricity.

That didn't mean that they couldn't do dangerous things at the railway, even if they didn't touch the high voltage wires. There were two level railroad crossings, one on the Hordyk where Adrie lived, and one on the Dortse Streetroad, which were very close together. In order to save money, they only had put up a railway watch house on the Dortse Streetroad. The railway watchman had to look after both crossings and close off the streets with a barrier before the train came through. He also had to put the train signals safe for the approaching train and had to sign the train through to the next station after it had passed.

Since there was no railway watch house on the Hordyk, the kids had free play on the railroad. Of course, when they saw that the barriers were lowered they cleared the railway. They were crazy but they weren't crazy enough to jeopardize their lives and be killed by a train.

As always, they started very innocently when they were playing. One of the kids put a penny on the rail and after the train rode over it, the penny was as flat as a dime or flatter. Adrie never had pennies and certainly none to be flattened by a train. The next day, he brought some spikes along to be flattened by the train. Usually, it was hard to find the flattened spike because the train had quite a speed which made the spike fly away. However, after a while they had a few flattened spikes. (*When they ran out of spikes, they should have written a book called "The Last Spike," but that would have upset Pierre Burton who wrote such a book much later.)* Instead of a spike they tried a pebble. The pebble broke into fragments of course and they didn't even find the slivers.

You could say that they were like cats; their curiosity was awakened and they were going to find out what made the thing tick. It meant putting some more pebbles on the rail but instead of one they put a whole row on the rail. From there on, the pebbles became stones and rocks. They got a bang out of it when the train rode over the rocks smashing them to smithereens. One time they were watching the result of their experiments while a biker was waiting for the train to pass. When the biker got a shower of rock slivers, he said: "Holy pope shit, what a bloody mess this railroad is." The poor creature never knew what hit him; neither did he know that the boys were the cause of the bloody mess on the railway.

This game was very dangerous; with all the rocks they put on the rails, the train could have derailed and then there would have been hell to pay. They were innocent kids and never figured that a big train could derail when you put big rocks on the rails. Luckily this never happened. If the train had derailed, the police would have been involved and it wouldn't have looked that good for them. Actually, putting rocks on the rail was more dangerous than touching a high voltage wire. People could have died easily if a passenger train had derailed.

A less dangerous game was the Kievit egg search. In Canada there are no Kievit birds but they are quite common in The Netherlands. This bird loves low wet lands and nests in shallow ditches in high grass. The bird shouts its own name, that's why it's called the Kievit bird.

The Kievit bird lays eggs, about half the size of a chicken egg and the shell is spotted with green specks. These eggs are real tasty and in Spring a lot of people go out in search for the delicious eggs.

The Dutch Queen in The Netherlands liked Kievit eggs too but she didn't search for the eggs herself. It was the tradition in The Netherlands that the first found Kievit's egg, in Spring, was offered to the Queen. To make it attractive for the people who found the first Kievit's egg to give it to the Queen, the Government paid 100 guilders for that egg. That was a lot of money in those days and it encouraged people to spend a lot of time seeking for the 100 guilder egg.

The Kievit bird makes it difficult to find her nest. When she hears somebody come towards her nest, she walks a considerable distance through the high grass away from her nest before she flies away. When you see her fly away, you think that's where her nest is but it never is. In vain you look for her nest because the Kievit bird has you fooled. You look in the wrong spot.

Adrie was looking too for Kievit's eggs and found a nest with three little eggs but somebody in Friesland beat him to it to be the first. Friesland is one of the Northern provinces of The Netherlands and there are a lot more birds than in South Holland where Adrie lived.

There were some people who didn't like the Kievit egg search, they said: "You rob the bird from her offspring. Those people eat chicken eggs which is robbing the chickens from their offspring too.

(A man went dining in a restaurant and asked the waiter what the special was. The waiter said: "Cow tongue." The man said: "I don't like to eat what a cow has had in her mouth, give me chicken eggs instead.")

"Would you like to go to the Meuse tunnel? It's only a forty five minutes walk!" Adrie's friend came one day to call on him and this was the question he popped. Adrie's answer was a foregone conclusion: "Of course, it sounds like fun."

The tunnel had just been opened which was quite something in those days. Two car tunnels had been made, one each way. They were separate tubes to avoid head on collisions. There was also a bike tunnel for bikers and a pedestrian tunnel which was underneath the bike tunnel. The automobile tunnel had a long slope, to get the cars to the desired depth to go underneath the water of the Meuse. For bikes and pedestrians it wasn't practical to have that long a slope in the tunnel. Instead, they had long escalators to get them to the required depth. When you were at the depth of the bike tunnel, the pedestrians had to go down an eight foot stairway to come underneath the bike tunnel.

The escalators were easy on pedestrians but were hard on novice bikers who wanted to get down or up the escalators. It was easy as pie once you knew how to handle your bike. When you go up on the escalator you push your bike on the moving stairs and stand behind your bike. That way, it's easy to hold your bike which is resting against you. When you go down the escalator, you step on the escalator at the same time that you push your bike on it and stand beside your front wheel. If you don't do that, it's hard to hold your bike and there is a good chance of falling down the escalator with your bike. This could be dangerous especially if you fell against other people with bikes, who might fall down the escalator as well. For safety, they had a tunnel watchman, who had to stop the escalator if such a mishap occurred.

They were interested in the tunnel alright but most of their interest was in the escalator; they never had seen anything like it. After walking forty-five minutes to reach the tunnel, they went down the escalator and walked for ten minutes to the other side of the tunnel. At the other side they made a thorough inspection to see if they really had crossed the river. Those people could tell you all kinds of things but they certainly didn't believe everything they were told. They had told them that there was a St. Nicholas which wasn't true so they didn't necessarily believe what the grown ups were telling them. When they were convinced that indeed they had crossed the Meuse underneath the water, they went back through the tunnel.

The boys had seen the tunnel but they hadn't had enough of the escalators. Up and down the escalators they went half a dozen of times, which didn't meet with the approval of the tunnel guard. He came up to the boys and said that when they came down the escalator, they had to walk to the other side of the tunnel, the escalator wasn't a toy. They already had walked to the other side and they had to walk forty-five minutes back home; this guy could forget it. All they did was walk down the eight feet stairway underneath the bike tunnel, waited for a few minutes and went back on the escalator. After they had played that trick three times, the tunnel watchman came up to them and said solemnly: "Why don't you kids knock it off? I told you that the escalator wasn't a toy? Can't you kids ever behave? Go home and pester your parents instead of misbehaving here."

This disgraceful, miserable tunnel watchman probably had forgotten that once upon a time he was young too and acted like a kid. It was decided to call his bluff and ride the escalator two more times before they were going home. They looked around the corner of the stairway and as soon as he turned his back, they stepped on the escalator again. After showing him that they weren't going to behave the way he thought they should, they started their trip back home.

That's the way it was in those days, kids couldn't do anything or they were criticised. All that they were expected to do was behave. It didn't harm anybody that they were riding the escalator; sooner or later they would have had enough of it, and gone home without being told. This was perhaps the reason that they were putting rocks on the railway and did other stupid things, just because of dingbats like the tunnel watchman.

The good old times had a certain charm which is gone forever. One of the amenities was certainly the horse market, not to be missed by anybody. It wasn't just a day for farmers to buy or sell a horse, there was something for everybody. Stalls with Deventer gingerbread, Dutch herring, and a whole variety of other merchandise were attractive to anybody who was hungry.

It was a very important day; the children even had a day free from school. Young and old were at the horse market that day. After arriving at the horse market, Adrie saw farmers who wanted to buy a horse. They were looking in the horse's mouth to determine the age and health of the horse they wanted to buy. Adrie knew a Dutch proverb which states: "One must not look a gift horse in the mouth." It means that if you get something free, you shouldn't be critical because you didn't pay for it. According to Adrie's philosophy, those horses were not gift horses because everybody looked in their mouth.

Adrie wasn't interested in looking a horse in the mouth to check his tonsils, so he carried on to find something that interested him. There was a big guy standing on a box, he was shouting that he was the "Shackle King," of the whole wide world. That Adrie had to see.

The Shackle King had all kinds of shackles and chains with locks. He passed them around for general inspection to be insured of an honest demonstration. After everything had passed inspection, he invited a few people to shackle and chain him to the tree. As soon as he was chained to the tree, he stated that he could shake his chains and shackles in no time at all. The speed of him shaking his shackles would depend on the amount of money that was donated. Donations were welcome, you could throw your donations on the carpet and the more money, the more he would be inspired to shake his shackles, which would free him faster. If he had depended on Adrie's donation, it would have taken a long time to get out of his shackles. All the money he had was three cents and the Shackle King wasn't going to get it.

A few coins were thrown on the carpet but the man claimed that those few coins didn't inspire him at all. In order to be motivated to shake his shackles, there had to be more money than that. More coins were thrown on the carpet. The man started rattling his chains and one fell off. "More money!" screamed the man. When more coins descended on the carpet, he was suddenly inspired and motivated and all his chains fell off. Adrie could even figure how he got inspired that fast. As soon as he saw all the money on the carpet, he wanted to get rid of his chains so he could grab the money before somebody else beat him to it.

After the Shackle King had liberated himself from his shackles, Adrie looked at a man who was swallowing a sword and another man who was eating razor blades. Walking some more brought him to one of the main attractions. It was a Fakir with a towel on his head who was lying down with his bare back on a spike bed while two fat guys were standing on his tummy. When he got up, the blood was standing in the spike holes in his back.

Of course, a donation was needed to make the Fakir perform; only the sun rises for free. The Fakir was even smarter, he went with his old hat around to collect money. A funny thing happened; he passed Adrie without even glancing at him. He probably figured that he was very rich and stingy and wouldn't donate money anyway.

The boys had fun during summer, but winter brought a whole new array of different pleasures. They knew how to entertain themselves winter and summer. When the snow was moist, they made giant snowmen in the polder that were so big that they needed three kids to roll the body of the snowman. A remarkable result was the outcome of this playing. In the middle of the polder was a field with a display of a dozen giant snowmen.

(The question was, "How did they know whether they had made a male or a female snowman?" Oops, I mean snow person. The answer is very simple. The one with the snow balls was the male snowman.)

They even made an ice fortress which was of course very interesting but there was a problem! It wasn't dangerous so there was no thrill to it. Something more exciting should be possible to satisfy their play. There was and they found it.

Adrie had a pricker moved sled. It was fun to lie down on it and go down steep hills at quite a speed. The quest for speed was always in his mind. When he saw the bus stopped, it was just a matter of time to hold the rear bumper and go with great speed through the snow covered street. His friend Jaap didn't have a sled which was no problem; there was lots of room on the sled for two people if you were lying on top of one another. Sometimes the sled upset when they hit a piece of the road with no snow cover on it but that was all part of the fun. A couple of holes in his pants told the story to his mother that something had gone wrong when they were playing with the sled. No use to tell her that they were holding the bus, she only would get worried.

One of their favorite winter games was ice cracking. When the ditches and channels were frozen over, they had to see if the ice was thick enough to walk on. If it was barely thick enough to hold them, they played their favorite game "ice cracking." They would run across the ice to the other side, back and forward until the ice gave up and they went through it, which usually meant wet feet or completely wet. The boys never quit until somebody went through the ice.

A lot of times Adrie came home with wet clothes and had to tell his mother a sob story about those damned windmills which had milled away the water from under the ice. Therefore as soon as you stepped on the ice you would fall through it. That happened once and it was a good excuse. Once he had been submerged in the frigid water and when he came home, his dry clothes were waiting for him. One of the kids had been kind enough to go to his mother, and tell her that Adrie had fallen through the ice. Just as well; he didn't even have to tell anything to his mother, she knew it already.

They always thought of something different. One time they went to the channel with an axe and cut a large ice floe. The idea was to sit on your sled and move the sled as fast as you could, across the ice floe with the prickers. It worked great; as soon as the sled moved on the ice floe, the ice floe went down on that side and it was easy to get off on the other side since it was a little higher. They cut the ice floe in two to make it more difficult and when it still went right, they cut it in four. Nothing could go wrong it seemed; it was as if they were performing in a circus; everything went perfect all the time. That was no fun; they had to put some spunk in this game to make it more interesting.

Finally, Adrie found it; he would go diagonally across the ice floe. This time it went wrong; his runner got stuck on the edge of the ice floe, and he had to jump off his sled, lest he submerged in the ice-cold water. To the disappointment of the spectators, he had only wet feet, but for Adrie it was good enough for that day.

There was a low lying area which was used for growing reeds during the summer. The reeds were used for the roofs of thatched farm houses. During winter they would bring up the water level to inundate it, and after it froze over it was a beautiful ice rink. It was too beautiful to be true, such a large ice rink. They leased it to a businessman, who put a barbed wire fence around it. He also put up a shed at the entrance where you could buy tickets if you wanted to skate on the ice rink. You could also buy coffee, chocolate milk, sandwiches and some candy. He was all business.

Adrie and his friends were all business too, but their business interfered with his business. How unfortunate! They were the crackerjacks in ice cracking and when they saw this large area frozen over, they couldn't help but do some ice cracking. The ice had to be strong enough before the businessman could get on it to fence it off, so the kids beat him to it. There were all kinds of holes in the ice surface and in many places it was full of cracks. With six kids they had ruined the skating rink and the man didn't like it. He went to complain to Baldy, their Principal, with the consequence that one afternoon, after school hours, they were writing lines: "We cannot damage the ice."

It occurred to Adrie when he was writing his lines that they had proven that they could damage it, so may be he should write: "We can damage the ice." Luckily, he had a second thought in which he decided that Baldy wouldn't appreciate his humor at all. All that he could think about was discipline so he was much better off to give him his satisfaction.

Adrie and his friends got into all kinds of mischief but they weren't as crazy as the two eight year old boys who were playing together. One boy said to the other boy: "Put your hand on the chopping block so that I can chop off your fingers."

The boy put his hand on the chopping block as he was told and the boy chopped off his four fingers as he said he would do. His fingers were put back on but circulation was lacking. It was feared that he would lose his fingers after all. As last resort they used leeches to suck the coagulated blood from his fingers. Luckily, the circulation was restored and he got the use of his fingers back again.

Even that early they managed to put severed limbs back on a person. On the news, there was an incident of a father in Los Angeles who had ordered his son to do a few things. When the father came home it hadn't been done. The father got mad, cut off his son's penis, threw it in the toilet and flushed it. Of course, the man was arrested for child abuse and the sewer workers were called in to look for the boy's penis in the sewer. Luckily, they found it and it took over thirty stitches to put his severed penis back in place in the hospital.

It's unknown if later everything functioned normally again. Usually there is a problem with circulation if severed limbs are sewn back on. Another unknown was if they used leaches on his penis to get the circulation going again.

There was very little entertainment in those days. The kids brought a book home from the school library every week and the books were read by the entire family. During the long winter people created their own entertainment. When they were visiting each other there were always story tellers.

In those days, people weren't only religious; they were also superstitious and believed in spooks, ghosts, werewolves and the almanac. People even believed that who got in bed first on their wedding night would die first. The remedy was to give each other a hand and they junped in bed at the same time.

Those story tellers didn't tell their stories to a kid who has to go to bed; no, they told stories to a crowd of adults and children who were present as well. Most stories were about werewolves that went on the prowl when the moon was full. Those werewolves were normal people but as soon as the moon was full they turned into a wolf. Once they were a wolf they recruited other werewolves, they bit people who then turned into werewolves, too. It seemed to be very contagious.

Ghosts probably provided more hair raising stories than any other fearful subject. There were lots of grown up people who didn't dare to walk past a graveyard at night because of nasty ghosts that came after them. When Adrie was about nine years old, he was never scared to walk past a graveyard at night but that was just about to change, thanks to a story teller who told a stupid story.

One night, Adrie was at his aunt's place and there was a man who was one of those stupid story tellers. He was telling a hair raising story about the graveyard. Adrie had walked past the graveyard many times and had read the inscriptions on the tombstones. It usually read "R.I.P." and then followed the name of the deceased with his birth-date and the date of his death. Never did he run across a ghost but this man said that there were a lot of ghosts at the graveyard and he told his audience all about it. The man had a squeaky voice which made it even more spooky. Here is his story:

"Last week when I came home late at night, I had to pass the graveyard. There had been an increased activity of ghosts lately and I was worried that I wouldn't get past the graveyard without problems. The ghosts had been quite restless and had caused quite a bit of trouble. I sure didn't look forward to walking past the graveyard in the dark. Luckily, I took the precaution of passing the graveyard on the opposite side of the street. That way, I could distance myself as much as possible from the big tombstones which are standing right beside the road.

This night was really spooky; the wind howled through the trees and the moonlight cast long dark spooky shadows from the tomb stones. I didn't trust it at all and hastened my steps in order to get past the tombstones in a heck of a hurry. When I came pretty close to the big tombstone adjacent to the road, I heard the sound of a rattling chain followed by heavy moaning and groaning. It scared the living daylights out of me but in spite of my fear, I looked at the big tombstone to see what was going on. To my consternation, I saw a ghost rise from behind the tombstone. The ghost was chained with one hand to the tombstone and he jerked heavily on the chain which made the tombstone wobble. It looked as if the tombstone would topple over but that didn't happen because all of a sudden the chain broke. After freeing himself from the tomb stone, the ghost looked in my direction."

Of course, Adrie had been hanging on the man's words when he told his scary story and had listened with his mouth wide open. He hadn't missed a word of what the man had said and had followed the story with due attention. Consequently, Adrie had a question for the story teller. The man had spoken about the ghost and had said that he jerked heavily on the chain. Since Adrie wasn't too familiar with ghosts, he wanted to know how he could determine the sex of the ghost. How could he tell that it was a he, all ghosts look alike according to Adrie? The same as all Negroes look alike to the white man and to the Negro all white men look alike. All ghosts have a long white night robe on so how could he tell that it was a male ghost? Thus Adrie popped the question: "How did you know that the ghost was a man?"

The story teller looked disturbed at Adrie because some people were laughing and that broke the spell of the moment. However, the story teller had an answer, he said: "I could tell by the moaning and groaning that it was a male voice."

That made sense to Adrie, he wasn't hard to please; the man could have told him that the ghost wasn't wearing any earrings so consequently it wasn't a female ghost but a male and Adrie would have believed it. It was probably a stupid question but when Adrie was taking in his scary story, it occurred to him that he was very scared when he discovered the ghost. It was hard to believe that he had established the gender of the ghost, by lifting the long white robe to look whether the ghost was masculine or feminine or perhaps it was a neuter gender, making it an it. Adrie could see that he had buggered him up with his stupid question. He had lost his momentum but he picked up the thread of the story again and continued.

"After the ghost had violently jerked himself loose from the tombstone my heart had almost stopped. When I saw the ghost jumping over the high gate which surrounded the graveyard, I knew that this was a matter of survival and there was not a second to lose. For a fraction of a second, it looked indeed as if my heart had stopped. My brain had given instructions to my legs to run like hell but my legs failed to move for me. I felt like a deer frozen in the head lights. Precious seconds were lost before I got my act together. Then I took off as if I was hit by a bolt of lightning; my life depended on it. Luckily, I still had quite a lead on the ghost but I couldn't determine with what speed the ghost was moving. Actually, I had expected that the ghost would catch up with me which would have been the end of me."

The man was a great actor; he could have had a movie career. He had started his story with a mysterious voice and when he came to the part where he discovered the rising ghost behind the tombstone; his voice had shuddered with fear. At the end for the climax of his story, when he was talking of the hot pursuit of the ghost, he started to sweat like an angry God. It looked as if he was reliving the anxious moments of the running period again.

The man took his hanky out of his pocket to wipe the sweat off his forehead and cleared his throat to underline the anxious suspense of the moment. With his little hold up, he had everybody hanging on his words again. It was like on T.V., just before the end of the movie when suspense is mounting; there is first a word from the sponsor. It looked as if time was standing still before he resumed his story.

He finally continued: "It was as if I had lead in my shoes, I wanted to run faster but my legs wouldn't do it. When I checked sideways to see how close the ghost was upon my heels, I could see a white glow. It was probably the light which was shining through the white sheet that he was wearing. I expected to feel the icy grip of the ghost in my neck the following moment, which would mean the end of my miserable life. Fortunately that moment didn't come; it seemed that I had a chance after all.

Some people I met were surprised to see me run like a horse that is pulling a stagecoach. They asked me what the hurry was and then I realized that the ghost had given up. Apparently, the ghost had returned to the protection of the graveyard. I was gasping for breath, but I was alive and kicking. I never had been that close to death in my entire life."

Those dumbfounded stories were actually rotten stories; they scared the hell out of kids and also grown up people. Before this idiot of a story teller had told Adrie about the ghost in the graveyard, he had never been scared to walk past the graveyard in the dark. After he had heard the story, the graveyard looked like a different world to him.

The next time that Adrie had to walk past the graveyard in the dark, he didn't feel good about it at all. For safety's sake he walked on the opposite side of the street; that way maybe the ghosts wouldn't notice him. Fearfully, he looked at the big tombstone across the street which was very close to the road, too close for comfort. He prepared himself to run for his life if needed. Luckily, there was no moaning and groaning so he couldn't find out what sex the ghost was. It must have been his lucky day, he didn't see anything. Maybe it wasn't quite dark enough; ghosts feel secure when it's pitch dark, they disappear as snow before the sun as soon as it gets light.

It took a while before he was brave enough to walk on the gate side of the street when passing the graveyard. He told himself that it were just stupid stories about ghosts. Yet, when he passed the big ghost tombstone, a cold shiver ran down his spine and he wasn't so sure of himself. Fear is easy to create but to lose it completely takes some doing.

By lack of spooky stories there were other favorites about people who were in perfect health and died of some kind of mysterious illness. Those stories were usually dished up in a very distasteful manner.

One night, when everybody was already in bed, Willie suddenly started to cry heartbrokenly. Her mother went to check what her problem was but Willie kept sobbing continually and finally told her mother that she had a deadly cancerous lump on her leg. When her mother inspected the deadly lump it was only a mosquito bite. Somebody had told a stupid story about a woman who had a little cancerous lump and in matter of a month she was kaput.

THE FORBIDDEN PLAYGROUND

Adrie's friends called on him all the time and asked if he would come to play outside with them. Playing outside presented a problem because there was no place they could play without being chased away by somebody. There was only one playground which was the school yard. It was surrounded with a high iron fence and after school hours it was locked. The Principal wouldn't allow the kids to play in the schoolyard after school hours because he was afraid that the kids would play soccer and kick a ball through the windows.

The kids weren't allowed to play soccer in the street either, it was too dangerous the police said. It didn't bother the kids that they had to play between the traffic that mainly consisted of bikers but the bikers didn't like it that playing kids were running into their bikes. Most of the time this resulted in a couple of bleeding knees for the kid and the biker usually fell flat on his snout. He was a lot worse off.

Where could the kids play? Nobody answered that question and the kids played in the street regardless. The policemen were riding on bikes in those days and they were always in uniform; you could see them coming a mile away. When the playing kids saw a cop coming in the street, they warned each other by shouting: "Cop, cop, ball in your pocket." They used a tennis ball to play football so it fitted easily in their pocket. That's all the kids had to play football.

If they didn't see the cop in time, he would jump off his bike, grab the ball and cut it into two pieces. This was vandalism but he got away with it. He gave the ball back to the kids which gave them two halves instead of one ball. The trouble was that half a ball doesn't roll very well.

Similar things happened when they kicked their ball into a flower garden by accident. A mad owner would come running outside with his pocket knife in his hand to cut the ball in two. Just to think that the very same people who cut the balls of the kids into two pieces complained about their vandalism. Where do you think the kids learned it from?

Whenever they kicked their ball into a garden, they would run through the flowers to retrieve their ball before the owner could grab and cut it. Nobody cared if they flattened the flowers; those ball cutters had it coming. There was one good guy in the street, who didn't cut their ball into two pieces but he didn't return it either; he gave it to his little son. Nice guy!

Not only was playing soccer in the street dangerous because of the traffic, many houses were standing close to the street and many a ball hit a window. This meant that the culprit had to dig deep into his piggy bank to pay for it. It didn't matter what age you were; if you broke something you had to pay for it. If you refused and your parents didn't make you, the police came to enforce it.

It was summer and a deaf and dumb guy invented spin top time. This was plain bull; it was supposed to be a dumb joke. In those days a deaf and dumb guy was seen as a stupid guy. (Dumb being translated as stupid.)

The spin tops were beautiful; the kids decorated them with silver paper and when they were spinning, they looked beautiful. They had some kind of a whip to hit the spin top and the art was to hit it hard which made it fly quite a distance away, for instance through a window. When you put a knot into the string of your whip, you really could make it go far, which made you a likely candidate to pay for a broken window. A beautiful spin top was bought for one penny but the broken windows cost more.

Actually, there was nothing the kids could do without running into financial difficulties. Fortunately, there was a solution to their problem. There was a large area without houses, where you could play soccer and throw stones without breaking windows. It seemed as if it had been made with the kids in mind and was exactly what the doctor had ordered for growing up kids.

It was "The Polder." A polder consists out of a large area of land intersected by ditches and channels with little windmills to mill the excess rain water into channels; from where it flows through the rivers into the ocean. There was only one problem; it wasn't only surrounded by barbed wire, it was also posted everywhere. Signs on the gates were stating: "No Trespassing."

The farmer even put a lock on the gate to keep the kids out of his pasture. That was just a waste of money, no lock could keep the kids out of the pastures; they just climbed over the gates even if there was barbed wire on the top. Kids saw the pastures as excellent football fields made to play soccer. Pity the farmer didn't agree. No barbed wire, sign or lock would keep the kids out of his pasture; the signs meant nothing to them! It looked as if the sign said: "Welcome Children. Have Fun!"

The children had very few toys in those days which made them think that everything around them was a toy. To the chagrin of the farmers, the kids were fascinated by those little windmills that maintained a proper water level in those ditches for irrigation of the fields. In case of pastures there had to be enough drinking water in the ditches for the cattle.

There is plenty of wind in The Netherlands and those little windmills could mill those ditches bone dry in no time at all, especially if it didn't rain for a while. Therefore the farmers kept a close check on the water levels and stopped the windmills as soon as the desired water level was reached.

When Adrie and his friends saw that the windmills were stopped, they decided to do some water milling on their own. That stupid farmer didn't know how to mill water. They turned the vanes of the windmill into the wind and in no time at all they were milling water, which made them think that they were experienced millers.

They had that right because the next day the ditches were dry and consequently, the cattle had nothing to drink. Evidently, something had gone terribly wrong and only because they had missed one little detail. When they were going home, they hadn't stopped the windmills and the windmills had milled water all night.

The farmer wasn't very happy with the kids' assistance in milling water; he called them "Little pests," for no apparent reason at all. He said: "If I see you even look at the windmills I'll break your bloody necks."

Of course, he had to catch them first. In vain he tried to compete with young legs which could run fast and jump across ditches. The only way he could get them was by sneaking up on the boys when they were playing their games.

In order not to look at the windmills, they decided to play soccer instead. Pastures were excellent soccer fields and in no time they were playing soccer. There was only one problem; their soccer game didn't do the pasture any good; they flattened the grass which angered the farmer. With the next game they had, the farmer came to chase them out of the pasture.

If they couldn't play in the pasture, they would play in the hay land. The hay was standing up to their middle; if they crawled through it nobody could see them. This gave them an idea to play hide and seek in the hay land. They would crawl on all fours through the hay and the one who was the seeker would crawl behind the ones who were hiding and try to catch up with them. There were all kinds of tricks to make sure that the seeker couldn't find the hiders. Double backing was a good trick or stepping carefully from their trail without disturbing the grass. Again the farmer was not impressed; he said that they ruined his good hay.

O.K. then, if they weren't welcome to play in the pasture or hay land, they would play in the channels. The channels were quite wide and the farmer made bridges across to have access to his land. First he put heavy beams across the channel and across the beams he put long, wide planks. He didn't nail the planks down which was noticed by the boys. "Look, beautiful canoes," they said and since a canoe is only in its element when it is in the water, they threw the planks into the channel. They took their clothes off so they wouldn't get wet and for lack of paddles they paddled with their hands. There was nobody to bother them because the bridge was at a narrow gravel road with hardly any traffic. The gravel road was used by farmers, the occasional bike and the boys of course.

Nobody had sold any tickets for the matinee to see the show but yet they had spectators. A couple of young girls, perhaps fifteen years old, biked down the road; they stopped and took a seat in the grass. They probably had never seen naked boys on planks in the channel. Maybe they didn't have any brothers so they had never seen naked boys at all. There wasn't much to see anyway; they were only seven years old and the cold water didn't improve it either. It didn't bother the boys at all that the girls were watching, as long as there was no farmer or a cop watching them. The girls couldn't harm them, they were still innocent. They threw the farmer's whole bridge into the channel but they were innocent. How about that?

Again, the farmer wasn't impressed with the inventive games of the boys. The next time they went to play canoe, the farmer had nailed down the planks so they couldn't throw them in the channel anymore. What else was there to do? There was a plough left in the field, maybe they could be of some assistance to plough the farmer's land. The problem was that you needed a horse to pull the plough and lucky for the farmer there wasn't a horse around. Ploughing without a horse was a futile attempt; they gave up and pushed the plough into the ditch. That darned plough wasn't good at all!

After the farmer had found his plough in the ditch, he was careful not to leave any more farm machinery on his land, which put the boys in the position that they had nothing to play with. When they were looking at the huge willow trees; they decided to make a tree house and play Swiss Family

Robinson. First of all they had to remove many branches so they would have enough room to move around. One of the boys' father was a carpenter, so he had the honor of going home to steal a saw. It was a lot of hard work but after a painful lesson, they managed not to saw their hands anymore. Considerable progress had been made and tomorrow they would inaugurate their brand new tree house.

It was a grand opening; there was even a ceremonial speech from a high official with the inauguration of their tree house. The high official was a policeman, who was coming with the farmer to investigate his complaint that he had pests on his land. Consequently, the farmer came with the pest control, which happened to be a policeman. All kinds of accusations were made by the farmer; he said that the boys dumped everything in the water including his bridge and his plough.

The boys told the policeman that they never had seen a plough in the field (of course not, it was in the ditch) and how could you throw a bridge in the water, that was a sheer impossibility. This farmer was completely out of his chord, the only thing they had done was saw a couple of branches out of the tree to make room for a club house. "A couple of branches," the angry farmer shouted, "The whole tree is ruined."

An extensive lecture followed by the policeman, he told them that they couldn't trespass on the farmer's land, and the way they were behaving they were heading straight for the gallows. Next, he took their names and addresses down and said that he would get in touch with their parents.

Whenever the farmers saw the boys in the polder they went after them even if they were doing nothing wrong, which wasn't very often. The farmers always had to even the score for mischief the boys had committed in their sunny past. It's hard to say what the farmers would have done to them if they had caught them, but they weren't interested in finding out; they took off for safety's sake. The reason that the boys were bellwethers was mainly because they had no playgrounds or other recreational areas.

Jumping ditches was really good Dutch entertainment for the simple reason that there were a lot of ditches in the polder. When Adrie was a novice in jumping ditches, it happened quite often that he didn't make it across which resulted in wet feet or worse. One of the problems was that his ditch jumping friends were all one or two years older than he was, which made quite a bit of difference with their longer legs. Soon he learned that when he moved his legs faster, he would get more speed which would see him across the ditch instead of in the ditch. It looked as if jumping ditches had been invented with him in mind. He took to it as a duck takes to the water and liked it as much as a piece of pastry or an ice cream cone.

Ditch jumping wasn't just a game, it was an art and it was also progressive.

There was always a wider ditch to jump which they hadn't tried before. One thing was for sure, they were never satisfied till someone didn't make it and jumped into the ditch. The most difficult jumps were the ones where you had to jump from low to high; you had to pull yourself up on the steep shore. You might make the jump but fall back into the ditch. There were usually a few spectators watching who would be cheering when that happened.

Most of the children were scared to get wet clothes which would be followed by a spanking by their mother. Consequently there were always more spectators than jumpers. As far as that was concerned, Adrie was lucky; his mother didn't mind it at all when he came home with dirty or wet clothes, as long as it was his old clothes. After school, he was supposed to come home first to change into his old clothes, which meant a pair of shorts and a shirt. In summer, he didn't wear underwear when he was playing in the polder and he also walked with bare feet. The fewer clothes he had on the better it was when he jumped into a ditch.

Sometimes the boys were jumping ditches when they walked to school. If this resulted in wet feet, they had to be careful because they were supposed to come to school with clean clothes, clean hands and no wet clothes. They wore wooden shoes to school and had to leave the wooden shoes in the hall under their coat peg. In the classroom they were walking in their socks on a wooden floor and of course if they were walking with wet feet across the wooden floor, they left a trail behind themselves as if they had thrown bread crumbs on the floor.

Whenever Adrie had wet feet, he would take his socks off and walk on bare feet behind his friend. That way the teacher wouldn't see that he walked bare feet. It was bad enough when his school clothes got wet and dirty but if his Sunday clothes got dirty there was hell to pay. If that happened it wasn't always his fault, it was more or less an unfortunate accident when his best clothes were full of mud.

One Sunday, he was looking at the tadpoles, in a muddy ditch, when Kees Vanderlinden decided to throw a big stone in the mud, right in front of him. With his best clothes full of mud; he could figure that his mother wasn't going to be very happy when she saw it. Kees Vanderlinden was a real pest, but the problem was that Adrie's mother wasn't going to listen to his explanation about why his best clothes were full of mud. After the damage had been done, Kees Vanderlinden knew that Adrie had it in for him, so he took off. He figured that Adrie was going to beat him up whenever he got him. As fast as his legs would carry him, he ran to a safe haven, home.

There was no worry that Adrie wasn't going to pay him back for what he had done to him; he was more worried about what his mother was going to say. Indeed, his mother didn't understand at all that there was a pest by the name of Kees Vanderlinden. She said, "If you had stayed away from that ditch, it couldn't have happened." For the rest of the Sunday he had to stay inside, except for going to church.

Kees Vanderlinden knew that Adrie was looking for him and tried very hard to stay out of his way. However, when you live in the same street, sooner or later you bump into one another. Everybody else knew that Adrie had to settle a score with Kees Vanderlinden and was going to beat him up. As always, there were many helpers to make sure that Adrie was going to get his boy.

A couple of days later, they were playing in the street. Suddenly, his friend Jaap Hoogland came up to him and said: "Say Adrie, Kees Vanderlinden is playing right in front of his house, you can beat him up easily."

"I might as well get this over with," he thought and ran into the street to beat Kees up, but Kees ran to his home again. He couldn't make it to the rear door so he had to settle for the front door, which was closed. Desperately, Kees rang the door bell to get in but Adrie wasn't going to let the opportunity go wasted and punched him in the nose. Kees fell against the front door right at the moment that his mother opened the door. Of course, Kees was screaming like a lean pig to get sympathy from his mother. That trick worked and his mother came after Adrie, shouting to her husband who was working in the rear garden.

Whenever somebody came after him, Adrie never ran home because it wasn't likely that his parents would take his side. That's why this time he found it wiser to run into the polder to get rid of his enemy. Vanderlinden, Kees' father, came after him right away to avenge his son and punish Adrie, which meant a beating if he caught him.

This was a silly situation, Kees was the culprit but in the eyes of his father and mother he was the villain and Adrie was the brute. They probably had seen too many Western movies where the villain gets his revenge. In their eyes it just couldn't be that their son was a real pain and deserved a beating.

When Adrie tried to run for the polder, where he was master in out-running and out-jumping people, he was faced with a handicap. He had a slight lead when the hot pursuit started and if it hadn't been for the gate that gave access to the pasture, he could have increased his lead in the following sprint. However, with the devil on his heels, the gate was an unwelcome obstacle that would slow him down in his attempt to scale it. It was very well possible that Vanderlinden would have been able to pull him back before he could get on the other side of the gate. While scaling the gate, he could almost feel a strong hand pulling him back to settle the account now overdue.

It was the second time that month that he had to scale a gate for dear life. The first time he had crossed a pasture where some horses were grazing. All of a sudden, he heard a horse neighing pretty close to him. When he looked back, one of the horses came galloping with enormous speed in his direction. He couldn't stop a wild mustang and tried to run out of the pasture but first he had to scale a gate. While he scaled the gate that time, he could feel the horse's bite in his behind. Luckily, it didn't happen but this time his luck could be running out when he was scaling gates to escape his pursuers; first a wild horse and now an angry man.

While scaling the gate, his ejaculatory prayer was probably heard by his guardian angel and on his wings he almost flew to the safe side of the gate. Luckily, unworthy people like Vanderlinden don't have any guardian angels so it took him a bit longer than Adrie to scale the gate. The danger hadn't passed yet, if he listened to the warning shouts of his friends. He kept running with the devil in hot pursuit and didn't even dare to look back to see how close he was. On the straight stretch in the pasture, the distance between Adrie and the bogy man increased quickly.

His pursuer kept following him and seemed to have no intention of giving up. In order to get rid of him he had to change his strategy. He was heading for another gate which wasn't a real problem, this time. His lead was big enough to allow him to scale another gate without being caught. Unfortunately, he wasn't going to lose that guy either. He had shown Adrie that he could scale gates, but could he also jump ditches? Jumping ditches was his best subject at school, (or was it after school?) He changed his direction towards a wide ditch in order to test the ability of Vanderlinden in jumping ditches. For this change of strategy, he had to give up some of his valuable lead because Vanderlinden took advantage of this situation by cutting the angle to the ditch. It probably gave him a false impression that he was gaining on Adrie and could catch him before he could jump across the ditch.

Usually, whenever he was jumping a ditch, he would look the situation over to see where he wanted to jump and what the conditions were. He knew the polder with its ditches like his pocket and knew from memory that he had to jump from a low shore to a high one, which meant he had to jump far but also high. This was a critical moment to shake his pursuer; he was very confident that he would make it across and that Vanderlinden would chicken out. He didn't even have to pray to his guardian angel; why bother him with a piece of cake? The worst that could happen was that he jumped in the ditch or broke a leg and those were the risks of the trade.

Without a hitch he jumped across the ditch and crashed with his knee on the high shore. There was no time to think about a little detail that some of his skin had scraped off his knee. It wasn't likely that Vanderlinden would jump the ditch but it's better to be sure than sorry. He kept going and when he looked back, he saw that he had figured it right. Vanderlinden was walking to the dam with the gate and took the easy way out. To make sure that he understood that he didn't have a snowball chance in hell to catch him, Adrie also jumped across the next ditch. When he looked at the arena again, he saw that his enemy had given up and had sounded the retreat.

This meant that he could rest on his laurels before returning home. Satisfied, he looked at the retreating enemy, which shows you that the good guy always wins because he can call upon his guardian angel.

After a short breathing spell, he decided to return to his friends but where was Vanderlinden? He was nowhere to be seen, which could mean that he was so far away that he couldn't spot him anymore or he could be lying in ambush to catch him on his way home. All of a sudden, he saw somebody coming in his direction. When he came closer Adrie could see, with his eagle eye; that it was his friend Jaap Hoogland. He came to see if Adrie was alright.

The entire street had been watching the hot pursuit; it was as good as a horse race with lots of suspense. When he was resting, they didn't see Adrie anymore and wondered what had happened to him. Jaap Hoogland's father said: "Jaap you'd better go to check if your friend broke a leg jumping those wide ditches; I don't see him anymore."

Jaap replied: "You don't have to worry; Adrie knows the polder and can jump all ditches without breaking a leg."

Jaap's father insisted that Jaap fetch Adrie back for a glass of lemonade to quench his thirst. This was an offer he couldn't refuse and to his surprise he was received as the local hero. He had supplied entertainment and came out as winner of the race. All spectators were on his side, except the Vanderlindens. Most people didn't like those people at all; they knew Kees as a regular pest and a thief. Whenever he came in the smithy, he always stole a hammer or another tool. Vanderlinden himself was a show-off and nobody liked him. Jaap's father was all in favor of Adrie and stuck up for him in a second confrontation with Vanderlinden.

A few days later, Vanderlinden saw Adrie playing in the street and thought it was a piece of cake to catch him. He came running at him but in time Adrie made it into his friend's yard. Vanderlinden followed him which was no problem. Adrie just went into the basement and bolted the door for safety's sake.

Vanderlinden was being stubborn again and rattled the door handle to gain entrance to the basement. Jaap's father came out to see what was going on and asked Vanderlinden what he thought he was doing. According to Vanderlinden, Adrie was a big bruiser and had beaten up his beloved son; he was no damned good and a tyrant in the street. Jaap's father told him: "Why don't you buzz off and mind your own business. Let the kids fight their own battles."

Vanderlinden left probably planning his next move to get Adrie. It was bad enough before this incident. Whenever Adrie played in the street, he had to look over his shoulder if one of the friendly farmers wasn't coming through the street, trying to get even with him. Now he had another enemy who was after him; Vanderlinden!

PESTS UNLIMITED

This is one of the stories for which a language warning is in place. It was the way people talked and reader discretion is advised.

There were a couple of farmers who could have drank Adrie's and his friend Jaap's blood. They would have paid if their heads had been offered to them on a silver platter. They were the Old Hook and the Young Hook. First there was the Old Hook and then there was the Young Hook who happened to be the son of the Old Hook. What a coincidence! The boys had given them those handy names to distinguish them from each other. That way they would know about whom they were talking. The young Hook followed in the footsteps of his father and they both worked for a rich farmer, Koos Vryland. Both Hooks were doing a good job for Koos Vryland, they were always chasing the boys out of the fields and pastures where they were playing.

It was a hopeless task for the two Hooks to keep them out of the pastures. No matter how often they chased them away, they would be back. The cat came back the following day but Adrie and his friends were a lot worse than the cat. They came back within an hour or as soon as the coast was clear, whichever came first.

The reason that the boys were very successful in jumping ditches, when they had to escape an angry farmer, came because of a progressive scheme with extensive training. There were about half a dozen boys who were doing very well in jumping ditches; most boys couldn't even jump across a trench. You could say that the ditch jumpers were members of an unfounded ditch jump club. They dared each other; it was a handicap if somebody of the club jumped a ditch and somebody chickened out to jump that ditch. If such a situation existed that you didn't jump a difficult ditch that somebody else had jumped, you were a "Sufferer." It meant that you were suffering and had earned the contempt of all other members of the guild because you were not a ditch jumper at all.

Those were the unwritten rules, it was an innocent contest and it was fun. Everybody tried to jump difficult ditches and then watch all the members of the club trying to jump them, too. It didn't matter if you didn't make the jump and got wet clothes, as long as you jumped that's all that counted. In that case it was still worth a bundle of laughs for the other honorable club members.

Since they were so much involved in jumping ditches, they gave all the ditches a name. They didn't put signs beside the ditches with the name on it, but everybody involved in the ditch jumping sport knew the names. Names were simple; there was the "Wide Ditch" and the "Very Wide Ditch." Other self explaining names were the "Channel" and the "Windmill Ditch." There was one name attached to a ditch, "The good for nothing ditch", because it was so small that you couldn't jump it, you could only step across.

Once when Adrie and his friends were playing football in the pasture, the Young Hook came riding on his bike into the field. They picked up their ball to get out of the pasture. The grass was short in the pasture which gave the Young Hook the opportunity to ride quite fast; it would be a matter of minutes to catch them. They had been playing soccer with 12 boys but by accident the Young Hook came after Adrie and his two friends. Those three boys were always together in the polder, and he had figured that they were the ringleaders of the pack. His philosophy must have been that if you want to subdue an unruly tribe, you have to catch the leaders first. The young Hook seemed to be busy catching the leaders; he was so close behind that Adrie could feel his breath in his neck. He was too close for comfort; all he had to do was to jump off his bike to catch one of the three.

It was high time to call up their guardian angels again because they seemed to be in trouble once more. When they were pretty close to a barbed wire fence, they dashed for it to get underneath to crawl to the other side. The danger was that their shirt would get stuck on the barbed wire but there was no time to think about those little inconveniences.

They got a little lead after the obstacle had been overcome. The Young Hook lost some time to get his bike on the other side of the fence, but once on his bike again he would catch up with them. There was no doubt about it; a change of strategy was in order. The pastures were divided into strips by shallow trenches and as long as they were running the pasture lengthwise, the Young Hook could stay on his bike but when they ran across the pasture he had to overcome the small trenches.

When they reached a ditch, they jumped across which gave them an advantage on the Young Hook. He probably could have jumped the ditch but it was impossible to jump with the bike on his back. If he wanted to chase the three boys some more, he had to leave his bike behind. Their strategy had worked again because he didn't want to leave his bike behind to chase them on foot. He gave up and turned back.

The three boys had a lot of fun after shedding their pursuer; they thought that he was a complete idiot to try to catch them. He would have been much better off if he had followed his jungle instinct and had tried to catch the weakest of the group. A lion always singles out an old or sick animal of the herd but never the strongest. Agreed he was no lion, he was just stupid.

However, he wasn't as stupid as the boys thought he was. They decided to go to the gravel road and walk to the highway where they were busy making an overpass. The Young Hook had watched them through his binoculars to see where they were heading. He biked around and approached them from the back, to ambush them in the rear like a coward. Suddenly he jumped off his bike shouting: "I got you."

An old Dutch proverb says: "Don't shout hooray if you haven't crossed the bridge yet." This farmer probably didn't even know what a proverb was but this was purely lack of education that the Young Hook couldn't help.

There were all kinds of little riddles, like: "What is the extreme of insolence?" The answer is: "Urinate on a cop's shoes and ask him where the urinal is."

There is another extreme riddle that applies better to the Young Hook. "What is the extreme of slipperiness?" Answer: "An eel in a pail of mucus." Yes, that's slippery alright, but there was one thing more slippery than that: "The three boys whom he couldn't catch."

Jaap said: "The Young Hook made one mistake; he opened his beak too early, that's why he failed."

The only way to catch them was to slam his claws in their flesh like a cat does to catch a bird. When he jumped at them, they jumped away from him. For the second time in 20 minutes, Adrie could feel his hot breath in his neck again. It was time for his guardian angel to interfere. That poor angel had to make overtime that day; hopefully he got paid time and a half because he was doing a good job. No sooner he did get Adrie out of trouble or he managed to get into trouble again, but one thing could be said about Adrie's guardian angel, he never gave up on him!

The Young Hook had longer legs than the boys, but they could move their shorter legs faster than he could, which made up for their handicap. They managed to increase their lead, which made Young Hook to resort to his bike again to pursue them. Soon he caught up with the boys and he thought he had them for sure. They were running on a gravel road with a wide ditch on either side, it was like being caught between the devil and the deep blue sea, or between the devil and the wide ditch. The trouble was, they could jump the ditch but they were running parallel to the ditch and there wasn't enough distance for the necessary sprint. Before jumping, they had to make a ninety degree turn which made them extremely vulnerable to being cut off by the Young Hook. It was a matter of jumping, swimming, drowning or being caught by the hostile Hook.

All three boys jumped at the same time, Adrie's two friends had wet feet and he himself fell into the mud. It didn't matter, anything was better than facing the angry Hook. Once across the wide ditch they didn't have to worry anymore; they quit running, feeling pretty safe. They said: "Bye Hook, see you next time!"

Disappointed, he jumped on his bike and paddled home. The boys learned from their mistakes; they kept an eye on him to make sure he wasn't going to prepare another ambush for them. Luckily he gave up, at least for that day.

The two Hooks must have had an obsession to catch the three boys whom they hated; they never let an opportunity go by to try to catch them. Jaap Hoogland and Klaas Hiemstra kept rabbits. A lot of people kept rabbits in The Netherlands for Christmas dinner.

Their rabbits were fed carrots, cabbage leaves, dandelions and grass. Koos Vryland with his pasture was the supplier of the grass. One night when Adrie came to call on his friend Jaap, his mother told him: "Jaap went with Klaas Hiemstra to cut grass for the rabbits."

Adrie went to the pasture just in time to see the Old Hook trying to sneak up on them from the back. He might have been successful if it hadn't been for a pest of a little boy, "Adrie," who came at the last minute to the pasture to warn them of the impending danger.

Adrie was shouting to them from far away, which drew their attention and when they looked up, they saw the danger they were in. In the nick of time they jumped up and ran away with the Old Hook close on their heels. They jumped the ditch to get to Adrie's side of the ditch and out of reach of the old geezer. At the other side of the ditch was the Old Hook gasping for air. He looked hatefully at Jaap and Klaas and shouted: "You damned pests, one of these days I'm going to catch you and I will beat the shit out of you so that for the next two weeks you won't be able to walk."

What language for a grown-up man to try to scare innocent little boys. He could just as well have shouted his threats at the ditch because it didn't impress them at all. They were merely doing their thing and if he didn't like it, he could lump it as far as they were concerned. However, they heeded his warning and whenever they were playing in the street, they were always watching if there wasn't a Hook coming in the street.

The Old Hook had given them a couple of ideas though; he had shouted that they were damned pests and they didn't want to make a liar out of an old man. In order not to disappoint him, they were going to behave as damned pests and they happened to know how to do that. He also had shouted that he would beat the shit out of them, which was completely unnecessary because they were going to give him all the shit that they could provide, free of charge.

There was a big barn in the pasture that was used to store farm implements and fertilizer. The Old Hook had a dairy cow which he was milking twice daily for his own use. He also used the barn to store his little milk stool, which he needed to sit on when he was milking his bull. (Jaap and Adrie said it that way. Instead of milking his cow they said that he was milking his bull.) That way he didn't have to carry his stool back and forth to home. The barn was well built and had a big door which was padlocked to keep everybody out.

When you are playing in the fields far away from home, it happens from time to time that you have to go to the toilet. The farmers didn't go all the way home when they were working the fields and neither did the boys. They copied the farmers and did their business at the edge of a ditch but now they had a better idea. Doing their business behind the barn right in front of the door was a much better place, so he had to watch not to step in it. After a couple of months, it started to look real funny in front of the barn door when more and more piles appeared every day. They were damned pests, the Old Hook had said and they had to honor their name; they made sure to make their daily contribution to make the rear of his barn look like a shit field.

After a while the novelty wore off, they had to find another way to vent their frustration at the ugly Hooks. They took a stick and covered the lock with fresh excrement, making sure that the keyhole was full of it. That way the Old Hook had to put his key in it or he had to clean the lock first. They knew exactly what time he came to milk his cow and made sure they were ready for the matinee. It was recommended to stay a respectable distance away from the barn, just in case the Old Hook wasn't amused.

The show wasn't disappointing at all; the result was better than expected. When the Old Hook was taking the key out of his pocket to open the door he couldn't believe his eyes. He took his glasses out of his pocket to put them on his nose and saw that the padlock was full of shit. First he got some grass to wipe most of the shit off the lock; then he opened the barn door to let the horses escape. And for the grand finale, he got an old pail from the barn, filled it with water and with a rag he cleaned the padlock.

There was a clean padlock on the barn door but not for long; the boys made sure that every day a fresh coat was applied to the lock. They had to protect the lock so that no rainwater could get in. And of course the faithful Old Hook was cleaning his padlock every day.

The boys were very serious that this was a life or dead battle; they had no playgrounds, were not allowed to play in the street, and the Hooks were going to take away the only place they could play. He could try but they were putting up a fight; the boys hated him as much as he hated them. The old Hook could try to stop them, but guaranteed, he would come away with a flea in his ear or better yet, he would come away with a shitty key in his pocket.

Yes, those were great moments in their lives; they made their presence known to the world. As proof, there were countless piles of shit behind the barn and there was always a shitty lock hanging on the barn, proving that "The Evil Shitter" had struck again.

The greatest moment in their lives was still to come. They knew they had enemies that wanted to get even with them but after a while they didn't think about this anymore, especially when they were involved in an interesting game. One night when they were playing a game in the street, the Old Hook came back from milking his bull and had of course cleaned his shitty lock. His blood was probably boiling and there in the street were his earthly enemies. Here was his chance; why not catch them and make good on his threat to beat them up? He threw off his wooden shoes so he could run faster, and was ready for his kill. Luckily for the three boys, the warning alarm sounded just in time. Cor Hoogland, Jaap's kid brother, had been playing in the street and saw what was happening, he cried wolf and away they were again on the races.

From playing games to running for your life is quite something; you ought to try it. They were close to Klaas Hiemstra's home and were heading for it. It looked like the basement was a safe place to be out of reach of the angry Hook. After bolting the door they were anxiously waiting for what would develop next.

The Old Hook was trying to open the basement door and when he didn't succeed, he started to bang on it. Behind the bolted door, the boys were giggling that they had escaped again. They never knew that the old geezer could run that fast, it came as a surprise to them. Apparently, his anger had given him a shot of adrenalin which made him run twice as fast. It looked like his anger was building up; he started to kick the door and he was shouting: "Come out you assholes, I'll kill you."

It sounded like their lives weren't worth a wooden nickel but help was on its way and for a change it wasn't their guardian angel. Klaas Hiemstra's mother had heard all the noise and came to check what was going on. She saw the Old Hook banging and kicking against the basement door and asked: "What is going on?"

The Old Hook shouted angrily: "I'll tell you what's going on woman, those damned good for nothing kids are a disgrace to this world; if I get them in my hands I'll kill them, eat them for breakfast and spit out the bones one by one."

Klaas Hiemstra's mother asked: "What in the world did they do?"

The Old Hook replied: "I'll tell you what those dirty dogs are doing. Every bloody day they put human shit on the padlock of the barn, pure people shit. I tell you woman, every day I have to clean it."

All three boys were snickering behind the door and remarked that he must have studied it good because he knew so well that it was pure people shit. If this had happened at Adrie's place, the outcome would have been different. To his surprise, he heard Klaas' mother reply: "No, no, this is terrible; I wish I could help you!"

The Old Hook kept going for a bit, using some more obscene language about rotten kids and assholes that put pure people shit on the padlock so the key was full of shit. Slowly, his anger was dissipating, he saw that he didn't get anywhere and finally sauntered home. But where were his wooden shoes? Cor Hoogland had been so friendly to throw his wooden shoes in the ditch. With a stick he retrieved his wooden shoes from the ditch with an audience watching from a safe distance.

Klaas' mother never asked the boys anything about shit on the lock. After the Old Hook left, she went inside the house with a mysterious smile on her face like from the Mona Lisa. After this incident, things changed. The Old Hook had either given up or maybe he had seen the light at the end of the tunnel.

He knew he was fighting a losing battle, he quit chasing the boys and in return, they had nothing to take out on him and quit pestering him. Whenever he entered the pasture, they would just leave and he would pretend he hadn't seen them. They would simply stay out of his way and they didn't put shit on his lock anymore. Actually, he wasn't a bad guy after all.

Hostilities had ceased after a hard fought battle and a lasting Armistice followed. They stayed out of each others hair. In a way they respected the Old Hook and he took them the way they were, understanding that they were part of the world and had the right to a rightful place in it. They belonged, and you can't change that!

WHEN YOU BURN YOUR BUTT YOU HAVE TO SIT ON THE BLISTERS.

This chapter deals with quite a different time as we are used to today. Reader discression is advised.

During the Depression, people were as poor as a church mouse. It was a desperate time in which people struggled to make a go of it. Naturally, theft was on the increase, and religion took second place. A person had to live. Adrie's parents weren't exactly stealing but they made extra money which they didn't report. Why should they, when they had a Minister President that was lying to them? If the Christian Reformed Minister could lie and cheat why should they be so honest?

Children were poorly fed and made up for it by stealing fruit. Adrie and his friends were well brought up and were as honest as gold but their honesty disappeared in less than a second, when they saw a fruit tree loaded with apples or pears. They came from a long line of apple thieves; even Adam couldn't leave the apples alone - they were merely a chip off the old block. The only difference between Adam and the kids was that they didn't need a woman or a snake to tell them that the apples were good. They knew that they were good, even if they were still green.

Whenever they saw an orchard, it didn't take them long to get into it. It was like walking in the Garden of Eden without the tempting woman and an apple-peddling snake. The only thing they could expect to meet in the orchard was an angry farmer calling them apple thieves, instead of an angry God throwing them out of Paradise. The angry farmer didn't have to throw them out of the orchard; they went voluntarily, in a hurry, as soon as they saw him.

They would steal like magpies if it came to fruit and chanced all kinds of things to get their fair share from the fruit trees. Most of the kids had an indescribable hunger for fruit but on their menu was also listed other produce such as turnip, sugar beet, carrots and cauliflower. Their teachers and parents had apparently given up on them; at least they were always saying: "Nothing good will ever come out of you boys."

Few girls would steal fruit; they either were more honest or they didn't have the nerve, but few boys could resist the temptation. They had at least the excuse that their parents were too poor to buy fruit so they had to take care of themselves. That's a poor excuse because they weren't starving. It probably was part of growing up.

With the ferocious appetite they had, they even ate horse carrots that were so big that you couldn't bite a piece off them. They had to gnaw on the carrot like a Doberman pincher gnaws on its bone. There were all kinds of clever ways to obtain all this produce; and they were smart enough that they could steal bunches of radishes right from under the producer's nose.

It all started very innocently, for they were as innocent as a new born baby. They knew nothing about stealing radishes and were told that stealing was sin. Not for long were they innocent; they were badly influenced by the Depression and the War. And of course of growing up; they can't blame everything on the War and Depression. There were few boys who could resist the temptation and stay away from fruit trees.

They never planned to steal radishes; therefore it must have been that nasty Devil that made them do it. One night they came to a ditch in the polder with floating radishes. The vegetable grower grew lots of radishes and when he pulled them out of the ground they were muddy which made it necessary to wash them. He dumped them into the ditch and while he was washing the bundles of radishes some radishes broke loose from the bundle. It wasn't possible to use those radishes anymore as he couldn't bunch the loose radishes. Therefore, he left them floating in the ditch for the snails. The ditches were loaded with snails and if you came a couple of hours later, the snails had already nibbled little pieces off the radishes. The boys fished the floating radishes out of the ditch, ate some and took the rest home.

They were fond of radishes and watched the grower when he was going to wash radishes again. It didn't bother the grower that the boys were fishing the loose floating radishes out of the ditch while he was still washing. The problem was that one night there were only a few radishes floating in the ditch. It entered Adrie's mind that he could help the radishes to break loose from the bunch, which would increase the number of floating radishes to fish out of the ditch. That would never work, he thought, the grower would see that and chase them away.

He knew a better way to get radishes. He could have gone to the land after the grower left and pulled them out of the ground himself. There was an easier way, he thought. He pushed a bunch of radishes into the mud and it stayed there. All he had to do now was to wait till the grower left, then take the bunch of radishes out of the mud. The water was murky so the grower didn't see anything; he left, and Adrie took the radishes. Of course, this was progressive; if you can steal one bunch, you can steal five or six bunches; same difference.

There are always sissies in the world who make it difficult for an honest thief to operate. One time when Adrie was busy pushing bunches of radishes into the mud, there was a girl watching him. All of a sudden she said: "I see what you are doing Adrie, you pull the bunches of radishes under water and pull some out to get more radishes floating in the ditch."

The grower looked angrily in Adrie's direction which made him act fast. He said to the girl: "You are nuts, if I had pulled radishes out of a bunch, you would see them float, wouldn't you?"

Looking at the water, the grower saw that indeed Adrie was right; there were no radishes floating. This dumb twit of a girl had it all wrong and really under-estimated his cunning. Now why would he pull a couple of radishes from a bunch if he could push six bunches in the mud. After that false charge, the grower kept an eye on him for the rest of the day; he had to cut it out and behave. First, he had to regain the grower's trust before he could steal radishes on a greater scale again.

The Sunday school teacher always said that if you do wrong things, like stealing, there is always this little voice, your conscience that warns you. Adrie must have been as deaf as a stone because he never heard a little voice. His grumbling stomach demanding radishes was the only noise that Adrie ever heard.

The Depression and the war years were hard times and even staunch Christians didn't feel guilty when they were digging up the potatoes out of the farmer's field. A guy has to eat. Vegetable growers weren't sharing either; they had lots of radishes, cauliflower, lettuce and other vegetables. On the other hand there was this problem that people didn't have money to buy the produce and the growers weren't about to give their produce away free of charge to the unemployed. They piled up the unmarketable produce and put poison on it to prevent the unemployed from getting it free. Everybody had a bad time, and in the midst of plenty people were starving. Adrie had heard about poisoned mushrooms but poisoned cauliflower and radishes was a new one on him.

When they were stealing apples and pears, they were always saying to each other that they had to help the farmers. The branches were so heavily loaded with fruit that the branches were bending. Some branches couldn't carry the load, and broke. They reasoned that when they took off some of the burden from the branches, they wouldn't break and that way they were helping the farmers. Actually, the farmer was indebted to them. There was only one thing wrong with that philosophy, the farmers didn't believe it.

Orchard owners tried to protect their fruit trees with high fences and barbed wire. No matter how strong and fool-proof you make a vault, there is always a thief who figures out a way to get in it. Same thing with orchards; no matter how high the fence was and how much barbed wire was used, the boys wouldn't rest until they had found a way to get into the orchard in order to save the farmer's trees. They could scale any barbed wire fence; even throwing them in jail would have been no solution because they could walk out without a problem.

There was an orchard surrounded with a high barbed wire fence. They scaled the fence and threw fruit across the fence into the pasture to retrieve it later. However, there was one thorn in their eye. It was an orchard that looked like Fort Knox: impenetrable. This orchard was right behind the farm house with pastures on either side, therefore the farmer could see the access to the orchard. The only place he couldn't see was the back of the orchard. However, the back was inaccessible; there was a wide channel which was very difficult to jump and even if they had managed to jump across, they would have jumped into stinging nettles, shoulder high. Furthermore, on the other side of the nettles was a high fence with barbed wire and even if you were across this fence, you weren't in the orchard yet. First there was a piece of land where vegetables were growing, with a narrow track for transportation of produce in the centre.

Only from the rear could they get into the orchard without being detected. The farmer wasn't worried that anybody would get in that way because this was impossible. There was more than adequate protection which would discourage everybody, he thought.

Jaap Hoogland and Adrie were more than friends; they were a team. Something like Mercedes and Benz. Sooner or later they would figure out a way to get in. It was sooner! One night they took a couple of clubs along, took their clothes off, and waded through the channel. The water came to their middle so they didn't have to swim. On the other side of the channel, they started to flatten the nettles with their clubs and after they were flat, they threw some grass on them to make it possible to walk across with their bare feet.

Scaling the fence was a piece of cake but when you are naked, you can't steal that many apples. To solve the transportation problem, they took a gunny bag along to put their harvest in. They walked naked, with their gunny bag under their arm, to start the harvest. After they had enough apples and pears, they left the same way as they had come. Everything went perfect and one could say that "Operation Apple" was a complete success.

As soon as their fruit supply was exhausted, they decided to repeat this successful venture. Everything went slick again but the third time they tried to re-supply their fruit cache everything went wrong.

After the farmer had noticed that he had unwelcome guests in his orchard, he was waiting for the fruit thieves. They only had a few pears in their bag when the farmer jumped at them and of course the race was on. Naked, they ran down the narrow track to the barbed wire fence which they had to scale in a hell of a hurry, lest they would get caught. There was no time to go to their selected spot where the nettles were flattened, getting across without being caught was all that counted. Stark naked they jumped into the shoulder high nettles, waded through the ditch, picked up their clothes and made their get away.

The nettles had done a good job; they had blisters all over their bodies. Making the blisters wet with cold water eased the pain a little. They also ate the few pears they had managed to steal before they were so rudely interrupted. When Adrie arrived home, he avoided his mother as much as possible which wasn't hard to do because it was bed time anyway.

Going to bed didn't solve the problem at all. His blisters were killing him and he couldn't sleep. Very carefully he had avoided his mother to make sure that she wouldn't see his blisters, but now he had to go to her for help. Of course, he didn't tell her exactly what had happened, he just told her that they had been jumping ditches and by accident he had fallen in the nettles.

It didn't surprise his mother at all that he had blisters all over his body; she knew that they often took off their clothes in the polder. That was alright with her, at least his clothes didn't get wet or dirty. She looked the blisters over like a skilled physician and put some vinegar on them. After that treatment, Adrie went back to bed hoping he could get some shut eye.

When a Chinese fellow saw the blisters Adrie had on his body and heard that he had fallen in the nettles, the Chinese said: "Those nettles aren't all bad, I use them as vegetables. When you cook them the sting disappears and they are delicious. You can also make a tonic of the nettles as a cure against arthritis."

When Adrie said that he didn't really appreciate all those qualities of the nettles when he jumped into the nettles, the Chinese smiled and said: "Yes, but you were dealing with the wrath of the sun and the moon. The nettles were a healing gift from the sun and the moon to the people. Nettles made the people strong and healthy but the people were rude and never thanked the sun and the moon. As punishment, the sun and the moon put tiny hairs on the leaves to sting them." With a grin on his face, the Chinese concluded his interesting story: "If you ever fall into the nettles again remember to say: 'Thank you' and the nettles will not longer sting."

It was hard to believe that Adrie would have said "Thank you," when he jumped into the nettles and even in the future nobody in his right mind would thank the Gods when falling in the nettles. But he could appreciate the tip to use the nettles as a tonic against arthritis when he got old.

The boys did better than Adam in their apple adventure. Adam was chased out of Paradise and they had to sit on their blisters for a few days. They never went back to the Fort Knox orchard; there were better ways to make a living. The main thing was that they had saved their honor in demonstrating that even Fort Knox could be entered.

THE TORCHES

There were all kinds of nice games, like ringing door bells. In the street was a long row of thirty houses, a row housing project, with the doors right next to the sidewalk. Adrie and his friends would run past the houses and ring all the door bells. When they looked back they would see all the people standing in their door opening which was fascinating. Some childish people, who didn't see the fun when they came for nothing to the door, rigged the door bell ringers by standing behind the door with a pail of water. They could hear the kids come and when they were ringing their bell, they would throw a pail of water on them.

This was a very interesting game since they could end up with wet clothes, but the most attractive game was making fires. Of course, this was forbidden, which made it even more attractive. When they wanted to make a fire, they had to do it secretly in a secret place like the loft of Adrie's house. They burned some newspapers and after they were finished playing with fire, the mess had to be cleaned up. In order to clean up all the burned newspapers, they just threw a bunch of gunny bags over the mess. That way, nobody could see that the firebugs had been at it again.

In their opinion, they had covered their tracks. On the contrary, they had made it more conspicuous. They had missed a few tiny sparks in the burned newspapers, which started to burn the gunny bags. Fortunately, Adrie's mother came home just in time to prevent the house burning down to the ground. There was only minimal damage. A little hole burned through the wooden floor and the house was full of smoke.

Adrie's mother wasn't impressed at all with his experiments with fire and when he came home she asked casually: "Did you play with fire?"

His mother had cleaned up everything and she had opened all the windows so the smoke was gone. Adrie wondered why she asked him that question and wasn't aware that there had been a fire in the house. He kept himself dumb and said: "Me make a fire? No, I never do that."

His mother replied: "If you don't play with fire, how come that there is a hole burned through the floor?" Adrie's punishment was to go to bed without food, which was a punishment often applied in those days.

One of Adrie's friends who also was a fire torch didn't get off that lucky. His father had a carpentry business which meant that there were lots of shavings around. When he came in the work shop, he saw a pile of wood shavings in the corner. That would do a good job he thought and said to his little sister: "I'm going to make a nice fire." And he did! It can be said that he was very good at making fires because the whole workshop burned down to the ground.

Adrie and his friends were almost the innocent victims of a circumstantial fire. One night when they were playing in the polder there was a farmer burning dry potato plants. Curiosity can kill the cat but it got them into trouble. After the farmer went home, they had to investigate, of course. Upon their investigation, they found that there were still some white hot ashes that ignited the straw they threw on top of it. Within no time they had a nice fire going with lots of straw to burn that provided them with a lot of fun. When all burnable materials had been burned, they left for home.

After a while the wind picked up, took some of the remaining hot ashes and dumped them on a nearby agricultural implement barn. The barn burned down to the ground and the farm implements, which had been in the barn, hadn't exactly improved either.

Somehow, the farmer thought that the kids had burned down his barn deliberately and went to the police. He didn't know any names of boys who could have been responsible for burning down the barn and neither did the police. The police went for help to the Principal from the school, who was trying to find out who had been playing in the polder. He went from class to class and asked innocently: "Which of you kids have been playing in the polder lately?"

Adrie and his friend didn't know that the barn had burned down but they could smell a rat. It wasn't hard to figure out that the Principal wasn't interested if the buttercups were already in bloom. No doubt there was another reason for his question. The Principal knew that Adrie and his friends were always jumping ditches, and asked if they had been jumping ditches in the polder. He was unsuccessful with his probe, they simply said very innocently: "We jump ditches alright, but never in the polder. We only jump ditches next to the roads."

It's hard to say if the boys could have been in trouble if they had found out that they had been involved in making a fire in the polder. The farmer hadn't extinguished the fire completely before he left; they simply had picked up where he left off and almost became the innocent victims of a circumstantial fire. In spite of that argument, they kept their mouths shut.

IT WAS ALL GREEK TO HIM

As far as Adrie was concerned when he was seven years old, he knew all about the birds and the bees. The bees were sucking honey from the flowers and could sting you. On the other hand, the birds were chirping in the trees and flying through the sky. What else was there to know?

He was growing up in an extension of the Victorian Era and no facts of life were ever revealed to him but this was just about to change. His sister Willie was three years older than Adrie and she came home with a story that was all Greek to him.

Sex was a dirty word and if children at school talked about it they were punished for making unchaste remarks. At home it wasn't much better; if you talked about it you were a dirty kid. Only dirty people had sex.

One day when they were eating supper, Willie had a story. She said: "One of the boys in my class asked me if my father and mother had sex and I said: 'No.' The boy said: 'They must have, else you wouldn't have been born.'"

Adrie's father and mother looked meaningfully at each other and remarked that he probably thought he was a smart boy. Nothing more was said about it and Adrie wondered what they were talking about.

Shortly after this incident, he was at his uncle's farm and found out that those grown ups were talking in riddles. It started very innocently, his uncle said to his farmhand Rook: "Say Rook, is that cow dry?"

Rook answered: "Yes, already for a week."

Adrie wanted to make sure so he put his hand on the cow's back and indeed the cow was dry, they had that right. His uncle said: "Good, this cow can see the bull tomorrow in order to get a calf."

Adrie made sure to be around when the bull was going to give a calf to the cow. It was a disappointment; he saw the bull come and go but he didn't see a calf. The next time he was confronted with those bull stories was on a different farm. It was the neighboring farm of Huib Zwaal where they had to pick up some stuff. While he was horsing around in the farm yard, Adrie observed some really strange things. He overheard a real strange conversation between Huib Zwaal and his farm hand.

Huib Zwaal said to his farm hand: "Which cow did you set dry?"

The farm hand replied: "The cow I tied up behind the barn."

Adrie looked at the cow behind the barn and saw that she was dancing in the cow shit and the mud. The farm hand hadn't done a very good job to set the cow dry, he thought. When they were talking about the bull that had to come pretty soon, Adrie was going to make sure that he was going to see exactly what was happening. After a while, the farm hand came running into the yard shouting: "Say Huib, the bull is coming."

The craziest things had yet to come! Indeed, a man with a bull entered the farmyard. Adrie was no bull fighter which made him go respectfully out of the bull's way. On the other hand, he stayed close enough because he didn't want to miss a thing.

The bull-man asked Huib Zwaal: "Which cow has to be impregnated?"

Huib said: "The cow behind the barn."

The parade moved behind the barn where the cow was waiting patiently and Cupid started to shoot arrows in the cow's heart. Next, the bull man said: "I'd better get the bull's marriage tools ready because he'll need them when they get married."

Adrie never had heard that cows and bulls get married and besides he didn't see a Priest to perform the ceremony. That bull man was apparently full of bull, he thought. When the man said to Huib Zwaal that the bull and cow were getting married, he winked with his eye at Huib. At first Adrie thought that he was standing in the draught when his eye winked, but he began to understand that they were taking him for a ride.

The marriage tools of the bull were well protected; they were hanging underneath the bull in a protective sleeve, to prevent the mosquitoes from stinging it, Adrie thought. On second thought, it looked as if the sleeve was holding up his marriage tool to make sure that it wouldn't drag on the street.

The bull man tapped the bull on his behind and said: "The bull is ready to play with the cow."

Adrie didn't know that animals played and moreover he didn't see any toys, which showed him that the man was full of bull again. The bull approached the cow from the back and jumped on top of the cow. Now Adrie understood; the bull was playing "Horse Back Ride" but for lack of a horse he took the cow. That poor cow almost collapsed under the weight of the bull. In normal circumstances when you have a horse back ride, the horse is bigger than the one that mounts it, but here it was just the other way around.

The bull started to bellow, which probably meant "giddy up." He didn't play very long; he had no stamina at all. After about four minutes, the bull's tongue was hanging a foot out of his mouth and he was sighing like a stagecoach horse that had been running for a few hours.

Suddenly the bull had to go home for a rest; the bull man put the protective sleeve over the bull's marriage tool and they were ready to go. Huib Zwaal gave the bull man some money, which made Adrie think that it was a tip for the bull but that was a wrong assumption. The farm hand asked: "How much stud fees did you have to pay for that sire?"

This Adrie didn't understand at all. To him a stud was a two-by-four and a sire was a king. No, he didn't know what they were talking about; it was all Greek to him.

Huib said: "For that sire, I had to pay fifteen guilders."

"That is a lot of money for one shot." The farm hand replied.

Huib Zwaal said: "Yes it is, but I can't do it myself. Beside, every day, the bull is fed a pail of raw eggs to be able to provide the studs which cost money, too."

At this time they started to laugh and were looking at Adrie to see if he was laughing too. This time he had those people figured out. Huib had told a silly joke and the farm hand had to laugh because if the boss tells a joke, everybody laughs. Well, Adrie wasn't working for Huib Zwaal so why should he laugh; he didn't like his stupid jokes and wasn't going to laugh.

Some time later at his uncle's farm, he heard his uncle say that the cow had to be bred. Adrie didn't quite understand what he meant because he didn't know the difference between breeding and brooding, to him it sounded that he meant brooding. This he had to see; a chicken broods her eggs for six weeks before you can expect little chicks, he wondered how long the bull would take.

Those cows had names. The bull man said: "Look Joe, what a pretty cow. Her name is Marie. Do your job Joe!" The way it worked out the bull did a snow job when he was breeding the cow; he was finished in five minutes and walked away with his tail between his legs. When the calf was delivered after nine months, Adrie started to see the bull differently. He was a fast worker; what the chicken does in six weeks he could accomplish in 5 minutes. Of course, he had it all buggered up because the bull was breeding and the chicken was brooding. It was just too complicated for a little boy to understand.

Finally, he had it all figured out and knew all about the birds and the bees. Wrong again; those people always came up with something strange which he didn't understand. A couple of years later his uncle said to his farm hand that the cow had to be bred, but this time he would take the iron bull to do it. A bull was made out of flesh and bones Adrie thought, so an iron bull sounded like bull to him.

The big day came and instead of a bull man with a bull, the vet came in his car. Adrie saw no iron bull and no beef bull and wondered what was going on. After the vet had examined the cow, he went to his car, came back with a little bike pump, put a little cylinder in the pump and shoved the hose up the cow's rear end. He started to inflate the cow with his pump and after a while he said that he was finished.

Adrie couldn't figure it out at all and asked the vet what he had in his bike pump. The vet answered: "It's not a bike pump, it's an injector and I put semen in it."

This was the craziest thing Adrie had ever heard, seamen in a little pump. He had seen a magician pull a rabbit from a hat but seamen in a pump? This guy probably figured that he still believed in Santa Claus so he could tell him anything. Why would he stuff the cow's behind full with seamen? Seamen are sailors; this cow wasn't a battle ship.

Of course they were talking about artificial insemination which made its debut in those days. It changed the life of the bull forever. There are no amorous trips to the farms anymore where cows are waiting with a heart full of love. It completely buggered up the bull's sex life.

The bull had a good life before, going from farm to farm to impregnate all those pretty cows. Now he is dreaming and waiting at the lab till the vet comes to milk him. Never thought to see the day that they would milk a bull, he has no udders but they milk him anyway. The bull thinks with melancholy about the good old time, when a bull was a bull. He had to do an honorable job, whispering love words in the cow's ear, while the cow's heart was full of love for him when he did his duty to keep the society going. Even a bull could become depressed and have need for a psychiatrist.

People are replaced by an iron machine and bulls are replaced by an iron bull; it's enough to make everybody crazy, bulls included. The days of the wandering bull belong to the past. Honorable professions such as bull walker and stallion walker, where a man with his bull or stallion goes from farm to farm to peddle studs have disappeared.

(Oh yes, the cow joke! I came to a farm and saw a cow with three legs and asked the farmer what had happened to the cow's leg. The farmer said: "The cow still gives a lot of milk and we can't eat the cow all at once. The cow can walk on three legs so we have started to eat one leg.")

Pigeons mate for life and when their mate dies they seldom take on another mate. The female lays two eggs in spring and the happy couple takes turns to brood the eggs. During the night, the female broods the eggs and in the day time the male has his turn. After two weeks of brooding the little pigeons make their entry into the world and are kept alive with pigeon milk for a few weeks.

When one of the pigeon owners told Adrie that pigeons give milk, he thought the guy was kidding. Pigeons are not mammals and have no tits so how could they possibly give milk? No, he didn't believe that. The story got worse when the guy told him that the female and the male pigeon both give milk. Who the hell did the guy think he was kidding? Adrie told the guy to tell such bull stories to kids who still believed that the stork delivers the babies.

Even if he had believed that the female pigeons give milk, it never happens that the male gives milk, he was sure about that. A cow gives milk but a bull doesn't and even with people, only the female gives milk. The guy got cheesed off and said: "Oh, a wise guy that knows it all, you think you know everything about the birds and the bees. Let me tell you, you don't know bugger all. Come to my shed and I'll show you pigeon milk."

Seeing is believing. Adrie had it right that a pigeon doesn't have any tits. Instead, male and female both have glands in their crops from which some kind of milk flows. Little pigeons can't suck tits anyway, so they drink their milk the way they take water. Adrie had to admit that the guy was right that he didn't know bugger all about pigeons, but he was learning. It would be better for him to go away from this smart guy before he showed him the stork delivering a baby. That would be the day!

EARLY SEX EDUCATION

Jaap Dalm was all set after he started to work for the ship yard Boele in Bolnes. With his job as crane operator he had a good steady income for his growing family. Actually, he could thank Farmer Beet for firing him and running him out of town. It had led him to greener pastures and a job with a future. Working for farmers for little money and being abused to top it off was no future.

With all the good things of life he had, there was only one short coming, he had four daughters but he didn't have a son. After the stork had delivered four girls, he made an exception and delivered a boy when he came the fifth time. Jaap was in the clouds from happiness and his little son was his pride. He was spoiled rotten and could do no harm in Jaap's eyes. When the boy was only two years old, he poked the stove. He had seen how his dad poked the stove and "monkey see, monkey do." Jaap had no objection; everybody who came had to see what a two year old boy could do.

The pleasure was short lived. One day, when the boy was playing, he pulled himself up on a tablecloth. Unfortunately, there was a sewing machine on the tablecloth which slid with the tablecloth off the table. When the sewing machine fell on the boy's head, it broke his neck and he died the same night in the hospital. That was very sad especially since the stork didn't come anymore.

Very few outings occurred during the Depression years. The reason for that was that an outing couldn't cost anything and that limits you quite a bit. Yes, that was the good old time. Only when an aunt or uncle had a birthday would there be an outing, provided that they didn't live too far away. If it wasn't within walking distance, they couldn't go.

There were a couple of aunts and uncles who lived a spit away. Make that a whole bunch of spits worth a five minutes walk. Aunt Dirkje and Uncle Jaap didn't live that close, they lived in Bolnes, a town about six miles from where Arie and Ko were living with their family. It was a stiff one and a half hours walk, which didn't kill anybody since everybody was used to walking. Arie was the only one who had a bike and since you can't seat four people on one bike, they had to walk when they went to Bolnes for a visit.

Adrie will never forget those outings. It caused considerable hardship for him to get there, not that he couldn't walk that far, he was a tough kid. You had to be tough in a tough time; he had little choice. The real problem was that he was only six years old and he couldn't walk that far without going to the bathroom. It was quite a busy road which made it impossible to sit at the side of the road with your pants down, lest he'd be caught red handed with his pants down. For a boy it wasn't hard to have a leak, you could always pee against a tree but if the big job had to be done Adrie was in trouble.

Of course, his mother insisted that he went to the bathroom before they left. He tried but if you don't have to go, you don't have to go. After he had walked for about an hour the situation changed in a hurry. All of a sudden, he had to go and if you've got to go, you've got to go. Adrie's mother said: "Think of something else, don't think that you've got to go."

It's easy to give that advice if you don't have to go yourself but it didn't help Adrie a bit. He was sweating bricks wondering if he was going to make it. On one occasion when they arrived, his mother said: "I thought you had to go to the bathroom?"

Adrie said: "Not anymore because I already did."

After dirtying his pants there was a major problem that his pants had to be washed and of course he hadn't brought a pair of spare pants with him. That created another problem; his aunt and uncle had four daughters but no boys so they had no small pants. Since he hadn't arrived in a nudist colony he had to put on a pair of panties and a skirt from his cousin. That sparked some objection from Adrie's side. No boy would ever put girl's clothes on, that wasn't masculine at all.

No use to tell you who won the argument. His mother was bigger and stronger than Adrie was and he ended up walking in girl's clothes to his chagrin. Nobody, but nobody, could persuade him to come and play outside, not on your life!

Actually, they were nice outings if he managed not to poop his pants. Cleaning up and walking in girl's clothes was plain murder. Adrie's uncle had four daughters which made him rather fond of Adrie. When the family came to visit his uncle, he was always glad to see Adrie; he probably thought of his own son who died in an unfortunate accident. He treated Adrie as if he was his own son and Adrie was allowed anything except pooping on the table. If he was pooping his pants his uncle didn't care; he didn't have to clean that up so that was alright. Adrie was even allowed to play with his radio, everything was o.k.; he could do no wrong. His uncle made good money and whenever they were visiting, there was always money for an ice cream cone and candies so it was no wonder that Adrie liked those visits.

On one of their visits, Uncle Jaap had just moved and lived in a house owned by the shipyard. The house was built within the extreme boundaries of the shipyard which was a row of 12 houses on the dyke. You could only enter those houses in the front from the dyke. If you wanted to enter the houses through the backdoor you had to go through the gate of the shipyard.

Another peculiar thing about those houses was that they didn't have a toilet. The inhabitants had to use the toilets of the shipyard. When Adrie visited their new house for the first time, he couldn't find the bathroom. His aunt said that he had to go out of the back door, walk across the shipyard and use the bathrooms of the shipyard. Adrie wasn't sure if he knew what she meant. This was the craziest thing he ever had heard in his entire life. Apparently he had the look on his face as if he saw water burning, but the problem was solved instantly. There were volunteers to show him where the bathroom was, three of his female cousins volunteered to walk with him to the bathrooms.

Those were the strangest toilets Adrie had ever seen, they were built right over the water. There was a two by ten mounted over the water on which you could sit with your pants down. Everything that you discarded fell right into the water and would be carried off with the current. This was probably the last practical invention of those early times; there was an ever lasting flush with no water bill to pay. A rope was strung in front of the toilets which you could grab so that you wouldn't fall backwards into the water. They had thought of everything; nobody wants to fall backwards into his own dirt.

Those funny bathrooms were closed on the front and the sides. The back was facing the river; nobody was there to spy on you. There were also dividers in this long bathroom so you had your own private cubicle to do your business. A plank with a hole in it was the only thing lacking. Probably an economist had built the bathrooms and he had cut all corners possible. It was a smart design geared for the Twentieth Century.

It was real nice of those girls to show him where the bathrooms were, except Adrie didn't smell the rat when they were so helpful showing him around, but he was soon to find out. They made sure that he used the end bathroom so that they could throw rocks behind him, from the side into the water, while he was sitting on the toilet. Barely was he sitting on the two by ten and holding onto the rope for dear life, when a couple of big splashes occurred behind him. He got wet to his belly button and he wondered what was happening. It didn't seem to him that there were such big fish in the river to make big splashes like that. When he heard his cousins laugh, he knew that they had something, if not all, to do with it. A couple more big splashes followed which made him cut short the operation considerably.

It wasn't hard to cut down on time because his cousins had been very friendly to wash his behind. You couldn't beat that with a piece of paper. This was a bathroom which was half a century ahead of its time. An ever flushing bathroom with a water bum cleaning apparatus was at least half a century away. You could say that this bathroom was very refreshing and it saved you a lot of time when you had to speed up the operation. What else do you want from a bathroom?

When Adrie came out of the bathroom, the girls were laughing. There was nothing that Adrie could laugh about, he was soaked and couldn't see the fun of it. To him, it was a sick joke to play on an innocent little boy.

One of the workers of the ship yard had been watching and told Adrie: "We also have a lot of fun with those bathrooms. If we want to play a joke on one of the workers, we throw bundles of straw in the river and set them afire. When they are floating with the river current past the bathrooms, the workers are leaving in a big hurry or they burn their butts.

It was Adrie's habit to study everything. Things he didn't know much about were the prime target of his studies. There was one such a thing he knew practically nothing about; it was about the birds and the bees, that's why he studied them.

After years of study, he was an expert in the bees and the birds and knew all about them. Everything has its reason, he found out. When in fall the birds migrate South they fly in V formation but one leg of the V was longer than the other one. Studying the problem gave him the answer why this was so. According to his humble opinion, one leg had fewer birds than the other leg which consequently made the leg shorter.

Kees Meuzelaar next door of the Demerwes had a son called Kees Meuzelaar. He was an only child and wanted a baby sister. When he asked his father and mother where the babies came from, they didn't tell him that the stork brought them but in this case they told him that boys came out of the red cabbage and girls came out of the white cabbage. Those people had it coming! Kees Meuzelaar was a vegetable grower and his son decided to get himself a baby sister. He took a big knife and cut open all the white cabbages but no baby girl was found.

(One stork was talking to another stork about her growing up stork boy and said: "This little stork wants to know where he came from.")

(When a little rabbit asked the same question of his mother, his mother said: "A magician got you out of a high hat. Stop with all those annoying questions!"

Most of the parents told their kids that the stork brought the babies and when the kids asked where the stork got them, the answer was that the stork got the babies from heaven. *(Today's stork doesn't fly with babies around anymore; he now has a test tube in his beak.)*

Actually, Adrie wasn't interested in where he came from, the question he popped was: "Why do girls wear skirts and boys pants?"

The answer he got was: "Girls can't pee through a fly when they go to the bathroom so they have to pull their panties down." That was a reasonable explanation, but actually Adrie knew that already because dogs are the same, the female sits and the male lift his leg. Females are sure different than males he observed.

Wolves and dogs are the same in mating; when they are in heat their glands secrete a strong smelling substance, which is mixed with their urine and attracts a male from many miles away. When wolves and dogs mate they become love locked to insure insemination. Adrie used to watch mating dogs in the street which were love locked. At one time the owner tried to retrieve his dog but he only could take two dogs, the other dog was attached to his dog. He went into his house, returned with a pail of water and threw it over the dogs. The dogs tried to run away and all of a sudden there were two dogs again.

When Adrie was growing up there was no sex education, even talking about sex was taboo. Naturally, growing-up kids were miss-informed; they have to get their knowledge from hearsay which is not admissible in court. Combining what they heard and saw, they got the wrong picture and thought that people are like dogs to become love locked when they have sex.

One time when Adrie was already grown up, he happened to over-hear an interesting conversation from a couple of kids. According to one kid, he had seen a young couple at the edge of a ditch having sex. He threw stones in the water to make them wet. The guy got mad and said to the kid: "Why the hell don't you bugger off before I grab you and beat the crab out of you."

The kid said: "I called his bluff and told him to go to hell because he couldn't get up when he was love locked."

According to the kid, the guy couldn't get up; it was exactly the way he had figured. Lucky for the kid, the guy didn't get up. Would the kid ever have been surprised if the guy had jumped up to grab him to make good on his threat.

At one time when they were visiting Uncle Jaap Dalm, Adrie went for a walk with his cousins. After they returned home from their walk it was supper time and after supper they played a game. When it was time to go to bed, the adults were discussing where everybody would sleep. They had a problem it seemed because you can't put boys and girls in the same bed they said. Adrie was the problem because he was the only boy.

They had three double beds; one was used by Uncle Jaap and Aunt Dirkje. Willie could sleep with one of her cousins on the other double bed and the two other cousins had to give up their bed for Adrie's father and mother. His two cousins had to sleep in the loft in a corner and Adrie had to sleep in the opposite corner on a home made bed. That was far enough apart Adrie's mother thought. Adrie was only nine years old and posed no danger for the girls and the girls wouldn't think about it to bother a boy. That was nice thinking but she had misfigured on the powers of nature.

Adrie's mother tucked him in and decided that everything was under control. She left to spend some more time with her relatives and Adrie was just waiting in his strange bed till Mister Sandman would come to close his eyes till the next morning.

Barely after Adrie's mother had left, his cousins started to call him; they said they wanted to talk to him. Curious as to what they had up their sleeve, Adrie left the safety of his bed to see what they were up to. When he was standing beside their bed, they wanted him to come in their bed and opened up the blankets. Both girls were stark naked and Adrie had no intention to sleep between two naked girls so he went in a hurry back to his own bed. Luckily Adrie was only nine years old, so nothing could happen. His mother might as well have tucked him in between his cousins but little did she know what growing up girls would do.

Adrie was never told anything about the bees and the birds. Nowadays there is sex education at school but in those days kids were never taught anything. Because of lack of education about the bees and the birds, girls didn't even know about their periods when they started.

(Of course, we have jokes about this. A growing up boy had always played with the growing up girl of the neighbors. When the girl got her first monthly period, she had no idea what was happening. Nobody had told her.

She thought she was bleeding to death so she started to cry. The boy asked: "What's the matter with you?"

"I can't tell you because I can't talk about it," the girl said.

"What do you mean?" the boy asked, "that you can't talk about it. We always played together, don't start acting stupid now."

The girl said: "I'm bleeding."

"Where are you bleeding?" the boy asked. "Let me have a look at it."

When the girl lifted her skirt, the boy looked underneath it and said: "No wonder that you are bleeding, somebody cut off your dink.")

(Back in Ireland, a boy and a girl were playing together. It was a sweltering hot day so they decided to go for a swim to cool off. They both undressed and the boy was looking with amazement at the girl. He said: "My mother told me that Protestants are different than Roman Catholics but I never had thought that they are that different.")

(There are even jokes about grown up men.

A woman on her way to the hospital to deliver her baby couldn't make it. In front of the hospital, right on the side walk, the baby started to come. She shouted to a passing man: "Pull the baby out!"

After he had pulled the baby out, the new mother yelled at him: "Spank the baby on the bottom."

The man spanked the baby on the bottom and said to the baby: "You naughty kid, you should stay out of there. This spanking serves you right!")

GOING APE

During the summer holidays, there was one day reserved to go ape. Going to the zoo was pretty well the only outing Adrie and Willie had besides the visits to relatives. It was a treat for which their mother had to save a long time to make it possible for them to see their distant relatives, the apes.

There used to be an old zoo where all the animals were caged in a little cage that gave them no more room than on Noah's ark. In the new zoo things were looking up for the animals. The zoo had improved quite a bit upon the old monkey cage of that time. Unfortunately, a zoo tried to get as many different species as possible but the new zoo had spent a lot of money to exhibit the animals in a more natural environment.

Indeed, the Rotterdam Zoo had quite a collection of different apes. There were gorillas, chimpanzees, orang-utans and some smaller monkeys, enough to go to the Planet of the Apes and return to the planet of the apes. There was also a huge aquarium for the fish and an aviary for the birds. There was no petting area as yet where the children can play with tame animals. Progress was coming but it went at a snail's pace.

In the old zoo, when Adrie was admiring a monkey through the bars, it always made him wonder who was the monkey because he was watching the monkey through the bars but by the same token the monkey watched him through the bars. The monkey could have thought that Adrie was the monkey.

A day at the Zoo was quite an outing. They had to get up early to make it worth their while because they were going to spend a lot of money that day. There were the three of them which meant three times ten cents for the tram, plus three times ten cents for admission tickets to the zoo. Top that off with a one cent ice-cream cone for Willie and Adrie and a bag of peanuts for the apes. And of course they had to return home by the tram wich was another 30 cents. That day's outing came to a whole guilder which three people spent in one day.

They walked to the electric tram. If they had taken the bus to join up with the electric tram, it would have cost them another 30 cents. In that case the day's outing would have cost them over one guilder which was too much for their budget. Their weekly income was only 10 guilders and spending a whole guilder on entertainment was a lot of money.

The Zoo was a treat for the kids but even the ride in the electric tram was something to talk about. It was just recently that the city of Rotterdam had replaced the old horse drawn streetcar with an electric tram. In The Netherlands, they were actually far behind with electric streetcars. In Germany and the U.S. they had already electric street cars by the early 1900's while the horse drawn tram still performed in Rotterdam. They were late having electric trams in Rotterdam but once they had them they never got rid of them.

(Today, the City of Rotterdam still moves its people with electric trams. Most cities in Europe and elsewhere abandoned the electric tram decades ago but Rotterdam is still going strong. In the meantime they also have a Metro but transportation with the tram is still a great way of transportation.)

Of course, they had been unlucky; the tram went every twenty minutes but slipped just away in front of their very nose. They had to wait almost twenty minutes before the next tram came but finally there it was. Adrie was going to make sure that he was going to catch this tram and his mother had to hold him back or he would have jumped on the moving tram.

The tram ride was an eye opener for him, especially when they crossed the Meuse bridges which were very big and long. All the bridges Adrie had seen so far were across a wide ditch to make it possible for the farmers to get into their fields. The longest was perhaps 30 feet long and 15 feet wide so that a horse and cart could go across. Those Meuse bridges were traffic and train bridges that opened for the ship traffic. Rotterdam was a big harbor city and ships were just as important as trucks, perhaps even more important.

There was even a train crossing the bridge; Adrie had never seen that before, everything was new and exciting to him. When they reached their destination, the tram ride came to an end. The zoo was in sight and Adrie wasn't sorry that he had to get out of the tram.

After they had obtained access to the zoo, they studied the program to find the time of day that different animals were being fed. That way they could also see the trainer and the tricks the animals knew.

Birds of the same kind flock together they say. If Adrie looked at all the throngs of people who were gathered around the monkey cage, he could say: "Amen." Who ever had made up that saying had it right. Luckily, the apes were well mannered. Sometimes you can have some ill behaving primates that throw dung at the people.

Apes are always funny but there were more exciting animals they wanted to see. The elephant was a big animal; it was even bigger than his uncle's horse. He wasn't the only one who was astonished at the size of the elephant.

(There was a man who said to his wife: "It ain't right that a big elephant has to stay in a little cage like that while a little bird has the whole sky to fly in."

Shortly after, a flock of birds flew over and made a deposit on the man's head. His wife said: "Be glad dear, that the big elephant is in a little cage and not flying in the big sky. If a herd of elephants would fly over you would have to run for your life.")

Next, they saw the giraffe which was so friendly that it ate peanuts out of their hands. There was a feeding trough for the giraffe which was placed high enough that the giraffe didn't have to bend over to eat. He could eat standing up like in nature. A little boy asked his father: "Why does the giraffe has that long a neck?"

His father replied: "He has a long neck so that he can reach his feeding trough." Ha, Ha, you can sure learn a lot in a zoo.

After feeding their relatives and looking at the elephants and the ice bears, it was time for a snack. They couldn't afford to eat in a restaurant, so they had brought along some sandwiches and lemonade.

The afternoon was spent viewing the tropical indoor garden, where they even saw a banana tree. One of the greatest attractions by far was a giant pond with a big water plant called Victoria Regina. Leaves of that plant were so big that a kid could play on it.

Actually, it's a meat eating plant. Mosquitoes are drawn to the honey of the plant but as soon as they are inside the flower, it closes and traps the mosquito. When the flower opens up again, the mosquito has been absorbed by the flower which is now pink instead of white.

One of the greatest things for the kids was without a doubt the recreation ground and a significant amount of time was spent on the swings, seesaws and merry go round. Back home, they had something to talk about; they had talked about it for weeks before the scheduled event took place and they would talk about their daytrip for a long time to come but not that night. They were tired alright when they came home; it had been a long day that had started with a brisk 45 minutes walk to catch the tram and ended with a 45 minutes walk to get home.

(Noah's Arc was the very first zoo and several other people have kept animals after until animal parks became a common thing in cities. We can thank Noah who saved the animals from the Great Flood. If it hadn't been for him we would have had no animals. In order to keep an adequate supply of animals, the zoos have to breed the animals which is a problem. Some species don't breed very well when they are in captivity and others breed so much that there is a surplus of animals. Euthanizing those animals has created problems with animal groups that are protecting their rights and went as far as suing the animal parks. In order to prevent those problems the zoos are now using contraceptives for their animals. This makes me smile because I wonder how you are going to talk an elephant into using a condom. However there is a pill nowadays for everything and vasectomies are also done on animals.)

(And how are you going to protect an elephant of becoming pregnant when she is having sex with an ant, when the ant is refusing to wear a condom? Explanation needed I guess.

An elephant in the jungle was being hunted by an ivory poacher. The hunter laid on his elephant gun and aimed at the elephant. Just when the hunter was going to pull the trigger an ant climbed on the hunter's leg and bit him. Luckily for the elephant, the shot missed and the elephant made her get away. The elephant was very thankful to the ant and said: "You saved my life, is there anything I can do to please you?"

"I'm as happy as a lark," the ant said, "How can you possibly please me?"

The elephant said: "Think about it for a while, there must be something that I can do to make you happy."

After a while the ant started to giggle and the elephant wanted to know why. "No, I can't tell you that," the ant said, "it is absolutely too crazy."

The elephant insisted that the ant would tell her what was so funny. Finally the ant said: "OK. I'll tell you but it is absolutely crazy. I always wanted to have sex with an elephant."

"O.K.", the elephant said and lowered her tail to give the ant an opportunity to get up that high. After the ant had been quite busy for a while, the elephant thought: "I better please this ant and pretend that I enjoy it."

In order to fake pleasure, the elephant started to moan and groan. The ant tapped the elephant on her behind and said: "Take it easy girl, the first time always hurts."

Why do we have pink elephants? It makes an elephant blush when she is having sex with an ant.)

THE BEACH PARTY

On the beach and at the sea,
That's where we love to be.

Uncle Jaap in Bolnes had taken his daughters to the zoo several times. One time when he visited he said to Adrie's father: "I'm fed up with going to the zoo to look at my relatives. I'm tired of looking at apes and feeding them. If I want to see an ape all I have to do is look into the mirror."

That remark was worth a laugh but everybody knew he had something else up his sleeve. They were waiting patiently till he was finished with his jokes and continued with the rest of it. He had seen an ad in the paper in which was advertised a day's boat trip from Rotterdam all the way to Hoek van Holland. You could board the boat in Rotterdam and after a two hour voyage you would arrive in Hoek van Holland. One could stay all day at the beach and swim in the sea and at night the boat would take you back to Rotterdam. He concluded his speech: "It would be very nice for the kids to go out a day like that."

Everybody agreed and the motion passed unanimously. The great day came when they boarded the boat in Rotterdam and sailed all the way to Hoek van Holland without sails. Of course Adrie had to ask that dumb question when the captain announced the sailing time. Adrie just wondered where the sails were. "All boats used to have sails so they sailed," the captain explained. "Now we have engines to get the boat where we want it but the term sailing has remained. They couldn't find another good English word to say what they meant."

It was a good thing they had learned their geography at school, at least Adrie could check up on the Captain to be sure if he knew the way to Hoek van Holland. The only geography Adrie had learned so far was from the province where he lived which was good enough for this trip. A row of city and town names of their province went as follows:

Rotterdam, Schiedam, Vlaardingen, Maaslous,
Hoek van Holland, here is the crazy house.

That rhymed and that way it was easier to learn and remember. Indeed there was a crazy house in Maaslous where mentally disturbed people were institutionalized. Whenever you acted silly, they would always tell you that they would take you to Maaslous which was the only place that they could help you.

It looked as though they had learned it right at school. The towns passed by in the right order. However, there was one thing they hadn't taught the kids at school. After you pass Maaslous the river water becomes salt. Fresh water flows from the mountains into the river and the river drains the water into the sea. Since the river has an open connection with the sea, with high tide the fresh water is pushed back by the sea all the way to Maaslous.

Adrie certainly was a good kid for finding things out the unpleasant hard way. When he got thirsty, he found himself a tap to have a drink of water. There were two taps sitting one beside another. The taps looked the same but of course Adrie didn't know that the one tap was fresh drinking water and the other tap was river water. They had passed Maaslous so the river water had turned salt.

Naturally, Adrie made the wrong selection and picked the salt water tap. With a few unorthodox words, which he wasn't supposed to say, he vented his dismay about the crummy situation. That helped, the mate came to his rescue and explained that he had taken the wrong tap. The tap he had drunk from was water which was pumped from the river; it was meant for cleaning only and not for drinking. He added to his explanation: "If you want to wash your hands you need special salt water soap, the regular soap doesn't work with salt water."

Even if the water wasn't salt before Maaslous, he still shouldn't drink it because river water was polluted and not fit for consumption. It was a good thing that it was salt which made him spit it out in a hurry. That sure was a new one on Adrie; one tap for drinking and one tap for cleaning. The house he lived in had only one tap in the entire house and the water was good for everything. However, the lesson he had learned was one never to forget, the salt water from the tap tasted awful.

As soon as they arrived in Hoek van Holland, they went straight to the beach. Uncle Jaap gave Adrie a dime to spend that day and he looked at the dime with disbelief in his eyes. Never did he get more than one penny to spend for an ice-cream cone, that dime made him instantly rich. Uncle Jaap had a good job and didn't have to turn around every penny before he spent it so he could afford it.

Now Adrie was rich. He tried to figure out what he could do with all that money. An ice-cream cone cost one penny, if he put his money into ice-cream cones he could buy ten ice-cream cones. You could also buy an ice-cream waffle for three cents but that was spending money foolishly, he wasn't going to throw his money away like old paper. Easy come easy go, they say but money didn't come easy to him, it seldom happened that money came his way. He sure had to study this project of spending a whole dime for a while.

There was a whole row of stalls which merchants had set up to sell their goods to the public. All kinds of merchandise were offered for sale which made Adrie head for the stalls to view the merchandise. One stall had delicious yellow plums which made him drool when he looked at them. When he enquired what the plums cost, the fatso of a lady said: "They cost ten cents per pound."

If he bought the plums that would finish his whole dime with one purchase and he would have lost his entire fortune buying one item. In no way he was going to do that but the yellow plums did look attractive.

Adrie started to figure; a Dutch pound was five ounces, if a pound cost ten cents, an ounce of plums would cost two cents. If he bought an ounce of plums, he would still have eight cents of his dime left. That was smart figuring for a seven year old boy.

Cheerfully, Adrie went back to the stall with the yellow plums and told the fat lady, with the double under-chin, that he wanted an ounce of those yellow plums. Adrie never heard anybody laugh like that before. He thought she was getting a living fit, her big fat tummy was shaking and her boobs went up and down from laughter. It made Adrie think that she was churning the milk pretty good and pretty soon she would have buttermilk. Still laughing, she said: "The plums are sold per pound and that's the smallest unit to sell the plums for."

Adrie didn't think there was anything to laugh about but this big twit didn't appreciate that he knew his arithmetic that well. She probably was after his money and wasn't happy with two cents, she wanted it all or nothing. Well nothing it was, he had her all figured out with his glass eye, she was trying to bluff her way but she lost.

It's understandable that she never before had anybody ask for an ounce of plums. On the other hand, she could have given him one or two plums for his two cents, that wouldn't have hurt her at all. In a Dutch metric pound there were probably ten plums anyway. Instead of laughing she could have thought: "Smart boy," and admire him.

Anyway, she kept her plums and Adrie kept his money. For a starter, he thought it safe to spend one whole penny on an ice-cream cone. That would give him enough time to think about his problem as to what kinds of investments were safe. Before he had money, he didn't have a problem in the world and all of a sudden he had money and problems as well. As soon as you have money there is always some pan-handler that tries to screw you out of it. That's what he learned that very day.

While he was enjoying his ice-cream cone, he was weighing the pros and cons of any further investments. In no way was he going to make ducks and dragons of his money, he was not that foolish and was too close fisted for that. His eye fell on some liquorice and chewing-gum and at the end of the day he still had money left to take home. That money was good for a hungry day; it could be quite a while before he would get money again to buy candy.

TOO MANY HOLY DAYS

The following chapter needs reader discretion. The man that explained Christian holy days explained it most of the times rather well. However, he had his own opnion about those things which makes the reader of this book not always agreeing with his sometimes unorthodox statements and opinions. Quite often he got carried away and was skeptical about things and made a joke about it.

There was a New Year again with a brand new calendar that showed what day your birthday was and what date Easter and Witsunday was. When Adrie studied the calendar some more, he found that there were a lot of Holy Days that he never had heard of. That raised his curiosity.

The first of the Holy Days was January 6th which was called "Three

Wise Men Day." When he brought it up with his parents, his father knew all about that, he said: "Three Wise Men Day is called in Brabant Three Kings Day which is quite a celebration among the Roman Catholics. It is the remembrance that those Three Kings brought presents to Jesus when he was born.

In the province where we are living it is just a celebration within the walls of the church but in North Brabant all young girls went in a parade through the towns with an old hat on their head. They would sing:

Three Wise Men, Three Wise Men,
Give me a new hat.
My old one is threadbare,
But my father doesn't care.
He says your old hat is not too bad.
It still has a lot of wear.

Actually, it was an early Easter Bonnet Parade on which the young girls cashed in by getting a new hat. Those girls had surely learned the tricks of the trade at an early age to get something that they probably didn't need. Their father had it probably right that the old hat was still in a good shape which made the girls call on the Three Wise Men. They probably figured that the Three Wise Men had money to burn. The trouble is that once you give them a new hat, they'll insist that they have nothing to wear. In my judgement, I go with the father. How could it be possible that all those hats were threadbare at the same time and next year again? That's impossible to me but young girls are the women of the future and they evidently learned that trick fast."

Adrie's father knew about that Roman Catholic celebration because he had been working in Government Work Camps in North Brabant. He said: "They have all kinds of celebrations in Brabant. One of the celebrations is "Rooster on a stick." They bake roosters from dough, put some eyes in the roosters, stick them on a stick and parade through downtown."

The next Holy Day on the calendar was February 2nd and was marked as Candle Mass. Adrie could figure that it was a mass where they burned candles but his father and mother didn't know the answer to the question "Why?"

One day Adrie got a lot of information from his Uncle Jaap who came one day a bit early when his father and mother weren't home yet. Uncle Jaap knew a lot because he had been reading a lot of books. When Adrie asked him about the Holy Days on the calendar, Uncle Jaap knew all about it and he also had his own opinion about them. He looked the calendar over and said: "The Roman Catholic Church has the entire calendar year Holy Days which are dedicated to Jesus."

When Adrie asked him about the Candle Mass, Uncle Jaap knew all about it, he said: "Jesus was born when Marie wasn't married yet and the Jewish Laws consider a woman dirty when she has a baby out of wedlock. Therefore, the woman has to be cleansed 40 days after the birth of her illegitimate child. According to the Bible, Marie was conceived by the Holy Ghost. Jews don't believe this. They don't even believe that Jesus is the promised Messiah."

Uncle Jaap looked some more at the calendar and said: "Here is a good one; March 25th is Annunciation Day, exactly nine months before Christmas. That's the day that Mary was annunciated - make it impregnated - that's easier to understand. This annunciation was actually an announcement from the Angel Gabriel to Mary that she was to give birth to Jesus. Even the Angel Gabriel had his hands in this Immaculate Conception. I always thought that Gabriel was just a trumpet player hired for Doomsday but since Doomsday was a long time away, they used him as a courier as well.

Immaculate conception is sometimes confused with Virgin Birth. According to the Roman Catholic Church doctrine: 'The Virgin Mary, though conceived naturally, was from the moment of conception free from the stain of original sin.' The pope must have thought that people wouldn't believe in Virgin Birth anyway so he came up with a doctrine which was more acceptable."

(Why was Jesus not born in Saskatoon?

Because they couldn't find Three Wise Men or a Virgin in Saskatoon.)

Uncle Jaap looked at Adrie to see if he was still interested in his story and when he saw that Adrie loved it, he continued: "In The Netherlands this Annunciation Day was translated as being the day of Mary's Glad Tiding. As far as I'm concerned this wasn't a glad tiding at all that Mary was expecting a baby out of wedlock. After Joseph found out that Mary was pregnant, he wanted to leave Mary and was planning to take to his heels. Thus Gabriel visited Joseph and told him that he couldn't abandon a sinking ship. He said: 'Fear not, it's from the Holy Ghost. The Holy Ghost had it in for you.'

First this Gabriel gives you the shock of your life and then he says: 'Fear not.' That's an angel for you. Of course it's up for grabs whether Gabriel prevented Joseph from taking off or Mary's father. This whole thing could have been a shotgun wedding with Mary's father presiding, telling Joseph: 'Don't you dare to leave Mary alone with her baby, you scoundrel, or I'll spill your guts.'

Since the shotgun hadn't been invented yet, Mary's father was probably standing with a club in the doorway as a sentry, to make sure Joseph would marry her. That would have made it a club wedding. Mary's father wasn't as easy to get along with as the angel Gabriel. He probably said: 'Don't try to make your get-away you dirty man, first you get Mary pregnant and now you want to abandon her? Forget it!' It's hard to believe that March 25th was a day of glad tidings for Mary or Joseph and Mary's father couldn't have been all that glad either, with Mary coming home with a belly full of bones.

It's not that I want to poke fun at the Bible or the Gospel but some things don't add up to my knowledge. There are questions such as: 'How come Mary was the mother of Jesus and Joseph wasn't the father of Jesus?'

Even the theologians and the Pope acknowledged that there were a few flaws in the Gospel story. This is where the doctrine of the Roman Catholic Church came in to explain what really happened, so dumb people like me could understand it as well. I know I am a pain but I can't help that; I think about those things."

Ash Wednesday was marked on the calendar and Adrie thought that this was the day that they took the ashes out of the fireplace, but his Uncle Jaap said that it was forty days before Easter and the beginning of Lent and also the beginning of forty days of fasting.

Adrie knew all about Palm Sunday, he had learned that at school. Uncle Jaap said: "Palm Sunday is the Sunday before Easter, the first day of Holy Week. It was the day that Jesus swiped a donkey. I'm not kidding; it's all according to the Gospel; read all about it in your Bible.

Jesus was walking with his disciples to Jerusalem. When they reached the town of Bethany, he was so tired that he needed a ride. You couldn't hitch-hike in those days, so he said to two of his disciples: 'Go into the village of Bethany where you'll find an ass with a colt tied, whereon yet never man sat; bring him hither and if any man asks 'why do you take the colt?' you'll answer: 'The Lord needs it.'

It never is difficult to find an ass; there are even people who make an ass of themselves. The disciples found it exactly as Jesus had painted it and when they tried to untie the colt, the owner asked indeed: 'Why do you take the colt?' and the disciples said: 'The Lord needs it.' It was that easy. The Bible doesn't relate what the owner said after the disciples made their get-away with the colt, but what was he going to say anyway, there were two disciples and only one of him.

I wonder if I could get away with that, if I could go to a farm to rip off a horse and tell the farmer that the Lord needs it. Maybe I can go to a car dealer and rip off a brand new Mercedes Benz and tell him that the Lord needs it. It wouldn't take long to get arrested and put in jail. Anyway, the disciples got away with it; the whole thing was real saucy. Those disciples were as bold as brass, but then they say: 'Fortune favors the bold.'

At one time, if you stole a horse, they would string you up on the highest tree. I don't know what they did with people that stole donkeys in those days, but I don't believe that there was no punishment. They could have crucified

Jesus for colt theft. However, they didn't know about it and tried to pin all kinds of things on Jesus, in order to incriminate him.

They didn't take any old ass, no, they took the colt which never had been used for riding purposes. Anyway, after Jesus had mounted the colt, people were putting palm branches on the road ahead of Jesus. That's why it's called Palm Sunday. In Jerusalem it's still customary that the Bishop rides on an ass (so you can see one ass on another ass) into Jerusalem the Sunday before Easter, accompanied by people who carry palm and olive leaves.

Every day of the Holy Week was a Holy Day. I don't know what people celebrated on Monday and Tuesday of that week. I don't know everything, but I do know that Wednesday was celebrated as the Day of Betrayal. It was the day that Judas conspired with the Jews to betray Jesus.

Maundy Thursday is next. This was the day that Jesus had his last meal with his disciples, the famous Lord's Supper. Jesus washed the feet of his disciples before supper because he couldn't stand the smell. This is all celebrated in different churches. On Maundy Thursday, there is a church service and Holy Communion is administered. Before the Holy Communion, the feet of the poor are washed. If you are rich you can wash your own dirty feet. It sure doesn't pay anymore to be rich.

Good Friday wasn't all that good in The Netherlands because you had to work and at night you had to go to church. It was a religious Holy Day but not a holiday, only Prince Bernhard and his kind had holidays. Those people you worked for weren't crazy to pay you for a day you didn't work; they didn't have a hole in their head, they never had heard about the stupid idea of getting paid for a day you didn't work. It would be ludicrous to pay your staff if they didn't work, you couldn't afford it.

Nobody worked except the farmer's hands. It was compulsory for all other people to have a day off to celebrate Good Friday. There was one more day that was a worry to the wage earners; it was Christmas when it was on a working day. If it was on a Sunday it didn't matter but on any other day there was a loss of wages. Compulsory Holy Days without pay were a curse; they were days of worry and concern to get through that week with one day without pay. If you didn't work you didn't get paid, it was as simple as that. I still can see my mother penny pinching weeks before Good Friday because she would have one day without pay. No, Good Friday wasn't good at all. I wonder why they ever called it Good Friday because it was also the day that the Jews crucified Jesus. It's the day that Christ died on the cross and some churches administer Holy Communion in that church service.

Holy Saturday was the day that Jesus was buried. It was a quiet day. After quiet Saturday came noisy Sunday when the angel rolled away the stone off the grave. Jesus didn't stay in his grave very long.

Sunday was the day that Christ was victorious over death. Some churches emphasize that Easter is a spring festival and they celebrate nature's renewal of itself out of the death of winter and stress that Christ did exactly the same. Some churches have sunrise services on Easter morning. At sunrise the service starts symbolizing the end of night (death) and the revival of hope in the hearts of the congregation. Actually those churches are half pagan and half Christian in their celebrations of Easter.

In The Netherlands they celebrate Easter Monday which is a Holy Day and a day you didn't work. Of course there was a Church Service on that day but most of the people didn't go to church and spent that day visiting with their family. That brought on some more Doomsday preaching from Reverend Young.

From the earliest times, Christians have kept Sunday as the weekly commemoration of the resurrection of Christ. They all gather (congregate) on Sunday because the first day of the week 'Jesus Christ the Saviour' rose from the dead. Sunday was actually a little Easter."

Adrie had been listening to all the revelations of his uncle with keen interest; he never had heard those things before. It was an eye opener. The way his uncle explained all those things was different than the Reverend explained things, his uncle made a joke out of a lot of things.

Uncle Jaap looked at Adrie to see if some of the stuff he was telling him had sunk in. He leafed through the calendar some more and said: "There was a day that Jesus was circumcised and a day that he was baptized by John the Baptist. There was also a Holy Day of Obligation. That was a day that Roman Catholics had to attend mass and weren't allowed to work. But there was a lot more to celebrate.

Sunday of Thomas.
Sunday of the Myrrh Bearing Woman.
Sunday of the Paralytic.
Sunday of the Samaritan woman.
Sunday of the Blind Man.
Sunday of the Pharisee.
Sunday of the Prodigal Son.
Sunday of abstention from meat.
Sunday of eating cheese.
St. Stephen's Day.
St. John the Apostle's Day.
St. Sylvester's Day.
Holy Mary Day.
Holy Joseph Day.

The people already observed all Fridays and were not allowed to eat meat. Fish was substituted at the meals. With all the Holy Days the people had two more Sundays on which they couldn't eat meat. First they had Sunday of abstention of meat and the following Sunday they had Sunday of eating cheese. That day they had to eat cheese so meat was out. They could have had Abstention of meat Sunday and Cheese Eating Sunday on the same day. If you don't eat meat you have to eat something so you could eat cheese. That way, they could have killed two stones with one bird, or was it two birds with one stone?

The Pope came to the conclusion that it was for the birds to have that many Holy Days. It was alright to pray for all those brave Saints but you couldn't see the forest because of all the trees. Therefore he started to prune the Holy Days. When he put down his pruning shears, the Holy Days were reduced to 36.

Roman Catholics had to observe all those 36 Holy Days. Only the Pope could cancel a Holy Day and he could also bring in a different Holy Day instead. The Irish managed to get permission to have St. Patrick's Day instead of Holy Joseph Day.

In order that all those Holy Days wouldn't interfere with doing work the Pope had all the Holy Days on a Sunday which made it easier to celebrate without interruption of work. However, the Pope decided that 36 feasts per year was too much. It came down to having three celebrations every month and he himself got tired of it.

The Pope must have been full of bull because in another Papal Bull the Pope narrowed the Christian Holy Days down to twelve after abandoning Cookie Eating Sundays. Through the years only six Religious Holy Days remained but they still put all the original Holy Days on the calendar. Not too many Roman Catholics pay attention to it."

Adrie wondered that with all those Holy Days why we didn't have Holy Cow Day. "Only in India," his uncle replied. In the meantime Adrie's father and mother had come home which ended the conversation that Adrie had enjoyed very much. Nobody else but his Uncle Jaap could tell stories like that.

Bad times didn't deter the kids from having a nice Christmas. Christmas was for the children and since Adrie was a kid, he could only benefit. He already had received his Christmas presents from St. Nick and was way ahead of the children who had to wait for Santa Claus to deliver the presents.

The reason that the Dutch children got their presents early was because St. Nick was hyper modern and came from Spain by steamboat. When St. Nick arrived with his steamship in The Netherlands, St. Nick was standing on the poop-deck waiting to get going. That's why the Dutch children had their presents way ahead of the English and Canadian children. Ha, Ha, Ha! Or is it Ho, Ho, Ho?

Actually Christmas is a strange feast, it is the only time of the year that you sing Christmas Carols in front of a dead tree and eat candies out of an old sock. Bon appetite! In The Netherlands, Christmas was a children's feast even though there was no exchange of gifts. The children in The Netherlands knew about Santa Claus but in The Netherlands he was called the Christmas Man, which was an appropriate name. Children in The Netherlands didn't care for the Christmas Man; they never got anything from him so why should they care about him?

Christmas is actually "Christ Mass," named by the Roman Catholic Church. In Canada it's also written as X Mass. The X stands for the Greek letter Chi of the word "Christas" which means "The anointed one."

Christmas in The Netherlands was a pure religious feast and that's where the doomsday preacher came in. This doomsday preacher could get very excited when he was preaching doom; he would hit his fist on the pulpit very hard. People always expected that sooner or later he would make firewood out of that pulpit. He had a religious complex and saw sin everywhere. According to him, people were changing the Christian Holy days to pagan holidays. Look who is talking; it wasn't that long ago that the Christians made Christian Holy days from the pagan holidays.

How soon they very conveniently forget! According to the doomsday preacher, the people took the meaning out of the Christian Holy days. When on Ascention Day the tulips were blooming, people didn't go to church, they were going to enjoy the endless tulip fields and to top it off, people had made a fair out of the Christmas celebrations, just to please themselves. It looked like the competition had moved in and he didn't like it a bit. He wanted all the people in the church, period! And all the time!

In England, people had altered one of the Christmas songs in 1936 after King Edward VIII had abdicated in order to marry Mrs. Simpson. Mrs. Simpson was a divorcee and marrying her was against the dogma of the Church of England so he was forced to step down. When Christmas came, the English people were singing:

Hark the Herald Angels sing,
Mrs. Simpson took our king.

The doomsday preacher didn't like it a bit; he said people shouldn't make fun by changing the lyrics of a Christmas Carol.

As children of Christian parents, Willie and Adrie had to go to Sunday School; that was compulsory. At Sunday School, the teacher would tell a story out of the Bible and the children would get some home work. Every week, they had to learn a verse from the Bible. If they knew that verse by heart, they would get as reward a little picture of Jesus with a Bible verse. They really poured the Bible right into the kids at a very early age.

Every week, the kids had to bring some money to the Sunday School. Somebody had to pay for the pictures of Jesus with the Bible verse. Wouldn't you know there was that catch again, it always cost money.

It is very interesting to know how Sunday School kids explain the teachings of the church. The Sunday School kids had a test and the children were asked what certain words meant. Some of the children came up with the following answers:

> "An epistle is the wife of an apostle."
> "Joan of Arc was Noah's wife."
> "Adultery is the sin of saying you are older than you really are."
> "With fast days you have to eat in a hurry."
> "A layman is a guy who lays in bed on Sunday morning."
> "Repent means shape up or ship out."
> "Fake doctrine happens when people receive the wrong medicine."

Not all kids are dumbbells; some kids are real bright and think.

The teacher at school asked the kids to dot down the "Seven Wonders of the World." Many kids dotted down, The Pyramids of Egypt, The Great Wall of China, The Panama Canal, The Grand Canyon and a few other well known important places. One girl was an exception, she wrote: the Seven Wonders of the World are:

1. Hearing.
2. Feeling.
3. Seeing.
4. Tasting.
5. Laughing.
6. Touching.
7. And loving.

I can see it that way that man made wonders are second to the wonders the little girl mentioned.

Now we are talking about how kids think about religion, we have the one of the Sunday School teacher who said: "Today I want you to write a letter to God."

One of the boys wrote:

"Dear God, I always read the fabulous stories in the Bible. They look a lot like the Wild West stories of John Wayne, who doesn't take flack from anybody. You are the same, when people didn't do what you told them to do. You booted Adam and Eve out of Paradise and you drowned all the people with the Great Flood except Noah and his family.

Another great story is how you helped the Israelis by drowning the Egyptian Pharaoh with his army in the Red Sea."

Once a year there was a big splash, called the Sunday School Party, which was on Christmas. The children had to learn all kinds of Christmas carols which they had to sing at the party. Their parents were also invited to give them a chance to see what the children had accomplished at the Sunday School.

A huge Christmas tree was in the front of the church and all children would get chocolate milk and a cookie. To top it off, each child would receive a whole orange. That might look like a meagre Christmas celebration but in those times that was great. Children were happy with very little.

The Sunday School teacher would tell an appropriate Christmas story which would bring the message of Christmas right home. And the children who had learned the Bible verses well had an extra reward coming. Each child would get a Christian book for the home library, which would get them a Christian library right at home. Those people thought of everything and didn't miss a trick.

Children who had been best in learning their verses would get the biggest and nicest books. Since Adrie had a photo copy mind, his score was perfect. Guess who received the nicest book? There were all kinds of incentives to learn your Bible verses well; first they gave you pictures and the ultimate reward was a book. The Reverend who handed out the books made a little hay out of this book business. He said: "The ultimate reward of learning your Bible verses is not the book I give to you; the greatest reward will be given by the Lord in the here-after!"

This was one of the times that Adrie couldn't agree with the Reverend. There were a lot of children who just couldn't learn a verse by heart; they had a low I.Q. and the Lord was going to punish them for that? Adrie was already blessed with a photo copy mind and got rewards; first with a picture of Jesus, then with a nice thick Christian book and finally with a better chair in the here-after or whatever other rewards the Lord had in mind. It looked that the Bible was right again with stating that "To the one who has shall be given." According to Adrie that was not righteous at all, but then who was he to say?

It's just that he felt sorry for the poor dumb kid; he was already dealt a poor hand to play with and then everybody gave him heck. First his parents raised the roof that he hadn't learned his Bible verse, and then the Sunday School teacher told him that he was lazy, followed by the Reverend and at last God would condemn him for something that he couldn't help!

The Christmas stories which the Sunday School teacher was telling were all fitting stories for the occasion and always had a message. One of those beautiful Christmas stories with a message follows:

It was on the day before Christmas Eve, that Jan Holm was steering his houseboat on one of the big rivers in The Netherlands. He lived with his family on the houseboat and they were on their way to the village where they all were born, to celebrate Christmas.

He had hoped to reach the village this day but drifting ice had slowed progress and he knew that he wasn't going to make it. It didn't bother him too much because he could do the last bit on Christmas Eve. They still would reach the village in due time to celebrate Christmas Eve in the little village church. That was, if the river didn't freeze over during the night. He steered his boat with a steady hand and glanced very worriedly over the icy river. Those icy floes were just too much for his wooden boat. The boat had some steel plates on the bow for protection, but that was all the protection there was against the sharp ice.

Sunset was near and there were a few hours boating needed to reach his destination. At dusk, he moored his boat carefully at the side of the river. There was a very cold and icy wind blowing from the North West which could very well mean that the river would freeze solidly during the night. His wife shared his sorrow after he went inside the boat for the night.

The next morning Jan Holm got up before the birds to view the situation. Wouldn't you know, the icy wind had done its work and the river was solidly frozen over. It looked like a dark and gloomy Christmas was in store for them. They couldn't reach the village to celebrate Christmas and moreover food supplies were running out.

Disappointed, he went down to the cabin where his wife was waiting for him. She could see on her husband's grim face that the news was not so good and made a meagre breakfast for Jan Holm and the children. All that they had left for supplies was some bread, coffee and sugar.

Before they ate their breakfast, Jan Holm said grace and added an extra prayer, asking the Lord to deliver them from the pack ice. They wanted more than anything else to reach the village and go to the little church to celebrate Christmas. In silence, they ate their bread with sugar and drank their hot coffee.

After breakfast, Jan Holm went to the deck for some fresh air and when he looked out over the river he couldn't believe his eyes. He saw an icebreaker coming down the river breaking up the river ice. Behind the icebreaker were some more houseboats that also had tried to reach the village. The icebreaker was leading the way and soon Jan Holm was following the icebreaker as well.

God hears all prayers, but he doesn't necessarily give what you ask. This time, God had heard their prayer and freed them from the ice bound river. He couldn't leave those people stranded in the ice floe; they wanted to reach the village very desperately to celebrate Christmas.

As soon as they reached the village, they prepared to go to church. They put their best clothes on and soon they were on their way. The chimes of the little church were already ringing and they had the nicest Christmas ever.

Yes, that was a heart warming story; you could get tears in your eyes from that. Even the Reverend was very much impressed; that story was right up his alley and he couldn't resist the temptation to throw in his two bits worth. He said that this was the true Christmas and that was the way Christmas should be. According to him: "Most people have made a pagan feast out of Christmas, just to suit and please themselves and Christmas has become a fair instead of a proper Christian celebration!"

It sounded like a broken record that repeats the same thing over and over again. To most of the people, it looked that he had some kind of a religious complex and saw sin and wrongs everywhere, instead of seeing good in his fellow man. The Reverend was probably a classic case of what the eye sees the brain thinks.

A year goes by fast and there was another Christmas story with a heart warming educational message:

There was a very run-down family living in town. The husband was a drunk, the woman was lazy and if she wasn't gossiping, she was lying in her bed. Her children weren't taken care of properly and were running around in rags.

Next door to them lived a very fine Christian family. (I suppose that it wouldn't have been a very fine family if it hadn't been a Christian family.) This year, they had decided to have a Christmas project with which they would bring Christmas to other less fortunate families.

They didn't have to look very far for their project; the less fortunate people were living right next door to them. On the morning of Christmas Eve, the woman went next door armed with cleaning equipment. She rang the door bell and told the surprised woman that she was going to help her clean up the place, so they could celebrate Christmas Eve together.

Soon, they were working like a team of horses and before they knew it everything was spick-and-span and was shining as if everything was brand new. In the meantime it was already noon and after a fast bite to eat, they went together to buy a Christmas tree and other Christmas decorations. They put the Christmas tree in the living room and decorated the room beautifully. After they put the candles into the tree they set the table for Christmas dinner. The daughter of the Christian lady had cooked the Christmas dinner and they were going to celebrate Christmas all together that night.

The sloppy woman couldn't get over it that this was her house. Her place looked always like a dump but now it looked beautiful and after they lit the candles, the living room looked real cosy. She was surprised at what a few hours of hard work could accomplish.

Her husband was still in the pub and finally he stood up reluctantly. He dragged his feet on his way home because there was nothing to go home for. In his house there was no coziness to be found, everything was a heck of a mess. When he passed some houses where the candles were already lit spreading a soft light through the living room, he got homesick for the time that his place was also a nice place. Where did it all go wrong?

Before he could make up his mind what had gone wrong, he had arrived at his house. When he stumbled into the living room, he was dumbfounded when he saw the attractively decorated living room. He must have entered the wrong house with his drunken head; this was definitely not his house. But there was his wife standing by the Christmas tree; she still had her old dirty clothes on. In the confusion and with all the hard work she had done there had been no time to clean herself. His wife said: "Sit down quick, drink some hot coffee and change into your best clothes. The neighbors are coming to celebrate Christmas with us."

When they had their best clothes on, they looked sheepishly at one another; they hardly recognized each other when they were dressed up. They looked like complete strangers in their best clothes; there never had been a reason to dress up, that was too much trouble. That was the reason that they had slid down to become lazy people and drunks.

The doorbell rang and when they answered the door, the neighbors came in with the Christmas dinner. As soon as they were all seated, the neighbor said grace and after dinner he read the Christmas story from the Bible. With attention, the distraught people listened to the so familiar story. It was such a long time ago that they had read from the Bible. Everything was very beautiful and it was the best Christmas they had had for a long time. The morale of this story is to get into the real Christmas spirit by bringing Christmas to others!

When the Reverend rose to his feet, he said that this was the nicest Christmas story he'd ever heard. He said that last year, too, and it wasn't hard to guess that he would say the same thing again next year. He always said the same thing but this time he surprised everybody by not mentioning that people had made a fair out of Christmas.

It seemed that the Reverend was very much impressed with the story and he wanted to hear it once more but this time out of the mouth of the children of the Sunday School. He said: "Who can tell this story in his own words?"

After this heart warming story, everybody had tears in their eyes and a lump in their throat, so there were no volunteers. The Reverend made it a little bit more attractive and said: "The kid who tells us the story will receive an orange as reward."

That helped to get some cooperation; one of the older boys, Kees Kraak, stood up and said that he would have a crack at it. He did a rather good job but the Reverend wasn't completely satisfied. Kees Kraak forgot to mention that after the Christmas meal, they read the Christmas story out of the Bible. The Reverend asked: "Didn't you forget something Kees?"

Kees replied: "I don't think so, Reverend."

"What did they do after dinner?" the Reverend asked.

Kees saw the light and said in haste: "They read the Christmas story out of the Bible."

"Good, my boy," the Reverend said, "Here is your orange!"

That might sound like a lot of trouble for a little reward. An orange was quite something during the hard Depression time. People had lots of apples and pears in their garden but the oranges had to come from Spain or Israel and imports were very expensive. The best oranges came from Israel which were the Jaffa oranges. They were big, juicy and even the pulp was edible, contrary to some oranges which are not juicy and have tough pulp which isn't digestible.

Yes, Kees Kraak forgot the most important part of the Christmas story; he really slipped up, but so did the Reverend. He really missed the boat by not mentioning that this was the real Christmas, contrary to the fair people had made out of it. Maybe the Reverend got old and mellowed some what.

After the Christmas celebrations, there was New Year's Eve. It was very lucky to have Christian celebrations, the church made sure about that. New Year's Eve wasn't classified as a holiday but if you had a good boss, he would tell you at 3.00 p.m. to buzz off; you couldn't make the year good at that stage anymore anyway.

It meant that you were to go home, put your monkey suit on to go to church at 7.00 p.m. You couldn't just say good bye to one year and start a new year without being told how timely and temporarily we are. For a welcome change, the Reverend had only a one hour service instead of the normal one and a half hours. He probably thought about the same line as the boss that you couldn't make the year good anymore at that stage so the heck with it.

If he hadn't saved your soul yet, he'd try again next year, besides he had to celebrate himself.

Of course, they had to thank the Lord for leading them and saving them throughout the year. The necessary reflections of the past year and the high expectations for the coming year were always part of the celebrations. When you walked through the streets in the afternoon, you could smell oliebollen everywhere. Oliebollen are a special Dutch treat and are actually oil dumplings, rather than some dumb translation that says they are donuts. They are even oilier than donuts and have a lot of raisins and sucade (Candied lemon peel) in them. Oliebollen are very tasty but also very oily.

Ko was very busy all afternoon baking oliebollen for the party at night. Aunt Dirkie and Uncle Jaap with their four daughters were coming that night to celebrate. There were six of them and four of their own which made quite a crowd. You needed quite a supply of oliebollen because that was the meal for that night.

A never to be forgotten New Year's Eve party took place when Adrie was only five years old. To him, it was a great party because he was crazy about oliebollen. His mother usually kept an eye on him to make sure that he didn't over-eat. She gave him a quota which she thought was sufficient for a five year old boy.

That night, she was quite busy with her visitors so she missed what took place. Uncle Jaap enjoyed looking at Adrie when he was eating. His delighted face told him that he was really enjoying his meal. When he had finished his quota, he gave Adrie one more oliebol and said: "Here is one more."

Adrie thought that was pretty nice of him, and ate his extra oliebol. Next, his uncle said: "I have a little bit of sugar left on my dish; you might as well finish it with another oliebol."

After Adrie had finished that one, he saw a very small oliebol; it wouldn't hurt to eat that one, too.

Yes, that was a great New Year's Eve party, Adrie really had enjoyed it. He sure had put a lot of oliebollen behind his teeth, and wished it was New Year's Eve every day. That way he could eat oliebollen every day. Not for long did he wish that he could eat oliebollen every day! During the night, the oily substance started turning his stomach upside down and in no time he was throwing up all those delicious oliebollen. His mouth couldn't work it all out and some of the contents of his stomach were coming through his nostrils. With the oily substance coming out of his nose, he got sick as a dog and this nice party had turned into a disaster.

When Adrie's mother learned what had taken place that night, that his uncle had given him that many oliebollen, she gave Uncle Jaap a scolding and was real mad at him. Even Adrie's father didn't get off with a whole skin, because he had been sitting there and never said a word to prevent the disaster from happening. They both got hell alright but it was too late, the damage was done. After a harrowing night, Adrie recovered but the repercussions washed ashore for a long time to come. He couldn't stand the sight of oliebollen anymore, even the smell could make him puke. If he smelled oliebollen, he still could feel them coming out of his nose.

For the next five or perhaps six years, Adrie's mother would bake pancakes for him on New Year's Eve while the rest of the family would eat the traditional dish of oliebollen. After that he regained his taste for oliebollen, but he never ate the quantity anymore that he ate on that one great New Year's Eve.

In spite of their poverty, New Year's Eve was an occasion for which the bottle of home made gin came on the table, for they had to drink the Old Year out and the New Year in, all according to tradition. After New Year's Eve comes New Year's Day which came along with Happy New Year's wishes. The children went from door to door to wish the occupants a "Happy New Year." For that effort the children were rewarded with one penny. People had a pot with pennies in the hall, for this occasion. In spite of the low return, Adrie managed to collect 65 cents on New Year's Day. It almost cost him a pair of shoes to collect that kind of money but it was worth it. It was a thriving business and a one time per year opportunity to make money.

Besides Saint Nicholas, Christmas and New Year's celebrations there was only one more important day that came with extras. It was Easter. On Adrie's birthday his Aunt Joh had given him a paint box with all kinds of colors of paint and Adrie was going to paint all the Easter eggs. Painted Easter eggs were a colorful display on the dinner table. The eggs weren't as colorful as the pysankas of the Ukrainians but they were beautiful. Whenever they were eating eggs, they would only get one egg but with this special occasion on the go, everybody would get two painted Easter eggs with fresh lettuce from the garden. That was the only treat on Easter, chocolate eggs and Easter rabbits hadn't been invented yet in The Netherlands.

(At school, the teacher asked Johnny to hand over his home work in arithmetic. Johnny said he didn't have it because he was watching his rabbit. The teacher said: "Watching a dumb rabbit won't get you your assignment done in arithmetic."

"Is that so," said Johnny indignantly. "My dad says that rabbits are very good in multiplying.")

HE PUT HIS FOOT IN IT

In 1939 there were new elections and after the debacle of Colein with his fish head policy, he didn't only lose the election, he was ousted from Government. Degeer formed a Government again and for the first time the Socialists participated in the Government. They should have formed the Government but they had to be satisfied to just participate.

In the Fifth Grade Adrie got his Third Grade teacher Mr. Kerselen back. He was the one who thought he was funny and punished you if you didn't laugh at his sick jokes. Adrie wasn't impressed at all.

In The Netherlands, they celebrate Pentecost or Whitsuntide which is in remembrance of the foundation of the Christian Church. Pentecost comes 40 days after Easter and in 1940 it was going to be on May 12th. The Pentecost holiday would start on Friday May 10th and would last two weeks. On that Friday, the children had to come to school but in the afternoon they would get off an hour early to start the holiday.

Three days before the holidays started, on Wednesday, the teacher said to the class: "It's the time of the year that the lilacs are blooming. They are so beautiful. Who of you children has lilacs in the garden?"

Being poor was a curse, they never had a thing but this was one thing Adrie's parents had. Their garden contained beautiful white and purple lilacs that also smelled very nice. Adrie was very proud that for a change, they had something. He raised his hand and put his foot into the teacher's scam. The teacher said: "Good, then you can bring me a nice bouquet of lilacs on Friday. That way I can have some nice lilacs on the table for Pentecost."

Adrie had surely walked into that trap. For a boy it wasn't masculine at all to walk with a bouquet of flowers. That was feminine! It was all right for a girl to walk with a bouquet of flowers but not for boys. No way! Mr. Kerselen had fixed his wagon but good. It looked more like one of his sick jokes you couldn't laugh about.

When Adrie told his parents about the request of his teacher, their response was very negative. His mother said: "What an impudence of that teacher to ask for lilacs from the students!"

His father's remarks were even less suited to be related to the teacher. He said: "Why does that asshole think he is getting free lilacs. Let him go to hell, if he wants lilacs let him buy his own. He is getting none from me!"

Adrie thought that was well said and he couldn't agree more. The problem was that if he repeated to his teacher what his father had said, he would be forever in the teacher's black book. He didn't have much of a chance to get in his white book since he didn't laugh at his sick jokes. However, this could be the final straw to break the camel's back and he would have that stupid teacher forever on his butt. In that case he could have told him to get off his butt unless he was a hemorrhoid, but that would never do.

He surely was in a predicament and had to find a polite way to tell him that he was an asshole and that he could go to hell. There was a way out. During his short life, he had learned a few important lessons that came in handy at this time. If the teacher asked him why he hadn't brought him any lilacs, he would simply say: "Ask my father, I asked him for lilacs but he wouldn't give them to me!"

In the few years at school he already had learned to be a diplomat to get himself out of thorny situations by putting the blame on somebody else. He knew for a fact that he wouldn't go to his father and ask. And even if he did he would come home with a cold nose. That was all right with Adrie, he had it coming.

Things worked out quite different than Adrie had expected, he didn't have to use his diplomacy at all. The question as to where the lilacs were was never asked. On that fateful Friday, May 10th, the last day before the holidays, nobody thought about lilacs. Adrie was quite sure that the teacher would have asked for his free lilacs but unfortunately the school was closed because of the war. Early that day, about 4.30 a.m., at dawn, the Dutch people were rudely awakened by canon fire and low flying aircraft. The Netherlands was attacked by Germany and all schools were consequently closed immediately.

Not even the teacher thought about free lilacs on his table from one of his least favorite students who wouldn't laugh at his sick jokes. There were a lot more important things to think about with the outbreak of the war. However, that is another story which I will tell in my second book of this series called "Winning Three Times."

WAS THERE REALLY A GOOD OLD TIME?

Whenever people are talking about the Good Old Time, they are talking about pre-war times from around the turn of the Century till the start of

World War II in 1939. Now let's forward the clock to the year 2000 and compare.

It was Saturday, the day that Adrie had to do his grocery shopping. He started his van and drove to the Super Store where he walked through countless aisles loaded with merchandise. There was a whole aisle with Maxi Pads for heavy days and Mini Pads for light days and half an aisle for family planning.

In the Good Old Time they had never heard about Kotex or any other brand for female hygiene. Old bed sheets and pillow cases were used for that purpose. Moreover condoms for family planning could only be obtained at the drug store and they weren't on display. If you wanted condoms you went to the counter and whispered in the ear of the pharmacist what you wanted. He would then dive underneath the counter and made sure that nobody saw what he was selling.

There weren't only groceries for sale at the Super Store; there was bread, cheese, milk, vegetables, meat and even motor oil on the shelves. All supplies could be bought in one store. In the Good Old Time, you had to go to the Butcher Shop for meat, to the Dairy Store for milk, butter and cheese and to the Vegetable Man for potatoes and other vegetables.

Adrie put everything in his shopping cart and went to the checkout where a girl scanned all the merchandise. Everything was automatically added and after the girl told Adrie what his bill was he gave her a credit card to pay for everything.

After he loaded everything in his car, he couldn't help but think about the old grocery store of Fleurtje Groenenboom where they had about thirty articles for sale. Everything was in bins and had to be weighed in paper bags.

Fleurtje also had a piece of pencil behind his ear which was needed to add the different items on a piece of paper. If Fleurtje had seen the Super Store in the year 2000, he wouldn't have believed that all the articles you bought could be added without a piece of pencil behind your ear and paying with a credit card was unheard of. The modern checkout at the Super Store replaced many Fleurtje Groenenbooms with a pencil behind their ears.

When Adrie came home he put the milk and bread in the fridge and the meat in the deep freeze. A fridge and deep freeze were unheard of in the Good Old Time; they were many moons away in the future.

After storing all the groceries, he took a bath in the jacousie and couldn't help but remember that in the Good Old Time he washed himself in front of the stove, during the winter, with a pail of water.

That Good Old Time wasn't all that great, yet when he lived in it, he wasn't that unhappy with all the primitive means. He didn't know anything else and was used to it.

There were certainly people from the upper and middle class who enjoyed the Good Old Time, those were the happy people. The hapless people could be found in the lower working class who were abused. They had no holidays and there was no unemployment insurance. When they were sick they had no income either. Few people, who lived in that time, certainly can't say that it was such a Good Old Time.

To Adrie this Good Old Time was good for nothing; the only thing that it did to him was to give him "**A LOUSY START.**"